MY BLUE NOTEBOOKS

LIANE DE POUGY

My Blue Notebooks

PREFACE BY R. P. RZEWUSKI

TRANSLATED BY DIANA ATHILL

ANDRE DEUTSCH

First published 1979 by
André Deutsch Limited
105 Great Russell Street London WC1

Originally published in French as
Mes cahiers bleus

Printed in Great Britain by
Ebenezer Baylis & Son Ltd
The Trinity Press, Worcester and London

ISBN 0 233 97141 6

PUBLISHER'S NOTE

When Princess Georges Ghika (Liane de Pougy) began to keep this journal, she thought that it might one day be published. Twenty-two years later, when she signed the last page, she thought the same, although in a very different spirit. It is apparent, however, that during the intervening years she often wrote in her blue notebooks simply because the habit of keeping a diary had grown on her. Often this increases the value of what she has to say, but sometimes it results in triviality. For this reason cuts have been made in this translation.

Material cut consists of comments on the weather or on minor ailments; passing reference to the news of the day (on this Liane is almost always more dutiful than enlightening); references to people who do not figure importantly in the events recorded and who are not described fully enough to become interesting for their own sakes; mention of books read, if not enlarged with comment; a few accounts of events, such as a purchase made, the receipt of a letter or a visit by an acquaintance which cannot seem as important to other people, now, as they did to the writer at that time; and the few entries which are dull and perfunctory because nothing had happened to interest, amuse, annoy or otherwise animate the writer.

When a cut occurs within an entry it is indicated thus: . . . .

When a whole entry has been omitted (in a few cases more than one), it is indicated thus:

. . . .

We have followed the French edition in using Liane de Pougy's spelling of names, e.g. Nathalie for Natalie (Barney).

ILLUSTRATIONS

PREFACE

by R. P. Rzewuski

My personal memories of Liane de Pougy, Princess Ghika, belong to two periods: the first about 1924 or 1925 when I was living in Paris, the second during the Second World War, when I often had occasion to meet her in Lausanne, in Switzerland, between 1939 and 1946.

I met her for the first time at a big luncheon given by Madame Ganna Walska, the wife of Mr Mac Cormick, a rich American manufacturer of agricultural machinery.

The luncheon took place in the big winter-garden of our hostess's house in the VIIIth arrondissement, where she had collected a considerable number of guests round a large oval table: a rather odd party, to tell the truth, though very smart. To begin with I looked in vain for a face I could recognize, and felt rather out of place; but the singularity of some of the guests and my own always lively curiosity soon dissipated this feeling.

I was sitting on our hostess's left, while the place of honour on her right was occupied by a rather strange-looking man. He was small and swarthy and at first I took him for a Latin American, although his elegance – in spite of having something slightly disquieting about it – was not undistinguished.

The lady on my left was ravishing. Very elegant, she was wearing a classic, very English-looking tailor-made of pearl grey. One could well have taken her for a visitor from across the channel had it not been for her pretty hat, the same colour as her coat and skirt, which contributed a wholly Parisian refinement to her appearance.

What was her age? Difficult to say. But in spite of her supple figure and the perfect beauty of her features I concluded that she was not in her first youth. Perhaps, I thought, she is between fifty-five and sixty. If so, she carries her years very lightly and well. Her perfect profile like that on an antique cameo, her radiant eyes and the charm of her smile had not yet suffered any of time's outrages. That smile – yes. It was certainly very pretty; yet – without preventing her personality as a whole from appearing restrained and genuinely distinguished – it did just verge on the raffish.

Our conversation during lunch gradually revealed that my charming neighbour was none other than Liane de Pougy, that courtesan so celebrated at the end of the nineteenth century and the beginning of the twentieth; and that the mysterious gentleman for whom protocol had reserved the place of honour at the table was the Roumanian prince whom she had married several years earlier, Georges Ghika.

The luncheon party went by very pleasantly, thanks to Princess Ghika's gift for agreeable conversation. She had a pleasing voice which still sounded young. She spoke with a slight drawl and expressed herself elegantly and always with precision. She touched lightly on subjects connected with the arts: music, painting, and especially poetry – without forgetting politics; and evoked in passing memories of Saint Petersburg to which she had made several visits in the past.

I exchanged a few words with her husband after lunch; and that was the last I saw of Liane de Pougy and her princely spouse during the remaining years spent by me in Paris.

It was in Lausanne during the Second World War that I met the couple again, in circumstances very different from the first occasion.

It was just after the start of the war in 1939, or perhaps it was already 1940. I had left Paris in 1926 to become a Dominican. I was the spiritual director of our international seminary in Fribourg, and used to visit Lausanne from time to time in order to see an exquisite old cousin of mine who was paralysed and had taken refuge for the duration of the war in the nursing-home at Bois-Cerf, headquarters of the French Trinitarian Sisters of Valence.

Coming down their big staircase one day, I saw in the hall a rather surprising couple. One's usual encounters in that place consisted of clerics who happened to be passing through Switzerland, old ladies learning to walk again with the aid of sticks, or children who had recently been operated on by the celebrated orthopedist Nicaud.

This couple was entirely surrounded by great quantities of very expensive luggage of every kind and gave the impression of having got there by accident and coming from who knows where – perhaps from another planet. He was fussing with the luggage while she, slender, tall, distinguished and very elegant in her mink coat and her little hat with its long, face-framing veil, appeared to be no less irritated than exhausted. She sank languidly onto a bench and let her head rest against the wall, with the look of one who is determined to suppress her impatience and accept bravely whatever happens next, come what may.

Days – perhaps weeks – then went by before I returned to Bois-Cerf. When I did, I was greeted just as I was about to enter the lift by the gentleman of this couple, who reminded me most amiably of that distant lunch in Paris at Ganna Walska's house.

'Liane,' he said, referring to his wife without ceremony – 'Liane thought she recognized you on our arrival the other day, in spite of your habit. To make sure, she asked the directress of the clinic. Since that distant lunch,' he went on, 'we have heard no news of you, and Liane was amazed to rediscover her young neighbour at table in a Dominican.' Prince Ghika told me that his wife had not been well and was much confined to her room at present. She would like to see me, however, and hoped that I would pay her a little visit.

So during the next six or seven years I often saw Liane and Georges. Sometimes, when Liane was feeling up to it, we lunched together in the big dining-room at Bois-Cerf. When she was feeling less well I would find her reclining on a bed covered with pale blue sheets, blankets and cushions: pale blue, she explained, in honour of the Virgin to whom her mother had consecrated her at birth.

In spite of the years which had passed since our first meeting she was still beautiful and time had not diminished her charm. Perhaps her face was slightly thinner and longer-looking, which gave it a touch of serenity, even of severity. Even in bed she was as elegant as ever. When she was well enough to come down to the dining-room she walked just as gracefully, though perhaps a little more slowly, leaning on Georges's arm.

The couple, knowing no one in Lausanne, were lonely and soon made it clear that they welcomed my company in spite of the irreligiosity of which Georges liked to make a display. He took the same pleasure in demonstrating his advanced and often exaggerated taste in literature, particularly in modern poetry, and he himself wrote poems which were not to Liane's classic taste. I should add that in spite of Georges's agnosticism he was always friendly to me and showed respect for my calling. Liane, on her side, took me very quickly into her confidence. I saw her every time I came to Lausanne and it did not take me long to understand the double role I was to assume: that of a friend who brought a bit of interest into both their lives, and – for Liane – that of a confidant from whom she hoped to get help for the advancement of her religious and spiritual life. For so long as I remained in Switzerland (before being recalled to France at the end of the war to become Master of Novices at the Dominicans of Toulouse) I played this part in her life.

It will be obvious, therefore, that I am not always able to make use of my personal memories when speaking of Liane de Pougy and her personality; which remained, in spite of her reputation, simple and often touching. There was also something in her, very deeply rooted, which made her reserved when talking about herself and particularly about what she used to be.

Reading these notebooks today, I think I see that under this appearance of control and discretion was concealed a wish to reveal fully what this ex-courtesan had always known to be her true self. It is to that, I believe, that we owe these journals, quite as much as to the encouragement of enthusiastic admirers among whom Salomon Reinach was not least.

The self-portraits which Liane likes to draw of herself throughout these notebooks are striking in their sincerity and sometimes even cruelty. She has a lucid view of her own deficiencies and faults. By nature changeable, she is almost unhealthily sensitive and susceptible. Quick to fall into enthusiasms and friendships, she is no less impetuous when it comes to breaking them off for no good reason; but she doesn't bear grudges and when the eclipse is over she is delighted to rediscover the friendship which one had supposed to be over for good and all.

The most typical example of these fluctuating relationships is her friendship with Max Jacob, which plays a large part in her notebooks. She liked him and admired his curious gifts, she often wrote to him and received many very good letters from him. She had him to stay in Brittany or Saint-Germain, and spoilt him tremendously. When he was ill she looked after him as though he were a child. Then Max would start to get on her nerves, she would start to run him down and soon she would be longing for him to cut his visit short. He would do so – but was it a final break? Far from it. A few months later Max was back and was again being cherished and admired. It goes on all through the journals!

There were, however, a few exceptions: she was, for instance, consistent in her dislike of Colette. Nevertheless, when the latter opened a shop selling aids to beauty, Liane lost no time – perhaps it was merely feminine curiosity? – in going to see it and buying some of its products.

And there is the odd and mysterious business with Nathalie Barney, friend of her early youth in Paris: her beloved and matchless Flossie. They were united by forty years of mutual affection. They were often apart, but whenever they met again the bond between them would seem to have become stronger, unbreakable. Well, it was not. One day – it was important to her, because she records it – Liane was in Toulon and unexpectedly met Nathalie – almost bumped into her – in a narrow alley. She thought she discerned a mocking smile on the Amazon's lips, turned her head away and went by without saying a word. She never saw her again.

How did little Anne-Marie Chassaigne, later the young Madame Pourpe, become first Liane de Pougy, then a Roumanian princess, and end her days aspiring to nothing less than sanctity?

Concerning the Pourpe-Pougy metamorphosis I shall quote Boni de Castellane, who told me about it before I ever met Liane. She married a ship's officer and left him and their child very soon afterwards. In Paris she stayed with a friend whose morals were light and was soon swept away into the city's turbulent life where her beauty earned her a high place among the pleasure-seekers. She met a gentleman who bore the name of Comte – or Vicomte – de Pougy and became his mistress. The affair did not last and when Anne-Marie left him she simply kept his name and tacked onto it that of Liane, which had been bestowed on her by the dissolute set in which she moved.

As I have said, Princess Ghika disliked talking about her past in the demi-monde; it lasted, however, for almost twenty years. I do remember one story she told me about receiving a contract to play quite a big part in a play at the Théâtre Michel, then the Théâtre Français, in Saint Petersburg. All she had done hitherto was appear on the stage at the Folies-Bergère to exhibit her beauty in a few dance-steps or by appearing in mimed sketches. She freely admitted that she never had any real talent. But Russia offered tempting prospects, so she decided to ask the great Sarah Bernhardt to be good enough to give her a little coaching before she undertook this adventure. Sarah agreed, but was not encouraging. Her lessons –

exceedingly expensive – always consisted of the repetition of the same verse by Sully Prudhomme, a then-fashionable poet: one beginning '*Le vase ou meurt cette verveine* . . .' (The vase in which this verbena is dying . . .). Sarah hoped that as she learnt different ways of saying these lines, Liane would show herself capable of an intelligent interpretation of the parts she was to play in Saint Petersburg. Alas! After five or six lessons she told her: 'My dear, there's not much I can do with you. Display your beauty, but once you are on the stage you had better keep your pretty mouth shut.' Occasionally, with a characteristic little smile, Liane would dispense a drop or two of memory of this kind.

When she got to Saint Petersburg she still wanted, nevertheless, to act at the Théâtre Michel. It was a fiasco. She resigned herself to the fact but stayed on in the capital of the tsars, where she soon found a café willing to engage her to give the turns she had already perfected for the Folies-Bergère.

In Paris Liane was famous for the splendour of her jewellery, her luxurious town house, the 'secondary residences' she owned in Brittany and Saint-Germain, and her luxurious carriages. The press was always publishing articles about her and pictures of her, and spoke of her as the greatest beauty of the day. The three great courtesans of the Belle Epoque, Otero, Cavalieri and Cléo de Mérode, were foreigners, respectively Spanish, Italian and Belgian. Liane, proud of being French, boasts in the journal of having become 'the nation's Liane', a sort of national monument universally known and admired. When her immensely valuable five-row pearl necklace was stolen in mysterious circumstances, she was not unduly afflicted. A few days later one of her admirers gave her another one – only two rows, admittedly, but each pearl was worth four of the stolen ones.

To everyone's amazement the career of 'the most beautiful courtesan of the century' came to an abrupt end while still at its most brilliant. Her marriage to Prince Georges Ghika (who was younger than herself) was announced.

Once she was a princess Liane had the good taste never to parade the fact. Besides which, her relations with her husband's family would hardly have allowed it, because they never fully accepted her. By the same token she was never able to create an authentic place for herself in society. Her past always weighed on her. Nevertheless her notebooks contain a whole string of names of people she describes as her friends.

This medley contains a good many personalities from the theatre: writers of the day such as Bernstein and Henry Bataille; actors and actresses such as the Guitrys, father and son, Balthy, Yvonne de Bray, Yvonne Printemps, Cécile Sorel and others. There is Reynaldo Hahn, and – later – Poulenc and Auric. And Jean Cocteau, of course, who was much admired by her husband. Great figures from the world of *haute couture* are often mentioned: Paul Poiret, the classical Doucet, Madeleine Vionnet and Coco Chanel – whose generosity as it appears in these pages contradicts her legend, because she became the leading benefactress of the Asylum of Saint Agnes which was so dear to Liane's heart from 1928 on. We also find the names of the main priestesses of Sappho, because Liane de Pougy does not try to conceal the nature of her amorous leanings.

We see her at those great Parisian social occasions provided by theatrical first nights, where people come over to her in order to congratulate her on her elegance and on the beauty which seems to be immune to time – and there it ends. Liane continued to be alone. Not wholly so, it is true, because after her marriage and up until a certain moment in her life, Georges Ghika was always there.

Liane states repeatedly that for the first sixteen years her marriage with Georges was a happy one. The couple lived in mutual fidelity. Can that really be possible with a husband about whom she writes later that he was always a degenerate, even abnormal, and hysterical?

But Liane had the will, in this case the good will, to make herself believe that her past had gone away, that her household was stable and that the two of them were faithful. And even after all the difficulties she was to have with Georges, she still showed him gratitude for having rescued her from 'the morass'.

Liane sincerely wanted to consign the years of her worldly success to oblivion, and even to forget them herself. Forget the princes, the grand-dukes, the politicians, the financiers who had heaped their crowns, fortunes, celebrity and talent at her feet. That world, however, continued on its way and was neither able nor willing to forget her; and – cruel as it can sometimes be – it did not do so.

By the time I met the couple in Lausanne it was possible to guess that their relationship had been less than good for some years, and that the happiness to which Liane had lent herself with so much good will had received some painful shocks.

The ostentation of Georges's attention to his wife's comfort gave a pretty clear hint of hidden guilt. Liane on her side treated him with a visibly forced maternal benevolence, and received his allegiance with a grace in which traces of pity and boredom were discernible. It was very obvious that this ill-assorted couple's existence was overshadowed.

As I was to learn later, what had darkened the horizon was Georges's flight, on which he carried off a cherished young friend of Liane's. I will not dwell on this sad event. Liane's notebooks tell about it at length, as they also do about the unfortunate consequences which this event had for a time on the moral equilibrium which she believed she had regained with marriage.

Then came the return of the repentant fugitive and the forgiveness which – I like to believe – his wife sincerely granted him. But the wound Liane's heart had received left a scar on their relationship which resulted in a reversal of their roles. It was no longer she who felt guilty opposite her princely spouse; it had become *his* task to earn complete pardon. There were times when it seemed to me as though this reversal did not displease the princess.

What more can I say about her? Some two or three years after we met in Lausanne, on the death of her husband, she confided in me her desire to be received under the name of Sister Anne-Marie into our Order of Saint Dominic, as a tertiary lay sister. I readily agreed, because everything I had seen of her during this time convinced me that the renewal within her made her worthy of our black and white habit. She received it at a little ceremony in the clinic's chapel. Having become a tertiary she was faithful in carrying out the obligations laid on her by her new condition: daily recitation of the order's little office, the rosary and the gospel. She was also greatly attached to the *Imitation of Jesus Christ*, of which she read one or more chapters every day. And it should be said that at Bois-Cerf, and later elsewhere, she was loved and respected by all who had to do with her: the Mother Superior, the sisters of the Trinitarian congregation, and the doctors and clerics who met her. A saintly bishop, Monseigneur Herzog, who was formerly charged with promoting the canonization of Saint Theresa of Lisieux, became very fond of her. He often came to see her and the new tertiary's reserve and other qualities earned his esteem. She in return felt the deepest respect for him.

Did Liane become perfect? Her husband was sometimes ironical about her little faults: pious Liane might be, he said, but she was still capricious and changeable in her feelings. But does not God allow some apparent imperfections even in His saints? It is hardly surprising that someone who had once been probably the most adulated woman of the century should still show traces of something which was so much a part of her temperament.

One afternoon when I went to see Liane in Lausanne I found her, as usual, lying on a bed draped with pale blue silk and lace, but very much upset. She told me that she had just that moment had a telephone call from Aunt Jeanne telling her that Georges had been taken ill at his aunt's hotel and that a doctor had been called.

I was wrong when I said the couple knew no one in Lausanne. Georges's aunt, Jeanne Ghika, was also a refugee there and Georges used to go to take four-o'clock tea with her every afternoon, returning to Liane in time for dinner. Aunt and nephew were very fond of each other, and since the difficulty in transferring Liane's income from England had made the couple's financial situation precarious, the aunt generously allowed Georges enough to supply their needs.

Liane asked me to go round to the Hotel Mirabeau and find out what had happened, which I did without delay. Princess Jeanne took me into her bedroom where I found Georges stretched on her bed, the death-rattle in his throat. He was in a coma after a stroke, and the gravity of the situation was obvious. The aunt told me, in great distress, that the doctor had just left after telling her there could be no hope. Georges was unconscious. Princess Jeanne, like her nephew, was a member of the Greek Orthodox church, but unlike him she was a believer. I asked her if she had any objection to my administering absolution according to the Catholic rite. She was very willing, so I administered it. A few moments later, while I was praying beside the bed with his aunt, Georges rendered up his soul.

I hurried back to Liane. She had apparently guessed how serious it was and had foreseen Georges's death, because when I came in she was sitting on her bed and she said simply, in an expressionless voice: 'He is dead.'

I must say here in Liane's favour that I could only admire her attitude and behaviour in these sad circumstances. There was no false note, nothing exaggerated or theatrical. Her commonsense emerged, with considerable dignity. In spite of what had happened between her and her husband, Liane had undoubtedly preserved a sort of maternal fondness for Georges. His death left her on her own – very much on her own – deprived of someone to whom she was bound by thirty years of conjugal life, and who had not been able completely to destroy the truth at the heart of their mutual affection even by the 'trick' he played on her – which was how she used to refer to his flight.

The practical woman surfaced, and she occupied herself gravely with the immediate material considerations which the death involved: the funeral, the question of what service to have and so on. She telephoned to Aunt Jeanne to discuss matters with her. As for me, I spent the rest of that sad day at Liane's side.

By the time I knew her in Switzerland Liane was far advanced in her terrestrial career – or perhaps I should say 'careers', because she had certainly had several and they had varied greatly, both in a worldly and material sense, and morally. This variety did not mean that she had ever lost her nature's basic sense of reality. So she fostered no illusions about the proximity of her end. Everything else seemed to her to be buried in the past. She wanted to end her life as a good Christian, and even more, aiming for the highest as she had done all her life, in evil as well as in good. By now it could only be a question of good.

She told me that she had rediscovered her faith some years ago. But had she ever really lost it? Even during the 'great years' of her disorderly life, when she was the most notorious and spoilt courtesan of the fabulous Belle Epoque, I doubt whether she had truly lost it.

But what had occurred in the life of Liane de Pougy to bring about the consistent serenity and patience which I witnessed when I visited her room in the Bois-Cerf clinic, and later – when their money troubles had become more severe – in an even more modest religious establishment?

It was because life had given her – and this more than a quarter of a century earlier – a beneficent shock which had transformed her existence.

Liane had always believed, from childhood. She had had faith from the day she was born into a pious family. As she grew older the good sisters at her boarding school trained her in the pious exercises of that time and place; they taught her her catechism, her rosary, and devotion to the Breton saint Anne of Auray. They also took care of her education, gave her her pretty manners and the good handwriting which still revealed the care taken in those days in the upbringing of a young lady. According to what she herself said, even in her stormiest years she never failed to go in and light a candle if she went past a church. When she came to be married to Georges Ghika in 1910 she wanted to be married in a Catholic church. There happened to be nothing to prevent it, because although she had been divorced by her first husband, the ship's officer Pourpe, he had been dead for over twenty years by then. But it was the death of her son Marco, the airman who fell on the field of battle in 1916, which dealt her the cruel blow which gave new life to her religious instinct.

One can conclude from the notebooks that Liane had never stopped trying to find and love God. But she did it in her own way, just as she liked to have recourse in her own way to the bounty of her beloved Saint Anne of Auray, mother of the Virgin Mary. Beyond that her faith came up against what seemed to her an obstacle: how could she bridge the gap between the demands and the purity of the Son of God, His teaching and His example, and what she knew to be the truth about her own life, her past and even her present? And besides – this, perhaps, was the crux of the matter – Jesus was a man. . . .

And yet. . . ! It happened to her in the most unexpected way, in 1928.

When the couple was out driving one day, in Savoy, they came to a long wall belonging to a convent. When they reached the door, Liane had the whim of telling Georges to ring and find out what went on in this withdrawn place. It was the Asylum of Saint Agnes, where nuns devoted themselves to the service of abnormal – sometimes monstrously so – children, struggling to give these afflicted ones a chance to open up and reveal what remained of the human within them.

The spectacle revealed to Liane was appalling, the work was impoverished, the nuns who did it were heroic. In spite of the crumbling walls the building was as clean and well-kept as was possible. The children's appearance was sometimes frightful. Liane was horrified to see these little beings in whom it was often difficult to discern anything human. There were dwarfs and hunchbacks; others with enormous deformed heads on tiny bodies; others with rudimentary, hardly visible limbs. Their eyes, usually staring, seemed neither to see nor to understand. And this sight was accompanied by gurglings and squeals and moans. What did life hold for beings such as this except the utmost misery? It suffocated Liane, but it also – extraordinary event! – won her over. Paradoxical though it may seem, it was here, faced by this image of degraded humanity, by the horror of this poverty, that Liane suddenly understood the depth of her own degradation – more than that, her own monstrosity, what she had been and what she still was. She, Liane de Pougy, Princess Ghika – was she not, in spite of her charm and beauty, the very essence of that human degradation which had made necessary the presence here on earth of our supreme saviour, Jesus Christ?

So it was there, in that poor Savoyard asylum, that the existence – better still, the presence – of Jesus came into her life, and the demands made by His worship became not only acceptable to her, but necessary.

In the notebooks for 1927 Liane laments over her existence: 'I don't even want to think much about myself, I want to keep busy, devote myself to something .... My aspirations are always lofty. Will they ever be crowned in keeping with their elevation?'

Five years later, after finding the Asylum of Saint Agnes, she wrote: 'What a long way I am now from Paris and its dissipations! Here is my wealth: the friendship of this saint and a little part in this work of abnegation and sacrifice. That is my road to Damascus! Oh! that my return to Paris does not make me forget this little corner! Please, God, do not let that happen! .... It seems to me that You put the Asylum of Saint Agnes and its inmates in my way on purpose, as though to tell me: "Help them, and I will help you".'

And Liane really did find in that place that which she had been seeking for so long.

I no longer remember the exact year of Georges Ghika's death: 1943? 1944? Whenever it was, I often saw Liane after it. In 1946 I had to return to France. Correspondence became difficult, on her side because she was now very old, on mine because an absorbing occupation left me with little time. I knew her, anyway, to be in the excellent hands of the Mother Superior of the Asylum of Saint Agnes, and as it were stabilized in her holy life as a Dominican tertiary.

After the war ended her material life became easier. She was able once again to enjoy the income from what had formerly been a considerable fortune. Her age and her health, however, did not allow her to end her life, as she wished to do, near the inmates of the Asylum to whom she had devoted her heart for over a quarter of a century. She became resigned to spending the last years of her life installed quite comfortably in the Hotel Carlton at Lausanne, and it was there that she departed this life on the day after Christmas, December 26, 1950. She was laid out, as she desired, in her Dominican habit. She was taken to Savoy and buried in the little cemetery beside the buildings which shelter the unhappy children who had been so dear to her.

My relationship with Liane did not, however, end with her death. In 1954 I stopped at the Hotel Terminus in Lausanne on my way through Switzerland. It must have been about a dozen years since I last set foot in that hotel, but on my arrival the porter handed me a letter. It bore a date in 1950. It had been written by Liane just before she died. She said that she could no longer find my address in France but remembered that I often used to stay in this hotel. She wanted me to know that she was faithful to the memory of our friendship, and above all to her vocation as a Dominican tertiary. It was moving to receive this posthumous message from Liane de Pougy, Princess Ghika.

It has certainly not been my intention in writing these lines to make a saint of Liane de Pougy, or to canonize her; but who can claim to discern the thoughts and ways of the Most High?

Did not the great theologian Saint Thomas Aquinas believe that when a human being foregoes by reason of his sins the grace which binds him to God, and then regains it by means of fervent repentance and authentic confession, that grace regained, bestowing love renewed, may be superior to what it was before?

An ancient talmudic Midrach expresses the same thought in a more picturesque way: 'Man is attached to Eloïm by a thread. If his sins break the thread, Eloïm then takes the two ends and ties them together in a big knot. This shortens the thread so that the man is brought still closer to Eloïm.'

1919

Saint-Germain-en-Laye – July 1 to September 10

July 1. I have been reading Marie Bashkirtseff's life, or rather her journal. It touched me to the heart and here I am, carried away to the point of longing to write my own. My husband is delighted. Our friend Salomon Reinach* is also urging me on.

Marie Bashkirtseff, that little girl who died long ago and who throbbed with such a feverish passion for life in all its forms and above all for fame – she haunts and inspires me. But my journal could never be like hers. She was an innocent girl . . . and who am I? Princess Georges Ghika, born Anne-Marie Olympe Chassaigne and then put together from Madame Armand Pourpe and the notorious Liane de Pougy. She had a thorough, well-planned education; I had six years in a convent and heaven knows how many of experience picked up at random.

July 2. It is my birthday. I was born on July the 2nd, 18—. Look it up in the parish register of La Flèche (Sarthe).†

Maman was on a visit to some military friends. She was not expecting me to arrive before August 15th. Why? Simply because the Holy Virgin had appeared to her in a dream, sitting in a beautiful white cherry tree, and told her: 'You will have a little daughter on my feast day. She will be called Marie. I will protect her. After an eventful life she will end up in Paradise as a great saint.' Maman said later: 'July 2nd is the Visitation. It's the most important of the Virgin's feasts so the dream came true.'

Maman was very pious, half Spanish on her father's side. At the time of my birth she was forty-three and a half years old. She had

* Philologist, archaeologist and art historian who was custodian of the National Museum of Saint-Germain-en-Laye. He died in 1932, at the age of seventy-four.

† Liane de Pougy was born in 1869.

gone to see my brother Emmanuel who was a pupil at the Military School of La Flèche, and had dropped in on her good friends the Chapelains. What a visit! A baby popping into their arms without warning – and into the arms of a most delicious neighbour about whom I will have more to say! Madame Navarre, née Atala de Monpeyssin, a creole from Martinique who became a sort of second mother to me during my early childhood. Because I couldn't pronounce the name Atala I called her Maman Lala.........

Maman Lala has been dead for some time now; she became the friend of the timid little girl I was, taking me for walks on Sundays, stuffing me with coconut, guava jelly and sugar candy dipped in the rum of her beautiful homeland, about which she told me such fabulous and amazing stories. Maman Lala always took me to her house on public holidays and when my brothers and their friends were home from school, to rescue me from their rough games. She did the most exquisite embroidery on linen, making dresses of it for her spoilt little 'Poupette'. I remember, too, that she used to say her prayers aloud, very loud, and that she would scold the saints and perhaps even God Himself if they weren't answered. I adored her. How bitterly I cried, the night when my parents thought I was asleep and I overheard them saying that she was going blind.

I left her when I was eight years old. Floods of tears, cruel grief. Then, when I was sixteen, I took my husband Armand Pourpe to introduce him to her. Seeing me again after such a long time, she said: 'My little darling, do you still have yo' teet' of pearl and yo' coral nail?' Then, in a whisper: 'Yo' husban' look too husbandish!'

I saw her twice more after that. I showed her a fiancé – who only half pleased her and pleased me even less – a stiff, narrow Englishman with whom I broke once I had thought it over properly. And then I went to embrace her a week before she died. She made me swear that I would never go on the metro – there had just been a fearful accident on it – and I have kept my word.

July 3. Young heart, young face, but the years are here, the aches and pains, the sorrows, the empty spaces . . . Oh, my dear departed ones! My brother Emmanuel died in 1886 (Lieutenant in the marine infantry, killed at Tonkin); my father (retired Captain in the Lancers, Pierre Blaise Eugène Chassaigne) dead in 1892 at the age of eighty-one. Dear old Papa, all white-haired and upright, who had me when he was sixty, so gentle and indulgent like a kind grandfather. Maman Lala dead in 1905 and Maman in 1912.

My most piercing grief, the one which came near to killing me and which threatened my reason (I spent fifteen months in cruel nursing-homes) was the death of my son, my only child, the aviator Marc Pourpe, a volunteer who fell on the field of honour near Villers-Bretonneux on December 2nd 1914. Time has passed, I have made myself accept the inevitable. And so many others have fallen since then. And anyway it is true that great sorrows are dumb. There is no consolation; it is a matter of regaining one's balance.

July 4. Friday, market day. I love to go shopping with my little Fatoum*. The noise, the bustle, the hurly-burly – all of it delights me. I love buying and choosing. I love carrying my booty back to the house. I am greedy; I try to be a good housewife. Things which might well bore me, which I have to do whether I like it or not – those things I really concentrate on enjoying. I got this from Reynaldo Hahn. One evening, when we were having dinner together, I hardly deigned to look at the menu. Reynaldo took it gravely, consulted it with much care, ordered some substantial and delicious food, then said to me: 'Look, Liane, the way to live is to bring all the enthusiasm you can muster to everything: studying, talking, eating, everything.' I understood him so well that I made it a rule of conduct. And that is how the prosaic Saint-Germain market has led me to the poetic Reynaldo.

We were devoted to each other. For several years he was certainly the sweetness in my life. Then I told him that I was getting married and he replied: 'Goodbye Lianon. I hate married people.' No doubt he disapproved of my stormy and disturbing entry into a family of such great distinction, which had reigned in its time. Nowadays I think too bad for Reynaldo, losing a friend like me. I have become a creaky old granny, a little fatter and a lot more stubborn and combative, turned by my sorrows towards thoughts of religion. I dare not say towards God, I still feel so far from Him. But I need to believe that we will all meet again, that I will see them again. I need God. I seek Him, and I feel that He has tested me so severely in order to bring me back to Him.

July 5. A day of migraine. It happens to me once a month – still! I stayed in bed till after lunch.

Read *le Jardin classique* – a collection of lectures at the Conserva-

* Her favourite little Negro maid.

toire by famous actors and actresses. I summoned my husband; I gave my imitation of Sarah (I do her very well. I also do perfect imitations of Berthe Bady, Lavallière and . . . Albert Brasseur!!! And beautiful Otero as well). Dinner was served. I made quite an effort. It was a mistake, the pain became atrocious. Georges crept quietly into a little bed placed at the foot of mine. Darkness. I went into a semi-coma, was flattened by it. But I wanted to say my prayers and in the middle of my invocation to my darling patron Saint Anne of Auray I got a clear vision of Georges lying in bed in Professor Hartmann's clinic. I took his hand and it was already ice-cold. I was alone; they made me understand that he had to be buried. I lit the lamp and jumped out of bed. There he was asleep, his beautiful brown wavy hair on the pillow – I felt completely changed. Had it been a warning? I was terrified, pouring with sweat, feverish, trembling. In September Georges is going to have an operation for a big stone in the bladder. I promise that if it's successful I'll go to Lourdes and to Saint Anne of Auray as well, and then I'll give a thousand francs* to the poor in one lump. That will not be easy for me, because since the war our income is much reduced.

I told that to Georges. The pilgrimages made him pull a face; the thousand francs made him furious!

July 6. My migraine has flown away! I can almost laugh at my terrors. I say 'almost' because I take my husband's operations very hard. He's had six already, three of them since we have been together........

July 9. No journal yesterday, not for lack of enthusiasm but because my migraine came back. I wrapped myself in God, because He is everywhere. It did no good. So I prayed to my two patrons, the Virgin Mary and Saint Anne. I offered them my pain and my resignation.

I once rejected the Church to such a point that she had no choice but to reject me. But still when I remarried I wanted it to be in my Church. I was obscurely attached to it by a thousand little threads. Having been divorced, it wasn't possible, but I had been a widow since 1892. So on June 8th, 1910, the civil ceremony was performed uniting Madame Marie Chassaigne (who had attained her majority – I paid them fifty francs not to say my age out loud) and Georges

* In January 1919 the franc was 26 to the £ sterling, 5.47 to the dollar.

Grégoire Ghika (also a major). On the same day, in the little chapel of the catechism in Saint-Philippe-du-Roule, the union between Madame Pourpe, widow of Armand Pourpe, and Georges Ghika was also blessed. I had been to confession the day before . . . For Liane de Pougy to make her confession must have been quite awkward, don't you think? She polished it off like this: 'Father, except for murder and robbery I've done everything.'

July 10. Jean Cocteau has sent us a copy of his *le Potomak* with a lovely dedication. Ever since *le Coq et l'Arlequin*, and particularly since *le Cap de Bonne-Espérance*, Georges has been very keen on Cocteau. He says that Cocteau ranks among the leaders of the modern movement; Gide and Cendrars are ahead of him, perhaps, then Apollinaire who died in the nick of time. He says in addition that Cocteau has risen superbly above his early work, and that now he's redolent of craftsmanship, originality and, in fact, real talent.........

On the 23rd it will be thirty-five years since my mother-in-law brought Georges into the world for me. I teased her once, saying that. She answered impertinently 'That was not my intention.' I stretched my neck and replied with insolent disdain: 'Too bad, Madame. It is an accepted fact.'

We have had our skirmishes, Mariette and I. In 1912 she came to Algeria to make my acquaintance. She had been told such horrors (with thirteen rs!) about me that she found me charming. She invited me to visit her in Roumania. We spent two months with her – one of those things you do only once! She visits us in France almost every year. She doesn't like me for my own sake (how wrong of her!). Nor me neither, because I can't love anyone who doesn't love me. She appreciates my elegance and beauty, she blows hot and cold. She is a bizarre woman, a true boyar by descent, decisive, authoritarian, great-ladyish and impulsive. She can be perfectly maddening. She is pretty, subtle, coquettish, extreme, unexpected, changeable, reads a lot – but can be very comic in her interpretations of what she has read. She is sensitive about outward appearances and adores her children, when they are there. Georges was certainly just the right husband for me, and I think that Mariette suits me no less well as a mother-in-law. She makes no secret of believing in neither God nor the Devil. She is quite without hypocrisy, and knows how to give way gracefully when she has to.

In Venice, when we were on our way to stay with her, we bought some pipes. I said to her on arrival: 'Madame –' (she calls me Liane and I call her Madame, because I can hardly in decency say 'mother' to a woman scarcely ten years older than I am) – 'Madame, I must confess to a vice: I smoke a pipe.' I wanted to test her a little. She looked at me with raised eyebrows and pursed lips, then said: 'So much the better. I much prefer the smell of a pipe to that of cigarettes.' The pipe stayed in my suitcase.

July 11. I've just finished Cocteau's *le Potomak*. It is fascinating. It disdains orderliness and classicism. It is modern with passion, and with control. So that slender Jean with his great eyes is a real artist! His book is full of beautiful things.

Yesterday an aeroplane flew over Saint-Germain and dropped leaflets. Georges picked one up in our little park: it was announcing the aerial victory parade. One of my friends said: 'But you are the mother of that young eagle, Marc Pourpe – they should have given you a seat.' – 'Ah no! To take advantage of something so terrible . . .' The idea made me shudder. Grief, and nothing but grief. I did not love my son enough when he was alive. I was all woman – woman, not mother. My love was not able – didn't really want – to make a place for itself in his gloriously beautiful, excessively independent life. Oh how I have regretted it, how I have wept and been punished!

July 12. We have talked about the war so much that now we really need to shut up! It was a toxic experience, and going back over it stirs up all the poisons. My son's death, my illness, my husband's devotion, a few former friends who revealed such a vile and cowardly spirit that we had to let them drop, money losses, a hard and simplified way of life, six weeks when my house was turned into a dressing-station, and the victory of France! From my point of view, that is how I sum up those five horrible years. And then there is the disappointment – where is the purification through war which we were promised? 'There is no such thing,' says Georges. 'The war lasted too long, and the further we advance into peace, the more obvious that becomes.'

July 13. Sunday, eve of the victory parade. Oh, my country! My first country, because now I have become a Roumanian.

Georges is deeply hurt if anyone says, by way of a compliment, that he has a tiny (!) trace of a charming foreign accent. He thinks they must be deaf or trying to insult him, draws himself up and replies with a barrage of 'I have a horrrrror of everrrrrything Rrrrroumanian!' Georges is an angel, a love, an exquisite little boy, an ancient sage, a boring philosopher, an erudite scholar, etc etc. He is sometimes accused of being – too handsome. People are rather beastly to him. After we were married, the first time we went to a first night, which is my way of going out and about, I caught glances, spiteful smiles in our direction, whispers. So in front of those three powerful, widely distributed news-sheets known as Henry Bernstein, Pierre Mortier and Pierre Frondaie, when one of them asked me how I was: 'I am happy and enviable, my dear. I live with the two bravest men in the world.'

'???'

'Yes, my son who is a famous aviator, and my husband who had the courage to marry me.'

It was at the Théâtre-Français, a performance of *Primerose*: it went the rounds in a flash, and I had won the mockers over to our side.

July 14. The literary supplement of *Figaro* has published interviews with some of our intellectuals about the benefits of peace. Henry Bataille's answer was short and good: 'Freedom of thought.'

I have known Bataille for twenty-five years. It was Lorrain who introduced us. I was still a flighty girl, he was living with Bady and was on the verge of becoming famous. We still feel a certain tenderness for each other. The memory of our youth, of all those years gone by. We have not gone down, we have survived: we meet from time to time, exchange a kiss and a smile, tell each other how well we are looking! There was never anything serious between us.

July 15. . . . . Dreamt about Blanche d'Arvilly, a friend of my theatre days who went all over the place with me. She used to pick up the crumbs of my frivolous glory, was often very useful to me and more often treacherous and disagreeable. When I had my serious motor-car accident and was immobilized in the hospital at Beaujon, I saw her approaching my bed. Instinctively I shut my eyes. She came right up to the bed and bent over me – I could feel her breath on my face – and then she turned to the nurse and said in a tone of voice quite impossible to describe: 'So she is not disfigured?'

How can I hold it against her when we shared so much laughter? We had met one summer in Ostend, working in pantomime. She filled the role of a gnome, I of a pretty columbine, seductive and seduced. She also filled a costume made of virulent green wool. It was a hot night, her dance was energetic – and she was found unconscious in her dressing-room, her tongue black, half-poisoned by the arsenic in all that green, mixed with her sweat. Her pals were moving on the next day. She was ill. I took her on and nursed her and she stayed round me for years.

July 16. One of Cocteau's jokes – thanks to *Potomak* we are all completely encoctocated at the moment. Talking of a chameleon, he said: 'Its master put it down on a tartan rug and it died of over-exertion.'

Let's come back to Georges. He has a very ironical turn. Because he is also rather heavy-handed, it can make him seem ill-natured. When he's got hold of some nice, spiky little tease against someone, he fairly lets fly with it! When I pointed this out in a reproachful way, this was his clever defence: 'I have noticed that whenever I put someone down, the opposite opinion instantly prevails. So when I'm nasty to my friends I do it out of niceness, for the pleasure of hearing people sing their praises.'

I have just finished *Clarissa Harlowe*. It's very good; I like this book better than *Liaisons dangereuses*. Lovelace has charm. I once knew one of those: Henry Bernstein, an Israelite sub-Lovelace, full of talent. From writing all those plays about love with their last acts full of melodrama, he'd started introducing it into his own life, and into that of others. In the course of one year I took from him just enough to amount to a charming memory. Oh the splendours and the miseries he invented for me! 'I shall kill you!' – or 'If you won't say you'll marry me I'll throw you down and grind my heel into your pretty face!' or again: 'Think! Soon you'll be forty, my girl. You'll be *forty years old* – ' leaning on the words. 'No one will want you any more and what tears of blood you'll weep when you remember your Henry, and how much he would have loved you.' I had just turned thirty-five at the time!

When I drove him out and hid in a little back-room, he disguised himself as a postman bringing a registered letter I would have to sign for. When my friend Valtesse gave me sanctuary in her manor house in darkest Ville-d'Avray, he broke his way through doors and footmen and came bursting into her drawing-room. He had employed detectives to find out where I was! At Cap d'Ail, where I'd left him flat and taken a train for Paris, he went so far as to report me to the police: 'Liane has made off with a necklace of thirty-one pearls, which she will be wearing. A case of morphine-addiction: she is a sick woman so on no account should she be alarmed, but her whereabouts must be discovered and I must be told where she is hiding. I will deal with the trouble. I will look after her.'

After that he went to see Clemenceau. His police spies had failed to find me and he was in a terrible state. 'Maître,' he said, panting and gasping (Clemenceau lived on the fourth floor and there was no lift), 'just look at how pale and ill I am. That woman has left with the deliberate intention of breaking my heart, and her spite is such that she has carried off the manuscript of *Samson*, a play on which I have been working for a year and which I have to deliver to Lucien Guitry almost at once, it really is a matter of life or death to me . . .' In fact he had written about four or five pages of this famous *Samson*. But he was very plausible and touching. They set off in pursuit of me and brought me back. Whereupon he fell at my feet, full of repentance and love. He wasn't one to abuse his victories: for two – sometimes three – marvellous days he would treat me like a queen. The rest of the time it was blows, threats, insults, sneers, brandished revolvers. One Christmas night, in front of his trembling and paralysed brother, he dragged me by the hair half-naked from the top to the bottom of my staircase.

I was often able to escape while he was in his bath. One day, I remember, he hauled me off to London with him. He would reverse our roles, so that he became the victim – almost believing it sometimes. 'If I kill you, people will say that hussy drove poor Bernstein mad. Yes, my girl, I shall have the star part. I'll get myself consigned to a nursing home for six weeks, and afterwards – the women will be madder about me than ever!' I loved his flashy, insincere smile. He was my last fling: Georges turned up, as Fate had ordained – that boy soon had everything in its right place, helped by Marie Murat who was quite determined to adore Henry. He was the storm necessary to carry me out of the unhealthy stagnant morass in which I was miserably stuck, back into life and under the eyes of Georges. Now when I hear from time to time about his adventures, I smile. His marriage made one rather anxious for that pretty little girl, but he knows so well how to make us happy, sometimes. . . . .

Did I mention my 'morass'? Ugh – the memory of it still sickens me. No hubbub and grand gestures there, nothing but whispers, sly looks, devious scheming, nasty little crimes. Perhaps I'll write about it, simply to get it out of my mind once and for all.

July 17. My house is big and well-run, polished so that it reflects itself, without a speck of dust, light and airy. It is a beautiful old wing of the château which the Duc de Noailles built for himself when he was governor of Saint-Germain at the time of Louis XIV. I have about three acres of well-designed grounds – traces of Le Nôtre's taste; the building is by Hardouin-Mansart. I have two historic and listed trees: a cedar and a Japanese copper beech. Their waist measurements are more than five metres! I have dungeons, old floors, old panelling; my reception rooms are six and a quarter metres high and on the little landing between them there is my Marco's dear little room, empty for ever but so full of memories. I can see him now in his sky blue pyjamas, with his smooth skin, his hair which grew so beautifully, his complete lack of mustache. He looked like a fifteen-year-old girl. I was always scolding him for not loving me enough.

I've got to talk about the 'morass'. It will be less easy.

I had an intimate friend, as intimate as one can possibly be, a girl of twenty-seven. I was thirty. She was Yvonne de Buffon, a descendant of the famous Buffon. She was with me always, ran my house, everything around me and within me. She was pretty, intelligent, cultivated, a liar, a schemer – vicious. She loved wine, women, disorder, deceit, dubious relationships . . . and she sniffed! All this often came between us. Whatever has happened, I have always remained simple and straightforward. I was often quite hard on her because of her faults, but I couldn't do without her. She slept in the room next to mine, our doors stayed open. She came into my big bed; there was something protective and masculine about her friendship and her charming face was adorned with a pretty little mustache which would have been the envy of any sixth-former. And above all, a limitless devotion.

I used – I abused – her tenderness, I even tyrannized her, and I loved her. I loved her for what she was, so hard that I truly believe I still love her today. She lied from habit, to everyone. She brought bad luck. No sooner did she arrive in my house and my life than a fabulously rich friend whose whole life was devoted to me dropped dead; and another, a millionaire who had delighted in obeying my slightest whim, told me he was getting married. My servants? Absolute apaches, stealing everything, breaking everything. My beautiful five-row pearl necklace disappeared (May 13, 1903, 13 rue de la Néva; I'd been in Paris thirteen years . . . oh that thirteen!) It was worth five or six hundred thousand francs in those days, so *what* would it be worth now? My son went into open revolt against me. My health, my nerves let me down; I became a mere rag. I wanted to be alone, far away from a world in which everything wounded me. Yvonne came after me relentlessly, I only loved her the more for it. I found myself a little rustic house between the fields and the sea, at Roscoff. I became a creature of nature, a recluse. The lies, the fantastic stories she told me! The purses she lost! . . . Never mind. That winter I had an engagement to fulfil at the Moulin Rouge, where they used to put on revues and operetta. We returned to Paris. I felt rather than saw the evil which engulfed me more and more, day by day. I was depressed, discontented, weary; my heart was empty of delight and full of disgust.

One day, backstage, I met a little Israelite with fine eyes and a high forehead, who seemed very shy. Lorrain introduced him to me, overwhelming him with praise: 'Max Maurey, subtle and cultivated, intelligent and clever – my friend. He admires you . . .' and he left us. We looked into each others eyes, disturbed and smiling, and on that day at least I think that both of us had the same thought: let's make happiness together. He daren't woo me, I led him on; he daren't visit me, I called him; he daren't love me, I set about adoring him and managed to communicate some of my fire to him. His success made him bold. He loved my love, that was all, and began to bully me, lie to me, deceive me. When I tried to escape he came running after me, sobbing, haunting the street where I lived night and day. I was touched, asking – alas! – for nothing better. Yvonne and he loathed each other. There were floods of tears, flouncings out, threats, appalling things were said. One fine day, however, light dawned in me; I felt that I could no longer endure their treachery their lies, their baseness. I left. I went to Cairo, then to Alexandria, Athens, Constantinople (leaving instructions with my solicitor to pay Yvonne de Buffon an allowance of 150 francs a month, against receipts. I include this detail because after my marriage, and perhaps after her own, she wrote an open letter to a newspaper declaring that she had never had anything to do with me!). I saw nothing, or very little. I gained a few vague impressions of landscape, home-sickness undid me, and the Orient Express soon carried me back to Paris.

In my front hall I found Max, a rose in his hand, and a smug smile on his face. Yvonne had vanished. He said he had seen nothing of her. Liar! They had met to cry on each other's shoulders over my brave departure. Then she had led him on to confidences; she was gentle and maternal to him and their attitudes towards each other changed. Their feelings for me, too. Soon they were tearing me apart tooth and nail, and the hour struck! The hour of love following on hate. Yvonne was pregnant and he was stuck with her.

They are said to be married; it was never announced. They had two, three, then four children. Max, I know, has become Yvonne's punishment, her grief. She is the maid of all work, prisoner of her duties. They live like convicts chained together, miserable and discontented. Yvonne, cheated in her turn, has wept useless tears.

July 18. Received a circular letter from Germaine Bailly, Poiret's head *vendeuse*, letting me know that the house of Poiret, shut when the war started, half-open during, is opening again properly this month with a marvellous collection. We have always greatly appreciated Poiret's taste. He was an innovator, very much discussed.

I considered him an extraordinary being. I invited him to my wedding. He came, presented his wife to me and they became friends of ours. Yes – except that it's not really possible to stay friends with people who sell you things. I still like his taste, I often buy his clothes and I'll continue to do so . . . and that way everything is for the best in the best of all possible worlds!

They have installed a dance-floor in the garden surrounding the couture house, and asked us to the opening. We didn't go. At present we are going nowhere.

Speaking of Poiret and his parties. He has quite sumptuous ideas but the execution falls short. One day, when the pre-war kings were still around, the Poirets called on us to invite us to a dinner dance. It was to be a big party and everyone was to come dressed as a 'royal'. Poiret himself was to appear as the King of Dress-Design. We accepted, and because there was a lot of talk at the time about the Albanian throne, the 'cradle of the Ghikas', we decided to appear thus: the King and Queen of Albania, with their Favourite. The favourite was to be the Italian greyhound wearing a collar of gold and lying on a velvet cushion carried by Halima Larbi (my little white Moroccan, who was given to me by General Bailloud), who would lead the procession in sumptuous raiment. We would pace majestically behind her. I had dug out my rich Roumanian embroideries, royal blue and apricot cloaks trimmed with beautiful fur. Our heads were crowned with heavy toques of fur, to which aigrettes were fastened with huge diamonds. Our costumes came off perfectly. As soon as we arrived I saw that they were far too good.

The others were the kind of thing you see in the streets at Mardi Gras. My two black Africans, Zorah and Fatoum, dazzling and covered with jewels, walked behind us holding up our trains. I wore all my pearls. I really can't bear to describe the chaos and squalor of that evening. It was after ten before we sat down to dinner. Everything was badly done, ill-prepared, disgusting. The wines as well as all the rest – the guests became drunk on the hubbub. Obscenity soon took over from unseemliness. It was sordid and deafening.

On our way home, in the darkness of the carriage, I bewailed the time we had wasted there, scolded Georges for having agreed to escort us. I begged my little ones to forgive me for taking them there, and my dog too – I even asked my dear pearls to forgive me for having worn them!

From that day we began gradually to withdraw from intimacy with the Poirets.........

July 19. Max Jacob* has sent a message that he is ill and has been taken by cab to some friends in Montparnasse who will look after him until he is better, and that they are letting me know because they found my invitation for the 23rd in his pocket diary. I am sorry, because he amuses Georges. He appeals to my compassion because he's so feeble. In other words, I don't like him at all. He's a poor creature, very gifted but doomed to come to nothing much. There is something grubby (in every sense) and demoralizing about him. Beautiful, ravaged face . . . He has changed his religion, which is something I can never approve of. Why want to deny his race? Ridiculous! And anyway he hasn't been able to change his nose! In 1917 he lived with us at Roscoff for two whole months. It was pretty difficult. I did everything I could to show it as little as possible. I am not very sociable. I attribute all kinds of qualities to people, then pouf! Everything changes into its opposite as though by magic just because of a word said or not said, a gesture, a look, a giggle. I'm wrong, obviously. But my nerves are so poor and I get more and more worked up until I explode.

July 22. A postcard this morning from Vivières (Aisne). It is Henry Bataille's portrait of Yvonne de Bray. Yvonne has been Bataille's besotted mistress for ages, and it never ceases to amaze those in the

* Max Jacob had a considerable reputation as a 'cubist', or *avant-garde*, poet. He was born at Quimper in Brittany and died in a German concentration camp at Drancy in 1944, at the age of sixty-eight.

know. She drove off Berthe Bady, then took her place. Bataille always loves the one who is there! When Bataille finally left Bady after twenty-five years of close intimacy, I wrote to him: 'Your separation scorches my heart. To me it seems like an amputation and the woman you are taking on will always be, for me, your wooden leg.' Bady stirred up a scandal, mobilizing all the men of letters; Henry had to promise her a fat pension; 'Which', she cried, 'he never paid during the war, taking cowardly advantage of the moratorium.' We met her about a year after the split, and when I enquired affectionately how she was, she gave me this nice answer: 'Better, thank you Liane, much better, I'm crying no more than once a day.'

July 25. . . . . Today we acknowledged that Paul (Poiret) deserved his nickname, the Magnificent. He arrived by car, at midday, surrounded by boxes, suitcases, his most elegant and favourite mannequin, Germaine his faithful ambassadress (her diplomacy earns her the title), and my *vendeuse*. Nearly twenty models, each more ravishing than the last . . . I chose three dresses: 'Tangier', in thick black wool with touches of white embroidery and fringed with the same. It's ravishing. 'Saint-Cyr', in black silk, rather full pannier-style skirt, black bodice with little short sleeves, and three overlapping flounces of white organdy making a cape fastened with two silver tassels and a bow of violet velvet. 'Agrigento', two splendid lengths of glitter knotted on the shoulders and at the waist – that's all, but such a ravishing all! He had some superb coats, one of them Venetian, black and gold with a collar and cuffs of sable! 7,500 francs, a mere trifle! But a dream of beauty.

He was charming, allowed me a discount of 800 francs on the three dresses, which made them 3,000 net. Georges was pleased. Poiret had returned to being our dressmaker friend, so nice, with no pretentions except being very good at what he does. We hugged, celebrated, paid compliments, made plans. Poiret promised me he'd look after the sale of my house; he could strike a rich vein, with his clientele. At my first hint he said: 'It's dresses I sell' – 'Yes, but there'll be a commission of 50,000 francs.' – 'Oh well that's different, that's interesting'; and then we talked about it seriously.

July 26. I feel sickened, exhausted, even fed up at having ordered three dresses! I said to myself: yesterday we babbled, we didn't talk; we told lies; we schemed. I allowed myself to appear inferior to myself! I am angry with myself, and with others, for spending a whole day so far from what is true, upright, sincere, beautiful, real – from God. We were spiteful, we behaved with a Parisian kind of flightiness, like theatre people. Any why? Poiret is scared of the future. He wants to sell up, realize the assets he acquired before the war and live in the country with fresh eggs, chickens, his family. Goodness, how bored he would be! He's a townee to the marrow of his bones, and a business man too. He has made it up with Cocteau – another encoctocated one! He prophesied ruin and disaster. He is anxious, lacks confidence. I foresee trouble for him. The impression made on me is really bad. He told me: 'In Paris Denise spends all her time dancing, she adores it. For the opening of our dance-floor I made her a full-skirted, short dress of silver lamé. She was lovely. She looked like an epergne!' Puppets! I am no longer up to date and don't want to be. I wear nothing but black, white and grey. My soul, too, is dressed in gravity, gentleness and nobility. In fact I have been quite unable to digest that frivolous, demoralizing day.

Ah, my darling Flossie*, with your high-necked black dress, your fur and your unpretentious little hat, how different you are, how comforting, and beautiful. I detest letting my thoughts dwell on nastiness.........

July 27. Georges wanted to celebrate my half-name-day, because I'm called Anne-Marie. He has ordered my favourite dishes for tomorrow, Sunday. He has written me a beautiful letter, a bit literary, but so much 'him'.

This morning I went for a long walk with Steinilber and we talked about gestures. Each period, each fashion, gives rise to its own. That of the snuff-box, mittens and curved arms over crinolines, handkerchiefs held by the middle. What a charming gesture it was to lift the skirt to show just enough to excite desire by suggesting the rest . . . Now we wear low-cut dresses. Is it cold? There's a pretty, shrinking way of spreading your fingers over a fur crossed at the throat. Skirts are short, no more need to lift them. One stretches an arm, lifts the wrist to eye-level: how else read the time from one's wrist-watch? There have been the charming movements of the lips against the mesh of a veil; the lipstick gesture, so frequent that one no longer notices it, and the powder-puff, which has become so

* Natalie Barney, an American whose salon in Paris was a centre of lesbian society. In their young days she and Liane had a famous affaire.

natural; the sharp little tap of the walking stick, or the way of tucking it very high under one's arm-pit when not using it. I like taking a stick when I go out. It gives my spirit a touch of virility! I feel protected, and truth to tell, when I'm a little tired – well, I'm quite glad to lean on it a little; not much, not so that you would notice.

Walking stick, spectacles! Last April my mother-in-law took me to her oculist to get my first pair of spectacles. I use them when I read or write by artificial light. Walking stick . . . spectacles . . .

Poiret's little mannequin has a pretty enough face, lifeless, and beautiful auburn hair. I said kindly: 'Your hair is ravishing, so young and such a colour! One can tell at once that its natural.' My civility earned me this answer: 'Well, I'm young. I've got years before I need dye.' – 'Listen, you pretty fool, I do not dye and it wouldn't take you long to count my grey hairs. May you have as few when you're my age, or earlier for that matter. And let me tell you that when I was twenty-four I'd have thought myself an old has-been if I hadn't already clocked up a husband, a divorce and a seven-year-old son!' Poiret looked quite embarrassed.

Mannequins have always struck me as pathetic. Poverty of spirit, of flesh and of digestion. Oh! That bad breath from eating too little, too fast, and that obligatory smile degenerating into a painful grimace. What a miserable fate: poor relations summoned from afar to the sumptuous banquet, just to be useful!

. . . .

July 31. Benjy [Alfred Benjamin, London stockbroker] arrived yesterday at eight o'clock in a superb car. The dear old thing is just the same; he seems to have shrunk a little, that's all. Same clever, long-nosed face, same bald head covered with down like a duckling, same good humour, same fondness for us. He is easy-going. He told me: 'I've brought you a little piece of nonsense that I'm sure you won't have,' and out of his golf bag he wrestled an umbrella with an aluminium handle which opens out into a camp-stool. The umbrella's pointed end sticks into the ground: it's too comic – Briggs's latest invention. He said: 'If it rains, there you are, an umbrella. If you are tired, you sit down.' – 'And what if it rains when I'm tired?' Hoots of laughter. He's brought me a big bottle of my beloved English scent, Penhaligon's 'Hammam Bouquet'. You can get it in Paris at Carnaval de Venise, but it's no longer so fresh.

August 1. Migraine on the left side. Very painful, particularly, with a deaf English guest, full of energy and refusing to speak a word of French! As charming as can be, all the same. I'm going to put myself on a diet and send him off to play golf........

....

August 4. Have seen the new honours list in the papers. Henry Bernstein has been made a *chevalier* of the Legion of Honour. At last! Yes, but Pierre Wolf has been made a *commandeur*. Oh dear!

Pierre Wolf was once brought to see me, Liane of the Folies-Bergère, at lunch time. I invited him to stay to lunch. Wolf was in bicycling clothes, britches and leggings, which put me off to start with. My mother was lunching with me that day, and four or five close friends. The witty Wolf elected to show off his gift of the gab on dirty stories, sparing us no obscene detail or word. I was seething. I controlled myself as best I could, and he noticed nothing. As we waited in the hall for coffee after the meal, convinced of his success, he suddenly remembered that as well as being the star of the Folies, I was his hostess. So he came over to me all smiling and gracious, still quite tipsy on his own talk and my wine: 'Liane, my lovely Liane, what an exquisite lunch! How delighted I am to have met you. Tell me, tell me – what can I do in my turn to give you pleasure?'

At these words I jumped: 'Give me pleasure? You would like to do that, really?'

'Yes,' he said, surprised.

'But really?'

'Of course,' – already a bit nervous.

'Well, that's simple. You can give me enormous pleasure this very minute.'

'How?' and he leant towards me, his lips pursed.

'You can get to hell out of here!' And I called to the footman who happened to be passing: 'Get M. Wolf's hat and stick. He's in a hurry. Goodbye, Monsieur.' And I left him standing there. Flabbergasted, he grabbed his stick and made off. That evening I received a magnificent potted palm wrapped in rich Japanese embroideries, with an apologetic note. We became the best of friends. He remembers that little incident and often tells the story.

August 5. Just back from Paris. We were met at the station by a fine car and were driven to Professor Hartmann's nursing-home in Neuilly [Georges Ghika was to have his operation there on September 15]. I went over it and chose our rooms. Afterwards we buzzed off to the Ritz and to Martine's and to Poiret's and to Linker's and to Rebattet's and to Panizou's. The car was loaded with cakes, scent, hats and coats for Georges and for Benjy's wife........ At nine o'clock in the evening the bell rang. It was André Germain on his way back from Etretat, wanting dinner. We were just going to bed. He had a friend with him: it was a bit bad-mannered, not to say impertinent. I made up my face, shook out my hair, put on a silk wrapper trimmed with valencienne lace, got into bed – then thought to myself: 'Dammit, no! I don't want to see them. André Germain never answered the friendly note I wrote him a month ago, he takes the liberty of turning up so late, without notice. He's not one of our close friends, after all, he thinks he can get away with anything because he's the son of Henri Germain, the founder of the Crédit Lyonnais.' But you can't refuse someone a dinner. Georges wore himself out making excuses and had them served some soup, noodles and bacon, cold veal, coulommiers cheese, cakes and fruit. They expected to see me afterwards but I held firm. They left rather embarrassed, and disappointed. How ill-mannered people have become!

August 7. Joncières announces that he's coming on Saturday, so we'll hear all the latest about everything and everyone. Joncières is not well-bred but he's a close friend. He is horrid but he answers letters. He takes liberties but he will be anxious for news of us if we are ill, etc. They are doing one of his plays at the Comédie-Française, *le Fil d'Ariane*, starring Piérat of course. He's on his way back from Bataille's, they are passing him on. He's the homeless one who is at home everywhere.

The Roumanians have entered Budapest as conquerors and the Americans are telling them to get out of it again. The poor Roumanians, betrayed, beaten, rent apart, ruined: they make a last effort and vanquish their enemy, only to be told to renounce the victory. It's a bit much! That new nation is abusing its youthful strength.

Salomon told me some charming lines which he has written in English about Flossie, who is grieving us all by leaving for America on the 9th:

Analyse her
You'll be wiser
Steel and gold
All is told
....

August 9. A thought from Alexander Dumas the Younger, picked up in the literary supplement of *Figaro*: 'Begin by marvelling at what God reveals to you and you will have no time left in which to seek what He hides from you.'

When I was at Roscoff this year I read the *Mémoires* of Alexander Dumas the father. The volumes came to me from the library of my grandmother Olympe. She was very cultivated and composed songs, both the music and the words. Among her papers when she died my mother found quite a correspondence with Victor Hugo . . . My mother told us this openly, but when we asked to see it she put on a prim and disapproving look and said: 'Out of respect for my mother's memory I have burnt them.' She had, too. Towards the end of her life I drew her into my own existence more tenderly and intimately than before, here and there, in London, Paris, Monte Carlo . . . She saw me being celebrated and sought after, admired the luxury and order of my household, was dazzled by my clothes and jewels. One day I heard her say: 'Oh daughter, if I'd only known! I think I'd have really loved to be an actress.' Perhaps at that moment she would not have burnt the letters of my grandmother and Hugo!

You can see clearly that Dumas exaggerated and played games in his *Mémoires*. In several places my grandmother has corrected him in the margin. For example, he's talking about a session of the Palais de Justice, something about Hugo and a trial. Madame Olympe has written at the bottom of the page: 'You are lying, Alexander. They didn't say that. I was there.' It's amusing and made me feel fond of my beautiful, clever, formidable grandmother who ruined us all by her luxurious way of life. She had herself carried off by the man who loved her because her parents wouldn't give her to him. Carried off and put into a convent, in order to drag the longed-for 'yes' out of them. Later, when her love faded, they separated. There was no such thing as divorce. She was capricious, managing, independent. And I can see myself in all this. No doubt she loved her three children, but she loved herself more! Oh Grandmother, why did you bequeath me that, too? I'm said to resemble her physically, which flatters me – but she died of a dropsy and that horrible illness, so ugly and deforming, really frightens me.

Grandmother, does everything have to be paid for? Or is life on earth sufficient punishment for everything?

Joncières is here. He's been staying with Bataille who, he says, is still tired and ill. Yvonne de Bray nurses him, adores him, and he can no longer do without her. Everyone is a bit puzzled by this: their house is a mess, their servants are untrained and their cook is unspeakable.........

August 10. Léonce tells us all kinds of tittle-tattle: a witticism of Bovy's, a clever Comédie-Française actress, about Robinne, also of the Comédie-Française. Robinne is superb, classical, voluptuous, magnificent, but everything about her is a bit overdone – her hands, her cheeks, everything. 'She looks like an enlargement.' We couldn't help laughing because that's exactly it.

For Joncières, when it comes to looks, intelligence and talent there is no one but Piérat. He loves her madly and follows her everywhere, wants to see her four times a day, telephones her every morning, goes shopping for her, sings her praises, does his best to push her reputation, leaps into bed with her at night, gives her good advice, makes jealous scenes, swears by her alone, talks of her alone, lives for her alone. It makes him exceedingly boring and puts one off her. She wears her clothes well but no one ever wants to copy her dresses. There's nothing ugly about her but she is ordinary-looking, stringy, a bit meagre – the look of a housemaid in a good house. She doesn't act too badly, her technique is correct........

So that's *my* Piérat. She is not at all like Jonce's. She's married to Guirant, known as de Scevola, and they live their separate lives together in a perfectly friendly way. A well-established modern marriage. They each contribute what they can to the common stock, horrors, money, merits. They have a country house in Provence, a corner in Versailles, a good flat in the avenue Villiers. They live handsomely and keep good company. Apart from Joncières they know only rich people. Their close friends change often, according to the . . . shall I say heart's? . . . barometer. But Léonce is always there. He is closely and deeply attached to them. When there is a crisis – it can happen – he packs his bags and takes himself off to us, either here or at Roscoff. Whereupon he suffers, and his suffering exudes in the form of bad temper, complaints and grumbles. Then – it doesn't last long, it can't – back to the nest and we are more or less dropped. I don't mind. It's funny, if only because from listening to Joncière's talk I am able infallibly to pin-point Piérat's lovers, and I entertain myself with this as though it were a game. Last time it was a rich carpet merchant. At present there's a military man on the horizon. Lightly, he let fall the name of Marshal Pétain. Too good to be true!

August 11. Joncières plays the piano well. He says ingenuously: 'I play by ear, I never had a lesson.' I have heard *that* before! Lucie Delarue-Mardrus woke up one fine morning speaking perfect Hebrew: she had never had a lesson. Neither had Colette Willy when she played Schumann's 'Nut-tree' right through without one mistake. Vincent d'Indy's daughter, the pretty Marguerite de Bec-de-Lièvre, said almost the same thing when she played 'something of Papa's' at a party of mine, in my studio. Although 'something of Papa's' is very difficult!

That one knew how beautiful she was and delighted in shedding her clothes so that people could say it to her . . . so that they could prove it to her! What a delicious scatterbrain! An exquisite nymphomaniac, childlike face, golden skin, brilliant black eyes full of mischief, fair hair, haughty mouth, perfect teeth. It was impossible to love her deeply – the thought didn't occur. She was easy and vivid like a passing breeze, a whiff of scent, a fruit which one picks casually, a flower one smells almost without thought . . . .

. . . Georges is made of stone. Everything breaks against him. It looks as though I lead him by the nose, but not at all! He does what suits him, what falls in with his own ideas, what he condescends to approve of, but as for anything else – useless to go on about it. No use crying, raging, threatening, loving, joking, reasoning. His stubbornness is impossible to budge.

August 13. Our friends are sometimes astonished at our living so much on our own. For us peace and happiness lie in shutting our doors of an evening and finding each other again, alone with the beloved Italian greyhound who seems to enjoy the moment with all the voluptuous tenderness at her disposal.

I have had a letter from Marguerite Roquet, née Godard. Her mother was the daughter of my friend Valtesse de La Bigne, the Tesse of the *Idylle saphique**.

* Liane published this fictional account of her affaire with Natalie Barney in 1901.

That charming woman's death has left a hole in my life which no one else has yet filled. She would have suffered from what is called progress, that's to say from the tendency to accept and excuse shoddiness. She would have suffered but she would not have let it show. She was controlled, self-contained, reserved. Very lovely, sensual and intelligent, making a distinct separation in her life between the pleasures of the body and those of the mind. She never told me she had a daughter, yet we were friends to the limit – both permissible and forbidden. I was unforgiveable. One day I took Flossie to her house, went into a bedroom with Valtesse, locked the door and refused her nothing, highly amused at the thought of Flossie speculating and suffering on the other side of the door. How remote I feel today from the part of me which used to foment such stupid little nastinesses. Valtesse, so haughty and proud, whose motto was a superb 'Ego' and who once said to me: 'I am a courtesan, and how I do enjoy my work!'

August 15. Mary, Holy Virgin, I offer you this day. I hail you and I ask your forgiveness for everything within me which might offend you. I shall be tolerant, kind and gentle. I offer you Max Jacob and André Germain whom I do not like, but whom I shall try to like in your name, with all my compassion.

August 16. I have been given a pot of white marguerites. I have put it in Marco's room.

Yesterday I reread the letter he wrote me for my birthday in 1914. His fame, courage, luck and success had enlarged his spirit. He no longer resented the things about me which had wounded him. We loved each other tenderly: I was proud of him and he was glad about my marriage. Everything had become loving and sweet between us . . . my darling, how glad I am that you left me this memory of our sweetest understanding following after our savage times, and quite effacing them.

Max Jacob, nervous to begin with, was soon reassured. I told him that I meant to make the day go smoothly, having offered it to the Holy Virgin. He was witty and full of friendliness. This evening he leaves for Brittany, to Concarneau after stopping to see his mother and sister in Quimper.

Madame Jacob, his mother, has an antique shop on the quay at Quimper. She is a charming period piece herself, in the midst of her antiques, with her rustling high-necked silk dresses, her white wavy hair, her caustic look and her subtle, ironic mouth. Her conversation is a delight – old house, old papers, spirit of the past. She becomes quite forceful and funny, one feels her to be formidable and trenchant, very amusing anyway, knowing how to turn everything to account. She would have been at home anywhere where there was a government to lead, people to direct. Max has modelled himself on her. One can see him in her along with something settled, calm and established. Her voice is dry but she ends her sentences with a smile which turns up the corners of her mouth and sounds the tinkle of mockery. She's quite small but she looks tall because of all that she emanates. She has a superior mind. She doesn't choose to believe in anything . . . a majestic bearing in spite of being tiny and a gracious manner in spite of being in business. I like her enormously for her natural easiness and gracefulness and for her tart quality, blend of great lady and old woman who in her declining years has acquired the philosophy to control and illuminate emotion.........

Mademoiselle Jacob, Max's sister, has a beautiful and gigantic head. Hair like Absalom's to catch in the chandeliers, huge dazzling black eyes, full plump lips, a nose out of which you could make three . . . she's the shopkeeper who buttonholes passers-by in the street. That was how she accosted us. She wears antique ear-rings of gold and coral which suit her. She's a handsome queen of the fair ground who looks as though she spends her life on a roundabout. She stands there knitting rapidly and ceaselessly with enormous needles, trailing fat balls of dust-coloured wool wherever she goes.........

August 17. I've ordered a mauve shift. And another of grey crêpe de chine. I've been thinking a lot about clothes for some time, since Poiret's visit I believe. It stirred up the dregs of my old frivolity.

August 19. Salomon has declared that he would have loved Pauline* more, and after her Flossie, and from a great distance me, if we had led lives of perfect purity! I gave him a violent and eloquent lecture to prove that dung is necessary to the blooming of lilies and that perhaps Pauline's genius was so admirable and special precisely because she had given free rein to the materiality of her earthly envelope. That Nathalie remained the Exquisite, the Incomparable in spite of having allowed every kind of touch; and that as for me,

* Pauline Tarn, an English poet with whom Natalie Barney had a famous love affaire, better known under her pen-name, Renée Vivien.

I kept myself pure in spite of all the filth, kept my soul above it all though my body was given over to desires, remained ME in spite of everything, always and for ever.

After a declamatory speech in the style of Tonia Navar, I amused and rather surprised Salomon by reciting him a scene from *Femmes savantes* with a great deal of poise. Reichenberg gave me lessons for six months when I was eighteen. I could recite simply, clearly, with intelligence, but my voice didn't carry. It was all breath, and anyway I hated learning by heart. Reichenberg exclaimed: 'What a pity! I'd have to teach you nothing but technique. If you weren't so lazy you could be making your debut at the Vaudeville in six months time, and not in a supporting part, either.' Dear little teacher, how she scared me. Tiny and blonde, with her candid little face, her soft blue eyes, she simply terrified me. I remember begging her to turn her back so that I could let myself go a little in my speeches. She was proud of me. One day she invited Ignace Ephrussi and Prince Sagan to come and hear me. I couldn't open my mouth. So she laughed and hid them behind a big velvet curtain, and her 'little pet' was able to show her paces.

I met her one day at Virot's, just after my debut at the Folies-Bergère in – a conjuring act! She came up to me and said gently: 'Little pet, what a shame! What you are doing is so silly. I shall never come and see you down there, you know.' Emboldened, I replied: 'Yes, you will, you must promise me to come. The king of England (Edward VII who was then Prince of Wales) came to my première. You must come too.' Then she said: 'You are a silly, and the people who go to see you are even sillier, and I am the silliest of the lot, you know, because I was there on the first day! Goodbye!' Such kindness. People nowadays don't have the time or the inclination to be kind.

August 20. Been reading some Marie Bashkirtseff. It has disturbed me. That child had the whole of life ahead of her, was full of desire and ambition. She wanted the Duke of Hamilton to fall in love with her, then she wanted fame. As for me, my active life is over. I contemplate my past, I ponder Good and Evil. Georges has given me a relaxed, intelligent and harmonious present. I shall never again create anything. It is a matter of enjoying what has been acquired; it is the beginning of the end.

August 21. I am furious! Ever since April I've been longing for a beautiful rabbit-skin rug in big squares of black and white, edged with bands of black and white and lined with black velvet. Lewis is selling it on commission and we have not been able to strike a bargain. A month ago Laxton, the furrier, wanted 1,250 for it. I hesitated, then wrote again on August 18, and now he wants 1,400! I'm afraid of setting my heart on it. Something in me recoils from it and another part of me wants it more and more. Is it really reasonable, just before an operation? Yes, but is it reasonable to be nothing but reasonable? I shall end by tossing for it. That's the way I have made all the most serious decisions in my life: my marriage, buying the property, etc. There, I've just tossed. It's tails. I have to renounce the rug.

I have had four pages from my Salomon. He will have two of mine, on the subject of the nine painful months which followed my legitimate initiation. That makes me feel embarrassed, I don't like talking about it. My poor mother adored describing her pregnancies which were the most important and treasured events in her life. She said: 'I would have liked to have a glass stomach so that I could follow my child's development inside me day by day.' What a beautiful thing for a mother to say! But what a frightful image, all the same! ....

August 22. I have to admit that I'm up to my neck in frivolity, buried in dresses to the point of ruin! Fifteen different garments! My wardrobe jam-packed! My girl, this is not the way for an old woman to behave – particularly since you never wear anything but black and white, or a little grey, so that you always look as though you were in the same dress. Why fritter away your money so absurdly?

August 23. Am I vain? At bottom, yes. Not outwardly. I am aware of my beauty, naturally enough – the nation's Liane could hardly have remained unaware of it – but age is here. I often say 'Every age has its happiness and its beauty'. So my vanity finds words to console itself. I know that I am not a fool. I am prouder of my friendship with Salomon than of my husband's love. I am immensely and painfully proud of being Marco's mother. But I have a persistently naïve side which makes my first reaction to anything one of delighted amazement, whether it's a dress, a painting, a house, a piece of furniture, a book, a poem, a gesture, a face. On second thoughts I return to reality. So I seem very changeable and in fact I *am* changeable, oh dear yes, tremendously so. I'm always turning coats completely, and doing it with the utmost sincerity. So I have intelligence, but it has holes in it! And I never get to the bottom of anything, I have neither the time nor the inclination. I learn nothing. It's like wearing a watch, which I've never dreamt of doing. If I want to know the time I ask whoever happens to be at hand. In the same way, if I want to know something – all right, I'll ask the encyclopedia, or Georges, or above all Salomon. The Gascon's prayer would be the prayer for me: 'Give me not wealth, oh Lord, but the company of those who possess it.'

Wit? I am quite quick-witted. It still comes spontaneously when I write but it is slower when I'm speaking. My attention is drawn and held by exterior objects and I don't even think about what I am going to say. As soon as I start thinking, there's the repartee, easy and clever – and biting, too.

I am kind, really instinctively kind. I can be devoted but only to special people. Then I am infinitely so. I'm generous too. I like doing without in order to give – the old Catholic side of me, says Georges. I can't refuse anything if I'm asked for it, yet I'm afraid of being deprived. I keep accounts. Like an American, I want to get value for my money. I'm careful over five francs and spend five thousand without a thought. I'm never wasteful in little everyday matters – the good order of a household depends on that. I haven't always been rich so I take money seriously as a means to an end and to liberation. I save it when I can. I can seem miserly even to myself, and that disgusts me! I pause to question myself, I examine the facts in detail, I calculate. No, I am not miserly, I am prudent. I have profited from some hard lessons and from the example of other people's experience. But it's just as well to examine oneself from time to time, because it's a slippery slope: method leads to economy, economy leads to avarice – and that is really dreadful!

That and laziness. I abominate idleness. I like to have plenty to do, to organize and to look after. On days when I've trailed lazily hither and thither and nothing special has happened, I feel uncomfortable when I examine my conscience in the evening, as though I had done wrong. There are heaps of little daily duties to be performed, that's where one should turn for occupation. How can one ask everything from those around one if one gives nothing oneself? Before the war everything was so easy and abundant. In this big house where now I have two little maids and a cleaning woman, I used to have four Arab servants, a cook, a lady's maid, a scrubber and a housekeeper! I never put my hand to a thing. It was one long party! Everyone talked at the top of his voice, swore, frittered, guzzled, had a good time. Sometimes I used to pull myself up and tell myself: 'Life is too good, it can't last! It's against nature. Georges loves me, our health is more or less all right, my son is famous, I have charming friends, almost enough money . . . any change would ruin it.' The war came . . . catastrophes, sorrows.

August 24. Shall I draw my physical portrait? Tall, and looking even more so: 1.66 metres, 56 kilos in my clothes. I run to length – long neck, face a full oval but elongated, pretty well perfect; long arms, long legs. Complexion pale and matt, skin very fine. I use the merest touch of rouge, it suits me. Rather small mouth, well shaped, superb teeth. My nose? They say it's the marvel of marvels. Pretty little ears like shells, almost no eyebrows – hence a little pencil-line wherever I want it. Eyes a green hazel, prettily shaped, not very large – but my look is large. Hair thick and very fine, incredibly fine, a pretty shiny chestnut brown. Hardly any grey hairs. One or two, to prove that I don't dye. Bernstein once gave me the pretty nickname, Sable. 'Fine hair, the colour of a sable.' Marco had my hair, same colour, quality, quantity, growing into seven little peaks all round the head. When he brushed it back he was a real beauty.........

August 25. .... Giorgio has had a telegram from my brother-in-law: 'Can I visit you on Wednesday afternoon?' Giorgio doesn't want to answer. Henri has twice made appointments with us and then not turned up. We are affectionately cross with him and can do without his condescending presence. He has married a woman who doesn't wish to meet me. She is ugly, red-headed and – no doubt – virtuous. Her mother was a Drosso, which doesn't amount to much. The Drosso grandparents were, I believe, grocers. That kind of person will never forgive a dancer for bearing the same name as they do.

August 26. A ray of light in my sky! Laxton has written to say that he will let me have the beautiful black and white rug which I covet so badly for 1,250 francs. I thank him; I shall try to get it for 1,200, I order it at last. I tossed for it and got 'no', but my mysterious guardians have decided that I've had enough troubles to deserve this fugitive pleasure. I will not order any more dresses for a whole year.

M. Simon, our neighbour who owns the Duc de Noailles' former orangery with 22,000 metres surrounding it, asks if he can visit us. Oh, if only he can buy our wing of the château, what a relief that would be! His gardener has been round our grounds – he admired the trees and the design of the paths and lawns, and he showed me heaps of little details overlooked by my own gardener. Ignorance and ill-will combined.

The other day someone asked me how old Emilienne d'Alençon is. Fifteen years ago I heard people saying she must be fifty, and she is not that even now. There is just a year between us. How pretty she used to be! Enormous golden eyes, the finest and most brilliant complexion! A proud little mouth, a tip-tilted nose you could eat, an oval face rather in the style of my own.

We were friends, she was my leading light in the ways of the theatre and of our pleasures. She could be beastly, but was really so pretty that one couldn't hold it against her. For instance, she said to me: 'I know you are going to be at this big dinner tonight. Don't dress, I shall be wearing just a coat and skirt and a blouse and one row of pearls. You do the same, so that we'll be alike – and send your carriage away, I'll take you home.' So at eight o'clock there I am in my simple little suit and one row of pearls – and at nine o'clock in sweeps my Emilienne resplendent in sumptuous white and gold brocade, dripping with diamonds, pearls and rubies, no hat, her curls full of sparkling jewels. 'Oh dear – am I late?', with a delicious little pretence at absent-mindedness! One careless, hardly even teasing, glance at me, and she doesn't speak to me for the rest of the evening. But as she leaves she says goodbye and offers me her lips with the choicest nonchalance. And I go home in a cab, confused and cross, brooding bitterly on these lines which I found in a notebook belonging to my grandmother Olympe:

> In each young girl with gentle eyes you see
> A sister, not a rival . . .

Two days later and it might never have been, on my side as well as hers. With an impudence as great as her beauty she had moved in on me, had installed herself in my bed, at my table, in my carriages, in my theatre boxes – and all, I must confess, to my great pleasure. I couldn't be strict with her. But fore-warned is fore-armed, and I no longer believed what she said.

We went to Nice together, to the casino and to fancy-dress balls. We gambled together at Monte Carlo. Everyone admired us and ran after us; we were fêted, we were spoilt. Darling little Mimi! Last year, at the Majestic, she came to spend an afternoon with me. It was very moving to see each other again after twelve or thirteen years, and we were pleased to find each other still so beautiful. Her face is still ravishing, mine too. We cheered each other up. Our lives have gone completely different ways. She laughs, she dances, she stays up all night, she smokes (opium), she enjoys everything just as she used to do. She is rich, she has lots of friends. Bad friends – but that doesn't worry her. Her expression is still childlike and amused. When you tell her a joke she chuckles like a delightful chicken. She has become a woman of letters and has published a collection of sensitive and well-turned verse. She never stops falling in love, following her whim for better or for worse. She is adored, she's always changing lovers. They weep for her a little – too little – and console themselves rather too soon, but they are proud that she was there. How often have I heard someone drop her name into a conversation with a smug little look! She used to be my favourite model, vicious and ravishing, not like the others. Nothing about her was banal or vulgar, not her face, nor her gestures, nor the things she dared to do. It was she who made me cut my hair. She turned up with a pair of scissors and 'snip', it was done. Then she said: 'Come along, we'll try some henna.' Three months later, we were corn-coloured. Then in a flash we became brunette. We did have such fun with ourselves – and how we laughed at others, both men and women. And then, little Mimi, your lips were so soft, your gestures were so coaxing and . . . but here we are, my dear, a pair of nice little old ladies.

I received Salomon like the Queen of Sheba, reclining in a mass of mauve and blue chiffon, lace, scent, cushions and silk with the Italian greyhound lying at my side. We sipped beverages from China, nibbled sweetmeats from the South and pastries from the Ile de France. I read him some poems by Vehaeren. We talked about Renée Vivien and Flossie.

Poiret is angry and doesn't want to take back the badly made dress. I'm sulking and trying to gain time. Georges telephoned him and came up to my room quite green from having had to listen to the Magnificent as he fulminated. It's impossible, I'm always letting myself be taken in. Poiret's models are lovely but there is always something wrong with the workmanship.

Lewis has sent me a beautiful box of chocolates. He is burying the lost rug under sweetness; it costs less, appears to be gallant and can't be answered. Let him continue! In the ranks of the unbearable, Lewis comes lower than Poiret – *he* really is the king of them all!

One day in Monte Carlo, when I was competing with Otero in the display of jewels and dresses, an old Austrian Jew suddenly asked me, without ceremony, to have dinner with him. 'Oh no,' I said. – 'And why not?' – 'I don't care for your manner. That is not the way kings get accepted.' – 'Kings? What kings?' – 'Yes, kings, I love no one but kings.' – 'But the other day you had dinner with M. Goudstikker. He's not a king.' – 'Yes he is, he's the king of jewellers.' – 'And I've seen you dining with M. Battard . . .' – 'He's the king of cooks.' – 'And M. Lewis?' – 'He's the king of milliners.' He went off baffled, but the night brought council. Next day he sent me marvellous flowers, kilos of chocolates, a beautiful doll and this note: 'Have dinner with me. I am the king of fools.'

August 27. . . . . I am devouring Rabelais. He has one chapter which exactly fits Georges: 'How Pantagruel meets a man from Limousin who counterfeits the French language.' Georges constantly employs odd, little-used words, which make his speech sound silly, pedantic and boring. And he believes that he speaks so purely!

. . . .

August 29. Poiret has sent me two letters in the same envelope, one business, one friendly. Taken together they are impertinent and mean: whether or not your dress is all right, you will keep it and you will pay, or watch out! I shall pay. That is what princesses are for. . . . .

. . . .

August 31. Madame Calmette wanted to do table-turning last night. Louise Balthy* is a great believer: she says that her sister Justine is a good medium and that the whole of her glorious and lucky theatrical career was foretold when she was only fourteen years old and working for a haberdasher who specialized in mourning. To think of comic Louise, immersed in funeral crêpe!

Louise has a rare elegance and chic, wears enormous hats no one

* Louise Balthy was known as Polaire.

else could get away with, dresses in black and white, wonderful shoes, the latest thing in jewellery whether real or sham, and knows antiques as well as the sharpest dealer. She strokes a glaze or a soft paste like a connoisseur – a gourmet – and has furnished herself a little house fit for a queen with the finest of fine things. She had a tremendously successful sale. The little Basque peasant has come a long way and could stand as a symbol and example. She laughs, sings, dances, loves, recites, lies, groans, jokes – what vitality! Everyone likes her because gaiety is the quality that lasts best. Her voice – grave, sonorous, well-modulated – has extraordinary charm.

One day I heard some pretty idiot tell someone, in front of Louise: 'Louise is ugly.' The person addressed replied: 'Louise is ugly only in the eyes of imbeciles.'

September 1. The Queen of Roumania has given the *Revue des deux-mondes* an article on 'Tsar Nicolas II: a Martyr of the Great Tragedy'.

I saw Nicolas in Petersburg in the winter of 1891 when he was still the Crown Prince. An officer of the horse guards was getting married and giving his last party as a bachelor, and I was invited. The Crown Prince made his appearance at the beginning of supper and hurried off ten minutes later because he had to get back to Tsarsko Selo, where he lived with his parents, by a certain time. He seemed to me timid, embarrassed, gentle, good-natured and very mediocre. A few months later he lost his father. I was back in Russia that winter, for an engagement at the little Marie theatre. My engagement fell through because of the public mourning – and because I didn't want to stay on for it. I was at the Tsar's funeral. I saw the Crown Prince in the distance, transformed into the great Emperor of All the Russias, more pitiable than ever under his heavy burden.

How well I remember the wonderful ceremony, full of legendary symbols: the 'Old Reign' personified by a man in iron armour, all black, and so heavy that the man condemned to fill the role died on arrival at the fortress of St Peter and St Paul – if not on the way there. The 'Old Reign' led a black horse caparisoned in funeral draperies. He was followed by the 'New Reign'. He was a knight dressed in gold, riding a magnificent white horse adorned with white and gold.

I wrote a long letter to Meilhac describing this famous funeral in detail. My letter was so vivid and well-written that he read it out to some friends. Arthur Meyer was among them. He asked if he could have it for *le Gaulois*, and my letter was published word for word . . .

Dear Arthur's readership was pious and aristocratic; and he was as brave as a rabbit and as sly as – an Arthur Meyer. He published my letter without putting my name at the end, describing the author as 'One of our friends, an elegant Parisienne who is at present in St Petersburg and was able to attend the funeral of the Tsar' – and that's how little Liane had the honour of filling several columns in *le Gaulois*, certainly a respectable newspaper if ever there was one. The following New Year's Day, Arthur sent me a box of Pihan's chocolates. Pihan let him have them at a discount . . .

September 4. This morning I found a ravishing pair of adorable little Louis-Philippe vases for 4.75 francs. I note the fact here because it's so unusual for me to do good business with an antique dealer.

Tomorrow I am going to confession. I have begun to examine my conscience: no big sins. I was talking about it to Georges in front of Steinilber, who said 'Those are primary school sins.'

. . . .

Neuilly – September 11 to October 5

September 11. Intense and suffocating heat for the journey. Arrived in the light, airy house. Our three little rooms – Georges's bedroom, my bedroom and a dressing-room between them – seemed like a palace. A dreary little nursing-home dinner at seven o'clock. Hartmann welcomed us very affectionately.

September 12. Agitated night, almost no sleep. A bad beginning, as far as I am concerned. Jeanne de Pallady came this morning with two sheaves of pink carnations. She had been to the station to meet Mariette. Poor Mariette – her train had missed the connection at Trieste and she won't be here until tomorrow. She must be hot and enraged!

Georges swigged castor-oil at five in the morning, then two big cups of some herbal brew.

Bernstein heralded his arrival with an enormous bunch of enormous roses. He brought us the dressmaker Gabrielle Chanel – the taste of a fairy, the eyes and voice of a woman, the hair-cut and figure of an urchin.

September 13. Hartmann has thoroughly examined yesterday's X-ray photo. My God, there is only You! Georges and I are one and it is You who made us so. Surely You will not separate us? Endure everything! Suffer everything! Accept everything: people's cruelty, unkind judgments, illnesses, grief, ruin – but let us be together, for always.

September 14. Tomorrow's the day. The operation will be more delicate – they have got to get past the peritoneum – and longer. I went to church, I tried to pray, but it wouldn't come. I entrust myself to God and His will with a beautiful resignation.

Giorgio is admirable in his serenity.

September 15. Last night Giorgio and I bade each other farewell, love's sweet, sad farewell. Dear Giorgio, all childlike profundity and wisdom even in your follies; fatalistic, resigned, loyal, generous, attached and devoted even unto death – tonight I see none of your faults!

It is morning. The nurse is here, the hour is approaching. Georges is calm. So am I. I feel cold and distant, almost like a nun.

It's over, the operation has been a success. Georges is beautiful, pale, his magnificent features so rested. Hartmann is radiant. He hit on the stone at once, the whole thing lasted no more than forty-five minutes.

Sacha Guitry sent me a *pneu* which arrived during the operation: 'We are thinking of you', with his signature and his wife's. It brought tears to my eyes. Balthy telephoned. Salomon was standing by his telephone waiting for my call and asks for further news during the evening. Jeanne de Pallady, kind as ever, came early and took me out for a walk at the actual moment.

Flowers, telegrams, telephone calls, visits. I'm at the end of my strength.

September 17. A bad night. I'm depressed. Georges who was very ready to sleep after his morphine injection, was kept cruelly and stupidly awake by an appalling din, an atrocious and endless cacophony. Motor traffic, and then towards ten o'clock, the time when ill people get their deepest sleep, the Richer company going by with all its paraphernalia: the clip-clop of heavy horses, the rumbling of heavy caravans, the yells and oaths of heavy drivers, whinnying, braying, bellowing, etc.

I have been beastly, I have failed to practise Christian charity today. Georges wanted the door between our rooms to be shut during the night so that if I had the luck to fall asleep I wouldn't be woken. I shouted: 'You know that I can't sleep, you know that I'm alone and I'm frightened.' He persisted – ponderously, as he does everything. So then I slammed his door and locked the second door. I refused to go in to see him, and I can tell from the hundred thousand devils inside me that nothing and no one will be able to make me set foot in there this evening, and perhaps not tomorrow either, for the whole day. Not a nice character, Liane.

I really do adore Georges, but I never give way to him. At the beginning of our relationship I gave way all the time and he started using me as his pin-cushion. So I treat him rather more toughly and our household is the happier. I have been suffering dreadfully for him during these past few days, I was ready to die for him, I feel all his mother's cruelty towards him and my love is increased by pity and becomes even more tender and maternal, and then he opposes me stupidly without a thought for the terrible trials my poor nerves have been through. As I write this my throat constricts. I'm almost in tears. I feel quite shattered by these nights without sleep, I no longer know where I am.

By Mariette's 'cruelty' I mean the destitution in which she leaves Georges. She has had plenty of money since the war, but she lets months go by without sending him any under the pretext that the exchange is unfavourable. Rich as she is, she keeps her sons in the most complete dependence; they have nothing of their own. She makes them an allowance of barely thirty thousand francs a year, by dribs and drabs. And she brought them up on the footing, and with the tastes, of three hundred thousand francs a year. They can count on nothing; she promises and doesn't send, she announces and nothing comes because she has changed her mind. It is shameful and sordid. Hartmann took out Georges's appendix in 1916; we couldn't pay the bill. Very kindly, he consented to wait. So now Georges asks his mother to pay for both operations and give Hartmann a present for his obligingness. This is the answer he got: 'What nonsense! The exchange is terrible. I'll pay for one of the operations, perhaps. As for a present, certainly not!' There's nothing sublime about *that* mother! A French family might have cut off a son for marrying Liane de Pougy, but since she seemed to want to preserve some dignity for her son and herself and didn't do that, why doesn't she behave better? She has the tight, thin-lipped mouth of a miser.

September 18. I can't go on staying here, it's impossible. It will kill me, and my presence is useless to Georges because he insists on keeping the door shut. I'm going to try to move across the street, to Cautru's place. We stayed there in 1916; it is possible to sleep. My devotion and my discomfort are serving no purpose, and it's really stupid to ruin my health when I have had years of trouble re-establishing my nerves. I shall visit Georges during the day, and at night he has an excellent nurse, there is nothing I can do for him. This morning I can hardly stand, I'm on the verge of tears, seven nights without sleep have left me shaken, trembling and distraught.

So that's done! Here I am installed at Cautru's in a dreary little room with a bathroom, overlooking the back garden. It has been quite hard. Except for Marco's funeral, we have never been apart. With the tragi-comic stubborness of a true Breton, I tell myself over and over again: 'I have done right to retire to this quiet little hole rather than die of sleeplessness outside his locked door.' I'm terribly stubborn, and he, who knows me, is incurably given to putting his foot in it. He never thought I'd do this, and neither did I for that matter! I'm a little scared. Darling little Giorgio, now we are apart I love you; in the next room I'd be bad-tempered and boring.

Heaps of visitors: Max Jacob, Lambert, Noblet the actor, René de La Jaille, Hélène Miropolsky, Duret. This evening I daren't talk to God, or pray to Him, and yet . . .

. . . .

September 26. . . . . I talked to Georges about his mother. I said to him 'She has a sad, anxious face, closed to every kind of pleasure, rather aggressive. We should be sorry for her, she has no pleasures, she has nothing but functions.' He answered: 'Not at all. She loves everything that affirms her personality. She has chosen her destiny. The only thing she loves is increasing the value of her Roumanian estates, and she gets her happiness from that.' Poor little widow, far away from her sons, struggling on in her oceans of corn, vines and forests. She lives almost alone at Mascatene, an hour's train journey from Jassy, under the thumb of her German maid who is the only being who has mastered her and whom she loves, confides in and always treats with much consideration.

September 27. . . . . A most touching surprise: Maître P. A. Huillier (eighty-four years old) has forwarded me a communication from Indochina in which he is asked to tell me that the town of Tourane (Annam), where my son made some magnificent flights in 1913, has just given one of its streets the name of Marc Pourpe! I am so happy and quite overwhelmed. Maître Huillier will send them my thanks and a copy of a codicil added to my will this very morning, bequeathing twenty-five thousand francs to the town of Tourane.

September 28. I have just written Mariette a letter full of good and soothing news. I can see her from here, pulling a face when she sees my handwriting, not because she hates me but simply because she isn't used to it. Oh, these Balkan types! When I first knew Georges I adored him. He was twenty-three years old and I was thirty-five. I analysed the situation, I still had enough sense left for that, and the conclusions I drew were hardly cheerful because the gentleman was giving me a lot of trouble: he affected vices which he hadn't got, he told me about his past and future conquests with just enough reticence to be tormenting, and finally he thought up this: he would say he'd be with me at two o'clock and would not turn up until six. When he did me the favour of arriving at last, I daren't even complain. Once I said gently: 'Georges, you told me you would be here at two o'clock.' I brought this answer down on myself: 'I know, but I couldn't manage it. I was lunching with Madame Paul Reboux and afterwards we went for a long drive. And Madame Paul Reboux is uncommonly pretty . . .' My blood froze. I restrained myself, however, and made an appointment for the next day. Two o'clock came – no Georges, naturally. Jeanne de Bellune was there, so I said to her: 'Janot, you've a motor-car. Take me for a drive.' Good fellow that she was, Janot whirled me off to Saint-Germain for a spin in the woods, then to Versailles for tea at the Reservoirs; and then she said 'You are coming to have dinner with me.' I accepted, and it was midnight before I got home. There was my young Ghika in a Japanese kimono, pale, bilious, anxious, looking really unhappy. When he hadn't found me at home he'd been unable to believe his eyes, he'd eaten no dinner, he was completely shattered. He threw himself on me: 'What have you been doing? Where have you been?' Calmly I replied: 'I've been following your example, darling.' Silence, speaking looks, raptures; and never another lapse. He told me: 'That day's upset taught me that I can't exist without you.' I understood his character, I based my own on it, and as a result you don't find many couples as deliciously harmonious as we are.........

September 29. A photo of myself as a dancer: the ballet was directed by Mariquita, terrible little old woman, as talented as she was horrid.

Dear Madame Mariquita! How she could fray my nerves and reduce me to tears, but she did drag something out of me – out of the wooden creature whose first steps on the stage she produced – I have to admit it – in the Folies-Bergère of 1894. You could hate her but you couldn't despise her. She knew and loved her job; she was its master, a genius, a pro. In the midst of my independent and disorderly life she represented authority, duty, order, restraint, education. She gave me my calling, self-confidence and grace. Posture by Mariquita, hair by Marcel, dresses by Callot, hats by Lewis, it really was quite a show! ....
....

October 2. Mademoiselle Mermillod, the ex-nun from the Companions of Jesus who had special charge of my soul (she taught me literature, history and geography and was my tutor at table and for games) and who has been wrestling with life as a laywoman since the closing of the convents, has written to say that she will be in Paris early this month and ask when and where she can meet us. I answered at once to tell her that we'd be back at Saint-Germain on the 7th. Dear Amélie, she operated on charm: beautiful, dark-haired, white-skinned, with pretty features and a most persuasive and eloquent tongue, she could get us to do anything she wanted. We made up fantastic stories about her – love stories, of course. We piously preserved scraps of her writing, stubs of pencils, threads from the fringes of her nun's shawl. What a fierce need to love children have!

Amélie was one of my first loves (she, and a bareback rider in the Bazola circus called Annette Secchi, whom I rediscovered some twenty years later training horses at the Olympia while I was miming the part of Madame Paralière in *Watteau*, a pantomime ballet by Jean Lorrain). I have seen her since and at first it touched my heart: poor bird, thrown so brutally out of the nest. She didn't know how to pay for a taxi; she was unable to believe that people could tell lies.

Amélie knew my father, my mother, Marco when he was a baby, and me in all my first candour and purity. The first time I met her again was after my car accident. She was rather stiff and embarrassed, and said to me: 'My dear little Marie, when you were under the motor-car, did you think to make an act of contrition?' I answered with a laugh: 'Oh no, Mother Gasperine! I was in too much of a rage at dying.'

I met her again after my marriage. In the course of a conversation I said to her: 'Amélie, you are still beautiful, you could perfectly well get married.' Startled, and rather indignant, she replied 'I may be out in the world, Marie, but I am still the servant and spouse of Our Lord, and so I will remain.' Six months later something happened . . . she had her hair waved, she began to go to the theatre and to make up her face, she was looking for a husband!

Dear Amélie, I have to dismiss thirty years of thoughts about you in order to get used to what you have now become.

October 3. A photo of me taken in St Petersburg in 1892. Hat by Lewis. It was a whim and not the theatre which took me there. I was nineteen and a half years old. When I arrived in the melancholy of that wintery Russia I felt so sad that I cried. Even though I had held quite a court on the train. One old count whose name I forget, one of the Emperor's chamberlains, had started to cry thief in the middle of the night. Panic, hubbub, explanations: 'My watch has been stolen,' he yelled. 'It's been stolen while I was asleep. I wound it before I went to bed and it's of immense value to me. It was a present from the Emperor. A thousand roubles to anyone who finds it!' Everyone started to look for it, people were searched, every smallest corner was examined and the watch was found . . . under the old count's pillow! He had been suffering from a copious dinner and a great many glasses of champagne.

That country frightened me. I returned there three or four times and I could have married a Russian or two – a handsome officer in the horse guards, a hussar: a great name, a fortune, but no security.

I have belonged to the Society of Authors since the day when Félix Faure died, I have forgotten the date. On that evening (when I was starting typhoid) they played a little one-acter of mine at the Funambules, directed by the mime Séverin. I even had the honour of being interpreted by Séverin Mars and Henriette Roggers, who have been accepted by many important writers since then. Bouchor made me write a letter to René Fauchois, president of the play-wrights' union, saying that I wanted to join them. I was all for it. I am always on the side of the weak, the oppressed, the rebellious! And also for whatever will work . . .

October 4. .... In the old days at the Folies-Bergère I was great friends with a pretty little English dancer, another shooting star, Mimi Saint-Cyr. She drank enormously. Once I saw her in Maxim's, waiting for twelve o'clock to strike. She had twelve glasses of kummel ready on the table. At the twelfth stroke the table was clear! What dexterity and what a capacity! I watched her with my mouth agape. Everyone crowded round to congratulate her. She wasn't very drunk, just as gay as can be, and believe it or not she danced with her usual skill. It was that evening that she made a long-lasting conquest of the little Prince of Annam.

My Georges has been for a walk in the garden and in the afternoon he went out of the grounds as far as the Boulevard Bineau. Great progress. I've written to Robert Goldschmidt, asking him to lend us his Rolls Royce for when Georges goes home. It's the smoothest car in the world. Goldschmidt is a flirt of mine but not at all a restful one. He can be shameless and rude, with the most discouraging candour. He is in Brussels at the moment and has both written and telegraphed that he's delighted to put the car at our disposal for Thursday. So I shall be rather less worried about the bumpiness and length of the journey.

My Roscoff friend Madame Garat, or Camille .... is a natural child recognized by her mother who gave birth to her in a charitable institution at the age of sixteen. Mother Besnier's amorous career took place in Mans, which she never wanted to leave. She became quite the thing and ended by owning almost all of the rue Verte, the most ill-famed street in the town. In her old age she went into antiques and acquired a name, even fame, as a dealer, and a fat fortune. She wanted her little Camille to be well brought up, left her for a long time with a foster-mother and then sent her to a very expensive boarding school in Neuilly. Later, when Camille's schooling was finished, she made her take courses at the Conservatoire, gave her Mademoiselle Dumesnil of the Théâtre-Français as a teacher, and entrusted her to the care of the Countess de Buffon, mother of my friend Yvonne. It was through Yvonne that I got to know Camille. Imagine what might have happened to my Camille in that setting! No punctuality, no order, no duties! As soon as her mother paid them her monthly rent, off they went to the theatre and to restaurants. After that they were flat broke and lived from hand to mouth. They planted radishes on the drawing-room balcony, and Camille, heiress and rich paying-guest, used to hear the Countess call: 'Camille darling, a horse has just plopped in the street. Here's a tray – run quickly and collect it, it makes marvellous manure.' And Camille would rush out into the street to collect this precious treasure. They would buy salad and my Camille would be sent round to the grocer with a little jar to buy two-sous worth of ready-made dressing. Three times they sold the same ancestral portrait by Philippe de Champaigne. Each time they sold it, it was on condition that a copy should be made for them to keep, for sentimental reasons. Then a handy man called Garnet would antiquate it with much care and skill . . . But on January 21, the anniversary of the death of Louis XVI, they all wore black and windows and piano were kept shut.

When she got back to Mans Camille started to take lovers because she liked them, and quarrelled with her mother. Then she got to know Jules Garat, a romantic writer and friend of Peladan, who was not without talent and possessed two hundred thousand francs. He had read Tolstoy and decided to rescue this lost soul. Eventually, when the first love and excitement had passed, he made her the most wretched woman on earth. He ate the hearts of the artichokes, Camille nibbled the leaves. He gobbled the plums, Camille sucked the stones. He picked out the perfect pears, Camille made do with the rotten ones. And so on. He beat her, bullied her, insulted her. Even worse, he read her all his outpourings – and that was, indeed, an appalling fate. He started roaming the countryside dressed in flowing red robes, with crowns of ivy or vineleaves entwined in his hair. At last he left her, came to Paris, took up with the aesthetes, second-rate poets and their women, and went right out of his mind. He committed suicide.

Poor Camille, abandoned by everyone, turned to God. She has become very pious.

October 5. Salomon came to pick me up most punctually at 9.45. The car was an open one and we glided off to the cemetery at Passy. Dear, brilliant Marie Bashkirtseff; dear, rather brilliant Pauline – you must lend me your beautiful voices for the celebration of this, my first visit to your tombs. I was so much moved when I saw the chapel where my little muse reposes! There are epitaphs in verse round the walls, beautiful poems, sad, desolate, definitive. At the far end, one of her paintings: a desolate woman in a fierce pose, seated, gazing despairingly into the distance. Nearby stands the misty figure of another woman, weeping into her hands. It seems that they put the furniture from her studio into her tomb. There is her bust in white marble, wilful and proud, and a little reading chair covered in bronze plush with a flowered strip down the middle, all buttoned. It was the period for buttoned upholstery. Her chapel is large and was designed by Bastien-Lepage, the ultimate offering of a loving and broken heart. She lies under a little dome, rather Russian: 1860 – 1884.

Pauline's chapel is long and narrow like a little bed. Yes, like her: long and narrow. A photograph of her, after Levy Dhurmer, is placed in the middle, under the altar; in front of it, an incense burner. The windows are yellow, with figures, bordered with violet; two ivory virgins, one Christ, two old Delft pharmacist's pots containing thistles dyed mauve, church embroideries flung here and there, little bunches of dried violets hung on the grill with lilac ribbons, a selection of her lovely poems carved all around . . . On the exterior wall two verses which went straight to my heart:

See, I have passed through this door
Oh my thorn-bedizened roses.
Gone is what used to be. For ever more
My dreaming soul with God reposes

Calmly asleep, forgetting strife,
Having with its last breath,
For love of death,
Forgiven that crime, life.

Dear Pauline, have you forgiven me? We were tender rivals for Flossie, then friends. When I was in hospital having been crushed by my car on the public highway, you sent me flowers and copies of your books with beautiful inscriptions. And then one day your intimate friend, that little gnome Janot de Bellune, told me something very tart which you had said about me. I was ruffled and wrote you a letter – also very tart. Later I learnt of your illness and your death. Bitterness vanished from my heart. This morning's little pilgrimage was my symbol of repentance. Pauline died an edifying death. She suffered; she suffered in many ways. The dead are on the road between God and ourselves.........

Georges has given Hartmann's nursing-home a name: 'The Cancervatory'.

October 7 and 8. Here we are, back home . . . . I have had a fire lit in my big bedroom with its Louis XIV panelling painted royal blue. It's nice, warming and cheering. Georges is in an armchair with his feet on a stool. He is progressing very well. I am tired, good-tempered, happy. The grounds have a distressingly forlorn look, we must find gardeners.

Georges's operation has cost us 10,930 francs. Fourteen tips had to be given, fourteen thank-yous and mementoes.

October 9. I can't help laughing when I think of the things we buy, of the way we satisfy our expensive whims, and of the expression Mariette's face would wear if she knew about it! In front of her we bewail our poverty better than any beggar at a church door. 'That's a pretty dress, Liane!' – 'I've been wearing it four years, Madame.' – 'That hat really suits you.' – 'This is its third winter.' – 'What a ravishing rug.' – 'I got it in exchange for my old moleskin coat which needed altering, but I really couldn't afford to have it done.' – 'Where will you be going this summer?' – 'To Roscoff, the cost of living is lower there and one doesn't have to dress up.' – 'How cold your house is!' – 'Oh dear, I know, but coal . . . but wood . . . It's all so expensive.' – 'Georges, I've never seen you looking so shabby.' – 'But, Maman, I haven't a penny to spend on clothes.' And so the litany continues – it's odious but essential. When we are honest we get nothing, all because of that famous exchange and also because of Mariette's . . . well, her *careful* temperament.

Joncières has telephoned twice. He must have had a tiff with his Piérat and need a little suburban repose.

October 12. I've been to mass, or rather, dear Lord, I crept into the basement of Your house, into Your sanctuary while Your faithful were at prayer. I did it out of obedience, and humility, and to prove my gratitude. Accept, o my God, all that part of me that reaches towards you.

October 14. Squalls of rain, an icy house. I walk about our rooms wearing a coat, a pretty coat, light and warm, which is two years old. It's not fashionable – it never was – but it has a period look: it's the coat Madame Hanska would have worn as she got into a berlin on the way to visit Balzac!

Salomon came. Such delight, walk in the grounds, tea and cigarettes, and the conversation which is one of the pleasures of our life, these days. He is re-cataloguing the museum and has to look at all the showcases: an enormous and exhausting task.

October 15. The Great Mademoiselle has made her appearance, on the arm of Goldschmidt, The Great Mademoiselle is Sorel [Cécile Sorel, the actress], who has well and truly made it. She's looking for a house in the country, near Paris, and she loves whatever is old and has a beautiful shady garden – in other words Goldschmidt thinks of doing us a good turn, and her too. She came lilting in on winged feet, her smile flowery, her face framed in ringlets blond *for ever* [in English]. She was wearing a lovely black velvet coat trimmed with skunk and a Louis XVI hat which shaded her face. She bestowed honeyed words on the invalid reclining among his multi-coloured cushions, on our discreet and exemplary love, on the happiness of marriage, on my childlike complexion, on Giorgio's curls, on the negress, on the staircase, on the white-veiled nurse, on my pearls, my trees, my bits and pieces. She admired everything most conscientiously, murmured a tactful word about Salomon – glad of a chance to let me know that she, too, has a Reinach who comes to visit her. She sipped an old plum brandy, was kind enough to nibble a biscuit, said nothing foolish, made Goldschmidt swear that he would bring us to see her one day, etc. Could hardly have been pleasanter. A second-rate creature at bottom, always tense, artificial, on her guard, with no intimate, inward life.

About twelve years ago, in my Liane de Pougy days, I wrote an article on her and Henry Bataille read it and said 'You catty thing!' Sorel didn't catch on, at first. She ordered fifty copies. Then someone enlightened her, and I was told 'I think she's got it in for you, you made such fun of her.' But did I really make such fun of her? I admire her without question, for a lot of things. She has made a magnificent success of her life, without a hitch. She is absolutely tiny, it's the fashion. She told me: 'It's terrible, I live the life of a jockey in order to keep my weight down, and it's no joke because I'm horribly greedy.'

Goldschmidt was all bustle and bliss, letting us tease him and giving us such fatuous looks that we almost giggled. Happily I was wearing a pretty Poiret dress, two years old, but Poiret is always *up to date* [in English] so it didn't show: a long dress of off-white bouclé wool – in the style of Peau d'Ane's moon-coloured dress – trimmed with black velvet and little mother of pearl buttons. Sorel admired it, naturally, and my coat too – though when I said it was Madame Hanska's coat for driving in a berlin, she looked a bit blank.

October 18. Yes, materially life is becoming more and more difficult. One wonders what will become of us. Our big house is so demanding, more than we are. Thinking of life's difficulty reminds me of something Sem* said, twenty years ago. He had been to dinner with me in my little house in the rue de la Néva which I sold later to Princess de Broglie (Princess Auguste de Broglie-Revel was Jeanne Thylde, a mime at the Olympia when I was there, my friend and often my partner. Two princesses emerged from backstage at the Olympia. Sem was very perceptive but I don't know whether he foresaw that). Anyway, after dinner, when my electric brougham came gliding round to take us to the theatre, heated, and upholstered in white cloth, Sem gave me a look and said in his Bordelais accent: 'Life doesn't half treat you well!'

The Olympia, Thylda, Sem, Otero! Otero and Liane de Pougy, the two stars. Thylda was a good performer but she wasn't a star. Otero and Liane . . . stars, rivals.

Two years ago, on the Champs-Elysées, I suddenly noticed a fat lady with a very lovely face and a good deal of style, wearing sumptuous furs, with enormous pearls in her ears. It was my Otero! It really is true that every age has its beauty! She was quite roly-poly in her fat, but she looked radiant and her marvellous face was still the same.

Cavalieri, too, was among the Folies-Bergère stars of that time. She was as pretty as a cupid, with a piquante, subtle expression, but she didn't have Otero's splendid presence. One day a journalist asked me 'What is your opinion of Otero and Cavalieri?' For answer I gave him this little comparison which depicts them both: 'It's like this: when Cavalieri wears real jewels they look false, and when Otero wears false jewels they look real.'

Cléo too, dear, sweet little Cléo was on the same bill with us. I saw her in Monte Carlo when she was almost forty. She was still absolutely a little girl, tiny and nimble, smiling and fragile, fresh in spite of a few silver threads in her long plaits. She had just been

* Sem was a well-known caricaturist whose real name was Georges Gourset.

dancing very gracefully in a ballet of Paul Franck's. I congratulated her and we chatted for a minute or two: 'I have to go now,' she said in her little-girl's voice. 'I want to go back to the hotel to play with my dolls before dinner.' It wasn't a pose. Genuine puerility – not that it hadn't served some very dubious ends with men . . . but let's not go into that.

Max Jacob came with a friend of his called Herz, a writer and critic, rather scheming, who wants to undertake the sale of my house. Max looked well and was in very good form. Among other striking things, he said that there is something 'metallic' about Jews. He talked with me, too, about God, Jesus and the Church. He is very much a practising convert, but it is odd how when he talks to me about those things I feel embarrassed and a bit pained, as though he were making me an accomplice in a sacrilege.

. . . .

November 8. They are doing quite an interesting play of Jean-Jacques Bernard's at the Théâtre-Libre. It made me think of our friend Count Roman Potocki. When the Cossacks overran his estates (Lansut in Austria) they found everything they could wish for in the castle. Roman was already old, but great nobleman that he was, he received them generously, simply and without bravado. When they left, they damaged nothing. Most of the neighbouring landowners had panicked and run away. Their properties were razed, looted, burnt. So the Austrians put their heads together, decided Roman must be suspect, and had his castle searched. He had to endure the sight of his beautiful Lansut taken over by the police who cruelly and systematically demolished the panelling, the floors, the chimney pieces, the ceilings, knocked down walls, took a criminal and brutal delight in ruining everything. Poor Roman was unable to stand the affront and the commotion. He quite simply died of it, victim of the war and of human stupidity.

He was a really great nobleman: such distinction of appearance, such charm! Roman had enormous chic. He was big in every way. A gambler! and he knew how to play. He adored Paris. He appeared there every year, the clubs welcomed him with delight. He used sometimes to play at Monte Carlo, too. I remember that when I was starring at the Folies-Bergère he appointed himself my *cavaliere servente*. Every day he would put aside five thousand francs from his baccarat money for the whims and the gloves of his little Lianon. He came to pick me up at the stage door and took me to supper at

Paillard's, saying: 'Lilisky, bring anyone you please: actors, actresses, writers, friends, whoever . . .' Sometimes there were twenty of us. Henri d'Orléans would rub shoulders with Sulbac, Mayo, Mimi Saint-Cyr. And Roman himself would help the waiters hand round the oysters and champagne so that the service could leave nothing to be desired. It was at Paillard's, and in that same room, that I wanted to have our wedding breakfast. To celebrate and bury the crazy life I had led as a dancer.

I loved him with an affection sincere enough to extend to his family. When I was in Lemberg I wanted to see their ancestral home. There was a great entrance on a beautiful cobbled street, and opposite it another great entrance. Their house, his house, a pair of beautiful, aristocratic old residences. Countess Yaworska, who was acting as my guide, told me: 'On rainy days, when the Potocki family wanted to go from one house to the other, they had themselves carried so that they wouldn't muddy their feet. You would see the old Countess coming out first in the arms of two footmen, followed by her green dwarfs, also being carried by two stout fellows; then came Clementine, Beta, Roman. A whole liveried household carrying Their Lordships, nonchalant and refined, dreading mud as much as a blot on the escutcheon.'

.... Roman's mother was a redoubtable old Boyar. Even in the years just before her death, her children still trembled before her. Very much a figure from the past, very grand, she lived shut away in her palatial house with some thirty servants and the two dwarfs dressed in apple green who never left her, slept in her bedroom and kept her amused. She spoilt them and tormented them by turns. They played tricks on everyone and the old Potocki adored them. I rather like the idea of that, I'd have enjoyed it. I made do with three Moors. The truth is that it was rather awkward, it can't work in our country. When my little Halima tried to poison my two Italian greyhounds, Madame Garat and my husband, I wanted to take a strong line and have her locked up. All Roscoff rebelled: there was talk of illegal restraint, tortures and cruelty. I fell back on a diet of dry bread: the men slipped her chocolate on the sly . . . Finally, quite discouraged, I sent her back to her family, her poverty and her rags.........

November 10. .... An excellent *choucroute* bubbling away with its hambone and its sausages, its aroma wafting up the stairs. In comes Georges, and starts giving orders, carping, disapproving and pulling a sour face into the bargain. I turned him out pretty smartly. He really does lack tact, that boy. He nags us pitilessly for misuse of the subjunctive and for the smallest domestic failing. Why isn't he sculpted in old wood? He'd give us much less trouble and the state of my nerves would improve!

....

November 17. Little Maurice Rostand, as no one can fail to know, lost his father to the Spanish influenza last year. This young man is very exaggerated in his manners, his morals and his speech. One of his acquaintances invited him to a musical evening, highbrow, rather tempting. He hesitated, thought it over, and decided, 'No, my dear, I can't. I'm *madly* in mourning.'

Our cold baths have driven away the last signs of our colds. They are really marvellous if you can bear them. As the hour approaches we begin to paw the ground, nothing could rein us in, not the icy house, the pleading of our friends, our aches and pains – we disregard the lot. Undress very quickly, in and out! You emerge merry and brisk, refreshed and ready for anything, rather proud of your heroism.........

....

November 21. Salomon dropped in this morning. He brought us the latest volume of the *Chronologie de la guerre*. He is very upset by the behaviour of the Americans who are refusing to ratify the peace treaty and no longer want to belong to the League of Nations. The idea of which – so difficult to put into practice! – came from them. Evidently this young America is lacking in tact.

I distrust Americans. They are a bit childish. When they arrived in Vittel in August 1917, we happened to be there. It was the height of the season. They had been billetted pretty well everywhere and they were scattered all over the park, near the springs and in the restaurants. They received a fraternal welcome. People smiled at them, greeted them, overcharged them in the shops! One evening my husband was walking his little dog round the hotel when a charming Sammy came up to him and drawled: 'That's a very pretty little dog you have there, sir.' Georges smiled, much touched. Thus encouraged, the Sammy went on: 'You have also got a very pretty wife.' At that, Georges laughed aloud. They shook hands. The next day Lorenzo Thomson was waiting for us at the springs, introduced himself formally and became my *cavaliere servente*. Eight days later he asked me to divorce Georges and marry him. He might well have said to me what that rogue Goldschmidt said when I mentioned my age in order to discourage him. 'I prefer a woman of forty to two women of twenty!'

....

November 25. No more punctuation! The literary pundits of futurism and cubism want no more of it!

Saw in the paper that Madame Jacques Goudstikker – fat old thick-lipped mother Goudstikker who guided me through the labyrinth of precious stones in the days of my youthful independence – is dead. Sarah spent many millions with them. I myself must have had about three million-worth of jewellery from them.

Lazarus, to whom I offered a beautiful copy of my *Idylle saphique* printed on vellum, has paid me huge compliments. He says that it is a very important document and very well composed. He was so caught up in it that he galloped through it in two hours, only to read it again in minute detail from beginning to end, immediately afterwards. It comes off, but because the subject is rather improper I fear that the only reason why it pleases some men so much is that it awakens the animal sleeping within them........

....

December 1. My garden looks like a marsh and smells of mould and desolation. I don't know which saint to call on. Life is sad and difficult. Georges is very far from being a support. He has no strength. Nor has he any guile.

December 2. At midday it was five years since my child died for his country . . . I had gone out, I remember, to buy something for a layette we were putting together for a poor woman whose husband was at the front. Marguerite Godard was with me. Suddenly I felt the most violent pain in my bowels. Almost fainting, I gasped: 'Margot, I'm ill – take me somewhere quickly – into some concierge's, anywhere.' Margot, frantic, said: 'Princess, you are quite near home. Try to get there.' I got back into the house as midday struck (I have my son's little gold watch, found on him, half smashed and stopped at two minutes to twelve). I rushed into the bathroom; the pain had gone. I felt so tired and unstrung that I went to bed. I was knitting some little socks. At six in the evening the telephone rang. Georges went down, spoke, and came back, *green*!

He said: 'They want me to go to the town hall, straight away.' – 'Why?' – 'Something about – Marco.' He went even greener. 'He's dead!' – 'They didn't say so. He has had an accident.' – 'Go quickly . . . quickly!'

He left and my heart beat and beat enough to break. Mesdames Pernet (billed these days as Tonia Navar) and Gregory were with me. We kept saying it might be this or that – something less cruel. We waited. The two ladies got on my nerves, combing their hair, powdering their noses, watching my pain. Georges returned, staggering. 'Dead!' I exclaimed. 'Yes,' he said, hanging his head. 'Poor kid!' – and that was all I was able to say. Everything inside me was knotted and tense. No tears, no screams. I was bent double and couldn't straighten myself. Haunted by grief and every kind of regret, I suffered agonies for fifteen months, it nearly killed me. Ah! When it came to grieving I was a mother.

And what a way to break the news! No trouble taken, Georges summoned to the telephone and then to the town hall so that they could stun him by brutally thrusting this telegram at him: 'Inform Princess Ghika that her son, the aviator Marc Pourpe, fell gloriously on the field of battle at midday today and that the burial will take place at ten o'clock on Friday morning at Villers-Bretonneux.' Poor Georges, laden with his own despair as well as mine, could hardly stagger home.

Yesterday Salomon came in with a bunch of carnations for my hero. Fatoum and Rose followed, each with chrysanthemums. Georges has ordered a pot of flowers and I am going out to get another. He will be garlanded. His bedroom has to be his tomb because it is still impossible to move him and he lies down there in a vault belonging to strangers.

December 5. Joncières is having a bad time at the Comédie-Française. The papers say that it will be Ventura who will star in his play. Ventura, not Piérat, his beloved, his muse, his friend, the one and only, the most beautiful, the most inspired. There's been a falling-out, that's for sure; his heart must be bleeding. Not that he will lose by it with an interpreter like Ventura; subtle, very pretty, elegant, full of talent, better quality in every way than Piérat, and – a foreigner, which, with us, is always an added attraction. Ventura is a Roumanian Jewess, charming and much admired – and as for me, I acquire great merit by singing her praises because she used to be Georges's mistress. Oh, it was long ago – two years before we met, he and I. She was one of my friends. Retrospective jealousy? Once I knew Georges I never again wanted to look at her. Of course I'm silly to be jealous of Ventura, but even hearing her name spoken suffocates me! Is this stupid? I have to admit that it's the same with all of Georges's mistresses known to me.

These days the Americans consider D'Annunzio the greatest (or rather the most famous) man who ever was. During the war he was brave to the point of gallantry, for which he is forgiven a great deal.

I met him in Florence when I was dancing there. It was in 1902. Yesterday I came on a book which he gave me then: his *Francesca da Rimini*, bound in parchment tied with green ribbons, and copiously inscribed. I remember . . . he praised me for my corporeal grace – his expression – and invited me to visit his Capponcina. I accepted. He sent his carriage for me, filled with red roses. It was May 1st, which is the date of the rose festival in Florence. On my arrival I was greeted by workmen and young boys making a hedge between the gate and the front door of the house, all holding handfuls of roses which they threw at my feet. Inside, a 'poetic' décor, rather rubbishy and designed to impress. His conversation was marvellous. But there before me was a frightful gnome with red-rimmed eyes and no eyelashes, no hair, greenish teeth, bad breath, the manners of a mountebank – and a reputation, nevertheless, for being a ladies' man, and a man who was, to say the least, ungrateful to the ladies. I used every possible trick to resist him, and escaped by promising to return. Two days later he sent the same carriage for me. I substituted my maid for myself, with a note – a long note – saying: 'Stellio (the name of one of his heroes), that which has not been done is still to do . . . one day, no doubt, and why not . . . One cannot get used to such happiness all at once' – agreeable and uncompromising clichés. He had flown to the door to greet me and recoiled in furious dismay at the sight of my sniffy old Adèle. He pulled himself together and showed her the dinner which had been prepared, the table, the lit candles, the path I would have trodden spread with embroidered chasubles and scattered with rose petals (from the roses of two days earlier, no doubt). He gave her a folded paper for me containing these words: 'You light candles from afar, as well as near by. Take care. Stellio.'. . . . .

It has happened – Carpentier has knocked out the Englishman. Splendid victory. Paris delirious with joy!

December 7. Here I am in bed for two days. Balthy calls it 'having your baddies'. She says it with a tiny touch of a Midi accent, which is irresistible! But like all women approaching old age, she speaks of it much more often than every twenty-eight days.

When I, a young Manon, arrived in Paris in 1890, Mademoiselle Balthy already had wrinkles, a public, a reputation, a tiny place of her own on the rue de Chazelles, a carriage and pair. I lived with a friend opposite, at number 34, two ground-floor windows and two rooms. I slept in the living-room (where we also ate) and used to fly to the window to admire Balthy as she came and went. The jingle of her horses' harness used to alert me. I remember her in a glossy, tight-waisted astrakhan jacket with velvet leg-o'-mutton sleeves. Oh, how beautiful I thought it! As soon as I could afford to buy myself something chic, that was what I started with. How proud I was to sport a garment costing more or less the same as Louise Balthy's! I was not yet twenty. As for the famous Louise, she must have been at least twenty-eight. And now . . . she is ten years younger than I am! And she says as much even as I quiz her with an indulgent smile. Afterwards she takes my hand, pulls a naughty face, looks me in the eye and pronounces in her beautiful contralto: 'Darling, how I do admire you!'........

I sent a pretty shell to Cocteau, who loves them. That was ten or twelve days ago, and still not a word. Poets are absent-minded – yet Cocteau is very fond of us.

Last April I invited him to dinner with my mother-in-law in Paris, at the Jean Simmonds's apartment which they lent us while they were in Haiti. Cocteau spoke of foreknowledge of events as though it were a scientifically established fact, explaining himself in these terms: 'For you, who don't know, it is folded up. I know, and for me it is unfolded. You understand?' Well, yes – we understood, but . . . what did it amount to?

Cocteau is a dazzling talker, passionate, ironic, vigorous, elegant and abundant. He is delicious, slightly . . . repulsive, and very disturbing. He will kill with a word, is immeasurably and ceaselessly wounding. His mockery is sharp and cruel, respects nothing, plays with everything.

December 8. In *Yvée Lester* I wrote: 'Friendship gives and receives.' Friendship does demand a reciprocal honesty and a certain amount of esteem. I admire the Rochegrosses. I thought I was friends with the Poirets, but it couldn't last. Salomon? I admire him, I adore him – is that friendship? Camille? Rather like Joncières – lost dogs – mangy dogs, adoption and pity. The Isch-Walls, yes. The de La Jailles, even more so. The Jean Simmondses? No, distrust reigns. The Rouveyres? Almost. My Flossie? Less and more. The list is open, never closed and often revised.

And then there is Lewis the milliner, whose flourishing career I have followed and fostered. He's one who has become a habit. I knew him at Nice; in the morning he himself would bring round two or three huge boxes of the exquisite hats he had made the night before. The creature had taste, and made us laugh. What a gossip he was, and how he laid on the flattery! One day he brought me a ravishing beret of plaid velvet. I was nineteen years old . . . I ordered six, in different colours, and coquettishly I flaunted them. Everyone wanted one!

My Lewis, who was living in the attic of a tenth-class boarding house, had to take on an apprentice and descend to the ground floor. Customers came in droves and remained faithful. His skill and his funniness kept them happy. He spread to Paris, rue Royale, could turn his hand to anything, travelled, was always there on great occasions and became 'fame-valet' (to borrow Jean Lorrain's title) to all the celebrities. He stuck by me, insinuated himself into Otero's favour, achieved Sarah, knew how to take advantage of everything, broadcast what he was meant to and concealed the rest. He became the indispensable confidant, the familiar.

He ran faster and faster, sped to Italy to make hats for queens and great ladies, then to Spain, followed the season wherever it was. He has become formidably rich. No one could possibly be more obliging, provided it costs nothing . . . but if it does his feathers ruffle, his buzzard's eye grows beady, his voice goes edgy and gruff, his words become stinging and perfectly clear. Taking shelter behind the solid defences of his greed, he backs out of sight for ever.

He has remained rather faithful to me, even though I never buy his hats any more. They are too showy for my age and my situation. He was a witness at my wedding. He gave me my big Louis-Sixteenth black straw hat, trimmed with a cluster of aigrettes. A week later he came to call on us. 'Princess, keep the hat, of course – but take off the aigrettes and let me have them back!' – 'Nuts to you, of course I won't' said I, quite the princess! 'But they are worth 1,200 francs. I told them to use only the best. Ah, if I had only known . . .' He looked so woe-begone that I laughed till I cried.

December 10. My niece Aimée writes to say that she is expecting a baby at the end of April.

Yesterday some people came to view my tapestries, panelling and groups of stone figures. I need to raise a hundred thousand francs in order to increase my income by six thousand francs and pay my new taxes more easily. I entertain my friends freely but modestly. In the past I served them peacocks dressed in their plumes, exquisite foie gras, champagne. Now everything is planned, costed and prepared economically, though pleasantly, because the exchange has ruined my husband and enraged my mother-in-law, who keeps her purse-strings knotted. The value of the shares I hold has dropped. Some – the German stock for example – bring in nothing. I find myself much impoverished, while still having the same needs. Before the war butter cost 1.40 francs a pound, now it costs 9 francs. I used to pay my cook 100 francs a month and that was a good wage; today I pay 300 and get little satisfaction for it. Everything else is in keeping, which is why we want to sell this big house, this lovely garden in which we are not happy, and adapt our way of life to the style of the times.

December 11. Salomon teases me rather about my religion which, according to him, is full of error and most untheological. I may not be a woman of great faith but I know I'm one of good faith. Marie Bashkirtseff believed deeply in God, which did not prevent her from consulting fortune tellers. That I do not tolerate. I don't deny that during my wild years, influenced by my friends, I have tried it. I came away sickened, feeling diminished, despising myself. Oh that visit to Madame de Thèbes, in that filthy, smelly little place on the Avenue de Wagram! Old house, dirty stairs, smell of frying. I could have cried! Common, crafty woman with a vulgar, snub-nosed face, foxy eyes, a gift of the gab, sly and pushy! Jean Lorrain wanted to be friends with her, more or less, in so far as someone of his intelligence can be friends with such a person! At least he used to see her quite often. She plumed herself on having been very close to Alexander Dumas. Lorrain inflicted her on me several times, among others at a dinner which took place at la Cascade, when Jean had primed her in advance about the lives of his guests. The prophetess held forth at length and told us extraordinary stories. There was a great admirer of Jean's there, the Baroness Boulard, a very rich widow fresh from the fields of the Landes. She had been married to a young lord of that region. The Thèbes woman, warned, could play that situation with one hand tied behind her. She did it so well that we were all overcome with admiration and the Baroness fainted. Complete success!

When I was taken home after two weeks in hospital, at the time of my car smash, all literary and artistic Paris came processing past my bed. The Thèbes woman got wind of it, and two days running she installed herself in the boudoir next to my bedroom. She clutched at people as they went by, introduced herself, intrigued them. One or two took off their gloves there and then, others made appointments. I was furious. She wanted to force herself on me and I was obliged to have her thrown out. Lorrain had died a few months earlier so I was not afraid of offending his friendly feelings for Madame de Thèbes – feelings which, in my opinion, didn't exist anyway, because Lorrain knew his world, manipulated it and made it dance to his tune like the clever Norman that he was.

December 12. The Prix Goncourt has gone to Marcel Proust. *A l'ombre des jeunes filles en fleurs* took all the votes. I am in the middle of reading it. It is dense, heavy going, elaborate – it's very good. One can point to something masterly on every page.

I once met Marcel Proust. He was, and no doubt still is, a friend of Reynaldo and of Madrazzo. He was always ill, shut away indoors, working without cease on the books he has published since then. My friends adored him. His delicate health and his retreat from the world made him seem a rare being in an ivory tower. It was the first night of Reynaldo's *la Carmélite* at the Opéra-Comique. I was there, very excited. Reynaldo, all in a twitter of nerves, had the kind thought of sending Marcel Proust to me in every interval (Proust had departed from custom for this great occasion) to give me his news, collect mine, learn what I was thinking, what my impressions were and those of my entourage. Proust brought the notes with a kind smile, transmitted my messages cheerfully. Everything went as well as could be. He gazed at me with his deep look, his deep blue look, very gentle and thoughtful. I knew the poetic and melancholy legend which surrounded him, and welcomed him with the most affectionate sympathy. I never saw him again, but I am very happy to have his talent and his success confirmed, and to learn that apparently he has overcome the illness which kept him down, isolated him and worried all his friends: bad nerves, persistent weakness, lack of vitality in short. A sort of 'brother-in-suffering' to myself.

December 15. I was not able to go to Mass, so to demonstrate my good will I went into the church during the afternoon. A priest was in the pulpit addressing the large congregation. I got only a confused impression of his words, but the sound of his voice prevented me from praying; so I left after making a short little act of deference in honour of my promise.

It's at night, in bed, that I pray best. I feel nearer to God's presence then. Yes, sometimes in the solitude and silence of the night I am able to pray with fervour. Out of doors, too, under the sky and among trees, in the wide open spaces, words come to me easily and soar upwards. At those times it seems to me that God is present and hears them at once. In church – that is something else again. The music, the flowers, the beadle, the handsome Swiss, the scraping of chairs, the organ . . . I am no longer there. For me, church is a duty which one has to perform. I am able to feel neither fervent nor attentive, but I know that it is good and necessary to be there, as our Church directs.

December 17. Gaby Deslys, the pretty Parisian doll, the richest actress in France, the one with the most pearls and doubtless the most enviers, is at the point of death.

Madame Charron, my new caretaker, is going to help in the house. She is the cousin of Madame Martet, wife of the Martet with whom we had our famous 'little hat' row and who perhaps was the cause of my getting married. I must tell that story once and for all.

It was Easter Monday. Georges, Liane de Pougy and la Gigolette [Blanche d'Arvilly] had lunched in Saint-Germain, done the rounds of the antique shops, and were proceeding sedately along the rue au Pain to take a four o'clock cup of chocolate at Jousset's. I was wearing a little black hat trimmed with coarse white lace, very simple, today's sort of hat although it was 1910, that swashbuckling period of wide brims, etc. We passed two stout parties beplumed with ostrich, who pointed at me, burst out laughing and said in a loud voice: 'Just look at that hat! It's Liane de Pougy, the Paris tart.' Georges heard, stared at them and exclaimed 'You should take a look at yourselves before insulting other people.' Their two husbands were behind them. One of them, Martet, threw himself on Georges swearing blue murder and punched him on the jaw. Georges, stunned, was unable to defend himself because in one hand he was carrying two ravishing East India Company salt cellars and in the other two pretty Directoire miniatures. Blanche called for help. I must certainly have done the same. A policeman appeared at last and took us, at our bidding, to the station. Explanations, reports, legal action. Georges was bleeding, old Martet was frothing at the mouth. He was quite a drinker at the best of times, and had been celebrating Easter Monday with friends. The fresh air, and rage, had undone him. We all appeared in court equipped with lawyers, the Paris press attended in full strength. It was there, in front of the magistrate, that we became acquainted with the talented humourist Géo de La Fouchardière. There were witnesses a-plenty in our favour; we won. I shared the money out among the poor people of Roscoff, where I was when it arrived, having no wish to pocket my dear defender's 'blood money'.

The papers snatched at the chance to spread themselves in nasty gossip about both our exposed personalities. They poured out low envy, old grudges, every sort of spite to their hearts' content. Our allies joined battle, which prolonged it all. I was often irritated and saddened. Georges, who admired me as much as he loved me, said to himself: 'It is not fair, I am going to put matters right with one gesture which will place her above all these allegations.' Six weeks later he married me. Naturally there was a veritable storm of articles, gossip from dear old pals, gloomy predictions from our friends. We received a number of coarse and threatening anonymous letters.

Time passes . . . My private happiness endures in spite of all, in spite of everyone! Basically that disparaged, vilified, much-sued Liane had all the makings of a good wife – credit which I must now share with my equally abused little companion.

Georges has invited Cocteau to come to lunch on Christmas Day. Jean answered with a friendly, charming, affectionate, even tender note which said in effect: 'I will come if I have nothing else to do and if the Christmas Eve party to which I may be dragged doesn't tire me too much.'

As for Max Jacob, he writes: 'Ought I to bring holly or a poem? Cocteau says I should bring the poem, I have written it.' They enjoy our company and are happy to see us, but not if they have to catch a train, so tiresome! Saint-Germain is remote, in the provinces – in the eyes of a cool, calculating friendship. Coming here is a proof of attachment.

December 22. First day of winter. It is mild. Yesterday evening the storm started up again, very violent, making me think of my fierce Roscoff.

I have had a horrid accident. I was combing my hair in Georges's study, using the comb from my chignon. As I smoothed the hair over my temples the comb hit the corner of my eye. I went into my boudoir, looked in my dressing-table mirror and saw something horrible: the corner of my eye was nothing but a great bubble of blood which was swallowing up all the white. We telephoned Venot who came running. I really have wounded my eye, but not in a way to affect my vision. The blood has spread right over the eye and will take a long time to clear away. I see clearly, praise God, that is what matters. Only my beauty has suffered. It is impressively hideous........

December 24. Dear Father Christmas, heal my eye! Father Christmas of my childhood, of my ancestors, of my church, bring me a brand new eye, all white and purified, or else the great courage needed to accept it cheerfully as it is! It is ugly and disgusting! I'm starting to jib a little........

The turkey has arrived, superb, fat, heavy. Raoul [de Galland] has brought three magnificent truffles from Paris, so we are going to give it the treatment it deserves. Let us console ourselves with food, which is also a gift from God. Raoul has also ordered a hundred oysters from Prunier's. I supply the traditional sausage on a bed of sautéed apples. Georges has bought a beautiful plum-pudding which he will set alight with Simmonds' rum. The champagne comes from Mariette, who would be enraged to know that something of hers was contributing to my little family reunion. Particularly as we shan't drink her health!

December 25. Father Christmas!!! My eye is pure tomato sauce. Too sad! We gave our presents yesterday evening. Great excitement over wrapping them up and keeping them hidden from each other. After dinner we set off in single file on the hunt for our shoes. So that is the modest Christmas of 1919's New Poor! ....

A mild, snowless Christmas. An intimate Christmas. I wore a dress of mouse-grey velvet. Max Jacob arrived with a beautiful holly tree. I feel as grateful to him for having transported it as for having chosen it. The dear boy is earning money and delights in spending it and in spoiling his friends. He went into the kitchen to wish Rose and Fatoum a happy Christmas, and scattered them with hundred-sous notes. He is selling his paintings. He is getting masses of orders and opened his wallet to show us with evident enthusiasm that it was stuffed with banknotes. He said: 'Look how many I have! I have heaps of them, and I'm going to get more!'

Cocteau didn't come. A long telegram at about four o'clock explaining that after celebrating Christmas Eve he woke late and harassed, and demanding that we send him word that we forgive him.

Max surpassed himself. Raoul played the piano, improvising on themes he set, and Max, in the artificial kind of voice used by masks, recited very funny little burlesque verses which made us roar with laughter. He was in a mood of boundless and amusing vitality. After 'The Jealous Vizir' he gave us 'The Little Cabinet Maker in the Forest' and 'The Aristocratic Motor Car with the Drawn Blinds', etc. Then he invented snatches of conversation between two dancers while Raoul played a slow waltz.

Max had an important engagement in Paris at six o'clock. He remembered it – at ten past six! So he stayed to dinner with us, was charming all the time and told us a play of his which is soon going to be put on by Barbazanges, Poiret's tenant in the faubourg Saint-Honoré. Our Christmas was gay, witty, graceful and affectionate. Georges was witty. Speaking of Baudelaire he called him 'the Musset of horror'. Neat? But a bit unfair.

December 29. Gaby Deslys becomes iller and iller. Perhaps it will be her fate to be spared old age and an actress's retirement, which is like burial.

I am reading Pascal's *Pensées.* I have begun his 'conversion of a sinner'. It could well be applied to me . . . but why are these pages, and all writing concerning religion, so full of exhortations to humble and abase yourself, to fall on your knees and smite your breast? Does God really want that from His creatures?

They say that D'Annunzio, like Napoleon, has been abandoned by all his friends. He continues, nevertheless, to live in Fiume.

December 30. I have read Max Jacob's *la Défense de Tartuffe*, which has just been published in its complete form. It is good. The passage about humility which I already knew is certainly the best part of it. The book is meant to be religious, but is it? The faith which Max has inside him fails to inspire him with a very sincere tone. One is always being shocked. I think he's aiming for 'the primitive' and one wonders if he is being serious, if he is being ironical. To my mind his writing is full of double meanings, dishonest, studied and without passion. Some of the prose is fine – is magnificent. He has made me think. According to him, too, it is necessary to humble oneself because of the sin one is constantly committing.

Confession bores me, and the mass, too, costs me an effort – I am not making progress on that road; I reproach myself for it. I am a poor soldier, at the least excuse I swing the lead. I don't rally properly to my flag, and I take the punishment for it inside myself: I am not happy.........

....

1920

Saint-Germain – January 1 to March 14

January 1. My God, I ended the year straining towards You, and that is how I want to start the year which begins today. My God! Bestow Your blessing on me and mine. Give us the strength to stay upright when it is stormy and good when we are happy.

Georges wrote me a beautiful letter. In the small hours of the New Year he came to kiss my forehead, my hands and my feet. Then we both went back to sleep. On waking I said my prayers, in my own way as always. Then the little ones came in to kiss me and give me their good wishes: I gave them presents of money.

January 8. Gaby Deslys has been saved: I wonder whether her near approach to the great mysteries will change and convert her? What an example she would provide if she sold her pearls and her real estate in order to give to the poor.

The really poor? They no longer exist! Washerwomen wear silk stockings, my butcher has bought herself a car. At Christmas and New Year my husband's barber sold his whole stock of madly expensive perfumery, above all Coty's which is prohibitive, to workmen. They eat roasts at forty francs, and the best poultry, go to the cinema several times a week, etc. Most of them, particularly the young couples, don't want possessions and choose to live in furnished rooms. They have got their insurance, haven't they? Their pensions, the backing of the boss? It is a change in the French character. As Lazarus wrote to me yesterday in his witty way: the shoemaker is getting the pleasure of the financier's money without the worry of it.

January 9. The Austrians have enough supplies left for only three weeks. After that it will be famine and people are saying that it could spread like an epidemic. At the word 'famine' I prick up my ears and hurry off to the grocer's. I do not approve of people who hoard too much, but one must have a little foresight. Georges laughs at me.

January 11. Like every morning I have had my enema, in order to preserve a clear skin and sweet breath. It is a family habit, approved of by Dr Pinard. One of Maman's old great-aunts, the beautiful Madame Rhomès, died at the age of ninety and a half with a complexion of lilies and roses, skin like a child's. She took her little enema, it seems, at five o'clock every evening, so that she would sleep very well. She did it cheerfully in public. She would simply stand in front of the fireplace; her servant would come in discreetly, armed with the loaded syringe; Madame Rhomès would lean forward gracefully so that her full skirts lifted, one two three, and it was done! Conversation was not interrupted. After a minute or two my beautiful ancestress would disappear briefly, soon to return with the satisfaction of a duty performed.

Salomon told me a very charming saying of Flossie's. When Rita Harry, a woman of letters, asked her for an interview, Flossie, who detests curiosity, hit on this delicious way of answering: 'You must forgive me if I refuse to disappoint you.'

....

January 16. I have taken a grave decision. Georges is stunned by it. I no longer want to sell my house. Yes, that is it! I have made a thorough examination of my feelings and I have come up with the following scheme: sell ten thousand metres of the grounds. That will abolish the cost of a gardener-caretaker. All I shall need then will be a man one day a week. What is more, it will reduce my taxes, augment my income. It is common sense. Because I cannot find the maid of all work I am looking for, I stop making use of my third floor. My little ones' work will become much lighter and easier with seven fewer rooms to keep up. I will arrange the rooms thus: kitchen, maid's room and boxroom, dining-room, drawing-room (these two delightfully proportioned rooms opening onto the beautiful terrace which overlooks my rosebeds), one big bedroom, one small one, a hall and a W.C. Every summer I will let them furnished for three months. That will cover my taxes.

No sooner decided than done. I hurried off to see a letting agency. Like Diogenes I set about looking for a man – that is to say, an upholsterer-furniture-remover-handyman – and I have found one Souris, with whom I have made an appointment for Monday. Georges is dumb with disapproval. What a wet blanket he is!

Furniture has been dancing in my head all night. I am happy, agitated, in a fever. I feel strong and resolute; I crush Georges with my scorn; I win him over to my cause. He has started to move and measure furniture. It is the thought of a tenant which ruffles him. Yet it is reasonable and carefully thought out.........

January 17. We are busy; we are exhausted. I have stripped my Marco's room. It wrenched my heart. Five years, and already I am demolishing – I am displacing his memory. I am putting it in the forgetting-box which, no doubt, I shall be unwilling to open ever again. And that is life, and that is for the best.

January 19. France has a new president: Deschanel! Father Clem has resigned on the eve of a set-back, rather angry. The preliminary scrutiny which took place yesterday revealed that he had a minority of nineteen. An inexplicable minority, but undeniable.

January 20. The house-moving has begun. My well-kept house in which we use so much bees-wax, so much turpentine, so many dusters, so many brooms, as soon as we start moving furniture my poor house reveals great clots of dust! It's heart-breaking.

This morning, when my face was dirty, my hair was a mess and my hands were black, Salomon suddenly loomed up before me in the open doorway. Pleasure equalled embarrassment. He understands this kind of thing and approves of the effort and the trouble we are taking. His visit relaxed me a bit. He talked to me about Flossie, whom he finds slightly tired, and about the election of the President of the Republic. In his opinion the right thing would have been for us to elect Clemenceau and then for him to resign after a few days. Concerning Flossie and her return from America, her friend Madame de Clermont-Tonnerre who travelled with her has given an interview in *Excelsior* about her impressions. She seems to have been wonder-struck; hardly surprising, in Flossie's company. She was enchanted by all the little details. For instance here, when we go for a drive in a motor-car, we are condemned first to bad roads, then to stopping in villages and getting out to ask the grocer who is sometimes kind enough to come and empty smelly cans into the fuel tank. Over there it is done as though by magic. You stop in front of a building, put the necessary money into a hole, turn a tap, and the liquid pours itself just where it ought!

I have begun a book by Rudyard Kipling. The brutal strength of his new ideas cracks my brain. I do like progress, but you need to slip into it gently, install yourself comfortably without being deafened and shaken up. No doubt I belong to my time, I mustn't be hustled too much. Certainly the wood fire which crackles in my room every evening, throwing its pretty lights, is much more to my taste than some disgusting stove! ....

January 23. .... This day, the anniversary of the death of Louis XVI, brings back memories of my childhood in that corner of Brittany where all the old, right-minded families indicated their respectful mourning by keeping their shutters closed all day, going to mass dressed in black and doing penance to compensate for France's criminal gesture. My mother, my old aunts and their friends set the example. My youth and cheerfulness were put to a hard test. Faces had to be long. Only the humble folk were allowed the privilege of passing this day comfortably, but they were regarded with an indulgent and disdainful pity.

I once knew an indirect descendant of Louis XVI, even knew him quite intimately. He was the eldest son of the Duc de Chartres, that charming Prince Henri d'Orléans who went exploring in Africa in the direction of Abyssinia. Sadly enough, he died down there, like the young Duc Jacques d'Uzès who preceded him by some years. Henri d'Orléans pursued me and loved my beauty, my wit and my delicacy. True descendant of Henri IV that he was, he had heaps of passions, but his faithful friendship gave the little dancer-mime at the Folies-Bergère a sort of halo. He used to write to me from those distant lands, tell me his exotic experiences, give me his books (he published several accounts of his travels). One day he sent me some heavy bronze rings and some circlets of old yellow ivory, saying: 'I have brought you back bracelets from your Abyssinian sisters, you won't think them very elegant. Use them for paper-weights.' I still have them at Roscoff; they are precious on the days when the wind rages.

Another time he gave me a white poodle from Syracuse, bought from a circus trainer. I couldn't keep it, it was so vicious. The mountebank must have beaten it dreadfully. Henri sent it to me washed, combed and tied with sky-blue ribbon, accompanied by these words in a letter: 'I belong to Liane de Pougy. I want to live for her. I know how to jump very high through a hoop of flaming paper, climb a ladder and count to twenty.' At first I was enchanted – then I had to think twice. The animal went for people's throats. It knocked down Emilienne d'Alençon and bit my butler. He opened the door for it and the animal flew out and ran away – to the house of the Duc de Chartres! Henri caught it and sent it back, thinking that it had escaped. Then I told him everything and begged him to rid me of it. He took it back, a little vexed I think, and after that gave me easier presents.

January 24. I slept badly and I prayed. I prayed to God and to Saint Anne of Auray. I consider her kind and merciful; God seems to me severe and alarming. My heart shuts against Him. The opposite of the state of grace. Instead of blessing, I curse, instead of praying I argue. Then I lament over myself and cry: 'Saint Anne, lead me to God bound hand and foot, grant me the blind faith of the simpler people whom I envy.' My God, I perceive You dimly, through trouble and discontent. I want to come to You, so do not hold me off like this!

Organizing all this furniture-moving, and actually doing it, is good for the nerves. My little kitchen is nearly done. It will be ravishing. The walls will be painted a sunny yellow; soon the windows will open onto a cloud of Persian lilacs which will fill the room with their scent. My tenants will be enviable!

January 30. Something strange is up: for some time the wireless telegraph has been registering mysterious signals. Our learned men wonder whether we are in communication with a planet – Mars, it would be. Oh, how wonderful it would be to see that in one's lifetime! There are people who laugh and think it's a hoax, but I prefer the explanation which gives my imagination play.

January 31. Henry Bataille has just put on a play, *l'Animateur*, which everyone is talking about. His beloved, his muse, Yvonne de Bray, plays the leading role. It is a huge success, the reviews are glowing. Bataille never writes anything commonplace. Yvonne is at the top of her form and has talent, certainly: their union is a fortunate one for them and for the public too.

I no longer care much for the theatre. In the last five years life had given us so much drama! I prefer the entertainment of a café-concert, amusing numbers, good, silly, funny popular songs. The variety programme at the Olympia attracts me; I shall try to get to a matinée some time this week. A new attraction, a Spanish woman, is spoken of very highly: Madame Raquel Meller.........

Sacha has a new play on: *Béranger*. Yvonne Printemps gives a clever performance in it as Lisette. The great Lucien Guitry plays Talleyrand; Sacha is Béranger. I am very fond of them in a sort of way, based on a sort of admiration. I know their defects and am indifferent to them; their good qualities interest me to the highest degree. They have always been charming to me. The father calls me 'Beauty'; the son tells me 'Nothing is prettier than you are'. Little 'springtime' smiles nicely at me. They make much of me and send me seats. At the time of Georges's operation they made the touching gesture of sending me a *pneu* as full as could possibly be of affection.

February 1. Salomon came and I had him to myself almost the whole time. He talked about Flossie: she is preparing two books full of marvels.

Salomon is not pleased with my poor little naïve faith. He thinks it is a pity that a soul of my temper should be so given to nonsense. He quotes passages from the Bible and makes me put my finger on errors and contradictions. What do I care for the Bible, sermons, conventions? I draw my consoling faith from the vanquishing of my own strength. Dear Salomon, don't blow away my pathetic conviction, so frail and weak. I have had so much trouble bringing it to this point. All my family believed in God, and served Him; I choose to stand beside them.

....

February 6. A lovely time at the Olympia. Good, amusing, varied programme: acrobats, shadow-play, songs, dances and Raquel Meller who was worth the journey. She is fragile, tall and magnificent, taking, touching. One's heart aches for this frail and slender creature whose whole being lights up at the word 'love', who shudders so painfully at the sorrow of love, who is left shattered by the beloved's death. A great artiste. She deserves her reputation. Her Spanish costumes are ravishing and underline her performance. She has fine, elongated features, eyes which are large and luminous, a rather poor mouth, sad when she isn't smiling, and very sober gestures. Her voice is fluent and pearly, grave even on the high notes, effortless, as though she knows profoundly well how to project it. Bravo Raquel Meller! It's a pleasure to have seen her.

Ozenfant writes to us on behalf of Max Jacob who is at Lariboisière afflicted with two broken collar-bones and a congestion of the lungs. The poor dear was on his way to see the Russian ballet at the Opéra, in top-hat and tails, when a car ran over him and now he is in a public ward with his top-hat and tails perched sadly on a chair beside his bed, his body mangled, his fever high, reduced to pain and immobility. He is thinking of us. He knows that we will feel for his sufferings. I am about to despatch a messenger with letters and fruit. We are too fragile to risk going there ourselves. Georges and I, who sped off to see Raquel Meller, haven't the energy to visit Max and I know that we are not going to have it. We are going to write to tell him that we love him and that we have caught colds.

We will take trouble for him. I have just prepared a beautiful basket of choice, juicy, golden fruit for him. He has my affection and some of my anxiety, but I shall not go to see him. I am woman enough to take him in to my home and nurse him through his convalescence if necessary, but not to go to that place. I really do not understand myself. If loving is preferring another person to oneself, as Tolstoy says, then I don't love him; and yet his fate, his appearance, often move me almost to tears.

February 8. Yesterday my little Charron went to Lariboisière. He saw Max Jacob who was talking to a friend. He was short of breath. He has been forbidden to tire himself and his oranges have been confiscated. Tomorrow I will send him some huge grapes, with a note.

I am exerting myself to make him feel that our friendship is on the alert, but . . . we do not budge. He will need at least a month in hospital. Then it will be less cold, and if he wants to come and convalesce here I shall invite him and look after him to the best of my ability. I have already had him at Roscoff for two months. He was calm and good-tempered and buried himself in the library – and managed, nevertheless, to make himself insufferable. Sharp words, quarrels, sulks . . .

February 10. At this moment I adore Max Jacob. I will be judged inconsistent, changeable, crazy. I have fulminated against the poor devil in my time . . . Everything is different. I am sensitive to a fault, influenced by the day and the event. This poor, crushed Max, I love! I began to love him when I saw him again last year and he had risen somewhat above his material misfortunes, had started to earn his living – and his socks. Before that he used to wear his friends' socks and underwear, their old clothes. I was sorry for him but I found that ignoble and it hurt me to see a gifted man so bogged down. I found him repugnant and turned away from him angrily. Now he has freed himself from Picasso and his charity, from Poiret and his old neckties. Since his painting sells, he has been painting and has thus been able to continue the philosophical and poetic lucubrations which bring him in nothing beyond admiration. His accident has moved me very much and I am going to prepare a pretty, sunny, white and red bedroom for him on my second floor, for a sweet, affectionate convalescence in the fresh air. I will plan meals and flower arrangements for him, delights, instant satisfactions; in fact I will take – with a great deal of pleasure – a lot of trouble for him and he will not feel the effort in it.

....

February 12. Letter from Max, highly delighted about coming here for his convalescence. His accident was dreadful. He was crossing the boulevard de Clichy on his way to the Russian ballet when he found himself threatened by five or six cars, took fright and clutched at the headlamp of the one nearest him. The driver didn't stop, Max fell, the vehicle went over him, he fainted after seeing 'all the underparts of that car', he says jokingly. When he came to himself he was lying in the Place Pigalle surrounded by three hundred people. He was rushed to the Lariboisière. The brutal driver was chased and caught, he will be sued. Max is happy in hospital, he is drawing a little with his undamaged right hand; he has lots of visitors; he makes jokes; he wins hearts. He is allowed one visitor a day and more on Sundays and Thursdays. His friends come crowding in and spoil him. He prays; not for a minute does he complain. I have written a rather reassuring letter to his mother because in spite of their incessant arguments the old lady will be anxious. Of course I know that distance lends enchantment, but I am infinitely fond of Madame Jacob; she may not be the mother he would have chosen, but his mother she certainly is.

February 13. Gaby Deslys is dead. Never will she know the wrinkles of old age, and all they bring, and all they drive away.

....

February 16. .... Lazarus informs me that I ought to sell at once in order to buy more Royal Dutch, and some Central Mining. I had said to him: 'I never touch anything of yours any more, life is so expensive.' [Lazarus dealt in jewellery] – 'All right, how much do you need a month?' – 'Not much, I could make do with twenty-five louis.' – 'Very well, you will have them, and without loss of capital, you are reasonable.' He explained to us that Tanganyika is a lake in the Belgian Congo surrounded by a very rich subsoil and that it has a tremendous future in the production of copper, coal and tin. The way he spoke inspired confidence.

....

February 21. The town of Tourane has sent me a very beautiful letter of thanks. At Lorient, where my son was born, there was to start with some question of naming a street after him. There were manoeuvrings and discussions. Finally this is what they came up with for me: 'We will wait for the end of the war so that we can choose among the heroes of Lorient.' Then last year the mayor came to see me and gave me to understand with considerable clumsiness that all I had to do was make over a hundred thousand francs to the town of Lorient and the thing was done. I gave this person a vague – oh, a very vague! – answer, showed him out and left it at that. I have absolutely no intention of stripping myself because my child died for France!

February 22. Yesterday, day in Paris.

We trooped off to the Champs-Elysées theatre, a pretty theatre up on the sixth floor. Cocteau's show has the very latest thing in music: overture by Poulenc. We expected something eccentric but it was charming, a flight of elegance. Then came songs by Cocteau interpreted by Koulitzki in a beautiful voice slightly muffled by influenza, to pleasant music by Auric. That was all. Childlike word-play by Cocteau: '*Miel de Narbonne, bonne d'enfant, enfant de troupe*, etc,' ending with this phrase dropped as though at random: '*Le trapèze ensense la mort*' – felicitous, and impressive. It was madly crowded. Friends came up to congratulate me on my appearance. I was the smartest: sable coat and shift-dress of glittering silver material with a large black pattern: a simple style with a touch of the medieval, clear-cut lines. It suits me better than elaboration and it's never out of fashion .... Saw Henri Bernstein and his wife whom I couldn't find pretty however hard I tried: little shopgirl's face, badly proportioned features, not ugly, not handsome, insignificant.

Women nowadays are so commonplace! Monsieur and Madame Valette (she is Rachilde of the *Mercure de France*) were sitting in front of me. We exchanged opinions, ran down Ajalbert, admired Flossie whom they see often, and waited for the rest of this charming and revealing show. Two clowns dressed all in black did marvellous tricks to music by Auric. That was good. The very young leader of the orchestra was extremely good looking and graceful. I leant forward and said to Rachilde: 'Look at the leader of the orchestra, he's the image of my son.' – She answered: 'Your son must be better looking than that.' – 'He was killed in the war, alas.' The little shock made her give me a very quick kiss on the cheek, then she sat back, thoughtful.

And we felt the same about Colette Willy, too – her insincerity, her affectations, her talent in spite of all, and her infernal spitefulness. The next part of the show was three pieces by Eric Satie, encored and much applauded. The composer had to come down into the auditorium. I had met him before. He pressed our outstretched hands warmly, thanked us for our compliments and withdrew, happy at his success. He was first introduced to us on a less triumphant occasion, at the Ballets Russes, that famous performance of *Parade* – Cocteau again – which was whistled, hooted and shouted down so that we could hear nothing of the music. To end with, a coarse farce entitled *le Boeuf sur le toit*, the characters in carnival costumes with enormous cardboard heads. It was coarse, childish, not new, not funny. I'd much rather have *Parade*. Darius Milhaud's music, which was played alone at first, was pretty and alive and could only lose by this buffoonery. It had its longeurs, but it gave the impression of a crowd, a multitude, masks, tragedy, comedy, which the action spoilt and diminished. To sum up, the musical side of the show was brilliant, full of charm and talent; but Jean Cocteau's side of it, to be honest, was deplorable. Parts of his books are admirable. There he has a dazzling gift, a new and bizarre kind of talent. He touches the sublime and overleaps good sense. He should stick to that. But . . . he is so completely *Parade*! He needs the stage, the scenery, the noise, a tickled public. Rachilde said: 'He knows his public and what it likes, he's rubbing our noses in absurdity.' These words and her amused attitude enraged Georges. But there was something in it, all the same.

February 23. Read in the papers yesterday that my friend the Duke of Oporto had died at the age of fifty-five, an exile in Italy. I was assailed by a thousand memories: my travels to Portugal, staying in the palace at Ajuda, the friendship of that good fellow, that bear not quite licked into shape with his simple emotions, our evening drives in the country, along the banks of the Tagus. He drove a phaeton with a team of high-spirited and beribboned mules, and their bells were muffled (see *Idylle saphique*) because the revolution was brewing, anarchy was grumbling. It smacked of ambushes, assassinations. Alfonso had preserved the spirit of a child in his sportsman's body. I remember noticing one day that his ears, cheeks, nose, fingers were covered with thousands of tiny pricks and scratches. When I asked him what they were, he told me: 'I'm raising rats, twenty of them, and sometimes they hurt me.' – 'But why are you raising rats?' – 'Because on Easter Day I'm going to send them to old Countess X, hidden in a basket of flowers.' – '?????' – 'She has said very nasty things about my mother (Queen Maria Pia), my brother (King Carlos, who has been assassinated since then) and me.' A prince's revenge! A courtly pastime!

I saw him carrying a wardrobe on his back when two of his servants had been unable to lift it, and freeing the mule-carriage by putting his shoulder to it when it was stuck in the mud. In civilian clothes he looked like any fat bourgeois. It amused him when he was not recognized and could fool about without constraint. If he met a pretty theatre colleague at one of my tea parties or receptions, and I asked him next day if he had liked her, he would answer candidly: 'Yesterday I liked her a lot; I had supper with her. Today she doesn't look so good.'

He was unable to come to Paris, the Paris of his dreams, very often; his means were limited. But they would send him to the English court with a wedding present, to the German court with a christening present, and that gave him delightful holidays. He pinched and scraped out of his travelling expenses so that he could stay longer in our capital. We often had a good laugh together, going over his accounts and the risks he took with them.

Once he made me come to Lisbon. He was not at the station, as he usually was. He was not in the hotel suite which he had reserved for me and filled with flowers and chocolates. They brought me a letter: 'I've got rather a headache, I'll come in a day or two.' I was so vexed that I was thinking of catching a train home after a short rest, when I was summoned to the Ajuda palace. A closed carriage was waiting for me. I jumped into it, arrived, and there was my Alfonso with his forehead laid open, minus the lobe of one ear, his face wrapped in bandages, one eye closed. 'What on earth . . . ? An assassination attempt?' – 'No, something in my motor-car blew up in my face.' He called that having 'rather a headache'.

He was my sincere and devoted friend and could refuse me nothing. He would have made a detestable lover, chasing any skirt which passed. When he was in Paris he indulged in it to his heart's content and every morning at ten o'clock he came to my little house in the rue de la Néva, sat beside my bed, listened to my news, gave me his, read me the newspaper and took my commissions. He adored his mother and always felt like a little boy when he was with her. . . . .

February 25. It's going wrong with Max Jacob. He is becoming impertinent. He feels that I am cossetting him and he is taking advantage of it. The other day he wrote complaining about how disgusting the hospital food is, and saying: 'I'm longing to eat some meat cooked by *people*.' I went off to the butcher and bought pork at 8 francs a pound, to the poulterer and bought a chicken for 18 francs, to the other butcher to buy rump steak. Fatoum roasted it all during the afternoon. We cut it up and arranged it in a charming china dish which we will never see again; we despatched young Marcel Charron who has to be paid for his trouble, he took it there, handed it over, Max opened it and pushed it away saying: 'But it's Lent, I can't eat that.' He distributed it round the ward. I am not complaining, but what manners! That renegade Jew is more Catholic than the Pope! A sick man, crushed, with congestion of the lungs, doesn't have to fast – and a man should always remember his manners!

. . . .

February 27. Max Jacob got Ozenfant to telephone us and let us know that he was very ill, that they have given him two punctures without much success and that they are going to give him two more. A pulmonary complication.

The poor boy must have had a temperature when he wrote us that vehement letter. I don't hold it against him, but I would rather not have someone to stay who is so irritable and still so delicate. Above all I owe it to myself to keep well so that I can care for my family, those nearest to me, those whom God has chosen to collect around me and in my house. The latter has become very precious to me since it escaped the profanation of being sold. I think it more beautiful, I adorn it, move the furniture around, take pleasure in it, embrace it symbolically, air it, warm it. It smells good, it is spacious and light. Every corner is tidy and clean. It was in ruins when I bought it, and I restored it. It is mine, I shall keep it.

....

March 2. The spring doesn't suit Georges: he is grumpy, discontented, languid, disagreeable, boring. He will read these lines and learn what I think. I think this stupid boy eats enough for four, takes no exercise, that at this time of year it is a good thing to take a purge and that he's sticking in his toes. To think that the happiness one expects from a man depends on castor oil or some sort of pill or salts! ....

March 3. Max Jacob is calmer and seems to be sorry for his outburst. He's almost apologizing. I have sent him an affectionate answer. Poor Max, he really is too weak and wounded to return to the usual course of his bohemian life.

March 4. Yesterday morning I went out early, exasperated by Georges's tiresomeness.

I bought some thick English tweed with a black stripe making a large check in the latest fashion. Rose will make it up into a skirt for me, and I'll wear it with a black silk sweater and cardigan. It will modernize them a bit.

On my return I had the nice surprise of finding my Salomon. I had been to see a delicious little old house which is up for sale. I like it immensely, but it's Cadet Rousselle's house without floors or ceilings. The price – including the most urgent of the necessary repairs – would come to between two hundred and two hundred and twenty thousand francs. It encloses a square courtyard, there is enough garden, a cedar tree, a splendid wistaria, old panelling, four ancient mirrors, five or six old chimney-pieces, and a roof of mellow tiles which any collector would love to lay his hands on. The roof is collapsing, of course. The whole thing is in a lovely countrified style, very snug, well planned, designed for a peaceful life in well-earned comfort, and it would all have to be done over.

Salomon admired my material; Georges too, but he doesn't like the idea of a home-made skirt at a bargain price – the dago!

Salomon teased me about the versatility of my decisions; not to sell my house, to sell it, to buy another. Look: if someone will pay me a very good price for my house, 700,000 for instance, I'll sell it; I will invest 500,000 francs through Lazarus and I'll buy the old house which is better proportioned, more secluded, more intimate than my Noailles folly which is only a small bit of a castle chopped off when the road was built, nothing more, really, than a stub-end of a house.

March 8. At about five o'clock the bell gave a feeble tinkle. Georges hurried to look out of the window and came back quite overcome: 'It's that poor Max clasping a sheaf of flowers in his damaged arms!'

I flew to let him in. The poor dear boy, thrilled to see us again, thinner, nervous, out of hospital on Friday, had made the great, the beautiful, the touching, the elegant gesture of staggering all the way from Paris with a heavy pot of azaleas in his arms. There are simply no words to depict what I felt at the beauty of it. He wanted to thank us again, to apologize for his feverish note.

He looked well. Apart from the damage he underwent, he has been able to rest his organism and has been cossetted. Life seems sweet to him. He took great pleasure in the train's progress through the fresh springtime greenery as it carried him along between the flowery embankments. He had his own little tea-tray, just for him, near the fire. And my heart throbbed, and I felt infinitely sisterly and loving towards him.

March 10. Cold, melting snow, a bit of hail. The workmen break their promises. They don't turn up, or else they begin their day at midday; they have forgotten most of their tools, they roll cigarettes. They stop giving a damn as soon as you stop chasing them.

Cocteau telephoned. He is enchanted by his success as author-backer. Houses have been so good that he has got to give an extra performance on Saturday. It's all too much, his voice takes on a dying fall. The Opéra is going to do *Parade* again. He has a new piece in preparation; he wants to visit us. Yesterday he went to see Max Jacob's play. Is it good? 'Ye-e-es. It's Maxish . . .' And no more need be said.

March 13. Sent Max Jacob proof of my restored affection: a pot of goose-liver paté and a delicious cake. Will he perceive my tenderness in it? I don't usually have much luck with my inspired gestures.

Yesterday I was reading about Heinrich Heine and I couldn't help comparing him with Max Jacob when it came to family feeling.

Like Max, Heine had it in for his family, loathed them and ran away from them. One day he even had the elegant cheekiness to write the following words to an uncle of his who was a millionaire and paid him a fat allowance (unlike our Max in that, alas!): 'The only good thing about you is that you bear the same name as your nephew.'

Paris – March 23 to 24

March 23. Hotel Terminus, room 142, second floor, looking onto the courtyard, twin beds, 34 francs a day, 39 because of the little dog. Twin beds! Snores, promiscuity, invitations, arguments, sulks! We have been here since yesterday. We were welcomed and installed with the manners refugees have to put up with.

We leapt helter-skelter into a taxi to go to Max Jacob's exhibition at Bernheim's. No luck, it was over.

....

Saint-Germain – March 25 to August 21

....

March 29. Yesterday Max Jacob arrived late; the asparagus soup had thickened, the risotto was over-cooked; he was impertinent, demanding, mischief-making, started smoking during the meal. He has his pockets full of money and a first-class ticket, if you please, for the Midi. Money doesn't suit him. He wasn't even funny.........

....

April 2. A portrait of me with the famous dancer Régina Badet. That young person is still thirty-two years old! She avoids me as though I were the devil and occasionally admits: 'At the very beginning of my career, when I was a little girl, I once danced with Liane de Pougy.' Without being spiteful, I do feel obliged to state that for a little girl she had very big arms, bottom and bust, not to mention a solid career at Bordeaux where she had achieved the status of *première danseuse*.

....

April 4. Easter! Christ is risen! It's going to be a grey, rainy day. Joncières is here, unrecognizably good humoured and charming, he has suffered a lot.

I must say in his favour that he shows no bitterness against Piérat. He simply reveals the facts. When I complimented him on this he answered: 'One should never tear oneself to pieces. Piérat was sixteen years of my life, after all.' He added: 'The other day I was having dinner at Madame Gillou's with Colette – who, by the way, rules the roost at *le Matin* on the literary side – and she started to malign Willy* quite terribly. She was really out to get him, omitted nothing, exaggerated everything, swore that he had never written a line of any of his novels, gave the names of the writers he exploited, burrowed in her handbag for revealing documents. It was painful.' A clever woman, certainly a glib one, talented, knowing the right people – but ill-bred and with a streak of silliness which prevents her realizing how odious and even ridiculous she looks in this role of hatred and disparagement. Her marriage to Monsieur de Jouvenel who she pinched from one of her friends, the beautiful Ida de Comminges – a brilliant marriage which gives her a high place in the world of letters – ought to have raised her above this low kind of bitterness.

Ah Colette! Of what metal is she made? She goes on being just what I, from unhappy experience, always thought her. Life neither softens her nor makes her more beautiful. It is rumoured that she is not very happy, deceived, rejected, ill-treated . . . Perhaps she still loves Willy who was her first victim, and her resentment is exacerbated by his sad fate. She believes in neither God nor the Devil, she fears neither sin nor death. I have watched her dancing and guzzling, with the corpse of a woman she loved lying in the room next door, shouting at the top of her voice: 'That's how we'll all end, the dead mustn't depress the living!' Poor, poor Colette, swollen with fat, puffed up with bitterness, envy, ambition. They say she's manoeuvring for the red ribbon.

. . . .

April 10. I have migraine. Georges is reading Nathalie's book and criticizing it heartily. As for me, I'm prejudiced in its favour, but I admit that it could be tedious to read all those fine phrases from

* Henry Gauthier-Villars, Colette's first husband, who exploited his wife by publishing her early work under his own pen-name.

end to end. Rather like eating too many delicious sweets, a bit sickly.

My park is ravishing. A real bosky grove full of birdsong which irritates Georges quite as much as Nathalie's book. I believe Georges would like to stay indoors for ever, his window bricked up, and could forget the rest of the world for the interest of watching a spider at work.

April 12. Lewis arrived late. He told us a thousand bits of tittle-tattle from his world: how Emilienne d'Alençon has 'debauched' one of his little mannequins, very pretty and young, for two thousand-franc notes. Emilienne rigged her out, did her up, trained her, introduced her to old Hennessy, took her to Monte Carlo and gave her the name Liane de Reck! She loves the name Liane, which I was the first to assume. She likes to speak it, to propagate it – in memoriam, no doubt. I spent so much time gaping at her in admiration between the ages of eighteen and twenty-two. She played so many wicked tricks on me, all of which I forgave as soon as her fresh and charming face appeared before me. Emilienne dances, tangos, dresses up as a naval officer in shorts (!!!), has her little curly head dyed red with henna, visits scandalous bars patronized by inverts, carries on with her vicious and fantastic little life, pays no heed to nature or to the Creator, enjoys herself according to her whim. She's a philosopher in her way.

Lewis told us how Gaby Deslys died after four months of suffering. A priest came to talk to her and advise her; a statue of the Holy Virgin was placed where she could see it; she made her confession, took communion, prayed. Religion gave her comfort.

Lewis wastes no time on sorrow or regrets. He says: 'Gaby was finished in America. They wanted no more of her, they'd soon had enough of her! People exaggerate the size of her fortune. She had a nasty illness in her blood,' etc.

Poor Lewis. His visit left us with an uncomfortable feeling of embarrassment. He explained quite naturally: 'Gaby left a life annuity of 18,000 francs to Harry Pilcer. Harry is very chic at the moment; he has just bought 300,000 francs worth of furniture; he's kept by a very rich old Greek.'

....

April 14. The other day Lewis and I spoke about Mata Hari. I deny that I was ever a friend of hers. She was brought to my house by

Hector Baltazzi, a gentleman of Greek origin transplanted to Vienna and washed up in Paris. Hector was an uncle of Marie Vetsera, heroine of the Mayerling drama, and a friend of the Empress Elizabeth. He used to ride with her and she nicknamed him 'my little pocket-handkerchief'. He was dreadfully small, very dark. My name for him was 'the Havana cigar-butt'. He was 'wagons-lits', always on the move, surrounded by foreigners, very international. Ruined, he lived luxuriously, was received everywhere and used to introduce well-born foreigners to the most charming of the Parisian actresses. Nothing has been heard of him since the war.

This photo of Mata Hari, so beautiful in her body and so ugly in her soul, who simply for love of lucre betrayed the France which welcomed her so kindly – this photo reveals her slyness. Though her eyes are beautiful her look is glowering, her expression is shifty, her countenance is hard and vulgar. I said that never was I able to feel friendly towards her, and it's the truth. There was something too hard in her which I found tedious and off-putting. She had a loud voice and a heavy manner, she lied, she dressed badly, she had no notion of shape or colour, and she walked mannishly.

....

April 22. Long talk with Georges last night, from bed to bed. I made my way of thinking perfectly clear to him. It will do no good: Georges is a stupid and ceaseless bungler. He becomes more like Mariette every day. I really can't stand any more of this dismal, bad-tempered, discontented, hostile and disapproving spirit of contradiction. When he assured me of his profound and faithful love I ended with these true and conciliating words: 'I don't mind about your love, just give me a little sympathy and kindness. That is what I need and that is what my conduct, my bearing and my efforts have earned me.' Sympathy and kindness! Those two words contain the whole secret of domestic happiness.

Royal Dutch have fallen to 61.000 francs after having risen to 66.400! We are very dejected. Georges telephoned Lazarus who doesn't care a jot for us. These fluctuations are the coquettishness of value, allowing clever speculators to play with it and grow rich. The carrot is dangled, then withdrawn.

April 23. Saint George! Happy feast-day to mine! Among the gifts I wish to bestow on him are sympathy and kindness, the two best of household fairies Everything is all right so far as it goes, but it doesn't seem to be going far – not at all far! I give warning in order to avoid trouble! I wrote him a dada letter which amused him very much and gave him a box of sultanas from Marquis and enough cigarettes to provide him with his eight a day for about the next two years. Tobacco is becoming scarce.

May 9. The day before yesterday Georges and I laughed for a whole hour till our sides ached, till we couldn't draw breath, till we cried.

We don't often get carried away by that sort of laughter. It hurts. It's the good old giggles of childhood, which you can't stop, which you suppress a little and then it bursts out even louder and harder. 'Laughter is characteristic of Man.' But I also say that 'Clothed, Man buckles on his principles. Naked, he is an unreliable animal, almost always dangerous.' Georges adores being naked, sauntering about naked in his bedroom and the bathroom. Savagery . . . When I was small my mother made me wear a chemise when I was taking my bath, for the sake of modesty and good breeding. When I began to fly with my own wings, at about sixteen, after my marriage, I deliberately left off the chemise on these occasions – which were rare enough, as it happens: three or four times a year. It caused a scandal in the house, scoldings, predictions of disaster. Modesty, even if only in her own eyes, was a woman's loveliest quality; losing modesty, she lost everything, even her husband's respect.

....

May 12. They say that today the strikers want to come out and prevent the non-strikers from working.

Ever since April 13 there have been strange-looking beings strolling the streets, idle squat males in thick corduroy trousers and flat caps, with their sturdy, weather-beaten, hatless ladies – what magnificent heads of hair these women of the people sometimes have! – and it needs no more than the appearance of a group of them, or a family, on the terrace and in the elegant places we give up to them on a Sunday . . . it needs no more than their undesirable and unaccustomed presence to make us feel threatened and flouted. One pretends not to notice them, but one sees and senses them, and terror is not far off.

I am reading Madame de Boigne. Naturally she knew that she was pretty, her portrait shows that she was, and she says as much. 'I was first made aware of it by the exclamations of working-class people in the streets.' It's a long time now since young men in the street have exclaimed at my beauty. It did use to happen, a bit. I went by quickly, in a carriage. Nowadays there are a lot of pretty girls, cosmetics diminish the gap between beauty and mediocrity; and anyway the working people have other fish to fry. My kind of beauty made its impact from close-up, in intimate situations. Above all I was distinguished. My beauty wasn't striking at a distance like that of Otero, Cavalieri or Emilienne d'Alençon; its action was delayed. Meilhac once said to me: 'You are so subtle, so perfect, it's comparison that reveals your prettiness. The greatest beauty ceases to exist beside you.' Reynaldo Hahn often told me the same thing and so did Helleu and Coco de Madrazzo, for whom I often posed.

Emilienne was the great object of my admiration. I spent hours gazing at her. Her looks enchanted me. The freshness of her complexion was dazzling, you could see the blood running under her skin. I have got her portrait wearing a petticoat. Because I wanted to be like her, I said to Reutlinger one day: 'Take a picture of me in my petticoat, like Emilienne.' He looked at me and started to laugh. 'Oh no,' he said, 'you are not at all the type, it wouldn't work. You were born to play princesses! Resign yourself to being a princess.' He was nearer the mark than he knew. Far from being flattered, I was very cross. I knew I was slim, incredibly so; I was always being teased about it in the gossip columns and I thought he had refused to do me in that pose because I was too thin. I returned to the charge a few years later. To please me, he draped me in a large shawl and did a semi-nude of me which came off quite well.

....

May 17. My son's birthday today, he is thirty-one. I longed passionately for a girl because of the dresses and the curly hair. My son was like a little living doll given to a small girl. I was very proud and forgot all the suffering I had been through. Yet fate was to make me a hopeless mother; all of life called me, all the different countries drew me away.

My Marco, who was not loved enough and who didn't love me enough! During the last three years we understood each other better and drew nearer to each other.

My God, thank You for awakening me under the spur of pain. I bless You for all the suffering which turned me into a real mother for my Marco.........

....

May 25. Spent the day, yesterday, in Henry Bataille's roost. Roost is the word, it's at the top of a tremendously steep path: a rustic and ugly villa called 'Paradise'.

The lord and lady of the manor were still in bed at midday. We had a look round as we waited for them. Yvonne de Bray appeared, fresh and smiling, prettily dressed in black satin embroidered with gold. We kissed, gushed over each other, exchanged compliments on each other's dresses and looks, etc. Then Henry made his entrance, stiff and large, pleased to see us and complaining about his health. He says that he can't walk, has tachycardia, is getting fat, sleeps well, eats hugely and works. His poetry and his plays bring him in an income sufficient to keep up his house at Vivières and pay a big rent for a handsome unfurnished flat in the Avenue Bois-de-Boulogne belonging to old Doucet, the couturier.

Henry and I, akin in suffering, talked about illness and doctors. Yvonne and Georges jokingly posed as the victims of our nervous systems – victims quite happy with their lot.

The day went quickly; we had so much to say to each other. We are very fond of each other: each of us embodies for the other something of his or her youth; we have survived so many vanished friends, been through so much, and we see each other so little, I really don't know why.

We promised them that we would spend a few days with them at Vivières. Georges can have a mattress on the floor at the foot of my bed, they invite our dear Lolotte as well and they urge me to bring Fatoum. They were so ready to meet all our conditions that finally I accepted in principle. They are our sort of people, and among the best of our sort of people. We speak the same language and share the same views. The only thing Henry and I disagree about is Flossie. He insists that she is spiteful and sly. I think she sided with Berthe Bady when Berthe and Bataille split up after twenty-five years.

May 26. In the middle of the night of May 23–24 some unhappy railway-track watchman had a horrible time. He met an old gentleman wearing white pyjamas who stopped him and said: 'I know this sounds very odd, but I am the President of the Republic and I have fallen out of my train.'

Malesherbes, with its lunatic asylum, was quite near, so there was our good man scratching his head and wondering what on earth to do. To his great relief the gentleman, having spoken, fainted. Our railwayman summoned whoever was available at that time of night and in such a place – his wife among them – and Monsieur Deschanel, for it *was* him, woke up reposing comfortably under respectful surveillance in the level-crossing keeper's house. The wife, quicker in the uptake, had recognized him from his portrait which has already been much reproduced all over the place.

As my learned friend remarked yesterday, we will be the laughing stock of Europe! We are all sniffing the air for mystery, crime, assassination attempts . . . Moral: a President of the Republic in the twentieth century must not sleep or indulge himself in the comfort of pyjamas. I was once told that Cécile Sorel – my Superb – remains armed throughout the night, discipline having developed into a graceful habit: a smile on the lips, arm folded under head, expensive and elaborate negligée, ostrich feathers arranged in carefully dishevelled hair – ready, in fact, to charm and tame whatever insolent being might have the audacity to intrude without warning, through door or window, into the presence of Célimène: of Célimène, who must never, never allow herself to be taken by surpise . . .

....

May 28. They announced the death of Chaliapin, hideously assassinated by the Bolsheviks. It seems that it's not true. Dear Fedia is doing well in Moscow, singing every evening and enchanting those people in their delirium. It was a French journalist, brave enough to undertake a journey to that terrible country, who told us appalling details and denied the many rumours. Our compatriots, detained until now, have just been allowed out. They are in a lamentable condition. There was a reception for them at the Saint-Lazare station, and the photographs of it in the *Excelsior* were very moving. They were crying; smiling nervously; faces were rigid in expressions of sorrow; some were on stretchers.

I am infinitely delighted by Plato's *The Banquet*. I'm proud of liking and understanding it. Modern philosophers use such a tortured and difficult vocabulary, you have to be initiated in order to read them, learn their language as though it were a foreign one.

....

June 7. Tumultuous day yesterday. My menu was phenomenal. Our guests were Bouchor, unexpected; Max Jacob, appearing like a jack-in-the-box with a beautiful bouquet of roses; Lucienne Rouveyre; Raoul de Galland, who came by car bringing his camera; Margot de

La Bigne and all my shopping. For tea we were joined by our future tenants who have signed the agreement, my uncle and aunt Burguet, Steinilber and Lazarus with his little Pierre. Lazarus – oh dear, not so good. He was embarrassed and uncomfortable in my presence. On my side I smiled too much and couldn't help feeling hostile, also embarrassed and uncomfortable. Oh dear, money! Damnable and necessary money, up to its tricks.

Last but not least we opened our big gates to a ravishing grey motor-car from which Andrée de La Bigne emerged, all golden in a dress of blue Japanese silk – really stunning, that girl – and loaded with chocolate caramels. She was followed by André Germain, resolute but staggering under the immense weight of his literary productions. Finally a delicious little grey night-moth came flitting out of the car, alighted beside me, fixed me with its tender and luminous gaze, full of childlike curiosity. It was Madame Clauzel, and I was conquered. Our arms linked, our hands met, our enchanted thoughts mingled. She is exquisite, gentle, authoritarian.

The friends left, the night-moth stayed – the night-moth and the clothes-moth. André Germain is a domesticated clothes-moth, we choose to spare him. He read us his articles on dadaism, on D'Annunzio. Meanwhile the night-moth was in my arms: delicate touches, caresses, kisses, nips and scratches. This morning I still have little marks on my wrist. Like me, she adores Salomon, loves Flossie, admires Pauline. We evoked them, we compared our pearls and the textures of our skins. There were ripples of laughter, exclamations. Stern André Germain came to a halt and drilled us with a coldly indignant look; his nose became even more pointy and he told us: 'I can't go on reading while you talk.' So we kept quiet and our hands squeezed each other with increased intensity. She is like Eva Palmer, my Yvée, recalls a slender Liane from those bygone days of fragility and delicacy. I gave my *Idylle saphique* to the night-moth, who opened enormous eyes at the idea of reading something which, she says, Salomon has forbidden her. Oh, Salomon!

My 'Maintenon' dress exhausted me, I was the slave of that white collar which crushes so easily. Lianon! Organdy's victim! It's impossible to lean back. Poiret is decidely impractical, doesn't know how to combine elegance with comfort.

June 13. My tenants moved in yesterday and I have sold my tapestries. I had to consent to a considerable rebate, 33,000 francs instead of 40,000. So much dust, so many moths and maggots concealed behind those lovely things. Like in people's minds, a mass of evil thoughts, bitterness and intrigue.

Yesterday I telephoned Lazarus to tell him that I needed 100,000 so he must sell my most valuable shares. He told me: 'You are a delicious friend, but as a client you are nervy, anxious, suspicious, cowardly. You are not up to it. A client who is, entrusts me with his money and doesn't give it another thought.'

June 16. Réjane has died of a heart disease. She was sixty-four, an immense talent, profound and moving. She could make me laugh and cry, make my heart thud while tears and mascara streamed from my eyes. Off the stage she was an exquisite being, passionate and not always very happy.

A big headline in *l'Intransigeant*: Paul Darde, former shepherd, received the National Prize for Sculpture at the Salon. I like that: a shepherd becoming an artist, a little flower-seller becoming a famous singer (Cavalieri), a prince marrying a dancer from the Folies-Bergère – it breaks the tedious protocol of life, it's a flash, a glimmer, a little triumph of fantasy over convention.

June 21. A delightful day yesterday. Max Jacob arrived at lunchtime with Georges Auric, a young composer much in the public eye, very futuristic, a protegé-friend of Cocteau's. He collaborated in *Boeuf sur le toit*. He's a mere boy, hardly twenty-two years old. He has a remarkable talent, plays admirably and fluently. His talent is geometric, architectural, I might say cubist. He has outstanding control. Long torso, fat hairless face, rather comic, a sensitive simpleton. He is massive with it, and unhealthy too. The war tortured and undermined him. He talks little – people say with difficulty. He has an acute look in his eye, but in spite of all this he seems to be very good-natured. A reserved creature, pouring himself into his abrupt and tango-like music. He charmed us all.

June 24. Auric has sent me his favourite piece, or ours at any rate, *Adieu, New York*, with a friendly inscription. That boy displays a gravity and dignity almost incompatible with his age. He sees a lot of Poiret – hmmm . . .

June 25. Salomon came yesterday and was cross and hostile. He works too hard, which wears him out and makes him irritable. He saw that I was mortified and finished me off with these words: 'Nathalie has one great advantage over you and over other women in general, she shows great steadiness of character.'

July 1. I've just been reading Claude Anet's *Ariane, jeune fille russe*, in which she tries to pass as a dissolute woman although she's just a foolish virgin, and it reminded me of a chapter in my own story.

At eighteen, when I sent the laws of society and the family flying, driven by my greed to know everything, by events and by my first husband's book-keeping which was very like Lazarus's – at eighteen I became the irresistible passion, the Ideal (so he said) of the Marquis Charles de Mac-Mahon. One day he was questioning me jealously: 'Tell me, my darling – how many men did you give yourself to before me?' I began to ponder, to count on my fingers, to recite whatever names occurred to me – names of countries, names of famous vintages. The twentieth was that of Lur-Saluces. Mac-Mahon was stunned: 'What, So-and-so Lur-Saluces?' (I forget the first name). 'Yes.' – 'But he's my brother-in-law! I would never have thought it of him!' – 'Oh, it was only a casual thing, very casual.' – 'Lur-Saluces! That serious chap! Sleeping with a little girl of eighteen!' – 'What about you?' – 'That's different, I adore you.' Rather disconcerted, I continued listing names. The marquis was spluttering with rage, swearing, suffering. When I reached forty-two I judged that I had made my little effect and stopped. 'That's all. The forty-third is you,' and I looked at him out of the corner of my eye. 'Little wretch!' (I gloated). 'Vicious little creature' (I was in seventh heaven). 'It's not possible at your age; forty-three men, it's appalling!' Now, I had in fact known my husband, my first lover (the ship's lieutenant Cronon) and the Marquis de Portes. Mac-Mahon was a mere fourth, but I thought it much smarter to create a whole list. For me there was nothing between being pure and being dissolute. After that I took refuge in the most absolute silence and refused to answer any more questions. So he suffered inwardly and his suffering exhaled great sighs. He gazed at me tragically, he shook his head, his eyes filled with tears: 'The forty-third! I'm the forty-third!'

One day he turned up and announced without ceremony: 'I've just been with Lur-Saluces: I spoke about you, yes, I said your name and he never even blinked.' I didn't blink, either. He went on: 'So I probed him a bit. He didn't give an inch, he admitted nothing.' Gravely I pronounced: 'All crimes can be denied. The man did right.' I was thinking: 'So this is how family quarrels begin! To think that I only picked on Lur-Saluces because I'd had some with my dinner the night before!'

Never did I grant him the only comfort he could have had, the truth. Perhaps he would not have believed me, perhaps he would have loved me less without that lie . . . Who knows? Anyway I didn't care two pins for poor Mac-Mahon who was too much in love with me and whom I ruined and embroiled with his wife (he had married Mademoiselle de Vogüé before he met me) as casually as I would have swallowed an egg. I wasn't faithful to him for a moment. I had a liaison, secondary to the one with him, with Evremond de Saint-Alary – the very same man who won the Grand Prix three days ago. Saint-Alary could outdo me in disloyalty, cunning, intrigue and lies! He took eight thousand francs – he was a gambler – out of a roll of ten thousand given me by Mac-Mahon, and never repaid them on the pretext that he had 'spent a lot of money' on me. That's a reason but it's no excuse. It will soon be thirty years since then. We probably wouldn't recognize each other if we met in the street, but when our paths used to cross in Paris I would give Monsieur de Saint-Alary a very cold look without bowing, while his eyes shifted in the other direction as he sketched the gesture of raising his hat.

The past, the ugly past . . . I am angry with Claude Anet for bringing it to the surface. My Giorgio! You alone have raised me above all that wretchedness.

July 5. We have quite given up the notion of staying with Bataille at Vivières. Delicate as we are, accustomed to considerable comfort and a healthy diet, we would adapt very badly to the hurly-burly of a house where grouchy servants are constantly giving notice. Joncières told me that there is one big bathroom in which people take turns. We need our comforts, our snug little corners all to ourselves. And then Bataille lies in bed till midday and makes up for it by staying up till midnight; that wouldn't suit us at all. I can't be up later than ten o'clock without risking a sleepless night. It would be better to stay where we are. We will not be moved however much they insist.

July 6. Torrents of rain all day yesterday, broken by a pleasant but too-short interlude: Salomon's visit. What an agreeable talker! What a charming reader! He read us Bossuet and tried to read Cocteau but threw the book aside, laughing. . . . .

Salomon has seen Flossie, who is not leaving her mother's side at present. Her mother, an eccentric old woman who can't be less than sixty-five and looks eighty, was reckless enough to marry – two years ago, I think – a young man of twenty-five. It didn't last. She has returned to filial love which will, no doubt, be kinder to her.

July 7. I am reading Lauzun's memoirs which Salomon lent me. Gallant and tender, rakish and charming. He sums up the spirit of his age in three lines: 'As was common at that time, I possessed very fine clothes to wear when I went out; at home I was naked and dying of hunger.' You don't see much of that nowadays, particularly not among upper-class people. They get themselves jobs in industry: Boni de Castellane is 'in antiques', La Rochefoucauld 'in cars', etc. They marry Jews and Americans more than ever. They are right, but the century loses charm as a result, and manners suffer.

July 12. Our little gathering consisted of Max Jacob, Auric, Joncières, Lièvre, Steinilber and Margot. We talked about everything. Auric played the piano, his *Adieu, New York*, then Chopin, Schubert, Glück, Spanish songs and dances. I dug out an old piece by Ketterer which Tamberlick used to sing, *Oh! Souviens-toi*, and he tinkled it for us in the wittiest way........

Lièvre and Margot found common ground. It was Lièvre's father who designed and made Valtesse's beautiful bed of many-coloured bronze, that famous bed which cost fifty thousand francs (and that was forty or fifty years ago!) and which was said to be the model Zola used when describing his Nana's luxury; that bed which is now displayed in all its glory in the Museum of Decorative Arts. I have often been in that huge bed, which stood on a dais and was surrounded by a grill. When I went to stay with Valtesse I had my own room and a comfortable dressing-room; but when morning came it was the custom to take breakfast in 'the Golden One's' bed. An hour often went by in cheerful, affectionate gossip. She gave advice, she drew one out, and she kept her own secrets. To think that I never knew she had a daughter! And she had two of them!

July 14. Yesterday evening I read Colette's new novel, *Chéri*, at one sitting. Salomon knows it and is delighted with it. Well, my dear Salomon, here's something else about which we disagree.

I find this book of Colette's muddy, demoralizing, depressing. Every detail reveals vulgarity. It is lively, well observed I suppose, well written. So I scold myself for withholding enthusiasm. I fear that it's due to my stubborn prejudice, my memory's inner voice, the insensitivity of bitterness in fact! I pick the book up again, I search, I reread, and again I reject it. I do not like it, it offends me, almost wounds me. Yet I admire Pauline, Madame de Noailles brings tears of enthusiasm to my eyes, Madame de Régnier moves me, Rachilde interests and amuses me, Lucie Delarue-Mardrus charms me. There are legions of women who win my approval and whom I'd like to equal. Colette . . . no! I look down on her with a grimace of disgust. And all literary and learned Paris, all my friends, are going to exclaim with admiration while I sit here crossly with my mouth shut. Is it just that I am unable to control my own unfairness? Colette appeals to her readers' latent sensuality, she titillates sex, shakes up the kidneys, goes to the head, tries to intoxicate, is well aware of the vulnerable spots and flavours her salad accordingly. It works; it works with everyone; not with me. Nor with Georges. I loved *Dialogue des bêtes* and was tremendously amused by her Claudine books; since then my enthusiasm has gradually melted away. Colette has beautiful cats' eyes, a comic look, vulgar, childish, rather catlike gestures. She also has the gift of the gab, wit, education, a lot of cleverness. It all adds up to a talent, a talent which her experience directs towards matters which I find hurtful. Let's leave it at that.

July 15. Anniversary of my first marriage.

The Mazerauds came back with a huge pot of pâté, an exquisite speciality of Pacy-sur-Eure. They overwhelmed us by offering it to us. They are such charming people, tenants such as we never dared to dream of! They also brought back an impresario whom I used to know: Theuret. His business is chiefly opera or operetta. He couldn't get over finding me 'so beautiful, so plump, so rosy, you who were formerly so slim, so pale, so long', etc. The truth is, his admiration of my full-blown charms turned the knife in the wound. In the days when everyone fancied big women, I was slender; as soon as everyone starts wanting slender women, I put on weight. No luck! . . . .

I have turned up a very funny and very incoherent note from my old dancing master in London, Daddy Espinosa who was about a hundred and seven and had once taught Mariquita. He paid homage to my suppleness and nicknamed me the Electric Shocker. This old boy with a nose as long as himself, small, appallingly dressed, absurd, red, bald, drunk, was the master of such an inimitable skill that with one gesture he could become graceful, airy, incomparable. He had danced before the tsars and all the kings of Europe between 1850 and 1870, and had collected proof of their admiring munificence: gold watches with royal ciphers, heavy chains, tie-pins, rings and portraits. I was very fond of him. He made me work very hard and managed to get some unexpected results out of me. Wife, sister, sons, daughters, the whole lot danced, worked at the bar, teemed, spread, scattered throughout every ballet in London and thereabouts. He was much in demand as a teacher and producer. His brilliant talent was recognized everywhere. Irving was always in his company – they were great friends. When I wanted to obtain some extraordinary favour I would mimic him and he would laugh and say: 'Cheeky! Why didn't you come to me when you were six years old and I could have given your bones a proper breaking!' His feverish and exultant letter proves that you are no less a man for being an old teacher!

July 27. The Duc de Morny died recently. He was the elder brother of our friend Missy, alias Mathilde de Morny. I possess a picture of her as Napoleon. She gave it to me with the inscription 'To my daughter, from her father-in-law'. It was Missy's way to call nice-looking boys her 'sons': Sacha Guitry, Auguste Heriot, Georges, were all her 'sons'. So when I became the wife of her 'son' she called me daughter and signed herself 'your father-in-law'. She wore men's clothes, cropped her hair, smoked big cigars – and would have let her mustache grow if she'd had one! She exchanged the name Mathilde for the debonair 'Uncle Max'. At bottom she was a charming, childlike creature, a bit simple, well brought-up but an exhibitionist and a worry to her family. We gradually let our friendship with her drop, which gave no pain to either party. Max-Mathilde loved dressing up and giving fancy-dress dances; her whole life was a masquerade.

Another of our friends, Sarah Bernhardt's niece Sarita who died some years ago, had the same little kink; although she used to wear skirts and was masculine only in the top half of her clothing, her manner, her style, her rings. She too favoured the cigar, which made her presence very disagreeable to me. Sarita who was intelligent – more intelligent than Missy – was very deeply committed to this line of conduct and used, between ourselves, to make a living by it, whereas Uncle Max was ruined by it. I ought to add that Sarah Bernhardt tried again and again to tear her beloved niece away from those circles and those habits, she reasoned with her, she gave her an allowance, she took her to America, she put her into plays. Nothing worked. Dinner jackets and love nests, short hair and the style of an invert . . . She was still young when she died of intestinal tuberculosis, after appalling suffering. Only when she was in the nursing-home found for her by her aunt, did she become more or less one of my friends.

I shall never understand that kind of deviation: wanting to look like a man, sacrificing feminine grace, charm and sweetness. To help the illusion, Missy used to flatten her breasts under a wide rubber band. How horrible to crush and damage such a charming gift of Nature! And cutting off one's hair when it can be a woman's most beautiful adornment! It's a ridiculous aberration, quite apart from the fact that it invites insult and scandal.

July 31. Cocteau has sent us a little pink compilation on which it says in black lettering: 'Carte Blanche'. A collection of all the articles he has published in *Paris-Midi*, lively, witty and biting. He never lets anything go to waste and collects even the least of his charming outpourings. In it he praised my friend Mistinguett with her unfailing, subtle, moving talent, so very Parisian. I'm glad. 'You need to come from Paris to understand that battered little girl's face, that drawling voice. Does Mistinguett sing out of tune? I don't think so. Whenever I'm in exile the memory of that voice pierces me . . .'

Mistinguett! When we last saw Bataille he fulminated against her: 'She's an evil woman, a bitch! It's shameful for an artist to be on the side of the police.' First, it has not been proved. It was made public, then it was emphatically denied. Mistinguett is good and very intelligent. Her adored lover, the excellent clown Maurice Chevalier, was a prisoner of the Germans and very badly wounded in the chest. Mistinguett went even so far as the King of Spain to get him returned to France. She achieved it; Chevalier was sent back. She nursed him with matchless devotion. Slowly he was restored to life. She got him wonderful engagements in the shows she was in. He repaid her by deceiving her with seductive little chorus girls and enthusiastic members of the audience. It broke Mistinguett's heart, but every night – oh what a cruel and ironic fate – she had to smile through her tears side by side with her unfaithful betrayer, because their contracts were unbreakable. She kept it up, and I hope she has consoled herself by now. She's such a dear little Paris guttersnipe, a real sparrow, a character. Her envious friends put their heads together and said: 'If Mistinguett could rescue Chevalier like that, she must have been a police spy ...' and the rumour got going. Personally I believe that if Mistinguett, always surrounded, always in the public eye as she is, was ever able in the course of one of her tours to do France a good turn, she did it, and she did it well.

We met each other more than twenty years ago. I was the visiting star at the Scala, and she was the established one across the way, at the Eldorado. Generously she came to see my act and gave me fervent applause and flattery. When I left she flew to the producer we shared, Madame Marchand, and said ingenuously: 'Oh Madame, please keep Liane's costumes for me, let me wear them in the next review!' Since then her indisputable talent has carried her far. Any number of beautiful costumes have been dreamt up, designed, created for her out of gold and jewels, fabulous period pieces, sumptuous elegance! – She knows how to wear them, how to 'manoeuvre' them as Cocteau says, with an incomparable chic that sparkles with wit. All in all, she is a great great artist. It does Cocteau honour that he wanted to say as much, to capture her in these eccentric and capricious pages which are rather like she is, unique Mistinguett whom I can't approach without my heart's beating faster.

August 1. . . . . Henri Régnier, a very old friend, has written a marvellous article about Colette, certainly far from impartial. On the other hand it appears that the well-known critic Henri Bidou has given her the most scathing review. So I am not alone; I am pleased about that, I was beginning to doubt my judgment.

Yesterday's conversation took a rather risky turn. In the course of it I learnt that the town of Bordeaux gave its name to the 'bordello'. I have visited them in many countries, out of curiosity and also because everyone else did. Each time I left one I experienced a feeling of disgust with human nature and hatred against men.

When I was at Bou Saada I passionately wanted to rescue that wonderful little Fally of the stormy eyes, slender and agile as a young gazelle; and her grandfather, like a good head of the family, refused to be seduced by even the most tempting offers. Finally, to convince me and get rid of me, I suppose, he told me: 'It is of the utmost importance that Fally should remain four or five years in the house of prostitution where her sisters, her aunts and her mother spent their youth.' I recoiled in horror. I tried to reason with him, to no avail. Nothing would shake him, sure as he was that he had made the right decision about the future of his wonderfully beautiful little grand-daughter who was alarmingly thin and shaken by a stubborn dry cough; his grand-daughter who at the age of eight was already dancing naked every evening in front of strangers. I sought out the commandant of the place, explained the situation and told him how I wanted to save pretty Fally's body and soul. He looked at me askance and sent me packing, politely but firmly. I heard afterwards that sometimes, after a good dinner, he made use of Fally.

So then, in despair, I went to see an elder sister of Fally's who was shut up in one of those houses, a café with dancing at night. The wretched girl's room had a dirty stone floor, its only furniture was a mahogany bed – like those of our country people – standing in a corner. On the bed, two torn and filthy mattresses. They made me feel sick. Filthy postcards and a few fair-ground ornaments on a shelf, a miserable white-wood table with bottle-marks all over it, and this sinister fat girl, her monstrous belly heaving with laughter at what I was saying. I left with gall in my heart. I can't even think about it without getting a lump in my throat, and to comfort myself a little I think: Fally must be dead. Surely, God, You must soon – very soon – have taken her away from this earth . . .

August 2. Yesterday a messed-up day if ever there was one. My bad nerves had to endure a rude assault, the arrival of these three soothsayers: Cocteau, Max Jacob and young Raymond Radiguet, a poet who is making a name for himself and who is only seventeen. (Max's explanation: 'My dear, infant prodigies stay seventeen until they are twenty-five.') Oh what a procession – starved-looking and dingy – led by Cocteau with his sharp, ravaged look like some vicious and anxious spinster, then shy, writhing Radiguet with shut eyes and open mouth, or vice versa, as though his skin were too tight. Max, always a bit of a carnival mask – Max had decided to live or die by every word which fell from the lips of Cocteau – of Cocteau patron of the arts, of Cocteau who puts on performances, organizes tours far from the theatres, who helps people even as he uses them as ladders.

Slovenly, incongruous and noisy, first they rumpled the rugs, smothered Georges's lavatory with tar, laid claim to our washbasins, our soap – and to other things as well. At table it was even worse and nearly ended in tears. Cocteau – and its not as though he didn't know how to behave because he comes from a perfectly decent family of scriveners – Cocteau began without ceremony to pick at a dish of fruit standing by him, and this during the first course! I signalled to Georges who smiled and said to the indignant Fatoum 'Take away that dish', which she did. First coldness.

At the centre of my table there was a rich and magnificent vase of dahlias, yellow, red and orange. 'I can't see Max because of the flowers' – 'I can't see Jean because of the flowers' – 'Well, what of it? You don't have to see each other' – 'Yes, we do' – 'Yes we do' – 'Too bad, there's no solution' – 'Take away the flowers' – 'Liane, they must go...' and Cocteau reached out for them. Outraged, I rose threateningly to my feet and said sharply: 'Listen, I am going and you can have my place, then you can give what orders you like.' Second coldness. Cocteau let go of the vase. Max was green, I was disagreeable, Georges was embarrassed and Radiguet was scared.

My food was exquisite and they did it honour. Thanks to its succulence, tongues were loosened; but I didn't take part, grumbling to myself that I'd worn myself out preparing this meal for such a lowdown bunch of clowns.

Afterwards, the reek of tobacco, and abandon. The gentlemen threw their ash on the ground, their fag-ends into the fireplace, their matches on the carpet, rumpled the cushions, knocked my books about, rummaged through our papers, etc. What a session! I took the line of clamping a smile – the professional smile of a dancer – over my indignation. The day dragged. I made them take a walk in the park; I took them to visit a neighbouring estate, I gave them the traditional chocolate and cakes at four o'clock. They left at seven o'clock. Not one witty or amusing word or thought.

Though Max did read three or four childlike and charming pages from his next book, and sang us some of his old songs. Cocteau, who has to hold the centre of the stage, didn't care for that.

They went away at last, leaving my poor house a pigsty, my spirits depressed, my mind full of bitterness. Never again! Never more than one writer at a time! How much I prefer Auric the silent, who knows so marvellously how to express all the sounds which inhabit him. Obviously there is a choice to be made; and made it shall be.

August 13. Salomon brought me some photos of Diane de Poitiers, on whom he is working. He thinks they are like me, that I have the same fine forehead and regularity of feature. I daren't really believe him. My arms are thinner, though very well shaped, my hands exactly the same (fingers with 'stomachs'). As for breasts, let's not talk about them: hers are pure marvels. Mine are placed in the same way, very wide apart, but less firm, little and – downy, as they say. Like her, I dress in black and white. She has an enigmatic, teasing smile, subtle and engaging. Mine can't be quite so charming.

....

August 21. Our trunks are locked, full to bursting [for the journey to Roscoff where they would spend the summer holidays]. We plan to cut down and take almost nothing, but they fill up as though by magic. Everything is *settled*, as the English say, our couchettes are booked. We are paying 65 francs today for what cost 12 four years ago.

Roscoff – Clos-Marie, August 22 to September 21

August 22. Arrived safely. Absolutely exhausted.

My Clos, my little Clos-Marie, which I nicknamed 'little house that's not so simple' (see *Yvée Jourdan*). Dear little unpretentious, welcoming house which everyone loves, our refuge from the heat of the summer, from the approach of the enemy and from the Gothas when they were bombing Paris. I never return to it without a pang, and memories come pouring in. I bought it in 1903, the year my pearls were stolen, after that great disillusionment. I did it up as best I could for later, for my mother. And my mother is gone, and 'later' has come. I am writing in bed, the window on my left is open. I can see the sky, the sea, and the top of my hedge of tamarisk and privet. This morning the air is soft and salty.

August 23. Everything unpacked. I know all the local news. I am still writing in bed. The old lady is taking a rest.

August 24. It is raining – November weather. Yesterday we did the rounds of the village and said hello to all our friends.

When we appeared at the hotel Madame Talabardon recoiled in horror with staring eyes. She couldn't utter a sound. I thought she had been taken ill. 'Oh, if you only knew, if you only knew!' she babbled. 'Only yesterday they told us the Prince was dead, and it gave me such a turn to see him there!'

It seems that there has in fact been a rumour that Georges was dead. The fishermen in our part of the village looked quite amazed when he appeared on the jetty. I don't like it.

I went to the end of the jetty and dipped my feet and my gout into the cold and salty sea. They soon became supple and burning hot. I am in need of this cure, and I shall follow it assiduously.

Georges is happy, cheerful and good-humoured. He is mad about this part of the world and my rustic domain. We go to sleep lulled by the waves. Few, if any, other sounds.

....

September 12. The sun is brilliant, bright and warm. The sea is calm and blue. One threat in my sky: Max Jacob, in Quimper visiting his mother, is going to come and 'say hello', or so he writes. Now – I know that he will stay here as long as he is able. Now – he is not livable-with. He will eat all the plump part of a fish, empty the cream jug without thinking of those who have not yet had any, take half a cheese, the best part of a cake, almost all the jam, scrape the bottom of the sauce-boat, cynically refuse potatoes, ask for coffee every day and sweeten it with three lumps of sugar. Such a guest is a real disaster, disorganizing his hosts' larder with an unfailing touch even while he tells them in a childish voice 'How you do spoil me! In Paris I often go without dinner after lunching on a pickled herring and a hunk of bread.' One smiles; one tells the maid: 'Don't put the butter on the table, serve it in a little shell for each person; make the desserts in separate ramekins, like in a restaurant; put the fish or roast in front of me, and I will do the serving.' One becomes thoroughly ratty, one mumbles and grumbles. At last the guest takes his leave and one says 'Ouf!'

Max goes to six o'clock mass every morning, waking everyone up. He upsets the serving of breakfast. He leans with all his weight on frail white-lacquered chairs as he puts on his dirty espadrilles. He broke a bidet worth ten louis without using it, and I have seen him lying in his filthy clothes and muddy shoes on a precious bedspread of white silk damask. Every one of this boy's loutish gestures irritates me like a fly buzzing perpetually round my head.

September 14. I am down with influenza. I am furious. Max Jacob says he will be here on Wednesday at the latest, for a whole day. God must have inspired him! The spare room is ready: I have had the bidet and the damask bedspread put away.........

September 17. Too ill yesterday to write a word. Max Jacob turned up beaming, well dressed, his hands full of Breton cakes and pancakes. It made it easier to welcome him warmly.

Kindly he took pity on me and was really accommodating, delighted to be back in the little Clos which gave him shelter for two months in the time of the machine-guns.

We chatted; he's a charming gossip, although rather destructive. He came from Quimper; everything went well between him and his family. Once fame has started to shine on someone, and money starts to clink in his pockets, even if one isn't going to profit by it, it does smooth out difficulties and soften asperities.........

Max found Georges marvellous, fatter, tanned, happy. As for me, I have almost no strength left and I am depressed and discouraged. I was so well! I flouted the cold and the wind, I went for long walks, I wrote, I read, I watched, I cooked, I did my embroidery and I tidied my cupboards. I was greedy and eager, choleric and alert, coquettish in my way, ironic, witty – alive, in fact. Now I'm pale, drawn, grumpy and melancholy; it hurts whenever I move.

I no longer care for people or my shelves, food fills me with disgust. As soon as I take the least drug my own nature, which is reaction itself, cancels itself and ceases to react. It seems as though something must be nourishing my illness – the bread, perhaps? It is horribly heavy and badly baked. It is quite impossible to get a good result with this appalling flour made, they say, of all kinds of war remains. They also say that this year's harvest is bad. A cheerful outlook!

I think Max and Georges despise me a little because I bought a complete set of Victor Hugo. Max gave me a sly look when he asked 'Is he a writer you like?' Today people speak of him scornfully – when they speak of him at all.

September 19. I asked Max Jacob: 'Do you often tell lies?' He answered: 'I don't often lie, but when I'm telling a story I almost always exaggerate.'

Sunday weather, singing our Lord's praises. The sea dazzling under the sun. Max celebrated Ember Day with vigil and fasting. He read edifying books. Bohemian artist that he is, with no precise rule of conduct, he finds a great deal of moral support in religion. A pity that it doesn't happen to be his own. A renegade always seems like an intruder, a sort of parasite, and race is always there.

A charming note from Salomon commiserating with my sorrows

and scolding Flossie who is still tucked away at Samois with 'someone'. Mystery and discretion. It enrages Salomon who loves our Flossie more than he admits – perhaps more than he realizes.

....

Saint-Germain – October 7 to December 29

Liane's influenza lingered for almost a month after her return to Saint-Germain, and her diary entries were consequently scrappy.

....

October 26. Very cold, winter is in a hurry. I saw the Roumanian princess again, she made eyes at Georges who didn't think her shoes any better than mine.

[*Liane had passed 'la Bibesco' in the street the day before, and had been embarrassed because she herself was wearing comfortable shoes while the other princess's were elegant.*]

Salomon left me a friendly review of *Chéri* by Jean de Pierrefeu. Salomon was hoping to embarrass me. 'No one has more genius than Colette.' See, Liane! 'Her precise and supple language adheres to the object (horrors!) and evokes the emotion (oh!)', then this long passage: 'The humanists of the Renaissance, culture's most admirable craftsmen, would have excluded this equivocal and fatiguing art of Colette's from the realm of that art which aims at elevating the soul and refreshing the mind. Quite apart from the fact that they would soon have grown weary of the strange, vulgar and uninteresting settings which appear to please Colette. It is time that she changed her characters; she has too much genius, surely, to persist in degrading it.' There! What did I say! I feel quite flattered at sharing the opinion of 'the humanists of the Renaissance'. Thank you, dear Salomon! ....

Marianne [de La Jaille] has been nagging at me to lend her my long pearl necklace. She is planning a little effect to be made with it! 'Cousin, show me your pearls. You don't wear them enough, it's bad for them. Oh how pretty this long one is, how I love it! I'll wear it for you if you like. Oh cousin! Look, it needs rethreading, let me take it to the jeweller.' I burst out laughing and so did she. 'Go on, child, take it: 406 pearls. Get it restrung, wear it, I entrust it to you for the rest of your stay.' She was enraptured. We began to count the pearls. Marianne found 416, Chochotte 408, Bouchor 420, Georges 417! It's always like that. Margot made it 407. A little society pastime.

November 3. I am feeling better. The cold is intense and Georges condemns me to the fireside. I go on crochetting my little dresses and reading Sainte-Beuve. He mentions Madame de Duras and depicts her in these terms: 'She had an extraordinary gift for adapting herself to each event, each person, and doing it naturally, without effort or calculation.' How totally I can see myself in that! I adapt, I assimilate. For example .... With Georges, with Max Jacob, Bouchor and one or two others I spring upwards, I fly, I soar, I really do display a sparkling wit at times, while with cousin Marianne I go to pieces, shrivel up and become as dull as can be. Salomon – with him it's the great pleasure of listening and learning, then some detail crops up, an argument, I rediscover myself, I become excited and I tell him cheekily, as though to get my own back: 'Dear Salomon, what a lot I could teach *you*!' In the presence of my silly, overbearing mother-in-law with her loud voice I go silent and hold myself in to the point of migraine. When she leaves I burst out, Georges and I go off like a cannon (he feels the same as I do and shares my irritation). If Mariette ever dissects and judges me, she must certainly think that I'm a great fool. Her buzzing eclipses one's personality: it's not possible to argue and it's idle to attempt a conversation. Actress . . . am I not always just an actress performing a role dictated by other people and the turns of events! It is before You and You alone, o my God, that I am able to find my true self.

....

November 19. Spent yesterday in Paris. Went in the metro for the first time. It's convenient, amusing, cheap, but people are glued up against each other, breathe in each others faces and travel underground.

November 24. Intensely cold. Salomon arrived while we were at lunch. Treacherous creature! He brought me Colette's short stories, *les Vrilles de la vigne*, and they really are very good. I come into one of them, the last, dedicated to Renée Vivien. It happens at Monte Carlo. This is what Colette says: 'Frail, delicious, supported, almost carried by young H and the no less young G, Mademoiselle L de P went by. She was smiling the lovely smile of a happy young mother leaning on her two big sons . . .' Behold – the claws hidden in the velvet paw! Colette is obsessed by the question of age. If you play little Claudine long enough you lose your sense of reality, you refuse to age, you fight desperately against wrinkles and grey hairs. And now comes: 'Less frail but no less beautiful is Madame CO (Caroline Otero), who is not playing today and whose brow wears a halo of melancholy . . . Alas, she says to her anxious admirers, it is because tomorrow I shall begin my twenty-ninth year . . .' There you are, any recognized beauty has to endure a scratch from the cat Colette. When I used to see the Willys, Moreno told me: 'Beware, my Lianon, Colette is vicious, cruel, jealous, she will envy your beauty, your features, your house, your pearls, your friends.' Young H – that was August Heriot (Louvre department store) whose mistress she became a few months later. She tried to make him marry her. The disappointment inspired her to write *The Vagabond*. Now, the 'no less young G' has become my husband, and it has lasted – no thanks to Colette! How she cried it from the roof-tops that it couldn't last, that G was marrying me for my money, that he would ruin me and abandon me to a poverty-stricken old age, doomed to the deepest despair. Luckily she has not proved much of a prophet – so far. When, two and a half years later, I married Georges, Colette's hatred expressed itself even more wickedly. The papers *Rire*, *Sourire* and *Fantasio* published ugly, vulgar articles striking at my dear little husband the better to hit me, all signed with meaningless pseudonyms. Some of our friends were moved to make a little investigation and they easily discovered the author: Willy – inspired and urged on by Colette. I did not hold it against Willy! God keep me from holding it against Colette!

To come back to Salomon, the beloved scholar came cheerfully into our icy dining-room on the stroke of half-past-twelve, asked for our news, then brought the *les Vrilles de la vigne* out of his pocket. The book was open and folded back at the fatal page. Pointing to this page 219 he asked me in a very interested voice who was the gambling woman referred to by Colette further down: 'Madame de la R . . . would that be Madame de la Redorte?' – 'Yes, it was her,' I answered stupidly. Now Madame de la R was given her scraping by the claws just after Otero. Salomon's pointing finger obscured her name and left clearly visible the passage in which I am mentioned . . . I understood. What a subtle fellow you are, my Salomon! What an amusing way of doing it, how kind after all, and how discreet! You thought: 'These lines contain the whole secret of

Liane's dislike of Colette. I am going to rub her nose in them to show her that I'm in the know.' It is even possible that Flossie may have tipped him off. No, my friend; these lines are the result of hatred, not a cause, and the hatred is Colette's not Liane's. Salomon, o Salomon, you ought not to stir up all this mud. I hope this malicious act will be the end of the matter between us for good and all. Go on admiring your Colette, chevalier of the Legion of Honour, and stop dinning it into my ears. As for me, I'm incorruptible!

November 28. Yesterday Salomon came to see us for a moment. I tell him a thousand things I wouldn't say to any other man. Confidence is complete. O Salomon, stay as you are but be a little less quarrelsome. Yesterday he spoke about my perfect (!) beauty and my prickly character. What cheek! Though it's possible, after all, because I do know that I am extraordinarily sensitive.

....

December 11. I stayed in bed with a terrible headache. I thought about Fatoum who has still not written. That little savage taught us to expect a magnificent indifference. So then I said to myself: one does not love one's parents. One never loves them enough. Look at me, I detested them, my judgment of them was ferocious. Think how I despised them for being old, poor, simple and having principles! I took everything as my due. Proudly I accepted every one of their sacrifices. I disdained their advice. Going away to the convent put the finishing touch to my indifference. When I came back, a child no longer, I kept all my kindness as well as my smiles for the young men who gravitated towards us. Yet I saw Papa wearing worn-out shoes and in all the sixteen years of my life in that house I knew him to possess only one single overcoat and only one single dressing-gown. I saw my mother going out furtively very early in the morning carrying parcels of precious family things to sell at the second-hand shop so that she could keep our little daily round going. I saw her coming back with empty hands, discouraged, silent and resigned. I was ashamed of my parents' threadbare, darned clothes, I was disgusted by my father's tobacco, I was irritated by my mother's prayers in church. I never shared any of my thoughts with them, I disliked kissing them. When I was seven I wanted to leave them, I escaped and ran off to ask for a job at Bazola's circus. Later, I dared to reply to some inquisitive fool who was interviewing me: 'My mother was a laundress who sold me when I was twelve.' My parents, did you have to die before you could find your place in your little daughter's heart?

There were moments when I threw myself furiously on my mother in floods of tears, all love and adoration. I hugged her frantically, overwhelming her with incoherent endearments. For her, those moments made all the others bearable! I used to sulk and pretend to be ill or to have a headache in order to claim their attention. I would refuse to eat in order to worry them, to make them pay more attention to me than to the others. And my lies . . . and all the ugly secrets and mysteries of my greedy and incomprehensible little soul, sensitive and stubborn. I was madly headstrong and never gave way. And my face was the face of an angel, sweet, candid, smiling, regular. Childhood is a state of the most appalling unconscious cruelty.

December 14. I am terribly disillusioned about Salomon. Yet another idol who has hurled himself off his pedestal. Georges is gloating and I have a sort of pain.

....

December 22. I have written a hai-ku in honour of Nathalie-Flossie, whom I also used to call Moon-Beam. I am sending her a picture of a little woman in a short frock smelling flowers in the moonlight; and because our mutual longing to see each other is not stronger than the times, places and circumstances which keep us apart, here is my work:

O brilliant moon
We see each other better
From afar. . . .

Then come our Christmas wishes. 'She will raise an eyebrow', says Georges.

....

December 25. Christmas! A warm Christmas, sweet and melancholy. Yesterday evening a knock on the door: it was Father Christmas in the shape of Rose dressed in a flowing white nightie, a white bonnet on her head and a long white cotton beard on her face. Marie followed, bearing the presents, subject of so much mystery and concealment. Georges gave me a ravishing black velvet dress, my two childhood cakes which had arrived from Lorient just in time, a box of splendiferous ecclesiastical purple writing paper, a pound of Jousset's delicious marzipan. I gave him, in addition to his shoe-presents, one thousand Camel cigarettes, three pairs of braces, a pound of marrons, a pound of pralines and – a litre of cod's liver oil! We laughed, smoked and nibbled, and everyone was happy.

The turkey arrived yesterday at midday, and is superb. We have stuffed it and truffled it. I have been sent fifteen kilos of green coffee from Haiti. Georges has written me a beautiful – and rather literary – Christmas and love letter.

December 26. I woke up rather unwell. I had a lot to do in the house, I wanted to go and hear at least a little mass. When I got back I shod myself in silk and robed myself in silver – a sumptuous dress from Lanvin – saw Rouveyre, the first guest to arrive, then suddenly my head began to swim and I only just had time to go and fall on my bed. When I came back to life I found – surprise, surprise – my dear Steinilber, very upset at my absence, and Max Jacob who had brought a box of Pihan chocolates bigger than himself ('all pralines, the ones you like best'). Auric, good brave little Auric had come too, even though he hadn't been to bed the night before. At about three o'clock I managed to get up, ate a little breast of turkey, and I kept going until the evening. Lunch had been men only, theories and discussions, almost arguments, but clean plates. In spite of his sorrow at my absence, Georges guzzled so much that he couldn't eat any tea, or any dinner either. We went down to the drawing-room, the stove was alight, the house was warm and good. Max, with a soft-pedalled accompaniment from Auric, entertained us with a rather incoherent but funny and charming little Christmas improvisation: the Virgin pregnant . . . and looking like me . . .

. . . .

1921

Saint-Germain – Pavillon de Noailles, January 1 to June 20

January 1. I had a long, clever, closely-written letter from Salomon yesterday, enclosing a copy of the impressions he recorded when we first met. Why does he send me that? I don't know. He says that I was lying down, not well, in black velvet and grey satin (my colours are sober and my dresses simple). He writes: 'She was wearing a necklace of enormous pearls and a ring of black enamel set with huge diamonds!' Well, why not? One ring and a necklace isn't much, not for the second floor of the Majestic! I'm no academic, I am Lianon the dancer at the Folies-Bergère, billed during a European tour in 1898 as 'Liane de Pougy wearing jewels worth a million'.

Salomon had got Flossie to introduce him to a chastened, suffering, unhappy little princess, wearing a black dress, one ring and her string of pearls, and he has to start criticizing! It's really too mean! He adds: 'That apart, she was irreproachable.' Thanks very much, you booby! For heaven's sake, if I never brought out my pearls they'd say my husband had eaten them!

Yesterday the goose arrived from Bourges in a huge basket, together with a fat chestnut cake in a mould and some delicious little coconut kisses. I quivered with delight as I unpacked it all. And my family's parcel was accompanied by another one, from Paris; a wonderful box of Boissier chocolates, with the good wishes of – Henry Bernstein! Well I never, what has come over him?

....

January 3. Rain, Sunday calm. Humanity stops its bustle, a feeling of peace descends on everyone. I went to mass – yesterday, too. The choir was hung with red banners fringed with gold, the flag of France was hung over the altar with the heart of Jesus embroidered in gold on the white band. Three glittering priests were officiating surrounded by children dressed in red and white muslin, and young priests wearing violet. All this red and gold and all these sparkling candles inspired the irreverent thought: sugar candy! But I listened to the organ, very beautiful and penetrating, and I lifted up my heart to You, oh Lord. My quivering, purified heart dares ask You for nothing, it submits, for itself and for those who belong to it, it does no more than make simple vows of courage and resignation. When one summons the courage to see what God is to us, the Infinite and All-Powerful, one can only submit to His will, do what is right and love Him in His creation and His creatures. It is in Him that we will all find ourselves.

January 5. Visit from Salomon, but I gave orders to say that we were in Paris. I want to help him space out his visits, so that it's not all on his side. He brought me *Madame de Caylus* and *La Grande Mademoiselle.*

January 9. Salomon came yesterday. I was in bed, nursing my migraine. Georges received him. Childish rhyme composed in his honour: 'Deserving a smack – how he does annoy – neither girl nor boy – Salomon Reinach.' My idol has fallen and is broken, now I trample it.

....

January 21. Charming surprise! My Flossie came to see me, after letting me know by telephone. She was dressed jauntily – Amazon style, what else! in a dark wool dress lightened by a green-embroidered white waistcoat. A caped coat over her shoulders, a plain felt hat on her blonde hair. With her brisk style, her implacable smile, her tenderness towards me, her instinctively caressing little hands, she looked very young and very happy. I plunged into this renewed contact. We spoke about Salomon. She made gentle fun of him, so indignation diminished. She stayed with me for a good hour. She has invited us to attend her Fridays, 'I'll have my Chinese music all over again for you, and you must bring Auric.'

January 23. Visit from Balthy, all in black, her ear-rings jet balls, her aigrette colossal, her eyes sharp, her laugh boisterous, calling up other laughs. She told me about her travels, New York, Los Angeles, etc, and swore that she had written from everywhere. Louise lies, but she does it so nicely! We talked antiques, works of art, theatre, fashions, cost of living. She is thin and her wrinkles have gone, her skin has become smooth. I suspect her of going to America to have her skin stretched and tightened, the way they do it over there. The shape of her mouth has changed a little, she no longer does her hair in the same way, no doubt because of the little white lines of the scars. She absolutely insisted that we should lunch with her on Saturday at Pépé's. I said yes. I can refuse nothing to my Louise when she fixes her black eyes on me and asks me for something in her vibrant, musical voice. Pépé is a Spanish grandee, José de La Pena de Guzman, etc – he has six whole lines of it! The luck of the draw landed him at Doucet's as a designer. He lives on the rue de la Ville-l'Evêque in a very big, very beautiful house belonging to Jacques Doucet. He lives alone with the most fragile of stomachs, sad, gloomy, immoral too, so they say. He is handsome, clever, distinguished and really too elegant! I used to know his wife, a former beauty, fat, rheumaticky, mottled, died in a lunatic asylum.

I was great friends with Pépé in those distant days when he made his debut at Doucet's. I remember giving him various little presents – sort of as tips – and even a few hundred-franc gold pieces brought back from Monte Carlo. He's given it all back since then! He has showered Georges and me with presents – dresses, linen, knick-knacks, furs. He is generosity itself, to the point of being embarrassing. Louise is living with him because she couldn't find a place of her own, and he's overwhelming her with them, too. We fell out because of incompatibility of temper. I'll enjoy seeing him again. He, like us, has come through a lot.

January 24. This morning I dropped in at the house agent's to discuss my house and my apartment. They suggested for us a little block of flats built in the Empire style with an adjoining lodge, also Empire, which has little columns and a pediment. It was once the Prince of Polignac's chapel.

January 25. The little Directoire house is dancing in my head. I hardly slept all night. Yesterday we went to see it. They are asking 70,000 francs. For that I would get responsibility for the upkeep of the flats and the income from them. The ground floor is let for nine years at 2,500 a year; the first floor is let for 900 francs to a tenant of long standing (eighteen years), three more years to run. It is worth 2,000. The second floor is let for 1,300 to someone who works in the Town Hall. The third lets at 1,000 unfurnished or 1,800 furnished.

It comes to 5,700. I reckon that upkeep would amount to 3,000. I would get a rent-free house and an income of 2,700. The little lodge adjoining the flats could be made liveable. It already has chic, with a little garden full of roses and a few shade trees at the back. The kitchen is a hole: a lot would have to be done. When one is reducing one's standard of living one must accept sacrifices. If I estimate my rent at 4,000 and it will be worth that once it's been done up as I intend, I'll have an income of 6,700. I don't think the necessary work will come to more than 100,000. It looks like good business, suitable to our decrepit budget.

January 26. Flossie has sent me some verses. She was supposed to come back on Saturday, wasn't able to, and apologizes in this charming way . . . .

I still have not got the little house, we are arguing over two or three thousand francs. Shall I get it? Shall I not?

January 27. The house is mine. Here I am with tenants, expenses, and rent coming in. I have paid a deposit of 17,500 and have deposited 50,000 with the lawyer, Maître Grebau. The former chapel of the Prince de Polignac is mine: I shall keep the repairs to the minimum and move in very gradually: I'm on my way down the slippery slope of poverty. I enter into possession on April 1, when work can start. What worries! But simplicity will be my foundation stone. Bit by bit I will become accustomed to the idea of leaving this large and expensive house, of living on little, of becoming content with even less. Each piece of furniture which goes will tear away a part of myself. Polignac will take the place of Noailles and when the modest little lodge is ready, so pretty and well-dressed, opening its little arms to me as wide as they'll go, I will let myself fall into them with a gentle resignation.

February 6. We have been to see old Pépé and sprightly Louise! The house is well heated and still richly furnished. It contains some fine collections: very valuable prints, Chinese blue and white. Pépé loves to rummage and accumulate. We were received with open arms, lunch was good, footman impeccable and well set-up butler.

In January my mother-in-law sent six thousand francs to her son, who is reduced to strict necessities. Good, we are glad, we are using the money. Immediately afterwards she wrote: 'It would be very helpful if you took out a subscription for me to *le Temps* for nine months and to *la Revue des deux-mondes* for a year.' A hundred and fifty francs to shell out! And a hundred and fifty francs is no joke to the poor boy.

....

February 10. Yesterday a day of migraine, but I still went to see the plumber and the joiner at my new acquisition. The little lodge will be very nice once it has been done up, but the doing up will be expensive: the whole staircase to be demolished and rebuilt in a different place, simply to make the kitchen bigger; a bathroom to be fitted in; and a thousand other details.

February 13. Salomon talks in a letter about the first novel I published, *l'Insaisissable.* Another piece of treachery. I dislike this very banal book, I have told him as much and said: 'Never mention it to me!' Is it forgetfulness, tactlessness, or yet another little bit of spitefulness? Into the waste-paper basket! Into oblivion! ....

February 27. We found Pépé having trouble with his stomach, condemned to yogurt and to having an x-ray on Monday. Balthy had pains in her shoulder and back; she forced herself to be cheerful and keep the conversation lively. A good lunch: boiled eggs, macaroni au gratin, mullet with mushrooms and truffles, warm custard moulds, which I abhor! They should be made the day before, they ought to wait and cool in their moulds, I have principles about it! Catulle Mendès used to say to me: 'Tapioca is a beggar which must be made to wait and thicken gently on the side of the stove. A soufflé, on the other hand, is a great lord on whom *we* have to wait patiently before welcoming him with admiration when he finally comes to the table in all his opulence.'

....

The next three months were tiring and rather dull: bad weather, uncertain health, continued irritation with Salomon Reinach. On May 22 Liane records that an American has bought Noailles for 550,000 francs. On June 20 she hears that her brother Pierre, who has been ill with cancer for some time, is dead.

At the beginning of July they moved into rooms in Saint-Germain. The Pavillon de Gramont seems to have been a school for young English ladies which didn't usually accept men but was willing to make an exception for Georges. Presumably the idea was that they should mark time here until their new little house was ready; but as it turns out, they never do move into the little house and Liane gives no explanation for this in her diary.

Saint-Germain – Pavillon de Gramont, July 1 to December 21

July 1. It's over, here we are rid of that ill-omened and oppressive house. I have been unable to write, ill and overwhelmed. We are all right here: quiet, airy, good wholesome simple food, friendly people. Flossie has been to see me with André Germain, she harmonious, he stronger. Salomon came and pedantized. Georges is thin and drawn, absolutely tired out.

July 2. My birthday. There's a gastric affliction going the rounds and Georges and I spent all last night paying our tribute to it. Now we are both in bed on a liquid diet.

They are very unhappy at Bourges [where her brother had just died] and want to hear from me every day. I do not want it to become a habit. What would be the good? I know what they probably feel about me. I may have forgiven the insults I received in the past from my sister-in-law, but I have not forgotten them.

It's nice to be ill together, to look after each other. To think that one can even contrive to manufacture pathetic little pleasures out of such a condition! 'Show me your tongue, how is mine? Goodness, it's medicine time again, let's have a tisane.'

Mademoiselle Hélou is something between a doe and a mouse. She is enchanting with her children who seem to love her and obey her without being afraid of her. Very little noise. I don't think we could have been luckier.

July 3. What an upheaval in our existence this house-moving is! I feel all scattered about in innumerable packing-cases and in the rough hands of the removal men – so scattered that I'll never be able to collect myself again.

Carpentier has been beaten by Dempsey, quite unable to return the blows he received. I'm ashamed, I don't like losers. Long live Dempsey! I'm quite taken by this thug. Rather beastly of me!

July 5. Salomon Reinach has – good heavens! – sent me some chocolates! Going through some papers I found a photo of Jean

Lorrain in summer clothes. It was in that get-up that he used to stare boldly at handsome young men and be amazed to find them 'sensitive to the power of the eye'. Poor Jean . . . basically sensitive and tender, flaunter of vices, valet to fame, intoxicated with the theatre and literature, heart of a child. Poor dear charming Jean, seeking after anything that might be described as a sensation of happiness. This photo is hugely like him.

I am no longer cross with Carpentier. He's all right really, and it was brave of him to take on that mountain. Poor fellow, he broke a thumb on it.

....

July 23. Georges was thirty-seven years old this morning. We did what we could. The day was lovely and very hot, the lunch good: all his favourite things, melon, radishes, sweet pimentos, lobster, roast chicken stuffed with foie gras, lettuce hearts with hard-boiled eggs, chocolate ice, a chocolate cake from Bourges made by my sister-in-law, peaches, almonds, cherries, coffee, sauternes from our own cellar. Mademoiselle Hélou sent up beautiful red roses and a pretty basket of pale pink carnations for the table.

....

September 9. Tomorrow an old lady and her daughter are going to come to stay here. These people knew me in Marseilles thirty years ago, when I lived in the rue du Dragon on the third floor of a building which had a girls' boarding-school on the ground floor. These ladies have told Mademoiselle Hélou all about it, saying that I was so young, so lovely, so alone! I used to play with the school-girls when I got the chance. It was from there that I escaped over the social barriers. My name became a scandal, I am still remembered. I hadn't a penny to help me leave my husband, but Grandmother Olympe had left me a rosewood piano. I considered it my property and wanted to sell it. Someone told me that a young man who lived in the same street was looking for one, so I went to see him. He received me, gazed at me, admired me, came to look at the piano and bought it without bargaining for four hundred francs, cash down. It was in the evening. An hour later I had left for Paris, for my dream, for fame and for filth – for my tumultuous destiny. Yes . . . but next morning, when the candid young man came to collect his piano he met with opposition, first from its owner, then from all the family. In spite of my receipt which was made out perfectly correctly, the young man never got his piano and may have felt that he paid dearly for the pleasure of my acquaintance! The one and only swindle of my existence, and quite involuntary at that. My husband was at Toulon and came to see me every week. When he arrived he found the nest empty and the bird flown. It was a very well-furnished nest. He sold everything on his own account to pay debts which we had incurred together: family mementoes, portraits – Maman at six months old in Grandmother Olympe's lap, with Uncle Gustave standing beside her . . . I have always regretted that picture, which had a damaged corner and could have had no value for anyone but me.

Rain and wind . . . . I am embroidering a blind for Polignac, a beautiful white blind with a Directoire vase appliqué in the middle.

. . . .

October 10. Salomon, after going round and round it, tells me: 'Flossie plans to visit you on Monday, with a charming friend who wants to make your acquaintance because she admires your books so much.' – '?' – 'Now, I shall be coming to fetch them, though I shall be too busy to come down with them.' – '?' – 'I want to ask you something.' – '?' – 'Don't be nasty to me in front of Madame R'. I roared with laughter. 'All right – but you are preaching hypocrisy, you know.'

And then my Natty arrived with Madame R – and she is absolutely charming!

She has ravishing white hair, a gold snake round her waist, a hat made of blue birds, a red coat, a black dress, silk stockings embroidered in royal blue, a swollen ankle, wit, a magnificent pearl necklace, sky blue eyes. She remembered meeting me in Switzerland, reading and loving *l'Insaisissable*, seeing me when I was ill at Oberthurs, my son's death. In short, she had followed my career. It is time that we knew each other. She took tea and congratulated me on being me. Flossie was putty-coloured from head to foot, complexion, teeth and hair included, and delicious and affectionate. I called Salomon 'maître' and 'Monsieur Reinach', and he was pleased with me.

I love seeing Flossie again, listening to her, watching her make her way through the world of her choice – easily the most charming of worlds. And she enjoys returning to me from time to time. To some extent I am her creation. Although she is younger than I am, she was my exquisite teacher and opened horizons to me.

My little house is coming along. It is taking shape. The contractors' bills are taking shape, too. Oh the brigands, the cheats, the shameless monsters!

October 11. I opened the *Imitation of Christ* this morning and chanced on a meditation on death. I read it attentively. It is sad and true. God led me to this passage, to counterbalance words spoken yesterday by Madame R, intended for my encouragement: 'One mustn't think about dying, one should keep going, keep one's mind busy, keep on the move: it's the only way to live. My father was still busily making plans at the age of eighty, so death crept up on him without upsetting him much.' I think that at my age one becomes more thoughtful and that it's no bad thing to get into the habit of thinking of death as a long rest.

....

October 29. On Thursday Salomon brought Flossie down, then left. We were alone together by my fireside for a good part of the afternoon. Dear Nathalie, so much grace and so much sweetness! So much kindness and charm! Nothing lofty was said, we just gossiped and exchanged opinions, and that was enough for the two of us, so happy at being together.

Georges tried to explain to Nathalie Einstein's theories, which everyone is talking about at the moment. He explains very well. We listened with concentration: Nathalie looked like a good and conscientious schoolgirl. As for me, I didn't understand a thing. I am furious at my mind's limitations. Nathalie got out of it with a smile and one of her pleasantly ambiguous remarks. We talked about my polar-bear rug, now hers. She said to me: 'He knew all your joys and sorrows.' I began to laugh: 'And some pretty comic moments, too.' – 'Tell one of the comic moments!' – 'Do I dare? All right. Once I was courted assiduously by a young, rich and silly Bonapartist. He heaped me with presents and money. He was always ready to obey my least – and most capricious – whim. He won over my maid, and one day, urged by her, I did an about turn and decided "So much devotion deserves a reward . . ." I thought of my bear. Getting into a sumptuous and very transparent negligée, I lay down on it. He came in, I opened my arms to him. Astonished, unprepared, he stammered – he gazed at me, unable to believe his luck – he bent over me . . . and pop! An enormous, a stupefying detonation rent the air, its origin only too obvious. I burst out laughing at the sight of my deflated lover looking over his own shoulder as though he were trying to see who had done this frightful thing. Then I was siezed with anger. "Get out of here! Get out at once! Open that door and disappear!" Oh, the excuses I had to endure, but I was unyielding and cruel. From then on I accepted all his gifts without feeling the least obligation, and as soon as I could I got rid of him. The dear old white bear saved me, that time.' Flossie laughed with all her heart and enjoyed the story so much that she made me promise to write it down here; which I have done because I can refuse her nothing.*

October 30. Salomon brought me a volume of old *Vie Parisiennes*, 1870–72. Very amusing. I told him the following little story.

One day in 1892 or 1893, old Meilhac came to ask me to be so good as to honour with my presence a performance of *Manon* (or it may have been *Carmen*) which was being given at the Opéra-Comique on the following day. I accepted. 'You must make yourself beautiful, beautiful. You must wear your tiara, masses of jewels, a lowcut dress.' – 'All right.' – 'You must arrive before the curtain goes up.' – 'We'll see.' – 'No, no you mustn't disturb the performance.' – 'I won't make a promise that I might not be able to keep.' – 'But baby! For me you can do this!' – 'I will if I can.' He left, satisfied with my promise, then back he came again: 'Bring some friends, you must have an entourage, I'll give you the stage box on the left.' – 'Good, I'll bring Marie de Lannoy and Blanche d'Arvilly.' – 'Yes, here's two thousand francs, buy whatever's necessary, wear your white cloak with the gold embroidery and the ermine lining, be elegant, be entirely Pougy in fact, and above all, above all, be punctual.' – 'All right.' – 'If you do as I tell you, there'll be a surprise.'

Next day, all flags flying, Marie de Lannoy noble and auburn in sombre jet-embroidered satins, Blanche d'Arvilly, dark and exuberant in sumptuous sables, flashing with diamonds, and me – oh me! A dream of diaphanous whiteness, enveloped in supple ermine, my dress white satin covered in pearls, we made our entrance into that beautiful box exactly a quarter of an hour before the curtain was due to go up. The theatre was almost full. The usherettes were obsequious. Nonchalantly I took my seat in the front of the box,

* Natalie Barney's biographer, George Wickes, reports that the polar bear was still on the floor of Natalie's bedroom at 20 rue Jacob even after she, as a very old woman, had gone to live at the Hotel Meurice where she died at the age of 96, in 1972.

haughtily I twiddled my ring-laden fingers. My companions surrounded me. Suddenly, as though at a signal, the whole house was on its feet and turned towards me, greeting me. Amused, I gave a gracious smile. The orchestra broke into patriotic music. Tumult. Carried away by the surge of emotion I rose to my feet, then sat down again. The house applauded. I had no idea what it was all about, although it seemed to me natural enough that people should pay homage to my youth and beauty. Blanche and Marie, serious and very beautiful, went along gracefully with what was happening. I whispered to them: 'It's some trick of Meilhac's. He promised me a surprise, we mustn't lose our heads.' Then the door burst open and in came Meilhac, rubbing his hands and speechless with delight. I motioned him to a seat and said: 'That was a very nice reception! I hope you're pleased with me? I think I played my part very well considering that I wasn't warned.' He was suffocating. At last he pulled himself together a bit and said: 'Oh baby! We're expecting the Queen of Sweden – in the box opposite – they thought you were her, it's too killing for words.' So all four of us collapsed into peals of laughter. And in fact the box opposite mine was occupied by a lanky, sad-looking woman, rather badly dressed, surrounded by quite an entourage. Her entrance had been ruined, no one noticed it. It was me, little Liane de Pougy, to whom the crowd had paid its homage – and the orchestra too, because it was the Swedish national anthem that they had played. I was flabbergasted and delighted, rather proud, too – and so were my friends. The enraptured Meilhac told the story to everyone, heaped us with presents and compliments, and announced far and wide: 'Homage to beauty! *Vox populi, vox dei*! How beautiful is our Liane! That is how people expect a queen to look, and she has proved it.' I should add that the noble lady and her courtiers opposite spent the whole of the rest of the evening examining and admiring the frail, luminous creature, its short curls crowned with jewels, which had been the cause of this 'historical' misunderstanding.

November 7. Yesterday, Sunday, we were expecting Bouchor and Max Jacob turned up instead, quite out of the blue. He spent the night here, in the best room. We found him very much himself, not at all sanctified by his sojourn in the presbytery. He is full of venom and bitterness, scornful and disparaging. He is bitter and anxious, tormented, difficult to understand. He is going back to Saint-Benoît because the life he leads there is conducive to work and meditation.

But what does he meditate? I get the impression that the evil spirits which possess him are hard to dislodge. He is spiteful about the curé, who seems to have used his authority to chastise Max's scandal-mongering. He seems to be more interested in the formal practices of religion than he is in his own development and his inner life. He must find life difficult. He is in a dilemma: either stay in Paris to protect his position – and lose his soul; or live in solitude in order to approach God – and lose his reputation. Memories are so short in the Parisian caravanserai!

....

November 27. I was feeling better and rejoicing at it, and now it's all collapsed and my ailments have renewed the attack. I try to behave as though there were nothing wrong with me. I rush off to Polignac to unpack and arrange things. It will be finished by the end of December. Had a long letter from my dear Rochegrosse. He speaks of Christ with a fervour which makes me envious. He misunderstood me when I complained that for me Christ doesn't exist, I didn't mean – oh no, indeed, far from it – that Christ in Himself doesn't exist, but that I don't see Him: a screen shuts in front of my eyes. I know what must be behind it, but I am unable to open it, to see, to touch. And that is what makes me the poorest of the poor.

My Flossie came on Thursday accompanied by little Clauzel, more faded and colourless than ever. Salomon arrived before they did and told me: 'The Baroness Clauzel is wearing a superb bison coat.' I was imagining her clad in a shaggy car-rug and what it turned out to be was a ravishingly light and supple mink! Dear old learned one! [Salomon's mistake came from the similarity between the words *bison* and *vison*, which is French for mink.] The night moth seemed shrewish. I prefer my Flossie peaceful and satisfied, calm, gentle and serene. Flossie has managed to find us two rooms and two dressing-rooms at the Palais d'Orsay with demi-pension at seventy-four francs a day. It's all arranged.

I have been working at Polignac, unpacking household utensils and books. In an English novel which I was given when I was in London in 1901 I found some of Nathalie's letters, impassioned, tender and full of devotion. Her passion has been scattered to the four winds but her tenderness is still there, and so is her devotion. Among these letters, two and a half pages from Pauline. They will make a present for Salomon. No doubt he will bequeath them to posterity, fully annotated, according to his habit. I don't think I could possibly give a greater pleasure to Monseiur Reinach, in love with a ghost. Pauline's letter is rather spiteful. Our relationship was never a very fond one: Flossie preferred me and I never made much of Pauline. In that world it's either adoration or hate.

December 21. Just had a visit from Flossie and the Duchesse de Clermont-Tonnerre. They were on their way back from Robert de Montesquiou's funeral which took place at Versailles. Plenty of visiting these days: Madame de La Béraudière has bought my lovely eighteenth century pastel. Lady M, who lives here at the Hôtel de Croisille, has asked us to tea. She is a Shakespearian being imbued with a thousand dramatic essences. She married a rather half-witted young Lord who, she says, did not consummate the marriage and dumped her here. She runs madly back and forth to Paris, raging and scheming, in order to recapture a gaga husband who is not in the least interested. A little Jew from the City came on the scene in the role of secretary to her father-in-law and has completely set this rich and noble family by the ears. When the old lord died he left him as much of his fortune as he could. Not satisfied with that, the young man seduced the widow and the imbecile son. He has declared war on the young rebel wife. It is a depressing story. I used to know that young man, rather a good-looking boy with a head of silky blond hair like Absalom's, blue eyes, an innocent expression, tenacious, intelligent and – I am very much afraid – quite without scruples. About twenty-years-ago Jacques, the maître d'hôtel at the Carlton in London, came up to me at lunch one day and said: 'Oh Madame Liane de Pougy, you could win me a horse! Mr – has promised that he will give me the horse he rides in Hyde Park every morning if I introduce him to you. It is such a beautiful horse, worth two hundred or two hundred and fifty pounds!' – 'Jacques – bring the young man over to my table at once!' Five minutes later the boy was sitting beside me, I was tweaking his beautiful hair and ordering him to send the horse round to Jacques at once, which he did. In those days he was still wet behind the ears, but he had a bold and optimistic view of the future.

Madame de Clermont-Tonnerre, née Gramont, told me that young Lady M is demented and quite dangerous; in their circle they call her 'Little Madame Landrue'. I shall disengage myself gradually – I don't like crazy people.

Flossie was affectionate. We drank tea, gossipped and talked about the Duc de Gramont, *le bel Agénor*, Madame de Clermont-Tonnerre's father. He was married three times and his wives were a Wagram, a Rothschild and a ravishing Italian beauty forty-five years younger than himself.

1922

Saint-Germain – Pavillon de Gramont

January 1. I am reading the *Imitation* and find it full of beauties. For example, this sentence about Jesus and the inner man: 'He often visits the inner man and his conversation is sweet, the comfort he offers is exquisite, his peace is inexhaustible, his nearness passes comprehension.' O Jesus, reveal Yourself to me this year! If only this veil between You and me would lift! I do so long to understand and feel Your love for me, and to reciprocate with passion.

Paris !!! – Palais d'Orsay

January 4. Here we are, and I am missing Saint-Germain! Here we are, and Georges exults! The Palais d'Orsay, huge and chic, offers us the shelter of two ravishing rooms on the fourth floor. It is warm, our little bathrooms are light and airy.........

The King of Roumania has finally abolished all titles: we are no longer princes! Or at least from now on we will only be addressed as such when abroad, as a matter of courtesy. Old families like ours, which have more or less fallen to the distaff side, have no choice but to accept it.

January 6. I can't resist the pleasure of quoting the pretty turn of phrase used by Duchess Elisabeth de Clermont-Tonnerre when she was giving her opinion about me: 'Where I expected to find no more than a whiff of scent, I found fresh air.'

Saint-Germain – Pavillon de Gramont, January 27 to February 9

January 27. It is a long time since I wrote. Naturally life in Paris was charming and eventful. Every evening fatigue threw me onto my bed, quite overcome. There was nothing for it but to pack our bags and return to the inhospitable fold provided by the Hélou ladies.

I stayed for Flossie's Friday. Madame Fabre-Luce was there, prepossessing and blooming and determined not to leave my side. Duchess Elisabeth arrived later, forced her way through the crowd, smiling from afar, with her hand outstretched, declaring: 'It's for your sake that I'm here.' Auric was there, and Madame Claude Farrère, alias Roggers, with whom I have had a coldness. The other ladies' friendliness infected her and she had quite a long and amiable conversation with me, very nearly confiding in me. Salomon appeared for a moment, kissed the tips of my fingers and slipped away, André Rouveyre joined us, then André Germain. Pierre Drieu La Rochelle was introduced to us: he is very agreeable and could claim successes in other lines beside poetry. Jean de Gourmont was there, shy and nice. We outstayed the crowd and had dinner with Flossie. It was eight years since I had dined out. I survived this debauchery very well, only to renew it on the Sunday evening at the Duchess's, a ravishing little Directoire house on the rue Raynouard, modernized with the most perfect taste. After dinner mattresses covered with velvet and cushions were spread on the floor of a little Chinese room, intimate and warm, and I was persuaded to lie down. Flossie, whose eye trouble was making her feverish, came and lay beside me and the Duchess sat close to us and quizzed us gaily.

January 28. The day after our dinner party Duchess Elizabeth left for Austria to look for platinum and jewels which, it seems, can be bought there very cheaply and on which we can make a good profit. The Duchess pooh-poohs the current rumours about epidemics in Austria.

Eating out all over the place like this is very funny. Our friends were determined to put on a good show for us, and at the moment the most expensive thing is chicken. So we could be sure that every meal would include the appearance of a beautiful roast chicken. Georges and I couldn't catch each others eye without laughing; we really went off it. Finally, when I got an invitation I said: 'I must warn you, I'm not allowed chicken.' – 'How very odd,' people said. 'Chicken – the white meat, anyway – isn't usually forbidden.' Then I would tell my story and everyone would laugh.

On Wednesday, lunch with Balthy. Louise was very gay, she had been dancing until three in the morning. At present she is collecting blue and white from China and Persia. She has blinds made of ostrich feathers and cushions made of fur. I caught her in bed, having herself daubed with oil of turpentine by her masseuse as she reclined on pink crêpe de chine sheets! Nathalie came with Romaine Brooks to pick me up; they wanted to see her close to, and seemed disappointed. Romaine was sporting the Legion of Honour. Nathalie took me to Madeleine Vionnet, the great dressmaker of the moment. A plain dress of black crêpe de chine, with no embroidery or decoration: 2,600 francs! 'What would its sale price be?' – '1,600 francs.' Nathalie was able to wangle it and got it for 1,000 francs. But that's still dear, for a reduction.

Then Flossie took us on to Madame R, who was giving a tea party in my honour. It was big, grand, cold and comfortable. I'm enormously fond of Madame R . . . but my Flossie! What a matchless creature she is, what a rare wit! She has it and she inspires it. When someone said that her house was very dusty she answered: 'But dust is pretty, it's furniture's face powder.' We saw her little old mother, frisky, alert, sparkly. Georges is mad about her. An incredible youthfulness runs in her veins, shines in her eyes, curls her white hair and vibrates the feather on her hat. Long ago, in our wild young days, she disapproved of my relationship with her daughter. I can hardly blame her. We didn't stir up the past, pressed each others hands and paid each other compliments.

The next day, lunch at the Rouveyres, then on to see the Countess de La Béraudière who was expecting us. Masses of wonderful things: Raeburn, Lawrence, even Greco – but everything liberally covered with . . . face powder!

January 31. I must have done with this visit to Paris, which is beginning to fade from my mind. At Flossie's brilliant party we were introduced to the old Marchioness of Anglesey, a dowager so beautiful that even at over eighty she draws all eyes. A lady wearing a coat lined with jaguar, who looked perfectly capable of having killed and skinned the animal herself, was bent on enflaming me with her conversation, her compliments and her burning looks. Flossie was ravishing in a white crêpe dress and a turquoise blue

Spanish shawl embroidered in white, her hair making a turban of gold. She was leaving for Saint-Moritz that very evening.

February 2. Duchess Elisabeth is a sensual, greedy, lovable child who uses all the gifts with which she is endowed to the top of her bent. When she laughs she stamps her feet as though she couldn't contain herself. Her hair springs up as though it were impossible to control it. She eats as though she were starving. No doubt she is a voracious lover. She has the most delicious thoughts: she ought to have them published. I have been told that she has shed bitter tears over Nathalie, but nowadays they have a very close and tender friendship.

February 9. . . . . I have read some of the *Almanach*, given me by its kind author the Duchess of Clerment-Tonnerre. It is a jewel of a book, sensual, enlightened, even erudite, and above all full of poetry. One learns delightful things from it: that quails are highly immoral and will marry anyone, the best seasons for eating this, that and the other. She despises radishes, extols the poultry of La Flèche and the strawberries of Plougastel. She quotes Nathalie Clifford Barney, Renée Vivien and others. It is written with carefully polished wit. Even apart from her blue blood, this duchess is quite someone and I feel more and more flattered by her good opinion of me: 'Aha! Princess Georges Ghika, the most charming of letter-writers and perhaps of women!'

Saint-Germain – Hotel de l'Aigle d'or, February 19 to April 16

February 19. At last we have escaped from those atrocious Hélous! We are not too badly off here, in the rue du Vieil-Abreuvoir. At first sight it is dreary and banal like any little provincial hotel, but our room on the first floor overlooking a tree-filled courtyard is handsome, with large windows and tall Directoire doors. It is light, quiet, large, warm, with a dressing-room and two good brass beds. The bathroom works, the people are clean, friendly northerners, and they charge less than those stupid people who treated us so badly.

In *l'Intran* they describe, without giving my name, a charming Roumanian princess, celebrated by Jean Lorrain, who is writing her Memoirs to be bequeathed to the National Library for publication in a hundred years' time. 'But who knows,' they add, 'whether the National Library will accept them?' I remain unmoved.

. . . .

March 4. Henry Bataille died the day before yesterday at six o'clock in the evening, in two minutes: a stroke. He was writing, he felt ill, he called Yvonne, got up and went out onto the stairs saying 'I'm suffocating – get me ether!', fell down and was lifeless for ever. Yvonne is in tears and his great family, the theatre, is stunned. We are all striken. It took place at Malmaison – it seems that he bought that house among the treetops just to die in it. Georges went there yesterday evening. He saw him. He was beautiful and looked as though he were asleep, the expression of his mouth so ironic and intelligent. Bataille was more than a friend. Whenever we were up to it we met with so much pleasure and affection, we wanted to know everything, we commiserated, we appreciated, we liked each other so much. In twenty-eight years he only had two mistresses that I knew of: Berthe Bady, who died less than a year ago, then Yvonne de Bray. Georges found her yesterday collapsed beside his bed, pressed against him, her face all swollen, unable to cry any more – it's frightful.

. . . .

March 11. An impudent and charming note from that little flatterer, Clauzel. She offers me the corners of her mouth – which are indeed extremely pretty, childlike and mischievous. She offers that, as though it were a pot of blue hyacinths, at my age! I am a bit tough with her; I don't really like her all that much.

I have been exercising all my felinity in playing with Salomon. I was kind, approving, unguarded. He was jubilant. I showed him the scar on my right thigh from my dreadful car accident. He was hesitant and disturbed – it's said that the only nakedness he has ever seen is that of statues.

March 20. On Saturday we were deposited in Paris at 27 rue de Ville-d'Evêque by a cheerful Salomon who was on his way to see General Lyautey. We found Pépé very weak, very pale and ultra-chic, sitting in an arm-chair with a pillow at his back, a black and white fur rug lined with violet over his knees, a shirt of fine linen with pretty pleated cuffs falling over his narrow wrists, a black velvet dressing-gown lined with violet, and a filmy white Shetland shawl over his shoulders. Splendid and touching! It was his saint's day and his drawing-room was full of flowers. We added ours, wall-flowers in two little Dresden china pots, very old and much sought-after by connoisseurs. The Baronne de l'Epée was there, very attentive; she takes a lot of care of Pépé and seems to be part of the household. He lunched in his arm-chair, near the table. Pépé had an operation for hernia in his own house. Now he is free of business, can sit in the sun all day, and is planning, much encouraged by me, to drive out next Sunday and drink his chicken soup in my Polignac cupboard. At about three o'clock my Flossie arrived. We lay down to rest in the overwhelming scent of flowers. She took me in her arms and caressingly . . . we were both equally stupefied by tenderness. The Countess de La Béraudière looked in for a moment to throw a charm on our voluptuous stupor with her caressing, slightly purring voice. Yvonne de Bray inherits the Château at Vivières, the property at Malmaison, the royalties from Bataille's four best plays, all the furniture in the flat on the Bois, and whatever liquid assets Bataille left. His other royalties go to his nephews and nieces. He made his will only two months ago.

March 21. Saw Yvonne de Bray; attempted to produce some sort of stupid and useless comfort. Her mother was there, and some men of business.

Time's patina
On precious things
And broken hearts –
Time's patina
Heals and erodes
In equal parts.*

She was pale and tall in black wool; no make-up. I stayed with her a good two hours. We must see each other again.

. . . .

April 5. Visit from Max Jacob yesterday. From time to time he has to leave his monastery at Saint-Benoît-sur-Loire and come to Paris to look after tiresome but essential money-matters. He agreed with his publishers to get three hundred francs a month on the one hand, five hundred on the other. Then he had to share what he was writing

* This is my wife's, unexpected and charming. Georges G. Ghika.

between them. This annoyed them and he stopped getting anything because each of them wanted to monopolize him. So – poverty, scruples, schemes. Max says that when he's in Paris he is a great sinner, so he makes his confession at the Sacré-Coeur before he goes back to Saint-Benoît because there he has to confess to the curé and since he lives with him he would be embarrassed........

....

April 14. I have been to confession. I told Monsieur le curé my big sin: 'I took pleasure in receiving over-emphatic signs of affection from a woman friend, and in front of my husband who wasn't at all angry about it, he laughed.' The dear curé looked quite embarrassed and told me: 'If you feel that it was wrong, you must not do it again.' I gave him a few more details in case he should think that it was worse than it was. He is a good and worthy curé. He is aware of the efforts I make and doesn't keep me on too tight a rein. The Laglenne sisters are urging me to take communion. I want this communion, I *am* seeking Jesus. One thing's for sure, at my first communion I was not seeking anything at all, in those days I was a heedless, greedy little beast, a hot-blooded young animal chafing at the bit, laughing at Hell, pausing at neither the Passion nor the Cross, glimpsing death only to cock a snook at it. I used to steal apples, strawberries, copy books and bars of chocolate, and then get myself caught by generously distributing my booty. I wouldn't have taken anything from another child, only from the community. I would have sold my soul for a beautiful box of coloured writing-paper with my initials on it in silver or gold. I learnt my lessons during church services, I recited La Fontaine's fables at prayers, I wrote impassioned letters to my best friends and I snipped bits off the shawls of my favourite nuns and preserved them between the pages of books. Now that I have been through every kind of suffering, have measured the infamy of human beings and the cruelty of fate, the insecurity of every living thing, God has become necessary to me. I want Him, I need Him, I seek Him, I call on Him, I pray to Him. Perhaps holy communion will speed my efforts towards success?

April 15. Madame R writes to say that her husband's health has improved. I like that woman a lot. She gives the impression of wanting to break out, but well-established habits are difficult to break: her chignon has no intention of being let down! Her voice has a decisive little ring, crisp and high, quite unsuggestive of voluptuousness. She's like someone in a theatre, sitting in a box. Yes, that's it, she has never had any role to play but that of spectator, and time is passing – and she would so much have liked to join the dance. Pretty bird in a cage, watching the world which it has never known.

April 16. Easter Sunday: sun and rain, the weather sad and cold. The hotel packed with noisy people.

I took communion this morning – I prayed to the best of my ability, I accomplished my religion s rites coldly and precisely. It is only in bed that I can pray properly, in darkness and silence, specially when the window is open. Then I feel God. As soon as it's a question of Jesus made man in order to save our souls, I might be trying to awaken a lifeless body. Nothing in me quivers, nothing responds, nothing speaks, nothing moves me. I will not despair. God has come down so low, I mean so far from Himself, in order to look for me.

Roscoff – Clos-Marie, July 4 to November 29

July 4. Two days ago I was fifty. I don't feel at all old. We arrived here on June 22; have spring-cleaned the house from top to bottom. Georges is enraptured, although we have had nothing but wind, cold and rain.

July 5. Our life in Pépé's house was nothing but joy, pleasures, parties and feasting. Everyone was so happy to see us, they danced attendance, they spoilt us. Pépé went off to work at Doucet's and was delighted to find us there, often with a crowd, when he came home. The servants were perfect, our first reception magnificent, the buffet (shared between us) sumptuous. Madame R was there, so animated, so joyful that she quite forgot her revived husband's mutterings. Nathalie came, the Countess Clauzel, Madame de Lubersac, the Countess de La Béraudière, the most famous actresses: Marcelle Lender, Germaine Gallois, Cora Lapercie, Amélie Dieterle, Madeleine Lambert, Vollerin, my dear Vollerin, devoted and sentimental though now he is quite swallowed up in Sacha Guitry's fame, being his secretary and his soul. In short, there were seventy of us, all having a lovely time watching, gossipping, flattering, tippling. Pépé received the guests in the big drawing-room, helped by the Baronness de l'Epée, and they were brought through to me in the little red drawing-room next to the dining-room where the monstrous buffet was spread. Robert de Rothschild made an appearance. We had three musicians: Auric, Poulenc and Eric Satie. They played some of their works. That was when Georges and I made the acquaintance of Francis Poulenc; Max Jacob has talked about him so often and was always on the point of bringing him to see us. Well, he is charming! I was wearing my black georgette peplum by Madeleine Vionnet, something quite unique, admirable, it works so perfectly that one can't describe it. Even Pépé, in spite of professional jealousy, had to bow down before this masterpiece.

What pearls there were! Madame Marthe Besnut, Prince Coloradi-Mansfeld's (?) fiancée, was wearing three millions' worth. Pépé was so enchanted that next day he gave me a beautiful grey wolf – the fashionable fur at the moment – and a very chic bracelet made of a circlet of onyx.

The next day we visited our neighbour Jean Cocteau, who was laid up all winter with a painful neuritis. He was preparing to leave for the Midi.

July 7. I have sent Pépé a beautiful lobster. He spoilt me terribly. The cook used to come and take orders from me. Our guests and his mingled to their hearts' delight. Nathalie came to Pépé, Pépé went to Nathalie. Her set is really select, their morals easy-going and their intellects unsparing. Lucie Delarue-Mardrus comes to sing poems while Armand de Polignac and de Chabannes play her own music as accompaniment. Auric and Poulenc come to play their new works. Chana Orloff, Madame de La Nux exhibit at Nathalie's: Orloff wood carvings, de La Nux boldly executed drawings, lightly coloured. She did a portrait of me for Nathalie, a very beautiful synthesis, the head tilted a little back, breasts bare, eyelids weary over a feverishly brilliant gaze. I sat for it at Flossie's house one thundery day in the poor light of a bedroom made even darker by a tree outside the open window.

We had five or six lunches at Nathalie's, plus her tea parties and her Fridays. Madame R took us for drives in the Bois, to Bagatelles among the roses, to the Cascade for tea under the trees. Once she took us all the way to Saint-Germain, back home, where I gave her a pot-luck tea. We kept meeting here and there, to our mutual pleasure; at two or three tea parties at the Countess de La Béraudière's, and another day at the Duchess Elisabeth's house. Madame R made me a present of a ravishing little silver-grey velvet handbag with a Chinese frame from Doucet's, where she took us one afternoon to see the models. There I was welcomed by Jacques Doucet, my former supplier, all shrivelled up and very changed. Pepito, enchanted, gave me four beautiful dresses and a cape – on the sole condition that I went to be photographed, which was done by Manuel and by Baron Rhebinder, Jacqueline de Pourtalès's husband – and then a superb wrapper in mauve crêpe de chine in which I could perfectly well dine, or even appear at a formal tea party. He gave me a beautiful sable muff which used to belong to his wife, who was very fond of me. We did everything we could to spoil him, too, and to make his life pleasant and happy. It was rather tiring for us to lead a double life like that, seeing his friends as well as ours, and then Georges was ill . . .

July 8. . . . very ill with amoebic dysentry which started suddenly, the day before our second reception. There was a wild and noisy Brazilian orchestra and eighty pleasant, happy and indifferent people to smile at. The doctor, called in at once, ordered bed, but Georges insisted on getting up and spending a short time in the tumult, which complicated his illness. He is still feeling the effects.

If it hadn't been for this tormenting worry, our second party would have been splendid. A buffet worthy simultaneously of Gargantua and of Brillat-Savarin. Madame R triumphant, Nathalie infatuated. As for Madrazzo, he was mad about the negroes and couldn't tear himself away from them, surrounded by Poulenc, Darius Milhaud and Georges Auric – not to mention Paul Morand, man of the year.

July 9. There has been a violent gale blowing in from the sea all night, the waves are breaking very high, the rain is falling in sheets. I do tapestry, write, read. . . . .

When we were in Paris we went to the theatre only three times, to matinées. Once to see Sacha Guitry . . . . I said to Sacha: 'You must have a child to carry on the brilliant line of Guitrys.' Sacha sprang to his feet: 'Princess, your wishes are orders, I will see to it at once,' and he left the dressing-room. I blinked, and there he was coming back in again with a beautiful tiny pink baby in his arms – how we laughed! It was the child of Yvonne Printemps's dresser. We had taken young Poulenc with us, thrilled to meet the famous Sacha. Papa Guitry made his appearance while we were there. He is terrific! An old man in a class of his own, who looks as though he had descended from Olympus in order to wipe a nation out or to load it with blessings. He dominates. Old as he is, masses of women are still in love with him. When he came in Sacha raised his head, got up, took one step backwards, stretched out his arms and threw himself towards the immobile old man in order to embrace him. Next the blonde Yvonne advanced lightly on tiptoe and reached up to the sacred cheek with her little pointed muzzle. Then me: 'I'm not going to be left out . . .' and there I was in Lucien's arms. Finally we tore ourselves apart. And that, no doubt, will be that for several years.

July 10. Still dreary and wet, the tourists are postponing their arrival. If this goes on it will be very hard on the locals.

To continue the story of our stay in Paris. We went to Sarah Bernhardt's theatre. They were doing *Régine Armand* by her son-in-law, Verneuil. During the first act the principal female part is taken by young Simone Fréveilles: a ravishing creature with charming regular features, long, slim, graceful and not at all bad. In the second act Sarah appears, seated in an actress's dressing-room. It's as though she were in her own. She looks much older, a shadow of herself, and she begins to speak in an undertone: the golden voice hardly carries at all. (It was a beautiful Sunday in May and the theatre was almost empty, no doubt Sarah was saving herself.) She shows nothing but her proud and beautiful profile, so clear-cut and regular (people used to say mine resembled it), her make-up is skilful, light, smooth, telling, unique. She knows better than anyone else how to use drapery, her gestures are marvellous, full of restraint, grace and style. At a given moment little Fréveilles has to approach her and take up a dialogue. Well, she simply ceases to exist beside Sarah! Sarah wins, and wins hands down, in spite of illness, age, the falling away of her voice, and a set of false teeth which threaten to follow suit and which is continually being brought to order between the measured syllables by a neat and clever flick of the tongue. Poor admirable Sarah! She will die on the stage like an old soldier at his post. One can only applaud and envy her.

July 11. This is what Sarah said to the person who told her that Réjane was dead: 'Réjane dead? It will be Granier's turn now.'

Today I want to talk about my conquests. Rediscovered Nathalie comes to coax and caress me, and murmur 'My first love, and my last.' I see her bending over to enfold me, and it seems that I have never left her arms. Inconstant Nathalie, so faithful, in spite of her infidelities. She celebrates my body down to the waist. That is all that I allow myself to grant. The rest belongs to Georges and no one else in the world can touch it. The rest would make the sin too big; and anyway that rest is so accustomed to Georges that it throbs for no one but him.

In second place comes Thérèse Diehl of the beaky nose, the wicked eye, the sensual mouth, very chic, candid as a child, unaffected, impudent, artful, simultaneously boring and attractive. She amused me; her skin is resilient. She is a good healthy Basque. She goes to mass every Sunday and doesn't at all allow her disorderly life to disturb her relationship with God. She shares a mad apartment with her brother Carl, a charming and well set-up invert who gets on very well with her and runs the family factory. Thérèse pursues happiness in pleasure, she drinks hard, talks too much, is a bad hostess, pays out generously, but lacks flair. Her head is charming when she tips it back. We went no further than kisses on the mouth. Then I went to dinner with her. There her furniture and her guests enlightened me: I was bored to death. I wrote her very charmingly, truly my letter was a song: 'Forgive me for having loved you because I can no longer tell you that I do.' That is a splendid sentence and always works. I have used it a good deal in my time.

It was then that poor Dora turned up. I had to pretend that I'd gone away. The telephone rang day and night. Pépé would answer: 'The princess is in Saint-Germain for a few days.' She loathed Nathalie and would never consent to meet us there. She did, however, bring her orchestra to the Countess de La Béraudière's. Funny little woman; she told me she was forty, because in an attempt to put her off I had advanced my fiftieth birthday. God! when a woman gets something into her head, how hard it is to get it out again!

My other conquest was Madame Bonin, heavy and hot. We met at Nathalie's and sat hand in hand during the whole two hours of that tea party. Another time I invited her to Pépé's house. I was alone. She arrived trembling and panting, fell on my bed and wanted to offer me everything. I drew her attention to the barrier raised by my principles across the bodies of women, just a little below their hearts and their breasts. She tore off her clothes to bare the latter, neither beautiful nor ugly, too big and a bit squeezed together. The top part of her arms was ravishing. She is a woman for men, designed to serve them, amuse them and then, very soon, to bore them. I took it into my head to offer her something to eat and dragged her into the dining-room where she devoured a bowl of cherries, reproaching me the while for getting her 'into such a state'.

July 12. Nothing amuses me this morning. Still, I would like to talk about my third conquest. At my request I met the daughter of an old friend of mine at Flossie's house. Betsy has her mother's superb fair hair, fashionably cut, a long face, a clear complexion and soft, roving eyes. She gives the impression of tempered steel, an indomitable character. She has her wits about her. At our second meeting, which took place at Pépé's house on a day when I was in bed, she threw herself into my arms, tremulous with passion. Astonished, I held her and began to stroke her hair. She offered me her lips. What could I do but kiss them? I did so with the utmost tenderness and with a touch of alarm, since the vivid impression made by Madame Bonin was still with me. Betsy was gentle and tender, she knew how the situation should be handled. She was a little bit lost for a day or two.

They were copying my dresses in Paris. We had dug out a poor little lady in reduced circumstances who was working on commission for a couturier. She could do a georgette dress embroidered pretty well all over for two hundred francs. Since we were going out a great deal, and in a very fashionable circle, I had to renovate my wardrobe a little and I ordered three: black embroidered with silver, grey the same, and white embroidered with dull white beads. These little slips of dresses had a mad success. All my friends wanted them, several of them at a time.

July 13. My photos have come from Manuel. The old girl doesn't look too bad now that she's fifty, wearing a lace dress in a couturier's advertisement!

I met Nathalie's sister again. Dear Laura seems frustrated and hard. One feels that she is hatching dark plots under her silence. When she speaks, the sentence falls – into emptiness! She looks down with disdain on her sister and her sister's friends, on her husband, on plates, glasses and desserts. I thought it would be nice to remind her how charming I once found her offer to save me from the life I was living by giving me her dowry. She shot me a glance heavy with unspoken thoughts and couldn't bring herself to answer. Her husband thought fit to say: 'How lucky Liane didn't accept. I had no idea that Laura could be so imprudent.'

July 14. We are having the doors and shutters of our little Clos repainted. I am giving it a summer dress in the hope that it will be welcoming Nathalie and the Duchess.

As soon as I arrived in Paris Yvonne de Bray came to see me at Pépé's, draped in a sort of toga of black veiling, very impressive. 'It's the costume I wore in Henry's last play. He saw me dressed like this, it was his idea. I can't bear to wear anything else.' Rather theatrical, no doubt, but very graceful. She took me to Saint-Honoré-d'Eylau and swept through the church and then through the sacristy as though she were in her own house. She walked fast, carrying a key, looking neither to right nor left and without uttering a word, as though she were accomplishing some rite. There was something moving in her loneliness and rapidity. She went down some steps into the crypt, stopped at a little door, opened it: there, by the flower-covered coffin on which I piously placed a bunch of Parma violets, she burst into tears. Two candles were burning at the head of the coffin which was raised on a dais. I took her in my arms and mingled my tears with hers. I have not seen her since then. She is busy – and it will do her good – with Henry's bequests, his plays, his memorial, his posthumous reputation.

....

July 20. .... Rochegrosse has sent me Giovanni Papini's *Story of Christ*, which is much discussed at present. It's in the form of short chapters each devoted to one of the facts of Jesus's life. It is easy to read, written very poetically and very accurately. I can read it with enthusiasm, soak myself in it, take in every detail – and the Gospels leave me unmoved, or almost so. I am still too thickly enveloped in flesh – and yet I really detest this tired, painful flesh. I despise it. Flesh ought to be alive and beautiful, firm, vibrant, animated. All that is over as far as I'm concerned. I hear a voice saying: 'Surely you don't want, after playing fast and loose with the flesh as you did in the days of your beauty – surely you don't want to turn to the divine consoler just at the moment when the ability to do wrong is leaving you?' Yes indeed, that is exactly what I want. And anyway, my crimes were not all that bad! Always so many arguments cancelling each other out, and me in the middle of it all with a sick body and an anxious soul. So then I fly to my beloved, tender, merciful Saint Anne! And suddenly everything lights up, I feel my strength renewed, I become resigned, I begin to hope. Saint Anne, do not abandon me, you are all I have! And through you I will find the rest.

July 21. This morning the painters finished dressing up the Petit-Clos. It was the least we could do for Gladness (the Duchess) and Harmony (Nathalie). Now we can face them without blushing.

July 29. The end of the world has been announced for the last days of August. Seventy volcanos are going to erupt, all at the same time. I wonder what I would do if I really believed that the end of the world was at hand? I would go to Flossie's house in Paris, be there between Georges and my darling, wearing my prettiest dress and my pearls. I would ask Auric to play the piano – or perhaps driving along a road in a car with those two, eyes fixed on the last landscape the earth's crust would ever offer us? Or there's church, of course – organ music, lights, the ardent prayers of the faithful, the exhortations from the pulpit. There would be danger of panic there; one can pray elsewhere. Alone in my bed and in Georges's arms? Rather frivolous ways of preparing to meet God!

August 4. Rain, grey sky. Everything looks dark and dreary in my eyes. Summer refuses to start. Even my roses – they are rotting before they open.

Letter from Max Jacob. Crafty – this is how he does it: 'Jacques Emile Blanche (painter and writer) is waiting for me in Normandy, the Lazarus family has asked me to Hacqueville, the Daudets want me in their country house – but, my dears, it is you I choose!' Thanks a lot! We are not going to answer. If he turns up we will accept him as a gift (!) from God, Whose will it is that His creatures should be put to the test.

....

August 20. The Duchess and Nathalie arrived at about midnight, exhausted but so charming! They had wanted to see Mont Saint Michel, call on Seignobos at Paimpol and heaven knows what else! They are still asleep as I write. How I hope the sun will come out to shine on our joy and this celebration of friendship.

August 21. Charming day with my charming friends. The regatta didn't disturb us, siestas, rest, good food and conversation. Afterwards I took them onto the jetty to show them my cliff kingdom and the twinkling evening lights of my village, which is all of Roscoff. The duchess is a delicious being, interested in everything; and how she does love life! How well she knows the art of living fully and beautifully!

They like the Petit-Clos. Nathalie is the connector, the bringer of order, she is redolent of an art which everyone ought to command and which she, with her smiling, silent grace, bestows on all of us. The Duchess played the flute. She is pure Watteau. She has brought some pretty clothes: pearl grey costumes, a pleated skirt, a duffel jacket, a little felt hat worn over one ear, black and gold pyjamas. I asked her: 'Duchess, tell me the first thing you can remember from your childhood.' – 'Aha,' she said, 'I've thought about that already, for my memoirs. I was two and a half. I had lost my mother so I was being brought up in England by my doting grandmother. She imagined that it was her duty to send me on a visit to my father, who was a brilliant cavalry officer, stationed at Melun at the time. When I got there I was stunned: he was the first person in the world who hadn't prostrated himself before me! Then he took me into a garden where there was a plum tree which he shook violently, bringing down a hail of plums on my little head and hurting me much more than he amused me.'

August 22. Yesterday I took them to see the beautiful cathedral at Saint-Pol, then to Penzé where we explored the mysterious alleys which I love so much. We greeted the tower of Berthe Bigfoot in passing and stopped at the illustrious calvary of Saint-Thégonnec. They bathed in the sea with Georges. The Duchess has a lovely swimming costume of violet wool. Undressed she is superb – dresses thicken her and spoil her shape. She soothed our siesta with the silvery accents of her flute. It was soft, pastoral, plaintive. She really does have tremendous style, always, in every one of her gestures, in her every attitude. Nathalie was sulking yesterday. It was obvious, so the Duchess made herself attentive.

After dinner we went up to my room. Georges and the Duchess smoked. I got into bed. Flossie came and lay down beside me . . . I committed the delicious sin of abandoning myself to her caressing hands while the Duchess and Georges went on talking literature with the utmost gravity. Nathalie and I were laughing like children at nothing and everything and it was infectious. The little Garat girl had come for the drive with us and was tired and happy, embarrassed at seeing us in each other's arms; she didn't know where to look, so then we teased her and she began to laugh with us. Goodnights were said. The Duchess came to sit on my bed for a moment. She was disturbed. She kissed the back of my neck, then my mouth.

August 23. Day follows day, fine, happy, golden within and without. Our friends are beautiful, cheerful, healthy, delicious and pleased with everything, all quite naturally, without effort or strain. At Santec we walked barefoot in the sea and the warm, soft sand. We drove back by the Isle of Sieck and by Saint-Pol, past the Danielou estate with the famous fig tree which spreads over six hundred square metres and is supported on ninety stone pillars. Our friends exclaimed: 'But it's a marvel! People go all the way to India to see giant baobabs or to Africa in order to rave about enormous rubber trees, and this beats the lot!' When we got home they went swimming, with Georges. Wrapped in her white towelling robe, the Duchess is as attractive as ever. No one else has such a majestic walk. For breakfast I give them toast, warm brioches, milk bread with raisins in it, tea, the freshest butter and our famous Plougastel strawberry jam, served on Quimper china. They make short work of it. We never stop laughing, we understand each other, we blend and mingle. In the evenings . . . the plot thickens. The Duchess came to lie on my bed and Nathalie snuggled between us. Caresses, loving kisses. It was charming – perhaps a little nerve-racking. Camille kept her head turned away so that she should see nothing. Georges read poetry aloud. Nathalie remembered something Marguerite Moreno said when she was staying with friends in the country, on a rainy day. Someone had asked 'What shall we do?' In her melodious, beautifully modulated voice Marguerite let fall the one word: 'Fornicate.'

I love my friends. Surely, dear Lord, it can't be a great sin? It is You who sent them to me all open-hearted, it's You who made them so sweetly fond and sensual, it's You who make them lean over me with such tenderness – surely it is?

'The Duchess is flighty,' says Nathalie. 'Elegantly, indolently flighty.' What else should Gladness be? No doubt the tenderness displayed by Harmony is more penetrating. As for me, I am Abandon: joyful, strung-up, with – this morning – a headache, a back-ache and my head in a whirl. But still a haze of happiness covers everything brought to me recently by my friendship with these charming beings. It is, in fact, an exquisite occasion in which we are all delighting in our true affection for each other. The sin would be if there were dishonesty or trickery in it, if there were an ulterior motive – snobbery or gross sensuality – or if decisive gestures had been made. Whereas these delicate, tentative caresses, like inhaling the perfume of a flower . . . ?

August 31. Read in the papers that at the celebrations at Caen Emilienne d'Alençon went up in an aeroplane piloted by an 'impresario'. When they were landing they ran into a tree, the machine blew up, the impresario was killed on the spot and Emilienne has been taken to hospital in Livarot with serious injuries. But what an idea, to get up to anything so dangerous, and at her age – which is the same as mine!

A card from my Flossie, another – exquisite – from Madame R and one from Salomon who has already heard about the radiant visitation I received. So he's grimacing and flattering and hinting. I am going to answer him without saying a word about it.

September 1. Such a charming note from my dear little Duchess. In my answer I am doing as she asked and describing one of our days in full. What a charming thought!

September 7. Everything the Duchess does is so charming – she has sent Georges a delightful poem celebrating our excursions in my beloved Brittany. It is very modern, and to tell the truth I'm a bit baffled by this kind of complicated thing which has to be read almost like a puzzle.

September 9. I am reading the letters of Madame de Maintenon. How that woman did love to give advice! She was only a school-mistress, but what a school-mistress! She seems willingly to have sacrificed herself and all the joys of a woman's life for the sake of directing and commanding. She never stopped beating time for other people to dance to. There is something very unattractive about this woman getting what she wanted by reason, patience and self-effacement. I prefer the actress who dances her way into the arms of a prince.

September 10. Cocteau has sent us a brochure which is entirely about himself. It's the fashion. They open their stomachs and say 'Look what I've got inside me!' The spectacle is neither clean nor pretty!

September 11. Madame de Maintenon asks the Abbé Gobelin for Saint Teresa's *Meditations on the Father*. It is my own bedside reading. It is very well designed for every day of the week, and I find it most helpful.

September 15. I am very kind, my kindness is measureless, but it doesn't last. It suddenly switches away from people, rejects them and turns towards others. And for those I have rejected, I feel nothing but indifference. I try to love Jesus. It is my constant effort, my daily prayer; and I cannot achieve it. Effort and reason have nothing to do with love. But perhaps this effort is in itself love? I don't see Jesus. I don't like the victims of persecution. It's like this: my reason wants to adore Jesus and my instincts jib. I lay my free will at the feet of my dear Saint Anne; I wait the divine love which must regenerate me, I accept non-love as punishment. Giovanni Papini's life of Christ, which I read every evening, is very beautiful; I read it, alas, as a pagan.

October 27. Georges becomes more and more disagreeable, hostile. He shows no consideration for the balance of my poor nerves, achieved with such difficulty. He no longer bothers about the harmony of our existence. To me this seems stupid, destructive. It is such misery to live like this after having chosen each other, as we did. I am losing my vivacity, my energy, my youthfulness of heart; in a word, I am being ill-used and that makes me bad-tempered and unhappy. I hate this man; I have taken a real dislike to him.

October 28. I think Georges is making efforts to mollify me. They are not very happy ones – they lack conviction. His mind is no longer capable of conceiving anything but outward forms. Perhaps he no longer loves me? Perhaps it is simply the necessary bonds of habit which link him to me? At the beginning of the war I hated him so much that I wanted him – in spite of his bad health – to join up. Our misfortunes and my grief had a hard time bringing us together. Travel? I would be dragging him behind me wherever I went. That's why journeys no longer tempt me. Wherever it goes that soft, evil paw treads, crushes, destroys. There isn't a landscape or an attempt at escape which hasn't been ruined for me. All my troubles come from that, from him.

October 29. I have had such a lovely letter from Nathalie. We love each other deeply; she has always given me so much pleasure intellectually. Our souls understand each other and mingle so tenderly; our bodies' gestures are dictated by the movements of our souls. There is no ugliness there, no brutality, no dirtiness. I love to lie down beside her, be in her arms, fall asleep lulled by the thoughts she breathes in short, sweet phrases. My Nathalie is a gift from heaven! Georges is stagnant, swampy, without strength, unwholesome; Nathalie's a luminous and subtle ray of light which gilds everything it touches.

November 18. Received this delicious letter from the no less delicious R. 'It is still quite delightful to go to Doucet's, and to Callot's too; but where are the sultans for whose sake one would wish to wear all this finery? Leave these temples of elegance and all one sees is appalling human nature under a foggy sky . . .' Madame Strauss is in mourning for her son. I shan't repeat here all her determined nastiness towards me: Princess Georges Ghika forgives the enemies of Liane de Pougy.

Naturally I had a dream about Madame Strauss, meeting her at the races, her youth and beauty restored. I also had other dreams, distinctly Freudian. I shall have to abandon myself to conjugal caresses this evening for my health's sake, and out of habit – and from love too, in spite of everything.

. . . .

November 21. Death of Marcel Proust. We have known forever that he was delicate, and became used to seeing him surviving in spite of it. His death has taken us by surprise. It has impressed and saddened us. He really did have talent, a strange talent: a sick man's rarified talent which weighed and pondered everything; an elegant talent, above muscular materialism; rather a mannered talent, a bit snobbish, but large, in spite of being diminished by the sick-room. When the Duchess was here this summer she had a letter from Proust who called her Emilie, although her name is Elisabeth; we laughed a lot about it. Perhaps he hoped for an answer putting him right? He was clever, loved titled and highly placed people. He was teasing and disdainful, vain and proud of his real importance. With all that, not tremendously sympathetic. His work is beautiful; no mystification there. It is short. He was approaching forty when he gave it to the public, just at the start of the war, and success came to him straight away. Last year he was given the Prix Goncourt.

....

November 29. I've received a photograph of the portrait Madame de La Nux did of me last summer, at Nathalie's house. Georges is crazy about it, he gazes at it, cooes over it, smiles at it, is dreaming up an ebony frame for it, or one of black lacquer. I like my eyelids in it, little half-melons, and my arms and my breasts. It was summer, or rather the very hottest days of spring, and I posed nude to the waist on Flossie's downy bed, buried by her in the softest cushions. I remember that Madame R took me by surprise like that. I seemed unmoved, but really I was embarrassed. The clever little artist, dark, with huge black eyes, had such pretty gestures. From time to time we exchanged a thought or two, or Nathalie, lying in her dressing-room next door, threw in a sentence. We and our two husbands had lunched with her. What, in fact, were our two husbands doing? Pierre de La Nux had gone racing; Georges was resting in the big round drawing-room on the first floor, smoking and burrowing about among Nathalie's scattered books and papers. He looked in from time to time, friendly and happy; I could feel that he liked the atmosphere and my pose.

1923

Nice – Langham Hotel, March 18 to April 16

March 18. No blue notebook for three months! For three months I led a dissipated, self-diminishing life without meditation.

I took New Year presents for all my friends, my intimate friends, to Pépé's house. Trunks unpacked, things put away; Pépé apparently happy, we too, smiling servants. We are going to have such a good time, give parties, go to them, eat, drink and be merry . . . Yes indeed! Saturday the 6th was the chosen date, five hundred invitations were sent out. Man proposes, God disposes . . . To be continued tomorrow.

March 20. I left matters at my arrival at Pépé's house, full of joyful promise. On New Year's Day we gave a large and splendid lunch. It was very gay. Pépé was just back from Germany feeling much better because of a strict diet, but not cured: and Pépé wanted to taste everything. We had endless trouble persuading him to stick to his noodles, his roast pheasant (Robert de Rothschild had sent me three) and his boiled potatoes. All day long there was a procession of his friends and our friends bringing good wishes, flowers, sweetmeats, kisses. I can still see Pépé coming over to me and saying in triumph: 'I've been eating the lot and it's wonderful, I haven't had the slightest pain' – whereupon he plunged into the chocolates and marrons glacés. On the second we lunched with Nathalie, the Duchess and Rouveyre, feeling rather anxious because Pépé had been smitten with a terrible stomach ache during the night. We went home early. We found Pépé in bed, pale, feverish, and groaning, his secretary at his side. He absolutely did not want us to call a doctor. I argued, I begged, I implored and at last he allowed me to telephone Jean-Charles Roux. Yes, but – J-C Roux was in Germany at a conference. Pépé continued to groan, I thought of Gaston Lyon. He came at once, palpated Pépé and ordered absolute rest, the strictest fast and bags of ice on the stomach. On the morning of the third I found Pépé up, green in the face, contorted, howling, insisting that he was going to the office. Georges and I forced him back into bed and the doctor came back: 'Keep absolutely still, not even a drop of water. I'll come back this evening.' I sent Georges off to lunch at the Rouveyres with Nathalie and the Duchess, and I stayed in. Pépé's howls redoubled, his face was haggard, his skin was waxy and he was frantic for a glass of milk. I prevented this until the doctor arrived at five o'clock. 'Keep absolutely still, not even a drop of water, I'll come back tomorrow morning,' and off he went . . . or rather, off he was going, because I caught him on his way downstairs and said crisply: 'Doctor, you simply cannot leave my patient like this. He is very ill indeed, his temperature is rising. It is essential that you come back this evening to check on him, keep him calm, prevent him drinking – and you must bring another doctor.' He gave me a look and said: 'Well, if you want to know the truth it's not another doctor I need, it's a surgeon. I was going to tell you tomorrow morning.' Something made me say forcefully: 'No doctor, not tomorrow morning. Now, this evening – and quickly.'

Half an hour later he brought us that great strapping Professor Le Senne, whom he'd had the luck to meet. After a careful examination Le Senne came into my room, shut the door and said: 'He'll be dead by tomorrow if I don't operate at once.' I pulled myself together. 'Very well, doctor; I'll take responsibility as though he were my husband. Operate on our friend quickly, don't let him die.' I was not proud. Le Senne went on: 'It's a dangerous operation, I'll see to everything. It will have to be done upstairs, I daren't risk bringing him down on a stretcher.' I went through three hours of atrocious anxiety. It was nine o'clock. I'd had no dinner and didn't want any. Meanwhile Georges bustled about watching over everything and making sure that everything would be ready. The Celer agency sent round six men and two women to turn the sitting-room upstairs into an operating theatre. It was really extraordinary to watch the speed and completeness of the transformation. Jacques Doucet came round. Georges told him the exact truth and he comforted and consoled Pépé by pretending to know that it was appendicitis. He offered to stay with us all night, and remembering his seventy-one-years I was tremendously grateful. The operation began at ten o'clock.

In the middle of it my room was plunged into darkness; the lights had fused. 'Oh my God!' I screamed, 'Pépé's up there with his stomach open!' Absolute panic. Georges flew out and came back beaming; the upstairs fuses had not gone. I was so stunned, so overcome, that I had not been able to pray.

It was all over by eleven. Pépé, carried back to bed by the benevolent giant Le Senne, woke up with no pain. The doctors told us: 'The gall bladder had swollen to the size of an aubergine and was on the point of bursting. We have excised what we had to, and have inserted drains; he is still in danger, great danger. We cannot promise anything. Till tomorrow!'

I am abbreviating. It really was marvellous, progress was so rapid. Pépé was up by the end of the week, eating chicken on the fourth day, playing up with his nurses, grumbling about his servants, wanting to know everything that was going on, listening to every sound in his house and becoming so intimate with us that it was soon perfectly insupportable. We wanted to leave. 'Don't forsake me! Don't make me unhappy!' So we stayed, pleased to have saved him and glad to see something of our friends. But day by day Pépé became more didactic, more demanding, even tyrannical, quite grossly rude. He no longer restrained himself at all. We had become things to him, slaves. We didn't belong to ourselves any more. He gave orders. His tone was sharp and peremptory. I understood Balthy.

The day after the operation, when the doctors were still forbidding visitors, Pépé whispered softly: 'Liane, if Louise comes, let her give me a kiss.' So at about eleven o'clock we went round to fetch Louise with Nathalie (who was almost as worried for us as she was for him). Balthy already knew all about it and nothing would shake her, she did not want to come. 'Shit!' she said. 'It's his wickedness that poisoned him. You're not getting me there.' – 'My darling Louise, he's dying.' – 'Shit!' – 'My darling Louise, he's asking for you.' – 'Shit!' – 'My darling Louise, he does love you underneath it all.' – 'Shit!' Nathalie added her urgings to mine. Finally Louise let us shove her, drag her, shut her into the car, carry her off. She was saying 'Shit!' all the way to the house. She went upstairs; Pépé saw her, opened his arms to her, they kissed. Then Louise made a silent and dignified exit from the room, gave me a look, murmured a last 'Shit!' – and departed, never to return. Faced with Pépé's behaviour to us, I understood, sadly I understood, and I wrote to tell her so. What a delightful holiday! What charming gratitude!

I saw Sorel again, splendid and sprightly, condescending and gracious, attended by her faithful Ségur. She had us to lunch one fine morning when the Seine was rippling like blue *moiré*, in her beautiful marble dining-room on the marble table which cost – so Pepito said – a hundred thousand francs. This table was covered with a pink cloth glimmering through gold gauze, strewn with multi-coloured tulips and fragrant mimosa among which were scattered peaches, pears, grapes and bananas. Célimène's lovely hands wandered about this flowery meadow, distributing fruit hither and thither. Everyone produced what was best in him or her. Sorel smiled, Ségur contemplated her – but without forgetting to do honour to the exquisite viands. Cécile's whole purpose is to dazzle and charm and it's done so nicely, so sincerely, that it works. Her apartment on the Quai Voltaire is grandiose, rich and in faultless taste. Everything is carefully chosen to provide a frame for a beauty composed wholly of artificial elements who is able, carefully and deliberately, to impose her own terms. Sorel brought me some beautiful roses to Pépé's house. I sent her a bottle of 'Liane', the toilet water sold by Delettrez with my picture on the label and a few approving words which I put together for him. Little Ségur is crazy about it. He wants to marry her; she resists. Will she ever do it? Backstage gossip has it that Guillaume de Ségur's mother is vastly rich and is against the marriage; so Sorel refuses and keeps him captive by love alone while she waits for the mother – who might conceivably dare to disinherit such a charming daughter-in-law! – to die. The little fellow is very well-off, and no fool. Sometimes when they are on tour he is given a part in a play beside his beloved. He has a good time, looks after the lighting, organizes visitors, has a hand in arranging tours, rehearsals, fittings, photographs, posters. We had a good laugh together. He knows how to enjoy life. He knows how to eat.........

March 22. .... Nathalie is miffed. She promised that she would come here with the Duchess at the end of March, and now she looks like going back on her promise. Having been offended, I wanted to offend in my turn. I wrote a very poetic letter to the Duchess suggesting that she should come with Mademoiselle Lefranc. Whereupon my Nathalie was stirred to wrath and wrote me a stern letter accusing me of not being pure gold. Nathalie is becoming cantankerous; it must be the change of life; she bristles at the least thing, her voice goes arrogant and pompous. I had a taste of it on December 27th or

28th; it passed, obviously, but it happened. For four days I flinched away from her as though she were a red hot poker. I called her 'Extra-dry, for the American market' and for a time withdrew the sweet name of Harmony. She was penitent and found charming ways of making up. I do like Nathalie, but she scares me and being scared does *not* suit me.

The Duchess was exquisite from beginning to end of our stay in Paris. She came to cheer us up every day, telephoned every morning, gave a lovely luncheon for me, then a tea party with the famous Ricardo Vines who played me marvels by Granados and Albeniz and insisted that I should sit by him as he played. The Duchess took us – Georges and me – to the Vieux Colombier theatre to see *le Carosse du saint-sacrement*, the most delightful comedy in twenty years, and so well acted.

March 24. A Spanish writer who is much discussed at the moment, Ramon Gomez de la Serna, has said in one of his books that women's breasts are incapable of sensation! How could anyone have the pitiful impudence to be so far from the truth as that man! Breasts – my own and almost all those I have known – the little points of breasts live a life of the most intense passion. What an idiot! Nathalie has put him right in a charming article under the signature 'The Amazon'. How can anyone publish and spread such nonsense? The man must be a brute.

March 27. Thérèse Diehl was with me almost all day yesterday. She was biddable and adorable; towards evening she seemed sad and languid. She's the same kind of person as Bernstein; like him, she can sometimes be carried away by her own play-acting. That reminds me of a funny story about Bernstein and Missia Edwards (now Madame Sert, née Godeski) when she was repudiated by Edwards because of pretty Lantelme and wanted to engineer a little scandal to her own advantage, in order to excite her husband and recapture him. Attracted by Henry's record, she picked on him. I had run away for the sixth time and had gone into hiding – very boring it was, too – in the depths of a little hotel in Passy. Henry knew where I was, came to bang on the door, implore, threaten. He tried to bribe the gardener to throw a sack over my head, tie me up and hand me over. Then it occurred to him that the trail laid by Missia might provide an agreeable diversion, so he went off to find her in Baden-Baden. The first evening Missia betook herself with precautions and abandon to Henry's rooms, complete with all her nocturnal gear including her pillow. Henry looked askance at all this and said to himself: 'This is going to be tough – the whole night, for heaven's sake!' He loved his comforts and could have cried at this depressing sight. Two more nights followed – the same thing all over again. In despair he began to shower me with emissaries, letters, telegrams, 'Come to me, Liane, my only love, the only sensible woman in the world, come to your Henry who is dying for love of you.' I was tickled by all this so I went to Baden. Henry drove to intercept me a few stations before. He threw himself on me, looking frantic, caught me up in his arms and carried me to his car. Pale, in tears, he babbled: 'Don't speak . . . don't speak . . . this is too strong, too beautiful for words.' At the hotel I found a most sumptuous suite. It was intoxicating. Missia and Henry had parted in a very ill-humour with each other. When they saw each other again they were cross and distant. Missia wanted her revenge and involved her first husband, the Jew Natanson, to this end. He picked a quarrel with Bernstein at the Authors' Society, and Henry flew into a passion and took it up. Oh that duel! What a performance my great actor made of it! Everyone round me was sworn to keep it from me, but an indiscretion – cunningly devised between Bernstein and Vanderein – took place by telephone; I pretended that I didn't understand. Lucien Guitry pretended that he'd made a mistake about the time and rang to ask the result: I got rid of him by simulating being cut off. When Henry left me he gave me long, speaking looks, his kisses were manly and reticent; I played the innocent. As soon as he had left I received a vast sheaf of roses complete with a letter on black-edged writing paper – a sort of testament of love meant for posterity and to drive me frantic. I roared with laughter. Marguerite Moreno was with me, she began to tell me about her love affair with Catulle Mendès and time passed cheerfully. Someone brought me the telephone, I heard a grave, gentle voice: 'My Lianon . . .' – 'Oh, so it's you. Aren't you dead?' – 'Oh Liane, how can you speak to me like that, at this moment?' – 'Frankness is suitable for any moment.' – 'Lianon, I'm coming round, I'm wounded.' – 'Are you? Where? In the tongue?' – 'Oh Liane, my knuckles are grazed. Did you get the roses?' – 'Of course. The ceremony was complete, except for the finale.'

March 28. Sarah Bernhardt is dead, the golden voice is silent. We almost believed – or wished – her to be immortal. Oh Sarah!

What a magical being, what a revelation to my candid sixteen-year-old self – that *Tosca* I was taken to by Armand Pourpe during our honeymoon! ....

April 7. Lord Carnarvon, the archeologist, is dead. He was my love when I was eighteen. It was here at Nice, at the Restaurant Français, that I first saw him. He was twenty-five. I thought he was so fine, so distinguished, so thoroughbred, so chic that I adored him. Just to watch him and admire him was enough for my enthusiasm. He was introduced to me that same year at the clay-pigeon shooting at Monte Carlo. Tremendous heart-fluttering, I could have died at his feet. He left the next day! What a dear little silly I was. A few months later I saw him again in London, at Covent Garden. Lady Dudley had the measles and the key of her box was for sale according to custom, and I had bought it. Carnarvon walked in absent-mindedly during the interval: flutterings, smiles, excuses, compliments, confessions. He was vicious, an invert so they said. He loved me all the same . . . and was a delicious, agonizing lover, full of charm and cruel grace. So I became the rival of Lady de Grey – Gladys. I had the upper hand. He didn't make me very happy; he was fugitive, a traveller, always off to India, the Baltic, Scotland. I have kept a pearl in his memory, the most beautiful of all my pearls, the one valued today at a hundred thousand francs.

....

Saint-Germain – Hotel de l'Aigle d'or, May 23 to 24

May 23. I lunched with the Lazaruses in Paris. After lunch Georges went to the Gare Montparnasse to prepare our journey to Roscoff, while I escaped to my dear Duchess in the rue Raynouard. She was in – and without Nathalie! The welcome she gave me was loving, joyful, tender, caressing. She was still my own Gladness. Dear, spontaneous, warm little Duchess. Her worldly duties are keeping her very busy these days, but she found time to tell me about the letters of Robert de Montesquiou and Marcel Proust, very curious letters. Montesquiou was so unkind to the gentle Marcel that it amounted to ferocity. It would be very interesting to see them. My Duchess has met Reynaldo Hahn, whom she likes very much. There were blue hydrangeas fading in her garden, and an African god commanded the entrance of the front court. She gave me some red roses. It's impossible not to love her! And how cross I am with naughty Nathalie, making me tell her lies like this, and avoid her! But I can't help it, I don't want to see Nathalie and they are always together. In the Duchess's bedroom I saw two pairs of slippers under a Louis XVI chest of drawers. I thought – the grey pair are Nathalie's, and I wanted to pull a face at them. Anyway, I showed Gladness my delight in being near her, in kissing her, in having her in my life, my thoughts, my heart. She was looking young and beautiful with a jaunty little almond-green hat, a chiffon scarf flung carelessly round her neck, a dark green satin Poiret-Egyptian dress embroidered in vivid colours. I feel quite impregnated with her tender warmth.

May 24. At about eleven o'clock I was just going out when I heard the magisterial voice of Salomon Reinach asking if we were in. He is no longer banned. I opened the door, and my little Duchess who was hiding in the alcove flew into my arms! She brought me a bouquet of purple roses and the delight of her sparkling presence. She talked to me about all kinds of things. With her everything is quick, vibrant, joyful and colourful. Salomon was rather left out but was happy to watch, analyse, calculate.

Roscoff – Clos-Marie, June 7 to December 30

June 7. At last! And for months . . . months . . . months . . . How happy we are together in our loving solitude surrounded by the endless space of the sea outside our windows, the fresh air, the simple little house. Here all is repose; wounds heal; thoughts become harmonious; bitterness sweetens. We retain only that which is charming.

June 8. It is thirteen years today since we took our love from the town hall in the rue d'Anjou to the chapel of the catechism in Saint-Philippe-du-Roule. They are cooking us turbot and chicken. The weather is magnificent and full of lovely promises because it's Saint Médard's day. It's also, and above all, the feast of the Sacred Heart.

I talked to Jesus last night. I told him: 'Jesus, I long to love

You. Perhaps Your incarnation makes me see too much of the man in You, and that puts me off. Men lack sweetness, generosity, justice and devotion.' An inner voice answered: 'What about your Georges? Isn't he sweet, generous, devoted, and so close to you?' Then I felt my heart growing tender. Oh my Saviour, help me to lift the impenetrable veil in spite of my unworthiness and my lack of merit. Come to me, Jesus, because I long for it and because I have suffered.

June 9. Salomon writes me a charming letter. He has regained his good opinion of me since he saw the Duchess kiss me. It's always a good thing to shake people up some way or another. Tacitly we have bestowed the name of 'Daughter of Louis XV' on my dear Duchess. Royal she certainly is: she commands a couldn't-care-less nonchalance, distinction, arrogance, condescension. Her fancy inclines towards me at the moment. I have become 'one of the good things of France' in her eyes.

June 16. Tolstoy wrote: 'To love is to prefer another to oneself.' Perhaps I prefer Georges to myself – sometimes; but if he preferred me to himself at the same time we would be like two polite people hovering in a doorway, doing that dance of hesitation and withdrawal. I offer Georges the best part of a cake, he offers it to me, and all three (I include the cake) get nowhere. I feel disinclined to make love; I'm unselfish and offer him my body; he knows how I feel and refuses – then what? We have to fall back on the mutual concessions which keep all successful households going.

....

July 28. Max Jacob has arrived. He has been having a bad time with his family, who would only be capable of understanding his talent if he could produce decorations, a car, a chauffeur and a profusion of thousand-franc notes. He's brought a trunkful of old documents. He intends to do an enormous amount of serious work.

August 1. Max is working hard. In the evening he reads us his poems. He has written two charming ones. He tells us anecdotes. He is amusing and likes being here. He claims that Roscoff suits both his piety and his work. He goes to the 6.30 mass every morning, he takes communion, he does the stations of the Cross, he meditates, he reads holy books. 'It would be impossible to be better,' says

Camille – she herself is falling off a bit, caught up in everyday life.

August 4. Max has caught the sun badly on the top of his head and his nose. He has made a cigarette burn in one of my linen sheets. His table manners are becoming bad. As soon as you indulge Max he becomes insupportable. He is going to force me back into cold looks and chiding words.

....

August 6. Max is a real fish out of water in our religion! His instincts are against us: sourness, arrogance, malice, insinuations. In spite of his masses, communions, stations of the Cross you can feel it all bubbling about in him. He fights it as best he can, he takes pains – really furious pains – to summon up his resistance, but it oozes out of his every pore. He is envious, jealous, slanderous, false, gossipy, blundering. It's a curious thing to watch. He is dirty, untidy, unwholesome, garrulous, pompous, greedy, either flattering or impertinent . . . he's inhabited by every sort of demon; his envelope contains a hundred-headed hydra. Georges is some protection against all this: pedantic, prudent, choosing his words and looking before he leaps. He can use his head. But he can still recognize the troubles with which other people are afflicted. And to those troubles he brings the most serene indulgence. He really is the pick of the bunch.

August 8. We are going for long walks. Max does not come with us. He works and meditates........

August 11. Max is in a good mood, good health and pleased with his work. He has given me a superb cake which he ordered from Quimper and I know he has a big box of pralines hidden in his cupboard for my saint's day. But his best present is his dedication of the new edition of his *Cornet à dés*.

August 14. Max has started to tell us the story of his life. We have reached 1904. First it's funny, then it's touching. He tells it with humour and irony. His early days were very hard, and that is how his life still is, in spite of his success. Max is only forty-seven but he looks sixty: no teeth or hair, a lisp, fat, short, a nervous cringing expression and a spiteful eye. But he has found God and that is the only treasure, true wealth, real magnificence.

August 15. My saint's day sung in by bells, by the wind, by the hearts surrounding me. Georges opened fire yesterday evening with a letter-poem, then Max with a huge box of chocolates and an adorable, miraculously preserved box of about 1830 with miniatures of little people under glass surrounded by delicate flowers and semi-precious stones – a little masterpiece of a knick-knack, really pretty and genuine. He had it sent secretly from his mother's antique shop in Quimper. I am spoilt, cherished, cossetted, loved, kissed, celebrated: cards from everyone and everywhere.

August 19. Max tells us about Doucet, the couturier who made a great deal of money and endowed a library for the State which bears his name and is full of very valuable manuscripts and rare editions. The manuscripts were procured at bargain prices because the Maecenas took advantage of hard-up young writers: he made them allowances – thirty francs, fifty francs, sometimes a hundred francs a month – on condition that they wrote him long letters, one, two or three, containing analyses of books by their contemporaries or of other interesting subjects.

As a couturier Doucet was only mediocre and as far as we women in the public eye were concerned his taste could add nothing to our elegance. The materials were beautiful, the dresses were well-made, but he had a hostile attitude towards the capricious movements of fashion and was determined to remain 'Doucet' through thick and thin! Poiret's enjoyable and spirited fantasies seemed to him like fancy dress. He fitted us out like good mothers of families – or at least like colonels' ladies! Basically what kept him fashionable was his address in the rue de la Paix and his enormous bills. His *vendeuses*, who were paid on their turnover, were well-spoken – and anyway we were mugs! Doucet's was a good meeting place, we could make the rounds of the neighbouring jewellers; actresses and great ladies brushed shoulders and the new rich had no need to manoeuvre their way in – they were welcomed, their chatter was smiled on indulgently, they were shown the greatest deference. It is all a bit different nowadays. Behaviour has become more natural, one goes out to dinner in a shift, one dances half naked. The ruined rich open studios and have fun designing dresses.

August 20. Yesterday Max was splendid in white linen trousers and a geranium blazer. I took him for a walk to show him off to the village as though he were a child delighting in new clothes. He spent the morning at his devotions: two masses, confession and communion. Saint Max all day. Jacob when he is naughty.

August 30. Max has seen me putting my pearls in a bowl of sea-water to freshen them. Yesterday he recited these two lines:

'The princess keeps migrating birds
Imprisoned in a bowl of sea-water.'

And Georges and he went on and on and on admiring them and declaring 'That is a really enchanting poem, to anyone who can understand it.' Max then said: 'Because you like this poem so much and it was the princess's gesture which gave me this happy inspiration, I am going to give it to you. I shall write it out and it will be just for you. I undertake never to have it published.' Well really! ... Is he making fun of us? Or is it ... I'm quite worried and must keep an eye on him. I must put them both on a healthy diet, feed them up – I'm afraid they may be going gaga from anaemia of the brain.

September 3. Yesterday morning, Sunday, Max devoted to church. He exhales all his piety there, and what he brings back to the house is cheek, tiresome whims, boorishness. We had words at table.

....

September 13. Benjamin has sent a telegram saying that he hopes to be here on Friday. Max is rather worried, he would be! He is wondering how a Jew will take his conversion; and he's also jealous at the thought of having to share our attention with another person.

I have been gardening. I have pricked out my pinks, taken some geranium cuttings and done some planting.

September 17. Benjamin has been here since the 14th. Max is sulking, suffering from held-in jealousy – and also from incontinence! His liver is playing up as a result of all this. It relieves him to be disagreeable to the point of boorishness and to exhale his rancour in remarks such as: 'It's the people I love, only the people. I'm one of them, and that's what I intend to remain!' Then – aimed at Georges, who makes a point of being absolutely polite whatever happens: 'If there's one thing I can't stand it's politeness.'

September 18. The little devil Jacob is stuck in bed under a pile of dirty old rags. The doctor has diagnosed a liver attack and a slight pulmonary congestion. So there we are! He's as tetchy as can be and lends himself very badly to the anxious care we are trying to give him. I have taken him up the vegetable soup the doctor ordered, and lemonade. Georges puts on his mustard plasters for him and has visited him a dozen times. Having friends to stay is not all pleasure!

September 19. I'm afraid that Max, seeing us bending so attentively over his couch – not that anything so dirty deserves the name! – has started to play the spoilt child. He is such a bizarre creature. He veers between being arrogant and humble, too much and too little, brash and sly. He is not without wit, but it's an ill-tempered, desperate wit which is turned odious by lack of manners, scruples and honesty. Max is certainly his own worst enemy, and he doesn't realize that he is frightfully difficult to live with.

September 20. Max is making the task really too much. Georges is becoming as weary and disconcerted by it as I am. It gives me no pleasure to see my beautiful quilted bedspread – so expensive nowadays – bundled up under Max's dirty chin unprotected by the sheet which he's managed to lose – the precious thing used as a towel, covered with pencils, open books, grubby papers, spent matches, spots of soup and lemonade. Our best course is to get him better and get rid of him. He will be furious about it, but we can't look after such a messy invalid right through the winter.

September 24. Max has gone! At last! We are disinfecting his room. He is now inspiring me with the sort of fond respect one has for dead people. I am sorry for him. He left without seeing me, mumbling vague phrases of so-called politeness. Madame Garat said goodbye to him for me, and told him I would pray for him. At those words he almost burst into tears and said: 'And I will pray for her, I do love her so.' Then a moment later he was seized by his demon: 'The truth is, you know, that I'm republican – I loathe royalty.' My old friend François asked me whether he was a bit mad. His daughter saw him in church making crosses with holy water all over his body, even on the tips of his toes. That is probably it: he is a bit mad. His chastity – if you can use that word for a negative condition – has gone to his head. I remember hearing him yelping genuine lamentations inspired by his fear of purgatory – 'Where everyone' he cried, 'will have to go for a very long time and the flames are as hot as those of hell.'

September 25. Yesterday a problem: two lovely Saint-Benoît cheeses – the same type as camembert – arrived for us, ordered by Max Jacob. He gave the order quite some time ago. My first impulse was to refuse them, but everyone contributed an opinion: don't complicate matters, don't insult the absent, they'll go bad, a pity to waste something so good, think what the poet spent on them and so on and so on. Then Benjy came in and said: 'Be *grand*, keep them.' So we kept them – and very good they are.

....

October 22. Sad letter from Nathalie. She is evidently haunted by the idea of death. She says that she hopes she will have the courage to die alone, as she has lived. It's a heart-breaking remark. I tell her to think of me, older than she is, ailing and always delicate, and follow me bravely and cheerfully. Nathalie has no notion of God to support her.

October 24. I am haunted by death. I see such appalling things that words fail me. When Georges has left me, or if he dies before I do, I shall shut myself up in a convent, I shall try to find the courage to die alone, as Flossie proudly says.

....

December 30. Can it be winter? It's hot, airless! I have had a present from my dear R – a marvel! A huge and sumptuous shawl in magnificent white crêpe de chine, with a big black pattern. Nothing could have given me more pleasure.

Enthusiastic letter from Max Jacob. How funny it is! After all that passed between us, here we are, possibly better friends than ever!

1924

Roscoff – Clos-Marie, June 22 to December 25

The Ghikas went to Paris early in January – Liane briefly records the fact that she is packing for the journey and that Lewis has promised her some hats – and have now returned to Roscoff for the summer.

. . . .

June 22. Corpus Christi: the bells are ringing, people in their Sunday best are thronging, the best hangings are being shaken out, gardens are being looted of their flowers, wayside altars are appearing in the squares; and the holy day is bathed in golden sunshine.

All the long time we were in Paris I didn't open my notebook once. I never had a minute for it, nor the energy, nor even the wish.

June 24. Missy has been here since yesterday, arriving in her beautiful red car with her chauffeur and her maid. Missy is Mathilde de Morny, daughter of the Duc de Morny, Marquise de Belboeuf, returned – since her divorce – to being Marquise de Morny once again. I have not spoken about her before because there was a coldness between us. She dresses as a man and has the ways and morals of a man. Her cigar used to give me a headache. Whereupon Missy grumbled to mutual friends: 'What a bore Liane is, with her migraines.' They repeated it. In short I let her drop, quite gently but firmly. This year Nathalie the despot said in front of me that she wanted to meet Missy so that she could introduce her to Romaine Brooks. I offered to act as intermediary. I wrote to Missy: 'Dear Father (she calls Georges her son), we never really quarrelled and we are dying to see you again. Write to me soon and tell me when it can be, open your heart and your arms to me once more.' Touched, Missy stopped being grumpy, unknitted her brows, changed directions and her mind, and came to see us the minute she arrived in Paris. We took up our friendship again with evident pleasure on both sides. But lo and behold, Romaine Brooks had gone to London and Nathalie – ungrateful, ill-bred creature! – disclaimed the whole thing and told me crisply that she wouldn't dream for a moment of receiving a woman of such ill repute who dressed as a man and had neither talent nor wit. Stunned, I told her: 'Do you consider that *you* have anything to be ashamed of as far as morals and reputation go? Missy sculpts quite as well as the Duchess. She's of good family. There's nothing to choose between you but a pair of trousers.'

I told all this to my dear R who at once began to long to meet Missy. I arranged a tea-party in our little nest at the Palais d'Orsay. In came Madame R, elegant, old-fashioned, smiling; candidly she offered an intrepid hand to the ambiguous Marquise, saying deliberately: 'Madame, when my husband was a boy he was madly in love with you. He was at Stanislas with your brothers and used to wait impatiently for Sundays in the hope of seeing you in the parlour. All the other pupils felt the same, full of admiration for your beauty.' At that Missy allowed her natural affability free rein; the two ladies had a long chat and were delighted with each other.

June 28. I saw Sacha Guitry again, and Yvonne Printemps, affectionate and full of success. I saw Jean Vollerin, a distant friend and Sacha's secretary. He asked us to dinner and we made the acquaintance of the Dolly Sisters, nice little acrobatic dancers, modern mechanical toys, funny, not pretty but made-up and dressed with enough charm and intelligence to take the place of beauty. Paris is crazy about them. They earn wads of money, bounce about the place to great effect, gamble in the casinos, dress at the great houses and buy and sell property wherever they go.

June 30. Missy decided to leave at five in the morning so as to avoid driving in the heat of the day. Sweet and contrary, she's perfectly impossible at meals. A guest to beware of! 'I can't eat eggs, or fish, or peas, or beans, or tomatoes, or veal, or pork, or cheese, or cakes, or strawberries, or apricots, or . . . or . . . or . . .' – the list is endless. Are you serving a salad? 'I eat only the ribs of the leaves' – scurry to cut out the ribs! Cauliflower? 'I eat nothing but the stalks' – quick, make a little dish of just stalks. Cucumber? 'Mine must be quite dry.' Chicken? 'Only the dark meat, please.' Rabbit? 'I dislike everything but the legs.' So this morning everyone is saying 'Ouf!' And it was supposed to be fun!

. . . .

July 3. Card from Madame Georges Menier who is the prettiest woman in Paris. Robert de Rothschild came to meet me at the first of Nathalie's Fridays. He was charmed by this amusing and ill-assorted gathering and enchanted to see me again and find me still so beautiful. So one fine Sunday he organized a luncheon at the Lebels – big industrialists somehow connected with the Meniers of Neuilly. It was dreamlike. Our photographs were taken in the garden, everything seemed intoxicating, we chatted, we smiled, we laughed, we wanted to shine with every facet. A few days later I had a telephone call from Georges Menier whose marvellous wife had just had an operation: 'My wife is allowed visitors since yesterday. She was so very sorry not to see you the other day at the Lebels' – I wonder if I dare ask you to drop in on her at the clinic?' When we went in to her room, which had been transformed into a blossoming hothouse, we saw a goddess nesting in flowers on a white cloud, in a snowy whiteness of fine cambric, entwined in yards of matchless pearls! A divine face, smiling, regular, pretty. A lovable, simple child, surrounded by four tall sons, her husband and her father-in-law. I gave her my white violets and signified my sincere admiration and my tender solicitude. She said all the right things. I had a friendly word with my old Gaston Menier, the senator, who often does helpful things for me. I like that beautiful, simple, friendly, perfect, irreproachable woman. All Paris admires her. When I talked about her to the Duchess she said: 'Oh, they say she's so lovely! But she keeps to her own kind of people, she's not a snob. It's a shame for our lot, whom she avoids so carefully.' In my opinion that's another thing in this charming woman's favour, and I am proud that she wanted me to come to her.

. . . .

July 13. When I'm thinking about this past spring I keep seeing the Cochon d'or, a restaurant at la Villette almost opposite the slaughter-house. All the snobbiest people were mad about it. One day my sultana, Madame Fabre-Luce, let fall: 'I never go anywhere, but I do, do, *do* so want to see this famous *Cochon d'or* everyone's talking about.' We went into action at once. Georges telephoned the handsome Italian *patron* and a menu was planned. The Duchess came disguised as a rake – little brown suit, hat over one ear, scarf flung carelessly round her neck – her dear little face alert and amused. Nathalie – grey – was the foreigner who is eager to see everything. As for my sultana, she was born along in her sumptuous car – after a detour to pick us up – her usual self: rich pastel finery from the rue de la Paix, pearls, rings, gleaming jewels, Cartier handbag with coral, ivory, onyx and diamonds . . . She descended from her chariot with a little amused look as though she were playing a practical joke on someone. 'Oh my God,' I thought, 'they are going to jeer at us! Whatever will happen?' I tried to shelter and surround my sultana. The *patron* conducted us to a little back room where our table was reserved. It was a Wednesday, market day. We were surrounded by huge, sweaty, red-faced men finishing their lunch, not very reassuring. They stared, but not unkindly. My friends' charm got to work. Voices became less loud. No one lit a pipe, no one spat on the floor, no one swore. It was as though we were providing them with a charming little performance. The commonest of the lot kept on winking at me. We ate like ogres. The pâté was really excellent, the chicken exquisite. As for the steak, we cried our admiration aloud. You don't know what red meat is if you haven't had it there: firm and melting, with an unbelievable flavour; you put it on your tongue and it evaporates – a marvel! We exclaimed with delight, our confidence quite restored, enchanted to be there. We felt that all those men were our brothers!

Certainly the Ritz, where we went five or six times, is good fun like a big liner packed with smart strangers; but the food there is horrible.

July 15. . . . . Georges doesn't laugh enough. When I scolded him for being sad, he answered: 'I'm not sad, just empty. I'm in pursuit of nothingness, of vacuity.' To my mind he's found it.

July 22. Max Jacob wants to come back here! And look at me – touched and softened, I tell him to come, that the Clos will open its doors to him and we will open our arms!

As for Cocteau, he's desperate to be in love! Mad with grief at Radiguet's death, he has fallen for that sweet little Garros. She's a charming creature who became drunk on literature while living with Mireille Havet. Jean, an invert in his time, is beginning to climb the slope – a real woman would have been too much to start with. Jean has celebrated her in verse as he celebrated that magnificent child

Radiguet in *le Cap de Bonne-Espérance*. May they live a virtuous and happy life together like Georges and me. Cocteau has already been madly in love with Madeleine Carlier, who was cruel to him. He expressed his suffering in a book which wasn't very good. Everything that happens to these gentlemen ends as a book.

July 27. Max arrived yesterday morning. Saint Anne's day – I think she must have sent him to me. I received him kindly and installed him comfortably, he feels at home, he was charming. We were mutually conciliating and ready to make concessions. Long may it last! He gave us a moving picture of the moral cruelties inflicted on him by the Abbé and some of the boarders at Saint-Benoît, particularly a young man called Pierre Robert who was his own protégé to start with. This young man had no money, no scruples, and a sort of commercial-travellerish cheerfulness which delighted everyone at the monastery so that he supplanted Max. He teased him endlessly, called him 'Monsieur Dumou', barged into his room whenever he felt like it, played practical jokes on him, used his paper, his pens, his books. On top of everything else, this young man of twenty-three became a lay brother at the last pilgrimage. Humiliated and tormented, Max became jealous and that's why he packed his bags and came to us. 'Being here is like Paradise after hell, my dears,' he said. He has started work already, his room upside down and his table loaded.

July 29. Max says that poems have started to flow. He read me some of them. Ho hum! I am not up to them. Here's one of them: 'Zambelli (dancer at the Opéra, past it) – elected legs – Brique Jean – go screw yourself – *Every Day*.' Georges is thunderstruck and heaps him with compliments. As for me – I say: 'Read it to me again.' Max gives a superior smile and goes on lisping away. I raise my eyebrows and try to raise myself to this intellectual level, but I always tumble down again, humiliated. Apparently it's euphonious and full of meaning.........

July 30. They have let me know that I have been granted the Military Medal in memory of my son who had the right to it because of his two citations. The address proclaimed 'Widow Pourpe'. I am absolutely *not* the Widow Pourpe, nor have I ever been, having been divorced. In law I then reverted to being Madame Chassaigne. So the Widow Pourpe is informed that she will be given the Military

Medal for her son Marc Pourpe, killed by the enemy; that if she wants the ceremony of handing over she must travel to Longvic, and that she will not be reimbursed for any expenses she incurs! If she prefers, she can have it brought to her by the commandant of her local police station. I feel shocked, bruised, wounded, ruffled and indignant. To be threatened with the police! The neighbourhood will think that they are coming to arrest me.

....

August 6. Affectionate letter from Nathalie – rather affected, I think. Poor fat old Nathalie, grumpy and cantankerous. The Duchess has vanished into silence. I no longer feel that I'm the couple's 'beloved child'. They are intelligent women, sometimes charming, often amusing, very superficial. When you want to go deeper you find that these intoxicating goddesses are banal and ugly. After that you have to manoeuvre to keep a distance between you and the banality.

August 7. Salomon made me reread the Epistles of Saint Paul. I don't understand them very well. He says that if you do not believe in the law but practise the virtues demanded by the law, then you are saved. That reassures me about Georges, and about me, too. Georges practises all the most serious virtues: gentleness, kindness, patience, and generosity. Honesty too. He sets me an excellent example. He denies everything without denying anything. 'Anything is possible' he says, with discouraging assurance. Salomon says that there is nothing but death and the smoke left by fame. Max insists at the top of his voice that he has an unshakable faith in every single thing taught by the Church.

August 11. A young poet called Malraux, one of Max's friends, has stolen some statues worth a million and a half from some holy temple in Indo-China. He was arrested, tried and given three years in prison. It happened at Pnom Penh. Max is in despair; this friend was always asking him out to dinner and paying the most immense bills in the very smartest restaurants. Max says: 'He is young – twenty-three – and fired by lyricism; lyricism raises a man's soul above the kind of scruple which constricts the bourgeois soul.' It's being discussed in the papers, they want to find excuses for him but it's difficult: his case is very weak. Max wrote about it to *l'Eclair*: I'm afraid that all he really wants is to draw attention to himself.

August 17. Missy arrived yesterday and Max took her for a man without a moment's doubt. She brought a rather commonplace and boring young couple with her. A sort of daily bread, not very well baked, heavy and indigestible. Max seems to be annoyed by this disturbance to his habits and his work.

August 18. Missy's guests are Swiss; the husband edits a review called *le Magazine*. They live at Lausanne and have an intolerably ugly accent, rather Germanic. Max is going all out to please them – saying to himself, I fear, that perhaps through them and their magazine he'll be able one day to reach the laggardly, gaping Swiss. He holds forth on literature, takes them for walks and flatters them. I dread the brick he's always on the edge of dropping.

. . . .

October 4. Here I am with a bad attack of gout in my right big toe. Georges made me smear the sick toe with glycerine and cover it with cotton wool, and the pain disappeared completely in five minutes. Uncle Max [Missy liked to be called Uncle Max] is on to a good thing there; I have just been writing her an unsolicited testimonial. Uncle Max has heaps of good recipes. There's one for polishing fingernails, another for copper, and one for building movable library steps. Tanks, she insists, were her invention. She is much drawn to the cinema.

The other day she caused a great sensation in my room. I was in the dressing-room with Georges when suddenly we heard the dear 'old boy's' high-pitched monotonous voice announcing: 'Children, I have a confession to make.' She's broken something in her bedroom, I thought. 'Go ahead,' I called. 'Well, listen: twice in my life I have slept with men . . .' Hearing that, and imagining it, was so comic that we burst out laughing. She went on: 'One of them was my cousin Alexis Orloff. He said he would kill himself if I resisted, so – well, I didn't resist, but I refused any repetition. The second and last was Lord Yume [sic]. He was a very good-looking boy and he adored me, he wanted to marry me. He wore me down, so at last I said "Let's try," and I was his mistress for ten days. Then I'd had enough so I refused his proposal.'

. . . .

December 25. Christmas! All the shoes left in my big granite fireplace were collected this morning by their owners. It was fun to have all these curious, greedy, cheerful, delighted, surprised people jostling round my bed.

We ate the truffle yesterday. Exquisite! I had bought a little brown casserole with a tight-fitting lid. When I lifted the lid we were intoxicated by a dizzyingly heady aroma. It smelt of richness, warmth, celebration, elegance, the triumph of gluttony! I had stewed this precious thing from Orangini for two hours over a low heat, shut tightly in with slices of ham, fillet of beef, some good white wine, a vegetable stock and rashers of bacon. My Georges ate it slowly, gravely, silently – and went on thanking me for it all day. There's nothing more sincere than the gratitude of a satisfied palate!

1925

Paris – Palais d'Orsay, January 28 to March 22

January 28. Paris, softened by sweet and premature spring weather! We are back in our two comfortable and pretty rooms which a cheerful sun has been illuminating all day. Everything unpacked and put away. I alerted only my furrier and Margot de La Bigne. The furrier has delivered everything and Margot has called in to give me a kiss. What a lovely girl, fresh, stylish, dazzling rosy complexion, the look of an archangel at the gates of heaven! Her skirt was very short and revealed her right leg, imperious and agile.

Georges seems very happy to be back in Paris. I shall make an effort to be a good and agreeable woman of the world, smiling, futile, indulgent, charitable, cordial. I have made up my mind – but I still feel wild.

February 4. Very tired by life in Paris, the constricted horizon, the thin air, the useless words .... When I was at a matinée at the Vaudeville .... Madame R sought me out. I was beautiful and sedate, in black. That afternoon I made a conquest of a charming little actress, Mademoiselle de Guise, who is working at the Palais-Royal theatre. At my age! I was astounded by it. Since this morning I have had – we, Georges and I, have had an apartment on the fourth floor at 64 rue Saussure. Simple house, vulgar street, pleasant little 'flat' which will do as a pied-à-terre.

....

February 13. Day spent with Nathalie. Georges left me with her this morning, then went to see his mother. Exquisite lunch with an affectionate, friendly Amazon, siesta, visit to an exhibition of Chana Orloff's sculpture about which I have nothing to say. Nathalie was very decent when she came to see our little hovel. She said: 'Don't spend too much on it. If we can find you something better you can sell it.' But I don't feel like moving house yet again. When you have not got what you like, then you must like what you have. I shall try to like my living-room. Went to Poiret – such a disappointment! Enormous premises, rich and tasteless. The struggle to be unusual has ended by making it impossible. It's like a sweetshop: green, pink, mauve, red. Poiret has a tartan motor-car. He is superb, fat, round, taut, a majestic buddha: black trousers with a thousand stripes and a white frieze frock-coat – very smart.

March 2. Yesterday I played the sultana. I draped my bed in the finest cambric and the rarest lace, I put on a tunic of violet crêpe de chine and a tiara of lace and pearls, and I received visits. I was shaken by a stubborn cough and it was agony when everyone did what they thought was their friendly duty and forced me to talk.

March 27. I have been unable to write during the mad days when my Thérèse was staying here in apartment 327. Yes, mad days . . . an enormous room, an immense divan, fur rugs, cushions, two beautiful and loving women dressed in gleaming satins, covered with pearls, and sparkling jewellery, surrounded by a constantly renewed crowd of elegant, laughing, inquisitive women; friends, a piano. Georges Le Baillif played – he's an excellent musician. Twenty-three-year-old Pierre Meyer, gifted with money, beauty, youth and a very beautiful voice, sang for us. Our mouths mingled. Georges, my grave and happy Georges, sitting opposite me, faint glimmers of light from neighbouring rooms; cheerful tea parties, improvised dinners, flowers, caresses. Quick, a drive to Versailles for some fresh air, or to the Bois, or to Longchamp, or to a fitting – and the endless, exhausting ringing of the telephone.

Challes-les-Eaux – Château de Trivier, August 20 to September 28

Almost five months have gone by since my last lines. Paris life: stupid, muddled existence, self-made occupations and duties, fatigue, uneasiness, laziness. One avoids thinking, it's a victory of the material.

Now I'm staying with Lucienne Rouveyre in an enormous old

château, comfortable, peaceful and well-kept. How many years has it been waiting here for us! Nathalie, who arrived before we did, left last night. Excessively hard-working as usual, she has managed to cram into eighteen days first a cure for her rheumatism at Aix, then one for her throat at Challes, then the preparation with André Rouveyre of a volume of a hundred letters which she received from her great adorer, Rémy de Gourmont. André helped her organize them, and illustrated them and the book's cover with his lovely woodcuts.

August 20. We spent four days at Honfleur with the Duchess: four charming, happy days, an island of calm in the exhaustion of our house-moving. We have stripped the de Polignac lodge of all our belongings and stuffed them into the living-room at 64 rue Saussure. It has become a charming spot, comfortable, cheerful, light and sunny. We like it very much – and would like it better if it stood in some other neighbourhood. Its own neighbourhood is within our means, makes life as dictated by the Roumanian exchange easier, and demands pots of geraniums on our windowsills.

The Duchess's house at Honfleur is a little eighteenth century lodge which used to belong to Admiral Hamelin. It's shabby, pleasant, a lawn in front and a shrubbery surrounding, big rooms with old woodwork which creaks of an evening. There's a view over the estuary and Lucie Delarue-Mardrus as neighbour. And neighbourly she is. The Duchess invited her to dinner; she brought her poems and began to read them as soon as the meal was over. In return we visited her at her place, the 'Pavillon de la Reine'. It's very pretty, a dream . . . one big room where the poetess works, the lavatory shut into a big cupboard, to the left a sort of little dining-room, shining with cleanliness. Flowers everywhere, and sweets of every kind. At present Lucie Delarue-Mardrus is painting misty-looking but brightly coloured flowers – after Odilon Redon according to Georges. She frames them in black, and here and there on the glass which covers them she places a spot of colour. It's amusing and original. She hangs them on the doors, which is unexpected. When I was admiring her taste and artistry she offered me one of them, and did it so sweetly that I kissed her. Afterwards I sent her a lot of sweets from Paris. She was very nice to us, to me. She told us that her little house was built for Marie Antoinette when she had to spend two nights near Honfleur. . . . . . .

Balthy's death! My Louise is no more, and treated me so badly during her last days that our friendship had already perished. I have not felt it a great deal – I reproach myself for that – and I am praying for her. I am really not sure what she had against me. When we met anywhere she would leave, she would walk past me in the Bois without greeting me. I don't go on loving people for long when they don't love me. She made fun of the modesty of my new apartment. I went to see Yvonne de Bray one day at Malmaison and she greeted me with brutal sarcasm: 'Liane, what's this nonsense about living in a lodging-house in the rue Saussure?' I looked at her in astonishment, and then I understood: Balthy had been leaving as we arrived.

She left a great deal of money for her sisters to share out in a friendly way without a will. She had suffered – she had cancer for several years. Sharp and proud, she defied the illness and took great care to conceal it. The blonde and attractive Béatrice Yturbe saw to it that her life was splendid. Her house was beautiful, her taste was sure, her relationships were stylish. She was openly scornful of my modest ways and resented the fact that my sober existence at Georges's side had saved me from her kind of life. She died on the crest of the wave, loved, spoilt, having just signed an engagement for the winter at the Apollo, which meant a great deal to her. She was in bed for two days, without suspecting that it was the end. Since her death, I met Pépé at Thérèse Diehl's. He threw himself weeping into my arms, weeping for his Louise who was never a bit nice to him. He loved her deeply, it was painful to see his grief. So now we have made it up, but I don't feel enthusiasm and Georges feels even less.

Lucien Guitry is dead. Sacha's grief really hurt me, the shock on Yvonne Printemps pretty face was striking. And then Lucien himself – he was magnificent, white, calm, imposing. I went to his funeral with Georges – it was there that I saw Balthy for the last time. She did not look at me. Her turn was coming, so near. I also saw Max Maurey and his wife Yvonne de Buffon. It awoke no feeling in me. Those are the people who are really dead, as far as I am concerned.

Poor Lucien Guitry was a tremendous eater, greedy, gluttonous. One evening after the theatre he had a supper of a hundred snails, twelve hard-boiled eggs, several slices of mutton, cheese, fruit and several glasses of beer. The next day he was laid up, very ill. He never got out of bed again. He died three weeks later. It seems that he often ate such suppers, for pleasure as well as to show off. 'There's nothing wrong with my appetite,' he used to say, laughing.

I had just got to Honfleur when Lewis telephoned me about Balthy's death. I had heard nothing. I was overcome and telephoned her sister Justine, a twitchy, bony little old woman of seventy-one. 'Justine, it's Liane, I'm appalled. Is there anything I can do to help?' – 'Yes,' replied Justine crisply, 'there is something you can do to help. You can send me some chocolates.' I almost dropped the telephone. I ordered 'la Marquise de Sevigné' to send her a bag of chocolates and enclosed a card with our condolences. That's Basques for you, a race apart!

....

September 2. One day we were lunching at the Ritz with Balthy and some friends when the Maharajah of Kapurthala went by without recognizing me. He wanted to carry me off to India in 1893. We were the same age. Rather annoyed, I said to the maître d'hotel: 'It's sad to grow old, Olivier. There's Kapurthala sitting opposite me and gazing at me, without remembering that once he wanted to marry me.' Olivier went over and whispered in his ear. Kapurthala got up and came over to greet me; I introduced my husband to him, he apologized and pretended that he had recognized me but hadn't dared to show it, then invited us to lunch at his pretty house on the Bois de Boulogne. It was charming, a lunch for twenty with two of his sons, some Egyptian princes, Turkish ministers, American mothers and daughters, etc. Perfect service, good meal, comfortable house. Nothing beautiful. I was on his Highness's right; we talked about our young days. He showed us his house. Two or three fine tiger-skins filled me with admiration and longing, which I expressed when we were drinking coffee alone with him on a little terrace overlooking the flower-garden. Two days later he sent me – a photograph of himself in a gold and silver frame! He is a childish sovereign, well-behaved and serious, more the slave of his ministers and the teachings of his religion than he is of the English. When we were walking along the well-raked paths of his little garden he said to me: 'The English don't like it if I come to France too often.' He has cut off the pigtail which used to crown his head when I first knew him, and has adopted European clothes. His accent is common, without charm or originality; he made me think of Ahmed who used to be our footman. He has vulgar tastes. Yet he is called on by the grandest and smartest people and his receptions are crowded. It will be a long time before Paris loses its taste for the exotic!

. . . .

September 7. I was telling Lucienne how, when the Tsar scolded the Grand Duke Constantine for using coarse language at table in front of the Tsarina, the children and the servants, the Grand Duke began clamouring for 'ches'. Baffled, everyone wondered what he wanted. What he wanted was *pea*ches! The Tsar saw red and Uncle Cogny had to leave the room . . . So, were those happy times? Not for me, flotsam stranded in Holy Russia, misled, seeking my true way. It seems to me nowadays that I wasn't truly myself; that only after Georges had entered my life did I rediscover my true self. I remember one day in Italy, at a circus somewhere, I was looking at myself very deeply in a little mirror. I did not recognize myself. Inside myself I asked: 'Is that you, is that really you, Marie?' I was there with some good-time people. I felt that at that precise moment I was denying myself and that my whole background was denying me. But I also felt a strong force pushing me forward. So I began to smile and chatter and fill myself with the belief that all was well, that I was having a lovely time, that I was destined for the most brilliant adventures, that neither Heaven nor the devil existed. There is nothing you can do against that force!

September 15. We have been told that silk will become very expensive this winter, so it's only prudent to lay in a stock. I have ruined myself: white crêpe de chine, black crêpe de chine, white and black satin-backed crêpe, white damask, cyclamen crêpe de chine. Let silk go up, I have nothing to fear. I have enough to dress well for two years.

September 21. Nasty little bits of gossip arrive from Paris. They are saying that I am kept by Madame R . . . That is the most dreadful lie. Georges and I don't deserve that! No one's life could be more proper than ours; it's almost saintly, people don't believe it because it's so very unusual.

When the engagement between Stanislas de La Rochefoucauld and the Roumanian artiste Alice Cocéa was announced, they said Cupid was paying back on France the trick played on Roumania by Georges Ghika when he married Liane de Pougy. All I can say is may they be as happy as we are, as tenderly close to each other in sorrow as well as in joy.

September 28. I'm reading some fine poems by Essenin in *le Figaro littéraire*. They bring that crazy Isadora Duncan to mind.

She wanted to 'procreate', if not with gods, at least with the most famous men of the age, the most intelligent in the world. About fifteen years ago she focused the full strength of her desire on the poet Henry Bataille. Yes – but Bataille was living with Berthe Bady! Fanatic that she was, she set about indoctrinating Bady: 'But darling, you must understand – no love or sentimentality, it's just the act I want, nothing more. Think of it, a child born to ME, by HIM – what a miracle! What a heritage to bequeath to humanity!' Bady was amused and agreed – having, anyway, an increasing reason not to be jealous. They agreed to meet in a beautiful Neuilly villa where Isadora happened to be staying. Disconcerted, weak and delicate, the highly strung, ironic Bataille took rather a long time to get going . . . Bady was called in. Bataille was beginning to rise to all this assembled good will when the party was interrupted by the sound of a key in the door: the arrival of a rich American who was supposed to be far away. Poor Bataille was shoved out onto the back stairs, clutching his clothes in his arms.

Came the war, Isadora made for Russia and set her heart on Essenin: a very free Russian-style marriage. She brought him to Paris. Nathalie captured the couple for one of her Fridays. Essenin recited his poems in Russian – she laughed when she told me about it because no one could understand a word but they all raved. From time to time he intoned 'Lou-pa-nar, sy-phi-lis'. Madame R gave them a lift home in her car. Two such irresistible forces could hardly meet without a thunderous din resulting in battles, struggles, separation.........

September 28. 'If I go down into myself and question my nature, what, o God, do I find? A mind full of uncertainty, always ready to go astray; inconstant affections; an inexplicable mixture of hopes and of vain fears; vicious inclinations; a mass of innumerable desires which agitate me and torment me without cease; sometimes a fugitive joy; usually a deep weariness; some sort of instinct for heaven and also for all the passions of the earth; a weak will which simultaneously wants and does not want; great pride in great poverty. Behold in this my condition as sin has formed it, and within myself I feel that I am powerless to raise a nature fallen so low.' I read this in my *Imitation* and I am sadly aware that it could be applied to me. There is some comfort in feeling that I am not the only one of my kind!

Paris – October 18 to December 2

October 18. At last! Here we are in our own home where we have been for eighteen days, having arrived at about midnight of September 30. No maid; in the hands of our concierge who is taking great trouble to see that we lack for nothing. The nest is charming! Now that it's transformed it gives the impression of being half of a quarter of a wing of a château. We still lack shutters and a maid. The fine white linen blinds embroidered with sayings which Nathalie gave me have been hung, delicate and transparent like my opaline glass – which I am beginning to go off. The stair-carpet is down; the lift functions; the telephone works. Everything is clean, light, blue, red, white and gold. Our shelves are beautifully tidy. In fact everything is fine except for the flu, which torments us both.

....

November 21. .... *Le Figaro littéraire* has devoted an issue to Courteline. I was much taken by an unpublished fragment of Boubouroche which someone found by chance in a café blotter: 'I am a bad adviser in matters of love because my way of understanding and practising love is rather special. No one in the world has loved more than I have; I have spent my life at it. When this little accident befalls me I play my part stoutly and I let things happen without doing anything to speed them up, *seeing that there is more delight in wanting a woman than in getting her, that a woman's power lies wholly in the desire you feel for her and that the intoxication of possession is always inferior to the dream one had of it.*' I underline the part which I feel and understand as a way of showing the opinion I share. The fever drops, the thing is seen for what it is and beauty is rare in this world ...

....

November 27. Lunch at Betsy Gautrat's with Nathalie. Archie had to leave very early, called to the Palais. We went to lie down on a big velvet divan in a Chinese room. The light was draped. Georges was on a low seat, smoking. Oh! such tender playfulness, such playful tenderness . . .

. . . .

1926

Paris, February 24. On Mardi Gras I had fifty-two people to a party! The day before I was feeling deathly. I was looking so ill that when I saw myself in a mirror I nearly fainted. My neighbour downstairs took pity on me and prepared a divan so that I could go down there for a rest if I collapsed. Well, on the day itself, in spite of my anxiety I stood up to it, I summoned up a cheerful greeting for my cheerful guests, I handed round innumerable pancakes, I talked to some, I introduced others, and from then on I have been going from strength to strength.

Pepito lent us marvellous Persian costumes: cloaks and head-dresses. Mine was bright red embroidered with gold, tall silver and gold hat embroidered and re-embroidered with emerald drops. Georges's was bright green braided with gold and sashed with violet, with a surcoat of deep pink fringed with gold. The Duchess came as Confucius: spectacles, mustaches, little pigtail, magnificent antique Chinese robe. Nathalie was a conquering hero – Attila, perhaps? – complete with embroideries and a sharp weapon, threatening and gruff, with a panther-skin slung nonchalantly over her glittering rags and a primitive little hat, rather Chinese. Madame Lucas was a Tunisian woman and relieved my tottering frailty of some of my tasks as hostess. Madame Beamish de Foras made a mysterious masked entrance in peasant costume with a basket on her arm containing two live ducks – her butler came in the car with her to take them back to the farmyard at Croizy. Betsy Gautrat was a Russian in pearl-embroidered red and a long veil hanging down behind, very beautiful. . . . . Margot, delicious in Nattier blue of about 1830, her mass of hair dressed à la Lawrence, mittens on her beautiful white hands. Madame Blanchon looked burly as an Apache in red and black; her friend Madame Renaud-Badet as his fancy girl in the same colours. They had prepared a little number with a leading dancing-master and performed twice, to tremendous applause, like two angels from the slums. Pepito came as a convalescent in a cyclamen dressing-gown of crackling silk, wearing odd stockings and slippers and a shirt with a pleated jabot ....

In fact it was a very successful party and everyone was thoroughly comfortable in our little living-room-turned-buffet – where the traditional pancakes made their mark, as well.

Saint-Germain-en-Laye – March 2 to March 24

March 2. Salomon Reinach left us here yesterday, in this nice little family pension, well within our means.

Our reconciliation with Max Jacob took place the day before yesterday: it was nice, and seemed to be sincere. The Duchess and Nathalie came to lunch and were charming to him. Nathalie made a conquest of him, looking after him at table, listening to him, strewing the precious pearls of her wit before him all the time. Max felt happy and celebrated, behaved well and we shall see him again.

March 24 .... They look after us well in this simple little place, it costs twenty-five francs a day, and the guests are an odd mixture. We are Roumanian; then there's a young Turkish woman who is recovering from anaemia. She is pretty and very young, not yet twenty: Georges has nicknamed her 'Albertine Imprisoned'. Then there's a really exquisite girl, my new little friend, Manon Thiébaut: an artist, trying to earn her living making woodcuts and drawings, and by illustrating pious books. She has wit, talent, easy manners, charm, wonderful eyes, beautiful tousled hair worn bobbed, a pale skin and an enchanting fragility which she has come here to cure. She shuts herself up to read and work and has hardly any appetite. She has been suffering badly from neurasthenia and is hardly over it yet. There is sympathy between us, we read the same books. I think we will see more of each other.

I have seen Lady M again, in bed just as she was when I left, under fine cambric loaded with fabulous embroidery and marvellous lace, a sheet worth seventeen thousand francs! When I raved about it she said she possessed them by the dozen!

I also saw my dear curé, Abbé Duchemin. He visited me here and yesterday I made my confession. So here I am, all tidied up. I like confessing to him. He's so good and gentle, so indulgent!

Paris – March 30 to May 14

March 30. . . . . Should I give thanks to heaven? Certainly it heaps me with physical ailments, but I think it has sent me a treasure, a friend: Marcelle Thiébaut, so full of kindness, wit, tact and courage. I love her already; she seems drawn to me. She has smiled on me, I have kissed her. She has had several affectionate impulses; I have had that of inviting her to spend the summer with us at Clos-Marie. She dreams of Roscoff, and we think of it greedily. These pages will reveal what comes of it . . .

. . . .

April 21. Letter from my dear Frédéric de Madrazzo who had invited us to visit him with the Tiny One. The Tiny One is Mademoiselle Marcelle Thiébaut, also known as Manon. As far as I'm concerned she is my Tiny One.

Tiny One wanted to paint on glass, and it's not easy. Joujou (Frédéric) has done it and at my request he was going to show her the technique; and Joujou picked that day to be somewhere quite else!

. . . .

Roscoff – Clos-Marie, June 2 to November 3

June 2. Tiny One arrived yesterday evening in torrential rain. Luckily an omnibus which plies to and from the station brought her up to the house, together with Georges who had gone to pick her up. Tiny One is enchanted with what she saw of Brittany out of the window of the train, with her arrival in Roscoff, with the Clos, with the drawing-room, with the bedrooms, etc. She went to sleep peacefully after a nice little supper which she ate sitting on my bed.

At about five in the morning the elements broke loose, the wind began to blow so violently that it shook our beds and the whole house, the rain became fierce enough to break windows, the sea roared. Towards six o'clock I ventured into her bedroom, wanting to reassure her – and woke up poor Tiny One who was sleeping soundly and who said at once: 'Oh how good it is to be here, what a marvellous storm!' Then she jumped out of bed and went to open her shutters, knocking over her letter-rack, her books, an ashtray – crying out 'How beautiful! How beautiful!'

Her little head must contain the most powerful forces, for her arrival to have put the elements in such a rage! Today we are far from the 'pearly sea-shell'; it's more like a copper kettle boiling over. Houses have been flooded, roads are under water, the wind is blowing skirts and umbrellas inside out.

Tiny One is here with her beautiful eyes and her friendship. It's a joy sent us from Heaven.

June 4. I have flu. One can't help exposing oneself to draughts while tidying, and my age makes me ultra-susceptible.

Tiny One continues to smile on everything. Her happy looks are our thanks. She has made a conquest of the whole household and the neighbours too. She understands how to look at our great landscape, how to feel things, how to appreciate the delights of comfort. She is unimaginably small, but beautifully built. I fuss over her and she allows it. Everything is going very well. She reads a lot. So do I. I have just read *Morvagine* by Blaise Cendrars. It's hellish! Today's taste for gloomy writing. People like horrors, they relish them. Cendrars has a powerful talent; he emerges splendidly out of the slough in which Aragon wallows so grossly. They made such a to-do over Zola's realism! These people leave it behind by miles. Even Cendrars's evident and moving talent can't make me like this kind of thing. Against my beloved landscape's infinity and in this fresh air the animality displayed in these squalid and deplorable offerings doesn't work.

June 8. The anniversary of our marriage. Sixteen years – and the bond has become closer. We have been kneaded and blended into one.

Yesterday Georges went to Saint-Pol to find me thousands of treats and collect – at last! – the fifteen thousand francs his mother has been promising since April. As soon as he left me I was racked by the most frightful anxiety; my nerves were on edge, I kept having the most gloomy presentiments. We went to meet him, darling Tiny One, Camille and I, and as soon as I saw him in the middle of the road my balance was restored. Thank you, God! I believe we are closer to each other than twins. Sixteen years! The dear sweet work of sixteen years! Even the rages which rumbled inside me and afterwards threw me panting into his arms, pinning us cruelly together; even the little secret tricks each of us had practised out of pity for the other's weakness or sensibility: all these miseries of human existence, all this space shared in the same atmosphere, the same pleasures, the same desires, the same tears in face of the same hopes, all of this lit by the most luminous sincerity. Yes, we really are embodied in each other. I offer thanks yet again, o God, for all the frail yet genuine happiness which this morning I can feel behind my dejection and which is swelling my heart with tenderness. I submit myself to these sweet familiar pleasures which bring me nearer to God and distance me from the world, because to some extent that is the consequence of our long days of solitude. Georges my husband, my love, my all, I bless you.

June 9. Yesterday passed pleasantly, except that I felt vaguely uneasy all the time. Rain, stormy weather, tiredness. I have let my diet slip: lobster, chicken, chocolate soufflé and champagne have all made their appearance on our table.

I have had a friendly letter from Cécile Sorel, now Comtesse de Ségur. It arrived aptly for our sixteenth wedding anniversary. I had congratulated her on exchanging her queenly crown for that of a countess, all for love. Guillaume de Ségur has been her lover for years and years. He is at least twenty years younger than she is. She hesitated; when we last met I gave her encouragement by our example, so she says in her letter. May Heaven protect them and preserve them in a state of grace!

We went round to our nice little Boignaus to hear Reynaldo Hahn on the gramophone. I was disappointed. I didn't recognize his lovely, arresting voice, warm and slightly husky. Perhaps its rhythms and easiness were there, but the machine's hard metallic resonance suppressed the charm and musicality and added touches of vulgarity. A wonderful invention all the same, but still a long way from perfection.

....

June 16. Yesterday Tiny One went in to Saint-Pol with Camille. They saw everything and did masses of shopping for me. They came home on foot in pouring rain, enchanted by it. Tiny One thinks the whole country is superb and Saint-Pol is beautiful, with a great deal of character. Tiny One knows how to see and how to feel. Her soul is as ready to see and understand as are her magnificent eyes.........

June 18. Sorted my old papers and family bits and pieces. At home at rue Saussure I have a few old portraits: Grandfather Lopez, his wife née de Montessuy, her mother Madame de Montessuy née d'Arey, Madame d'Arey née de Ruys and Madame de Ruys née Embito. There's a paper concerning the last after she had become the wife of Hyppolyte Thomas Marie d'Arey, affirming that in the terrible year 1793 (the second year of the Republic) she had not emigrated and had paid her patriotic contributions, etc. That paper can have been no joke and must have frightened the good woman and made her get rid of her title by marrying a little magistrate from Rennes, Monsieur Delacour, whom Maman could remember from her early childhood. Leafing through these papers I noticed that during the years of the revolution this former Mademoiselle de Ruys who had married a d'Arey wrote her name as one word: Delacour. Soon afterwards she retrieved her 'de' – de Lacour; and later still she made three words of it: de la Cour! ....

These, my old family papers, are my title deed to possession of my Brittany, and also of a few fine feelings, principles and prejudices. I inherit the utmost frankness from all these proud Bretons, and I have the faults which go with it.........

June 20. The weather is trying to be fine; can it bring it off? They are saying that it's the waves transmitted from the TSF which have caused all this rain.

My little Thiébaut is charming, her mind is so open, so broad, so subtle. And such pretty manners into the bargain. She is gentle and authoritative at the same time. She is perfectly well-bred. Every day she thanks us for having her. She works away at her little wood- or lino-cuts, her painting and drawing, for three or four hours every day. She has quite a few orders, and they are repeating. Her work is good, clear, witty, enjoyable.

June 22. Letter from Max Jacob. I think he wants to come here in July. And I think turning a deaf ear is the best thing to do. I am neither strong nor patient. Max's presence is a gruelling test which I always fail sooner or later.

. . . .

June 27. The local people arranged a pilgrimage to Lourdes. All Brittany went on it. The sister of my cook, Marie, took part. She prayed for me and asked that what I wished for should be accomplished. She came back yesterday, and no later than that same evening I had a telegram from an agency saying: 'Have found firm purchaser who sees solicitor tomorrow, drop all negotiations.' A little miracle! Coincidence, a sceptic would say, but I prefer to believe in miracles. Is not every person's existence a miracle in itself?

. . . .

July 4. Georges loves Tiny One! Tiny One loves Georges! Crack, it has happened! Is it worse than cancer?

Georges admitted it this morning, then Tiny One was summoned and came in very white.

I have been saying to myself for a long time that something was bound to happen. Georges is so much younger than I am, he has given me eighteen years of happiness . . . I must think! It's a very banal situation, after all. I don't want to make a grand tragedy of it, and anyway love carries the day. If it is a true love it will bend us to its laws. If it's a passing fancy it will pass. Yes, but . . . my nature is a difficult one. I don't yet know how I'm going to react and how I'll behave to them or to myself. Tiny One is adorable, well-bred, very intelligent, has lovely eyes, a young body. She has neither health nor money! Perhaps she is a bit of a schemer? Georges is hooked, but he insists that he adores me and can't do without me. My great, splendid, complete, pure happiness is over.

July 5. I am going to put this notebook away for a while. Georges has left me. He went away with Mademoiselle Thiébaut yesterday morning and here I am quite alone with the ocean and my disaster. I have not yet shed a single tear. Eighteen years of magnificent happiness have brought me to a quite atrocious resignation.

July 10. My god-daughter Margot de La Bigne has come. I leave with her for Paris on Wednesday the 14th, to start another life. To make use of my life! That is all I ask.

Liane put her journal aside for three months after her husband left her. When she returned to Roscoff in September she took it up again, starting by summarizing the events which followed his departure.

September 23. After a great deal of coming and going, packing and unpacking, here I am back at Clos-Marie. Here I am back with Camille and with a friend called Mimy Franchetti, an adorable young Italian who was brought to me by Nathalie and has been my consolation.

October 8. I thought I would die . . . I was unable to sleep, I was taking far too many drugs in order to get two or three hours of sleep a night. Here I have rediscovered everything, peace and natural sleep. Basically it has all been a deliverance.

Ought I to describe it all? Why not?

On July 4, curtains drawn on the appalling day that was about to start, I heard footsteps in my bedroom. I opened my eyes and could just make out my husband's silhouette in the duskiness, standing by my bed. Only half awake I said: 'Georges? Is that you?' – 'Yes, my darling. Have you slept well?' He got into bed with me, took me in his arms, covered me with kisses and said in a rather strangled voice: 'Listen, I've got a confession to make.' Accustomed as I was to him as the being from whom all sweetness came, I imagined some clumsiness; yes, the only thought to enter my head was that he had broken one of my ornaments, a piece of opaline perhaps. I smiled and said 'Confess!' Then he began mumbling that he couldn't do without me, that he adored me, that he would kill himself an hour after I died, but that he couldn't do without Tiny One. I didn't want to understand. I stammered: 'But Tiny One is here, you have got her.' – 'No,' he said, 'but I shall have her. I've got to. I've never deceived you, I want to tell you everything. Yesterday evening we kissed for the first time, we told each other of our love. The child loves me as I love her. I'm a bit old for her, but she doesn't mind. If you agree, nothing need change. The three of us can live together. I can't be happy with you and without her, or with her and without you.' My whole body began to tremble. I said to him: 'But you are murdering me. It's appalling, get out of my bed.' He hugged me tighter. 'But I adore you. You'll see, you'll have two people to adore you instead of just one. We'll cherish you, we'll take care of you, we'll make you so happy. She's mad about you – she'll obey you, you will always be the mistress, the queen. She will take second place, she will submit to you. I have told her all that and she has accepted it. Everything will go on as it is now except that I will go to her at night. No one will know anything about it, not even the maids or Madame Garat.' I prayed to God, with open hands I said to Him: 'Let Your will be done, oh God! Make me say what You want me to say. Help me, Saint Anne! This is the worst blow fate could give me. Don't let me cry like a fool, don't let me faint, but I wouldn't mind dying. Protect me!' Georges went on: 'You'll see, we'll be gay and happy. In Paris she can sleep in my bedroom and I can have the little divan in the dressing-room. During the day it can go in your big cupboard.' – 'Get up,' I said, because I didn't want him to feel me trembling. 'I have got to think. I have got to go away and think without hate or anger or torment. I shall go away with Camille for a week, somewhere far away from here, from you two, and then I shall tell you what we are going to do.' – 'If you leave,' he said, getting up at last, 'if you leave I shall hate her. I'm going to bring her in. She is waiting. Neither of us has slept all night.'

October 9. Then Manon came in, pale and trembling, trying to look me in the face. She threw herself into my arms as though to kiss me. I pushed her away gently and said: 'Do you love my husband?' She cried out: 'I love you both! I'll do what you say. I'll kill myself if I must.' I replied: 'That's beside the point. I see now that you're both mad, I'm the only grown-up here. I am going to think this over, somewhere far away from you. I shall leave.' Then Georges began again: 'If you leave I shall hate her.' This annoyed the girl, who sat down opposite my bed and said. 'No, I'm the one who will leave.' I made up my mind: 'Yes, Mademoiselle, that in fact is the best thing you can do. It is better that I should be the one to stay in my own family house. Go, I accept that you go. Madame Garat will fetch your trunk down. Go to your room.' Georges, furious: 'If you drive her away, I will follow her.' Me, calmed by the decision made and the completeness of the renunciation: 'I am not driving her. Mademoiselle Thiébaut says herself that she would like to leave, I accept. As for you, YOU HAVE GONE ALREADY!'

They brought me up my breakfast. Making a great effort, I ate it, then I gave the cook her orders. I got up and dressed. Rigid and tense, I simply tried to get through the activities of every day. Then I went into Mademoiselle Thiébaut's bedroom where the trunk was not yet packed. Her expression had changed. She had lost her child-like look and seemed ill-natured, older, formidable, evidently on the defensive. Yet for her this was the moment of triumph.

Georges was packing her small case. Having filled it he was bringing her things which she put into the trunk as I watched. I said: 'Don't keep my husband up too late. Don't make him drink or smoke; he is delicate, he needs a lot of looking after – and so do you.' Then I said: 'It's quite natural, if he loves you he'll have to follow you. You would have a frightful life with me. You have to consider my temperament: I am not dissolute, and then I have a violent nature. I would probably make your life quite impossible. Where will you go?' Georges – yellow, rattled, incoherent – muttered something about Brest or Morlaix. I advised; 'Paris would be better, it's the easiest place to hide in. Or why not Roumania? Life would be easier for you there.' Georges's eyes were pinpoints. He seemed to be suppressing a frightful rage. In all the eighteen years of our life together I never saw him look like that, but it's only like that that I see him now. I have lost the memory of all his other faces.

I saw that they wanted to gain time, so I said: 'I'm going, I'll go out and leave you alone. Georges, give me all the keys and put labels on them to help me in all the chores which I shall now have to do by myself. Give me my passport and my resident's permit. Go to the lawyer here and get me a power of attorney so that I can sell the two houses in Saint-Germain without you (we were well advanced in serious negotiations about them). When you are in Paris go to my lawyer, Maître Collet. Tell him everything and ask him to look after me. From now on you must write to me at his address, only to that address and only about business.' He said with difficulty: 'I have got sixty-five English pounds of yours. I'll get them for you.' I refused; 'Keep them! You are going away with a woman, you will need money.' He accepted and I went downstairs calling out: 'Goodbye! Be happy, if you are able to build your happiness on my distress!'

They left. The girl said to Camille: 'The worst of it all is that now the Princess will never believe how much I love her. Because I do love her.' – 'What do you mean?' said Madame Garat. 'She won't doubt it for a moment. Look how well you are proving it!'

October 11. At the age of eighteen I had a husband and a child. At that age I ran away from it all, driven by a fatal destiny.

Up to the age of eighteen: family, principles, routine and gentleness. From eighteen to thirty-six (another eighteen years) I lived in turmoil and among passions – every kind – either experienced or endured. I learnt to know the world, a sad distinction. At thirty-six I met Georges. And now, after another eighteen years, my life is renewed. Now I am alone and free, purified by that long period of duty, tenderness and trust. Alone and free: proud words, let them be my rule and my message. Alone, I will draw nearer to You, oh my God. There lies my longing and my will.

And yet . . . close by, under my roof, just opposite my bedroom door, there sleeps the most beautiful, the most ardent, the most seductive of women. Is it one more test? Is it consolation?

October 12. We have cleaned out the cistern, we have checked the roof. The garden has been tidied up. All the rites governing life are going smoothly, both within me and around me. More smoothly than before, yes, more easily, more gracefully and naturally than when he was here. Georges is a hostile person, clumsy and ill-natured. Stupid and without principles. One has to face it, he was a brute! I knew it, but I believed he was loyal, bound and attached to me with the full force of his evil nature.

The day after he left – it was a compensation from Heaven – every trace of my rheumatism suddenly vanished; every pain in my body fled away. Nervous shock, said the surprised doctors. I felt refreshed and rejuvenated and everyone said as much, both here and there: 'You are looking so young and beautiful' – I, who thought I would die!

October 14. I shall write to my husband through my lawyer, suggesting that he asks for a divorce. 'The Princess cannot do it except by the formality of making a confession, but she can submit to it and it would relieve her of a difficult situation which, although it was brought about by you, can hardly be agreeable to you either. The Princess is constantly in need of signatures and authorizations which still have to be given by you. For example, on the eve of her journey abroad last summer she almost failed to be granted a visa, lacking your permission. She was forced to renounce the opportunity to make a film, which would have given her an interesting and profitable occupation, for the reason that she did not want to depend on your consent.'

How much more freely I would breathe! How much less heavy

my burden would become! I am constantly afraid of what my assassin may do; even, and especially, that he may come back.

October 16. This morning we are driving to Morlaix to spend the day, Camille, Mimy and I – because I have a little Mimy in my life.

Mimy followed me, led by friendship, drawn by my grief. She followed me, ardent, passionate, true and beautiful – oh, so beautiful! Mimy never leaves me by day or by night. She is here with her fervent and splendid soul, her fierce Italian love.

My husband is in correspondence with Maître Collet, to whom he writes false and insinuating things such as: 'Do everything you possibly can, dear Maître, to help my wife, of whom I never stop thinking with immense grief.' Then: 'If my wife considers our separation to be final – something which I am unable to believe (!) – I ask that she send me all the letters I received from her, which are in a casket together with all her photographs.' – And then this: 'You hold my will, which is in my wife's favour. It will remain so. Be good enough to attach this letter to it in confirmation.'

Nathalie Barney flew to my side as soon as she heard of my arrival at Margot's little flat at 91 boulevard Malesherbes. She knew Eugène Thiébaut, a former diplomat at Washington, who was Manon's uncle. Nathalie brought him to see me. He showed me a letter dated July 6 in which Manon asked him to let her family know of her 'departure with Prince Ghika for abroad, and for many long years.' She had no doubts about it, but she did add that she was very sorry for the distress which she was about to cause her family, and for ruining Princess Ghika's life. At bottom the Thiébauts are divided between shame and the wish to see their Manon become Princess Georges Ghika as soon as possible. As for the Ghikas, they must certainly be satisfied at our separation, but worried about what that idiot Georges is getting up to now! At twenty he wanted to kill himself for Ventura (of the Comédie-Française); at twenty-six he married Liane de Pougy! Now, at forty-two, he lets himself be abducted by a little schemer. All this is likely to cost money, and Georges has none. I have my little income; while he was with me he fell into neither debt nor folly.

October 17. By dint of putting rouge on my cheeks and listening when they tell me I am beautiful and rejuvenated, shall I end by forgetting the burden laid on my heart by life?

October 18. I have Mimy. It happened like this: during the summer Nathalie wrote me a line saying that she was in love, madly in love with a woman, and that this love outstripped all her other loves by a long way. Rather vexed, I answered: 'The best in your life was me! Me! Me!'

As soon as I arrived in Paris, in Margot's charming little flat, I called Nathalie who came to me, affectionate and approving: 'You have done the right thing, Liane, I am so glad. You must keep it up . . .' She held me in her arms, listened, advised, sent flowers, took me to the Duchess's, showed me the sweetest and most compassionate tenderness. My friends rallied round, adorable to me and indignant at Prince Ghika, saying: 'It's abominable! How could he fall so low! You were his whole truth. He will be sorry – but don't ever take him back! He was such a bore; he got on everyone's nerves; he diminished you.' I heard endless versions of this. In short I was made much of, comforted, smothered in flowers, almost celebrated. Jean Cocteau came, very shocked, to pour out calming words, floods of healing poetry with which to express my agony. As he will also come, I hope, to sing my deliverance.

October 19. My little Margot offered me a room and a bathroom in her new apartment at 15 rue Verniquet, and it was a life-raft. I accepted with affection and enthusiasm. Camille had a little mattress in the bathroom. She never left me, my faithful newfoundland, devoted, alert, rather crusty, a little bit mangy, but mine come what may with all her loyalty and love.

And Nathalie was there. I – who am so scared of her thunder and also so afraid of doing her the least harm because through it all I love her deeply – this is what I did or rather had done to me, because nothing was started by me except a loyal and determined struggle in which I was defeated because Mimy, my Mimy is here, she's asleep in the room next to mine as I write these words and I shall soon be going in to kiss her awake.

Nathalie, sitting by my bed one day: 'Liane, the one I love is waiting outside. You are so beautiful, you have been so great, so admirable, may I bring her in to see you for a moment so that she can contemplate you, so that you can see her?' – 'Yes,' I said without much interest. 'Bring her in, go and fetch her.' And in she came, tall, slender, white as a magnolia flower, her enchanting gestures so graceful, small, rare, precise, fiery eyes, an almost unreal fineness. She bent over me, over my cruel suffering.

Nathalie smiled. It was Nathalie herself who prepared her own fate.

We talked. I told my pitiful story for Mimy. She didn't say a great deal. Nathalie wanted them both to carry me off to the country. I refused, overcome by weariness. They left me. But did they really leave me? Two minutes later a bunch of fresh roses was brought in which they had left for me at once, before going right away.

October 20. They came back. It was in the middle of the night. I awoke to hear Nathalie's voice calling me. Camille went to open the door. It was her, then Mimy with a violinist friend of theirs, Pola (who was a pupil of Sarasate). It was like a lovely dream. Nathalie on one side, stroking and caressing me; Mimy on the other, her lips on mine; Pola playing for us in the next room . . .

They came back – often. They made much of me, they took me out, they dressed my wounds. Mimy and I loved each other. Her presence was my heaven of joy and forgetfulness.

Nathalie became jealous. Nathalie loves in her own way. She wants her friends to be happy up to a certain point. She is dissolute; she adores directing love's revels, leading them on, halting them, starting them up again. What she loves is bodies, and reactions. We ran through the whole gamut – but Mimy loved me and I found her adorable.

October 21. Before I left for Deauville with Margot and Camille I decided to end things, avoid goodbyes, behave as though I were indifferent.

I arrived at the Normandy and I had not yet taken off my hat when I saw Mimy's maid pop up in front of me with a note from Mimy telling me that she was there, loving me and waiting for me. I stamped my foot in a moment of rage at my courage being wasted like that; then, with my heart leaping, I followed Suzanne and fell straight into the arms of Mimy: a tired Mimy, a Mimy in bed, a Mimy who loved me and wanted me and pursued me.

October 22. In joyful gratitude for this fresh dawn which illuminates my awakening, I want to record here my forgiveness: I forgive Georges, and Manon. They have gone right away, they are dead to me. They have suffered their fate – the fate they chose and which they deserve. This morning, oh Destiny, I accept you with the utmost submission. I forgive. And you, my Heaven-sent love to whom I open my arms, will make me forget.

October 23. Clos-Marie is no longer mine: I have just leased it for eighteen years to my Mimy, to the adorable woman who has shown me that I can still be loved – oh joy! – and still love – oh happiness! She is beautiful and vital, fervent, subtle and fine, amusing and gay. She brings together every one of Heaven's gifts. She is charm itself. She laughs, and everything around her becomes joyful. She walks, and the dance of her graceful body dazzles those who watch. She speaks: her voice is serious and soft, arresting, a little husky. She sings: one is conquered to the very depths of one's being by the warm, velvety, harmonious, enveloping timbre. She is tall – the tiniest bit taller than I – fine boned. She has the prettiest gestures. She is white, her eyes gleam, a greenish hazel, her eyelashes throw shadows, her eyebrows are delicate. Tiny blue veins are visible under the transparancy of the skin on her face and neck, on her body too. She has the most ravishing legs in the whole world, long, with amazingly delicate joints.

October 25. Mimy's love is ardent, impassioned, whole, jealous. Love in the Italian style! It sings, it shouts, it howls in keeping with her beauty, her gestures, her fiery glance. Mimy is a creature of excess.

We stay in bed late of a morning; we have breakfast; we tease; we laugh; we kiss. We open our letters. She gives me an Italian lesson: verbs, vocabulary, dictation, translation. We have a very good time. She sings me the blues, which I adore, or else Italian songs, in her deep, vibrant voice. We separate, then meet again on the little rock-beach. Mimy hunts for pebbles. She loves stones and discovers marvellous ones with bright colours and unusual shapes. We trim the shrubs in the garden. We go into the town. Everyone loves my Mimy, everyone smiles at her and gives her flowers. We take heaps and heaps of photographs. We come home again and Mimy plays the gramophone. She opens a book: D'Annunzio's poems or the stories of Mark Twain. I read too. Time passes so quickly. Everyone is amazed by my cheerful face, suddenly so much younger. They all say to me: 'Your expression has changed. Monsieur le Prince never used to laugh, you used to look as though you were bored.' It was true, yet I thought I possessed a marvellous treasure!

Sometimes we have quarrels: Mimy has already accumulated so many memories! Me too. We tell each other – and that's a mistake. The one who is listening suffers and becomes angry.

October 26. *Comœdia* have asked me how much I would want for my memoirs. I've turned them down.

October 27. I have written to Eugène Thiébaut, Manon's uncle. He answered that his niece had spent the whole summer with my husband's mother.

By the same post I had a letter from the lawyer warning me that my husband had given him a new address in Switzerland and that no doubt he would be coming to Paris, which would simplify the divorce. I am thinking of Moro-Giafferi for my advocate. I shall need the best!

To return to Mimy and her determined amorous pursuit. When I got back from Deauville I tried to escape yet again. I refused to sleep with her. That was when I accepted an invitation to spend two days with Madame R at her château. There again Mimy turned up, arriving with Nathalie at eleven o'clock in the evening simply in order to see me, kiss me and tell me: 'We are at Barbizon, we will sleep there and tomorrow we will come for you and drive you back to Paris.'

The next day I saw Nathalie who overwhelmed me with reproaches to start with, then cradled me in tenderness. Mimy took me out to dinner in Montparnasse. We came home, and all veils were rent asunder. We abandoned ourselves without remorse and without restraint to the delirium of our love. Days went by in sweetness and tumult.

We packed our bags for Venice, Margot, Camille and I. Lolo (Margot's friend Monsieur Lopez) and his family went on ahead. I had trouble with my passport and was almost stuck for lack of my husband's authorization, but finally my lawyer managed to get the necessary visa and stamps.

I departed, leaving my Mimy breathless and Nathalie full of hope. So there I was in Venice. My room at the Grand Hotel – a pretty double bedroom on the corner of the Grand Canal, with an enchanting bathroom – was perfumed with carnations. I stayed six days. Mimy was impatient, hatching plans, hunting for her passport which Nathalie had pinched and hidden. We went back and forth between the Lido and the Grand Hotel. I met friends: handsome little Pierre Meyer (son of the proprietor of 'Old England') and his lot. There was much talk about the Lido and sun-bathing. Pierre had a cabin on the famous beach. It was because he invited me that we were there every day, Margot, Camille and I in pyjamas! We lunched at the little restaurant underneath the Excelsior where they accepted pyjama-clad and partly-pyjama-clad people. Camille, sitting with us at Pierre's big table, had an English neighbour who wore nothing but his pyjama tops, giving his naked thighs a look at the summer weather which caused his red hairs to stand on end in astonishment.

I met Bernstein, who came to offer me compassionate condolences; Guillot de Saix who did a drawing of my profile which appeared in *Comœdia*; Baroness de Meyer, the Lioness of the Lido; Kapurthala; de Meyer's friend the Prince of Prussia. I said to Pierre 'You mustn't introduce me to the Prince of Prussia. I don't mind that he's a pederast, but I can't forget that my son was killed in the war.' – 'Oh Liane,' said Pierre, 'the war's gone quite out of fashion, we don't think about it any more.'

The days went by very cheerfully with this crazy group of young inverts, all quite unrestrained in their behaviour, displaying their vice with the greatest nonchalance. When I got back to the hotel I would feel rather disgusted. My life felt empty of meaning, stupid, hectic. In the daytime we laughed a lot at the thought of my husband's expression if he could see the three of us dressed in his finest pyjamas!

October 28. The Lido was madly crowded; cabins became drawing-rooms, arranged like the most mysterious of opium dens: cushions, mattresses, divans, embroideries, scent. Skins were oiled with rare and precious substances, people walked about naked or nearly so, took the sun, the air, the water, dried themselves, smoked, drank, loved. It was relaxation, a break in the year's complications. Beautiful bodies displayed themselves proudly: our Pierre's was marvellous. It was all for the sake of tanning, that was the pretext and the excuse! At lunch the women, more coquettish, looked as though they were acting in a fairy-tale: Schéhérazade, Salomé, Salammbô – oriental ladies from rich harems. They went by in sumptuous pyjamas of silk or figured velvet, brilliantly coloured, glittering with sequins and stones. Fantasy reigned, at its wildest.

There was a big fancy-dress ball. That evening all my Lido friends came to have dinner at my hotel. I was starting bronchitis. I had a temperature, but I enjoyed my little party all the same.

October 29. The whole happy – and depraved – band came up to my room to make themselves up before leaving for the ball. The handsomest, as always, was Pierre Meyer dressed as a Scot in a delicious little kilt, with his bare bronze legs, his cheerful boyish face and his great height. One couple (!) went as pierrots with pink roses in their mouths. Antoine, the hairdresser, was a superb Byzantine empress followed by his heart's beloved dressed as a Chinaman. Antoine had a gilded gondola decked with lights and flowers and filled with musicians. Antoine is rich. He has the taste of the sculptor he used to be and all the audacity of the pervert he is. His gondola carried Margot and her court to the Fenice. César Mauge de Houcke was in midnight blue, a dress which was once Lady Abdy's, and was very proud that the pretty lady's shoes fitted him. Rheims was a Neapolitan in pink and white. Guillot de Saix looked much as he usually does as Alfred de Musset. Having a beard, he always adopts this easy disguise. Monsieur de la Pena collapsed under the weight of a rich and heavy costume which made him look like an exhausted old Shylock. Everyone apart from him was laughing, joking, singing, dancing. They wanted me with them and tried to drag me along. I was stoic. They were all very full of the young inheritor of the Italian crown whose presence was going to give lustre to this charity ball. They told me that Antoine made the greatest sensation. We – he and I – were honoured by *Comœdia*. Yes, they wrote as though I had been at the dance, and one of the most beautiful there. They even published a drawing of me lying on my bed, which Guillot de Saix had made during the evening. I look like a queen reclining carelessly on her litter. I said to myself: if Georges sees this in Roumania he's going to think that my efforts to take my mind off stop at nothing!

Two days later I left Venice, and hardly was I in the train before my temperature shot up. My companions didn't know what to do. I had the courage to carry on as far as Lausanne. There we left the train at dawn and I was put into the Royal Hotel. A doctor was called who diagnosed congestion in both lungs. Margot sent a telegram to my Mimy who answered at once: 'Will be in Lausanne today all love.' The darling! So Lolo, who had to be in Paris urgently, was able to continue his journey after finding a flat for me and my friends, paying for it and leaving me some money. Margot was ready to stay with me but I know how crazy she is about her Lolo and how she needs him, so I insisted absolutely that she should go with him. I was getting better. Stuffed with drugs and shattered by that frightful journey, I plunged into sleep and my body's natural defences did the rest. When Nathalie came into my room next morning, followed by Mimy, they found me so far on the road to recovery that – although Mimy dared to rejoice – Nathalie was quite cross with me for not being dead after upsetting them with such an alarming telegram.

I had to stay at Lausanne for five days. Meanwhile Nathalie sent to Paris for her car, her smooth, shiny, silent, Buick; and after entrusting Camille to the express and her own resources, Nathalie, Mimy and my almost recovered self set off.

The first stage was as far as Thonon. The Hôtel du Parc welcomed us agreeably: two nice communicating rooms, one with two beds, sharing a bathroom. That was how we lived for five days. We covered 1,500 kilometres, laughing, singing and – Mimy and I – loving. We restrained our love in order not to give too much pain to Nathalie who began to torment me with the most bitter reproaches, really absurd, and to make the most unexpected suggestions: 'Do this to her, not that; give her this and not that.' I told her: 'Nathalie, I am me. It was you who brought her to me and threw her into my arms. Instead of frivolity and naughtiness, what happened was the birth of feelings which both of us need.'

October 30. One evening we slept at Bourg. Still Mimy in the double room chosen by Nathalie and me next door in the little single room as though I were their daughter. Although we did try very hard, Mimy and I ended by joining each other. She made me laugh so much when she said plaintively: 'Since when have mothers-in-law insisted on travelling with young couples?' We were cruel in the way we let ourselves go. All day in the car we held hands, our lips met.

November 1. We left for Roscoff like two children going on holiday. Nathalie left for the South of France. She must have been furious with me.

When I and my burden came into Mimy's life she reached out to offer me help. She sensed the truth of my grief and my life. She loved me, she still loves me. It cannot last – nothing lasts. But it's so beautiful, so simple, so complete. Perhaps this morning, when my kiss wakes her, I shall feel that her love has vanished during the night . . . I am alert for anything, I clutch at nothing, I let myself drift. I pay attention only to the present, I let the minutes run through my fingers and see only the last of them. Grace is refused me. I love Mimy, but whether she stays or whether she goes my love will not be transposed. She is there and she is not there. I hold

'Georges, la Lolotte and me on St Thegonnec's calvary at Finisterre.' The date is 1910, the year of their marriage.

The living-room at Clos-Marie, Roscoff.

Mimy Franchetti, bringer of timely consolation.

Natalie Barney,
sometimes called 'Flossie' and
sometimes 'Harmony'.

Manon Thiébaut, nicknamed 'the Tiny One'.

Top: Salomon Reinach (*left*) and Jean Lorrain.

Bottom: Prince and Princess Georges Ghika, in 1932

her and I can't feel her. I hold her and I see her going. I believe in her love and already I'm sacrificing it. When she tells me 'Always', it is I who want to leave as the word is uttered. When I answer 'We will never part' I feel the wish to disappear for ever, to flee without looking back. I don't really know what I want; I don't really know what I feel. If I spend an hour apart from her I truly believe that it will be for ever. Georges killed all the trust in me, even trust in myself. I say to the Lord: 'My God, it is You I love, it is You I want to serve, it is You I want to find! I do not live according to Your law, but what am I to do? I deliver myself utterly into Your hands. Tear out that which displeases You, make me what You would have me be.'

November 2. Collet wrote to Georges about divorce proceedings to be taken out against him and at the instigation, more or less, of both parties. He had revised my draft because he said my husband could not ask for a divorce on the grounds of his own errors. Prince Ghika's response stunned me! He declared that he was not envisaging divorce, that he failed to understand the difficulties created for me by my present situation, and that he acknowledged yet again all the wrong he had done me. Never shall I understand that creature. Never did I understand him. I see things straight and distinct and clear; he is obscure and tortuous.........

The idea of Georges in Paris is not a pleasant one. Meeting him would be disagreeable and useless. That little viper wrote to her uncle: 'Abroad, and for many long years.' What can have happened to make them change their minds?

November 3. Mimy has the flu but we are going ahead with our preparations to leave on Friday. I like the idea of taking action, pushing on ahead, tackling seriously this divorce which will free me completely. A sad freedom which I never foresaw, but still a deliverance! ....

I am very resolute, very calm, I shall even go to the conciliation interview. I hope I don't meet my husband there.

November 4. I have Moro-Giafferi as advocate. He is the champion of champions and he will deal with my case himself.

We are packing. Mimy is exquisite, easy and tender. Our intimacy is going to be somewhat interrupted.

Paris – November 7 to November 24

November 7. Here I am installed with my Uncle and Aunt Burguet; Mimy has gone home to 44 rue du Bac, feeling ill with a bronchial infection which she thinks has been building up for some days. Away from her and her charm I breathe better, I feel more myself. I think more freely, I live more healthily. Mimy never stops smoking, loves sauces, rich cakes, staying in bed, making scenes, reading funny magazines, running down her friends. She is fanciful, bossy, wounding, inconsistent. She is a conquest-maker. She loves me, but she indulges in a lot of little affectations which don't, in fact, conceal much. I have to say all this in order to recover my freedom of thought and action; and I am able to say it because I am clear-sighted and at present am incapable of a great love or even of a serious infatuation.

November 15. The most frightful things are going on! Georges demands that I should forgive him and says that if I don't take him back there is nothing left for him but death. So that is what the little schemer has reduced him to. I sent my answer to Madame Morel by Mimy. 'There's nothing left to hope for. I am going on with my divorce.' I see Maître Moro-Giafferi every day. I am not a good Christian but I have been brave in my renunciation, oh God, I have given myself over entirely to Your will. Come to my aid. I say today, as I did then: 'Make me say what You want me to say; make me do what You want me to do.' But . . . what a terrible confession I am going to have to make to Your representative. I dare not approach it. Help me!

November 19. Article announcing my divorce in *le Journal*. The rags have picked it up and repeated sentences out of it. The editor of *la Cigale* wants to see me. They come here to interview me. Orders are strict: they are told that I am in a nursing-home. My first application has been signed and despatched.

November 20. Maurice de Rothschild has invited us – Mimy and me – through Marthe Hollier-Larousse, to have dinner with him on Monday evening at the rue de Monceau. I long to see all his lovely things, and him too – I knew him when he was eighteen.

He was an adorable creature in those days. It seems that he has changed a great deal! That was twenty-seven or twenty-eight years ago. I was his first love. Mimy is his cousin. If he imagines that we are going to give him an evening of depravity he is much mistaken. We have made up our minds; at the first offensive word we put him sternly in his place. If he goes on, we leave.

November 23. Maurice behaved quite properly. He enlarged with pleasure and feeling on memories of our amorous youth. He showed us his house and his museum. I rediscovered the little Momo I used to know, a bit swollen and distended. Mimy was ravishing; I was all right in glittering black.

November 24. An atrocious day yesterday! Waiting at the lawyers. Waiting at the Palais de Justice. My divorce is going all right. Today I am quite shattered from the ordeal undergone by my nerves. I've still got the 'conciliation' to get through. Since Georges's legal domicile is 64 rue Saussure, we are sending the documents there. As he has left the conjugal home he won't get these documents and will probably fail to turn up, which is what we hope. Oh! please, dear God, forgive him as I do and grant me the favour of never seeing him again! I want him dead, not savagely but simply to end his suffering and his wrong-doing. All his and my responsibility I lay to the account of Manon Thiébaut, because in spite of her big innocent eyes she is tough, energetic, greedy, a monster of selfishness and cynicism, very responsible.

1927

Paris, January 1. 1926 over and done with: a year which – without doubt – I must consider one of deliverance. I welcome you with open arms, oh my destiny! Thank you for the flame which lights my hearth, for the good fire which warms me. Thank you for friends, for gifts. Thank you for what I am still able to detach from myself and give to others. Thank you for Jean Cocteau's intelligent and soothing telephone call, for Max Jacob's feeling letter, for the dear Burguets' heartfelt hospitality, for Mimy's love.

What a lot of blessings I owe you already, first day of the new year! Smiling resignation, calm, cheerfulness.

Thank you, God, for everything.

That entry is followed by two months of silence. When Liane takes up her pen again Georges is back. She does not explain how this came about. Her new name for him, 'Gilles', is evidently an attempt to convince them both that they can make a new start.

Boulouris – March 1 to April 28

March 1. My shipwreck has cast me up here, in a pretty white house standing quite close to the sea among mimosas, pines and eucalyptus. Georges Ghika has gone away. He has gone away for ever. But I have a certain little Gilles at my side, grave and sweet, affectionate and very pale, thin, sad at having hurt me so much. I do not think that Gilles can cure me of this hurt, but he might perhaps be able to help me to endure it. I have with me Camille, loving and bustling, awkward and clumsy; and I have Pauline Morel. I have a duty, an ideal. I am totally immersed in learning to know myself. I am here to straighten both of us out, to care for him, to do him good even if it means doing some harm to myself.

With him I am alone. Gilles still contains Georges Ghika, his faults, his instincts, his baseness. He gives me all of it, wrapped up in his love and remorse, and in a good deal of reserve. So the gift he makes of himself is complete! Ought I to feel sorry for myself? I let my life drift; it carried us along, separated us, brought us together again. I have left Mimy Franchetti who would have liked me to live against my inclinations, against what I firmly believe to be my truth. I am afraid of every word we pronounce, I don't speak unless I cannot avoid it. I also distrust the silences.

Gilles is shrunken, older, grinning, maniacal. We are living in the house of Jane Henriquez, the former singer reduced to this work by the cost of living – really rather hard for a nightingale! We go for walks . . .

Mimy Franchetti was dreadfully unhappy when I left her. I was unhappy. Our sensuality had its dear little habits. I tore all that up in one minute.

Gilles spent three weeks in a nursing-home at Chatenay near Paris, to rest, rediscover himself, try himself out, tidy himself up. I went to see him every day but all I saw was crime and darkness. Gilles has no gift for throwing light on things, nor any wish to do so. Our story has done nothing to illuminate him. I returned from these visits tortured, overcome, so tired . . .

My divorce was left unfinished. I stopped it for an indefinite period. If I no longer have Georges Ghika – if he has changed so much that I have had to invent Gilles – then it is true that I am not the same, either. New things have taken hold of me, have been unleashed in me. I used to be a magnificent creature, I have become a poor unhappy woman, desperately damaged, hurting all over.

March 5. Yesterday the sun gave nature and its creatures a rough shaking. Today it's rain, wind, storm over a grey sea, cruelly narrowed down. We huddle among the palm trees and mimosas surrounding this house, a nest buried in greenery. A train goes by and breaks the silence in which we live.

How I wish I could bypass this crisis in my life, this bankruptcy of my heart. Jean Cocteau met Georges Ghika and Manon Thiébaut in a Paris cinema. He told me: 'She's frightful! She's like a little monkey. One wanted to offer her a nut!' I answered: 'Her nut is my happiness.' He exclaimed: 'My love! You'll find your happiness again!' I know perfectly well, I feel very strongly, that I shall not. Besides, I am not looking for it; but I am waiting for something before I die – yes, I am waiting . . .

March 10. I am so unhappy I could die. I told Jean Bouscatel to introduce Mimy to Emilienne d'Alençon. Today Bouscatel wrote to say that he is going out with the two of them all the time. And it pierces my heart! My Mimy is going to forget me, to find consolation. She is with Emilienne; for me it's all over, over for good. I loved her so, so much . . .

Letter from Salomon Reinach. He is ill. He is wrong in supposing that the present blue notebook will be edifying and fascinating. Our life is pretty awful and I absolutely refuse to expatiate on it. I don't even want to think much about myself, I want to keep busy, devote myself to something . . . My aspirations are always lofty. Will they ever be crowned in keeping with their elevation?

March 20. Gilles and I wanted to have a little party: dinner in our room, with champagne. This morning we gave Camille the impression that we had remarried. As a matter of fact it happened on the first day. What would be the use of denying pleasure to our bodies?

Gilles tells me that I intimidate him dreadfully. No doubt his amorality is afraid of my purity – because I am all purity. And then, he loves me. He trembles before me, before the beauty he admires; he represses and restrains himself.

April 4. We spent a sweet day walking in the woods at Esterel among balsamic perfumes, under a blue sky, in the sun. Our sadness was still there, latent . . . and perhaps it has to be there. It's our point of contact, our way of communicating. Apart from exasperated embraces our sadness is now the best we have to give each other.

April 6. Gilles is tired, nervy. He is not smoking much and is not even thinking of getting drunk; watches me all the time with sorrow and affection – I daren't any longer say with love. He needs to be leaning against me, or in my arms; then his suffering diminishes and peace descends on him.

April 9. Moral collapse of Gilles: his idea – he confessed it to me – is to go out and solicit women wherever he sees them – unknown women – and do it very fast! 'Because if I have to talk to a woman for twenty minutes I stop wanting her.' He would like to bring them back to me, to go in for the most obscene and lewd games. So now what! I am going to consult my confessor and Father Sanson. I asked my dear Pinard for his advice, and according to him the calm and dignity of my household depends on soothing baths and doses of cascara. Dear God, I have no one but You!

In between times Georges tells me that he adores me, that he can't look at me without wanting to burst into tears (and there are tears in his eyes), and that he is unable to control himself any longer. He begs me to shut him up in a mad-house, or to kill him. It is complete disaster.

....

April 17. I can't bear any more! He's a sort of madman, erotic and hysterical to the highest degree. He has told me that we ought to live together 'lightly'. That means – so he explains – having other women, taking me to brothels whenever he feels like it, sleeping with me every day – because he adores me . . . I am adored! I think he is really ill, his health completely undermined.

April 18. Enough of all that, time will sweep it away.

Letter from Sonia. I had sent her Vladimir Miatleff. Vladimir is a poet and a madman. I knew him in 1894 when I was playing in pantomime at St Petersburg. He ruined himself for me, just for the pleasure of looking at me.

He had married the daughter of General Richter. On his marriage night Vladimir realized that he was impotent. His wife deceived him with Prince Gagarin. Miatleff fought a duel with Gagarin – his wife was pregnant and Mia didn't want any bastards in his family. The Miatleffs belong to the highest nobility, more ancient than the Romanoffs. On the evening after his duel, honour satisfied, Miatleff, who was a guards officer, gave a big dinner for his fellow officers. They drank as they do in Russia, and towards the end they began to talk about the recent arrival of some beautiful tarts from France. Mia, who was over-excited, yelled: 'Beautiful they may be, but there isn't a whore who is better than my wife!' In a second the unfortunate, staggering Mia was surrounded by a circle of lowering comrades who thrust a large sheet of paper in front of him and said 'Sign this, resign your commission. You are no longer one of us. You have dishonoured yourself, speaking about your wife like that!' Mia signed, red to the top of his head with shame. His comrades embraced him and had to watch over him – drink with him too, I think – for several days, to prevent him from killing himself.

I turned up two years later. Mia had cheered up. He was still impotent and had become a terrible masochist. He took me to his estate at Goloubin in the region of Kursk, and heaped me with gifts.

One day he summoned a Paris jeweller, Jacques Goudstickker, so that I could choose a row of pearls and some rings. Jacques – the tempter! – spread a million and a half's worth of jewels on the table. I was recovering from a fever . . . I came into the room and stopped, dazzled. I looked at this, tried on that, and couldn't make up my mind. There were ruby and diamond tiaras, emerald necklaces, diamond chains, a parure of turquoises and diamonds, etc. Mia was pacing the room – I can see him now – with his hands behind his back. Finally I cried out: 'I simply can't make up my mind! Mia, you decide – they are all so beautiful!' Then he gave me a charming smile, looked at me with his big black eyes and said simply: 'Take the lot.' I took the lot. He was a great nobleman.

Paris – rue Saussure

May 7. Here I am back home, with Gilles. I am looking after him. He has seen Vinchon who says we must take care of the body in order to reach the mind, and has prescribed to that end. Doctor Paul Emile Levy, on the other hand, claims that we must heal the mind in order to reach the body. Professor Sicard has declared that my husband could have no better doctor than me and that his idea of living beside me as calmly as possible will be the best thing in the world – for *him*!

After their return to Paris Liane put aside her blue notebooks; from then on she never wrote while they were in Paris, only when she was away – which was quite often. Except for a few pages in May 1928 there was to be silence for sixteen months. When she began to write again it was to record an event which marked all the rest of her life.

1928

Versailles, May 4. I am here so that Gilles can breathe a fresher air than that of rue Saussure.

Gilles is deteriorating rapidly, worn-out, maniacal. I look after him as I love him, with the greatest tenderness. I too am deteriorating fast. I am failing under the weight of the burden, and if I didn't have the burden I would have nothing. Nothing worth taking trouble for, nothing capable of entering into me: an egotist's bliss.

By dint of sharing the pleasures of an hysteric who is not responsible for himself, I myself am becoming hysterical – and it is my misfortune to be responsible. I measure, I analyze, I accept. By doing so I have almost reached the cheerful resignation that I have so often asked Heaven to grant me.

Because of all this I have put aside my notebook. I take it up again rather like someone turning round for a last look when they reach a bend in the road, or like someone opening an old chest, going through old drawers.

Mother Marie-Madeleine of the Faithful Company of Jesus has just died. I loved seeing her and listening to her. She said 'My little one – ' and it was so sweet to my heart to listen to someone who could still call me her 'little one'. She said to me: 'My little one, your husband has done a great deal for you. Remind yourself how he found you in very dubious company and raised you to the altar. What would he do if you left him?' I answered truthfully: what he did when he left me, he'd smoke all the time, drink as much as possible, lead the basest and most riotous life, quite without control. 'So there you are,' she concluded. 'Your duty is clear, you must stay with your husband.' She also explained to me that giving up things and people is nothing because we will lose all that anyway; the vital thing is to give up self. 'So you see, my little one, in taking back your poor wretched husband you have renounced your self, because you had quite a good idea of what lay ahead for you. That is the greatest of all victories. It raises you and strengthens you, it is pleasing to God and He will help you.' Dear Mother Marie-Madeleine! She had known me since I was eight years old. She had a superior mind and great authority, and her piety was limitless and well-directed. Thanks to these gifts she became Reverend Mother and Assistant to the Superior General. It was she who took care of their relations with the outside world, and in effect ran the whole thing. She could get what she asked from everyone, she knew how to touch the soul and move the mind.

I saw her this winter, alert and very much alive, still supple as she knelt in the little chapel where she had taken me to pray with her. Now she is praying for me in heaven – the day I heard of her death I made her an inward promise to do my duty by Georges to the end, neither to leave him nor to send him away.

Mother Marie-Madeleine, I can feel you within me in the sweetness of my resignation and the firmness of my resolution. I am well aware that I do not live exactly as you would wish, but that will come. It is difficult to sort things out. I am so unworthy and so imperfect, still so closely connected with base considerations. I was unable to confess everything to you, I respected you too much. Now you know everything and you will rescue me from this sewer.

Uriage – September 23 to October 1

September 23. I have neglected my notebook again for quite a long time. The summer has gone by, a difficult one as far as I was concerned, atrocious on the one hand and very wonderful on the other.

In July various people urged us to come to a so-called 'convalescent' home situated on the hill which overlooks Grenoble. There we found no chance of convalescence, no peace, no care, dirt, discomfort – we had been completely had! Nothing but noise, day and night: trains whistling, slaughter-houses and factories, smell and smoke. Too exhausted for a long journey, we let ourself slide into this hotel at Uriage – to us it seems like Paradise – which is run by the widow of Serge Basset who lost his life as a war reporter for *le Figaro.*

One day when we were going past an old grey house buried in vines and fig trees, we decided on a whim to pull the bell beside the big door on which was written: Asylum of Saint Agnes. Perhaps the curiosity we felt, Gilles and I, was rather unhealthy. We knew that this roof sheltered children who were idiots from birth. The door opened and we found ourselves face to face with a woman of impressive calm and simplicity, clearly marked by nobility and dignity. We asked if we could visit the chapel, and innocently put ten francs into the box for the poor. We thought we might see some of the unhappy inmates. We saw none of them, but I at least left that place shaken to the quick, vanquished by the Mother Superior. She is one of those beings whose gaze could make water spring forth from rock. Georges was won over, too – in his way.

The next day I went back alone. I was welcomed by the Mother Superior as though she had been expecting me. She is so completely natural that when you are with her nothing seems surprising and she herself seems surprised by nothing. I gave her fifty francs, apologizing for having left so little the day before. I talked to her for a long, long time about myself. She listened to me with pious attention and told me to come back that afternoon, with my husband, so that she could show us 'her children.'

We were punctual. She took us to a playground . . . and there I saw sixty-seven unhappy creatures between eight and sixteen years old, scarred by the most inexorable suffering. I nearly fainted. Georges Ghika went green . . . Oh! Those cries, those contortions, those grimaces, that smell . . . once you have seen that, never never again can you complain of anything! I was ashamed of having talked so much about myself to Sister Marie-Xavier. I pressed the poor tremulous, rather dirty hands which reached out towards me. I searched those wandering, fixed or mad eyes for some glimmer of light. I laid my hand on those foreheads, tumultuous or stunned, feverish, so pale . . . To think that I had given them no more alms than a heedless passer-by might have done! I gave five hundred francs, Georges Ghika gave a hundred, and I knew that he was more disturbed than he liked to admit.

I have been going back there every day, and that is how I have given myself. I have come to know almost all of them, one by one. I have written a very good letter to all my friends explaining the nature of the work in a most moving way; up to now I've collected nearly five thousand francs including my own offering, and that is only the beginning. I will move heaven and earth to help them. I will go begging everywhere.

Sister Marie-Xavier is slender, tall, dark, clear-cut and direct, intelligent, active. She distils an atmosphere of peace and trust. I am hers. I have laid my burden at her feet. She has become my friend. She says: 'I forbid you to desert. You must stay where God has put you.' I said to her: 'Mother, when I look at these poor children and think of my devastated life, I could almost envy them for their inability to understand.' Promptly she answered: 'They are certainly to be envied for their inability to offend God.' I told her the story of my life because I did not want to gain her affectionate interest under false colours. She bent towards me and confided; 'I too had to struggle. It took me a long time to become accustomed to this hard task. I have been here for fourteen years; well, for the first five or six of them I often had to repress the idea of killing myself in order to have done with feeling disgust day after day, minute by minute. I conquered myself. I love my children. The more they are tested the better I love them. Now I don't ever want to leave them. I help them to suffer and I help them to die. And I love you, Princess, because you love them.'

They lack so many things! There are no baths or showers. They have got to have all that. They will have all that. What a long way I am now from Paris and its dissipations! Here is my wealth: the friendship of this saint and a little part in this work of abnegation and sacrifice. This is my road to Damascus! Oh! that my return to Paris does not make me forget this little corner! Please, God, do not let that happen! Never again would I be able to believe in myself. It seems to me that You put the Asylum of Saint Agnes and its inmates in my way on purpose, as though to tell me: 'Help them, and I will help you.'

September 24. We are packing to go down to Grenoble tomorrow. This hotel is shutting. It has started to be cold, white frost is making its appearance in the mornings. My heart is a sunless world, but when I think how cold my little patients will be it warms up at the touch of a charitable thought: go begging for them!

An amusing letter from Jacques Bonjean giving us news of Max Jacob, who is more faithful to Brittany than he is to his friendship with us. I love him at a distance. By that I mean: I wouldn't like him to be unhappy or ill, but I no longer have the courage or the wish to expose myself to his hypocrisy. They say that he has definitely left the monastery of Saint-Benoît, which was such a wonderfully peaceful and pious refuge for him. Max needs peace, he needs to accomplish his religious duties. Now he is unrestrained. He is living a life which wastes his energies, his money, his heart, his dignity as a man and an artist. He is surrounded by a crowd of second-rate young people who make fun of him. We are a long way from the fine meditations which Roscoff used to inspire in him every day.

September 25. I wrote to tell Sister Marie-Xavier that I wasn't well, and had the lovely surprise of a visit from her, in the company of the Reverend Mother General. Their visit made me better. I mean to improve conditions for their patients, carry a begging bowl round Paris on their behalf to all those people who don't know what to do with their wealth and are dying of a surfeit. I am haunted, gripped, vanquished, ready for anything.

....

October 1. We will soon be leaving this sweet and charming place. Gilles is better physically, but his renewed strength simply serves to nourish the strength of his delusion, his dishonesty and his obscenity. He expresses himself only through that.

Yesterday evening he said to me – while his left hand never stopped plucking out hairs from above his left ear – 'I've thought of a very interesting film such as has never been seen, an obscene film – I mean one with absolutely nothing in it but obscenities . . .' Whereupon he began to describe for my benefit everything that his poor sick mind had been able to think up. He returned to the subject again this morning. I don't check him, it is better that it should come out. Being his confidant enables me to know where we are. He talks about it in pedantic detail, listening to himself, choosing his words, ponderously, his voice serious and sad. I play patience on my bed as I listen. I say 'Oh!' and 'Ah!' I try not to let my face show my disgust and sadness; I invent a nice affectionate little smile, the smile of a fond and indulgent comrade. And to think that for eighteen years we were such an amorously united pair!

We are leaving. We are going to Grenoble. We are thinking of going on to Aix-en-Provence and elsewhere, elsewhere. As far as I'm concerned, whether it's here or there it will be nothing but sorrow and desolation.

Aix-en-Provence, October 20. This morning I wrote to the Maharajah of Kapurthala on behalf of my work. Kapurthala is my friend. When I was twenty he wanted to number me among his wives and he's grateful that I became a princess, kept my beauty and my fame and a certain amount of money, and never made any appeal to his generosity. I knock at this door in the hope that it will open! I no longer use the words 'idiots from birth'. I say 'chronically ill, and poor – so poor!'

Return to Paris caused another interruption to the notebooks. Liane remained silent for almost three years, and says little to explain the fact. From then on she wrote chiefly when she was alone, during her husband's visits to Roumania to be with his mother who had suffered a stroke.

1931

Cap-Brun – August 14 to August 30

August 14. I have opened this notebook and reread the sheets tucked into it from time to time over the last four and a half years. I was rather ashamed of them. I would like to tear them up. That packet of love letters from Mimy Franchetti – I would like to burn them. I shall not do so. I am so remote from all that, purified by pain.

I have now spent five years with this unhappy Georges Ghika, irresponsible and debauched, suppressing actions but overflowing with evil words. He has been drinking, smoking endlessly, reading atrocious books, blaspheming against everything which contributes to a sweet and serious life: against love; against marriage, the blessed union of two people who love each other; against order; against punctuality, regularity, good manners; against religion, beliefs of whatever kind; against divine law as well as against human laws; against everything. Poor discontented, bestial being, with his great ability to illuminate directed towards the most hellish landscapes. I have suffered in my mind and in my body. I used to go out to take my mind off it and to stoke up some courage; what met my eyes was as bad, or worse, but it did not belong to me. Intrigues, lies, dirtiness, hypocrisy: I fled my house to find it all elsewhere, but there I was not closely connected with it. I was there as a spectator of these dreary comedies. I would get home exhausted. There I would find Georges Ghika, high on alcohol, damaged by tobacco, drunk on his reading. His hair was greying and falling out, he was losing his teeth. He had lost his virility – he was lashed by the desire to rediscover it. So at night he would direct all his evil ardour onto me, would try and fail and begin again, all to no avail. To him that, and nothing else, is what is meant by love . . . He would fall asleep and snore while I, in despair, would pray . . . I pray with all my distress and with all the pain of a crushed and imprisoned woman who can see no way out but death. It's at these times that I say: 'God, let me die, let me die tonight, now. I am in an abyss of desolation. I no longer recognize my husband, my lover, my friend, my Georges. He has become my torturer. Of course he is not responsible for what he does, I know that I must not accuse him, condemn him, hold it against him! He is my punishment, my atonement, my salvation. May Your will, o God, be done.'

On the 13th of March in this year 1931 my horror broke all bounds. I could stand no more. I cried to God with all the power of my suffering: 'God, it is too much, too much. I can bear no more. Deliver me!' And behold a miracle! On the morning of the 13th my mother-in-law had a stroke followed by irreversible paralysis of the left side. On the 16th, when I was out, my husband received a telegram giving him news of this disaster. On the 17th, he left with his brother! They were pitiful, both of them; they were afraid they would find their mother dead.

He writes to me all the time, vague, hollow letters empty of what I long to find in them. He tries to inject them with love. Mariette's agony is long and terrible. I pray for her and for Georges: I ask for courage on their behalf. I give them to God – that God denied by both of them – and I ask that I may never see them again.

Tomorrow it's August 15, the feast of the Mother of God, my saint's day in the midst of flowers and a splendid decor under a burning sun. Georges Ghika has sent me his wishes and a cheque for two thousand francs. He does not know where I am. My good and charming notary, Maître Collet, has agreed to receive all my correspondence, so my husband writes to me care of him. I want to put him off the scent, introduce a bit of vagueness and mystery, avoid direct contact, escape the possibility of being taken by surprise.

August 20. Everything has gone well for Saint Agnes. I found donors. The old grey house, that sacred shelter for the worst of suffering, has been repaired and improved. They have magnificent central heating even in the chapel, running water, lovely shiny brass taps flowing with hot and cold. Gabrielle Chanel was spontaneously and splendidly generous. I collected nearly three hundred thousand francs. The repairs and improvements cost over two hundred and ten thousand; the rest provided linen, coal, comfort.

This work has become my reason for staying alive. Those unhappy ones and the admirable sisters are now my only family.

This corner where I am now is ideally pretty. By the sea, by the hills, there rises the blessed mount, the Mont du Soleil, with its unkempt gardens exhaling the intoxicating balsam of their sun-warmed perfumes. The doves start cooing early in the morning. I wake up to this soft sound, a gift from nature. You would think that all the peace on earth had collected here, making everything more beautiful. My heart, too, has found peace. Five years ago I suffered atrociously, suffered from being abandoned, from not being loved any more. I offered it all to God. And I want it to be like that for ever: a pious accomplishment of duty, a humble submission to the divine will. I am so deeply committed to this way that it is perfectly easy for me to avoid whatever might weaken my will and interrupt my progress.

The *Imitation* encourages, advises and guides me. I consult its magnificent words every day and they enlighten and console me. Every time I open this marvellous book I draw on resources of strength and enthusiasm. I read a chapter every evening.

August 28. Georges Ghika writes, writes, writes . . . A registered letter arrives from Roumania every day. I can foresee that he will come back to Paris at the end of the summer, that he is preparing to return to my house, to me, as though nothing had happened. His letters are affectionate, insinuating, full of detail. Anyone who didn't know might be taken in by them and feel very sorry for him, might accuse me of being hard and dry. No, really, I have forgiven; I have forgiven his mother, too; but with forgiveness there came a feeling of immense indifference.

August 30. Today I read my mass in my bedroom. I read it well and thoughtfully, responding with emotion to the sacred words on which my eyes used to rest every Sunday as I sat beside my mother in church. In those days I repeated these words like a little parrot while I looked at the people sitting round me, particularly the women. I remember Madame de Vogelsang. She would come to mass alone, or else with her mother, rather pink in the face, ploughing through the rows of people to get to her place, which was just in front of us. I would sniff at her; she smelt good. I would study her dresses; she was elegant and everything suited her. I wanted to get to know her, to kiss her. I was passionate and always drawn to women, nervous and disgusted in the presence of men. Their smell of tobacco made me wrinkle my nose. I loved the bishops and the officiating priests in their sacerdotal robes, the choir boys, the censors, the perfumes and the music of church, without bothering much about what my catechism taught me.

No doubt Freud could find plenty of clues to my character in all that – and a chance to prove himself wrong into the bargain. I went off the rails, but that was not my true direction, not my essence. My debauched husband was caught out when he married me. It was Reynaldo who understood me. I realized that one day when he was talking about my life. He looked deeply into my eyes; his own filled with a great tenderness and he quoted these words of Goethe's: 'Child! Even when you do wrong, you are never guilty.' How he touched me that day! Nevertheless I have been gravely guilty. I have offended my God and I have broken my parents' hearts.

My husband still doesn't know where I am. I tell him that I am moving about rather more than in fact I am. I answer his daily letters about once a week, according to what I have to say or what is passing through my mind.

Mourillon – Le Prieuré, September 2 to December 15

September 2. Here I am in Paradise, in an animated solitude. I have a room with bath in the Pavilion of the Romantics. The proprietor is very interesting: he has been abroad a lot and the seven or eight houses which comprise his little kingdom are full of amusing Chinese objects. We are 'paying guests'; it's the latest thing and very nice.

September 16. My peace here is rather threatened. Georges Ghika writes that his brother will be taking his place beside their mother and that he will be in Paris between the 23rd and 25th of this month. If he does not find me in the rue Saussure he says he intends to wait for me with the Brothers of Saint-Jean de Dieu.

One of Paris's 'lionesses', Fernande Cabanel, has turned up here quite by chance! The other day she appeared suddenly in a blaze of sunshine just as lunch was ending, wearing sumptuous pyjamas by Schiaparelli and followed by her companion, the young Greek

Xanaris. We exchanged lots of 'darlings!' and kisses and we see each other all the time.

Fernande is very beautiful in a sunlit garden, much more so than at the Ritz in Paris. Yesterday she was wearing adorable very wide pyjamas combining several shades of blue. I admired them, I do so love blue! When I got back from my walk this morning I found these ravishing trousers on my bed with a charming card. I am confused and pleased. I have thanked her. I sent her a box of red gladioli and I said: 'Fernande, I am going to send a hundred francs to my unhappy ones at Saint Agnes whom you have already helped – a hundred francs in your name, not more, because I want to be in your debt.'

September 19. I have been on the spree two days running.

On the 17th my dear old friend Mayol came to have lunch with me. We were once on the same bill at the Scala: he was singing his famous songs, I was dancing in sketches. I came downstairs on the stroke of twelve and saw my fat Mayol standing in front of the house in the sunlight with an enormous bunch of dahlias in his arms, dahlias like himself, splendid and colourful: champion dahlias! We fell into each others arms. Suzanne de Callias arrived. I introduced Mayol who said to her: 'I read a book of yours signed Menalkas and Willy, but I knew it was you . . .' – 'I'll sign a copy for you tomorrow,' she said. 'Done!' said Felix; then turned to me: 'Would you like to eat aioli at home?' 'Aioli with Mayol – Oh yes yes yes!' I replied. – 'I shall count on seeing both of you, I'll send my chauffeur to pick you up – he's my secretary too, a very nice boy.' – 'And your sweetie-pie as well?' – 'Yes, of course.'

By the time we reached dessert we had collected the whole of the Prieuré around us. Mayol was delighted – he has to have his little audience. We ran through the 'have-you-seens'. 'Do you remember, Félix?' – 'Do you remember, Liane?' 'And after the Sunday matinée, those dinners in my dressing-room with the artistes of our choice and Yvonne de Buffon. Our director used to contribute two bottles of champagne, one sweet for you, one dry for me! And then Good Friday, when everyone else closed but we didn't. The Scala was bursting. The packed house was resplendent with all the lady-butchers from les Halles – they crammed the boxes, attentive, merry, sumptuous in shiny satin and crackling silk, sparkling with heavy gold jewellery. Up went the curtain on Liane.

Cheers, applause. Encouraged, I gave of my best. I was much better than I usually was, I gave myself, I took off. I got an enormous bouquet on behalf of all the leading slaughter-house families. I blew kisses, I got them back – it would still be going on if the curtain hadn't been brought down.

'But now – now it's Mayol! How they clapped, how they clapped! The orchestra kept on having to stop and start again, Mayol opened his mouth, then shut it. Finally he pretended he was fed up and going off, then the "Shsh-shshes" began. Mayol sang. It was very moving, absolute silence. He bowed, he had finished, he disappeared. They called him back, thunderous applause, yells, stamping. Mayol came back. It started all over again. Usually he sang three songs and gave three encores. That evening he had to sing more than twenty. They simply wouldn't let him go. They pelted him with flowers. They weren't yelling any more, they were roaring: Mayol! Mayol! And he gave and gave until at last he simply couldn't utter another note.

'I was in the wings, hidden by a flat. "What a triumph, love! What a house" – "Sez you!" he spat as he scurried past. "I must fly – they are waiting for me across the road at the Eldorado, I've got to go through the whole thing again." And it was true. He hardly had time to gulp a soothing drink when he was back in the arms of his frenzied Good Friday admirers.'.........

September 20. Mayol lives on an estate surrounded by eight or ten pretty villas bought to mark the stages of his triumphal progress. As a whole it is called Clos Mayol, but he's given each of the villas the name of a music-hall where he used to sing: the Scala, the Ba-ta-clan, the Eldorado, the Moulin Rouge, etc. In spite of all this he has somehow managed to keep plenty of open, flowery space and a big open-air theatre where he gives benefits for this or that on every fine Sunday. Artistes from Marseilles, friends on the wing and people living near by all collaborate. It's very popular. In September they close down for the grape-harvest. He has a big vineyard which produces two thousand bottles of a light, heady, and treacherous red wine – as I learnt the other day to my cost and the household's delight.

There are two fountains in his courtyard made of multicoloured tiles. It is cool, sheltered from the hot sun by fine trees. He has had big fountains constructed all over the estate, all with basins of many-coloured tiles. It's pretty and unusual, very characteristic of the laughing Midi which makes the most of nothing and where everything grows easily thanks to the blue sky. It is the retreat of a great artiste.

So I had been invited to aioli. There were two kinds, one with lemon, the other without. In addition: a huge dish of cod, several dozen hard-boiled eggs, octopus stewed in wine, a multitude of snails, lots of bowls of fat winkles, a mountain of potatoes and carrots, beetroots, chick-peas, green beans, etc. More than a dozen dishes of aioli! A vast green melon as sweet as honey, an ice from Philippe, the best cake-shop, and champagne to follow the Clos Mayol wine and complete my tipsiness. The last beautiful grapes from the stripped vines, blue figs – their skin splitting as though wounded – peaches, pears, delicious coffee. 'A liqueur?' suggested Mayol. 'I have a little Marc which is not to be sniffed at.' – 'Stop, stop!' I cried. 'I couldn't manage another mouthful.' So he took us to visit his museum. Mayol everywhere – paintings, drawings, posters, photos. Portraits of all of us: I found three of myself, rather pretty, inscribed to my dear friend. There were also mementoes of the war, letters to Mayol from soldiers grateful for the gift of a song or a little money. Then he took his secateurs and cut us yet more great sheafs of his matchless dahlias.

September 23. Yesterday Fernande Cabanel and her companion Sacha Xanaris, took me into Toulon for the afternoon. On the way Fernande said to me: 'I have some very urgent shopping to do. I'm completely out of something which I have to have. It is making me ill. Yesterday I tried to use some of Sacha's drug but it's too heavy, too strong for me. It upset me dreadfully. Jean Cocteau is here, we'll look him up and he's sure to be able to give me an address.' – 'Fine,' I said. 'Jean is an old friend of mine and I'd like to see him again.' She took me down to the port, near the Arsenal, and led me along a horrible street with reeking gutters which ran parallel with the quay. It was lined on either side with the most frightful shady-looking hotels. She said: 'Oh God – Jean is living in one of these.' We went into a foul slum called Hôtel du Port et des Négociants. She asked for Jean; the proprietor was smiling and eager, all amiability and complicity. He sent for Liou, the Annamite boy – a prince's son, it seems – who serves Jean. Fernande scribbled a note. Liou took it away, then reappeared with three words of answer: 'In an hour.' We left the hotel by another door, through a fairly clean little bistro opening onto the quay. There was an antique shop next door. Sacha and I went in and began bargaining for all kinds of things. Fernande kept watch by the door. While we were looking at ornaments in the back of the shop Sacha told me: 'Two cops followed us down that street and saw us go in. They are over there now – look. This hotel is often raided because of drugs and pederasty. The proprietor procures little sailor-boys and it's not expensive.' Five minutes later we were sitting at table before some excellent coffee, croissants, butter and jam – four-o'clock tea is always when they eat their first meal. They sleep late in the mornings because they go to bed late. When they saw us sitting down the policemen came back to the hotel, suspecting something. Sacha was paler than usual, Fernande very nervy and agitated. We went back into the antique shop and Sacha gave me a Louis-Philippe glass, a blue one. We saw Liou go by, looking for us. He led us away along the quay and said: 'Jean is expecting the two ladies. Will Monsieur be kind enough to have a drink in the hotel restaurant. The ladies should follow me.' All this went on while the policemen were watching the house. On our way upstairs we passed two little sailor-boys running down very fast, their heads hanging. Liou opened the door of a sordid room, letting out a strong whiff of the drug. It was sinister – what an extraordinary pleasure it is! Jean was lying on the floor covered with a disgusting bedspread, behind a horribly filthy bed. His voice was deathly, dull, dry, hoarse. He said: 'What are you doing Liou? Shut the door. Don't let anyone in. I'm very ill.' I backed out onto the narrow landing, but Fernande went in: 'Jean, for pity's sake give me an address. Liane is here with me.' What can he have thought? That I too have started to smoke? He answered almost inaudibly: 'Liou, give her some of my special supply: three francs a gramme. Forgive me, if you knew how ill I am! Lock the door, Liou.'

I got a glimpse of Jean, thin, pale, drawn, a shadow of himself and he was already a shadow. He had a three-day beard and his clothes were in disorder, dirty and crumpled. We went into Liou's room, even more sordid. On the wall a drawing of Jean's, signed and inscribed 'To my dear Liou,' and a page of poetry in his handwriting: 'To my dear Liou.' 'How Jean squanders himself,' whispered Fernande while Liou opened a mould-smelling cupboard. Liou: 'Here are 700 grammes, Madame, that will be 2,100 francs.' Fernande: 'That's too much for me. I'm afraid of overdoing it if I have that big a supply.' He went back to the cupboard and took out a smaller pot. 'Here are 150 grammes for 450 francs.' – 'That will do,' said Fernande. 'That will keep me going for two months.' She paid and we left. Xanaris, very nervous, was waiting downstairs. 'The cops are still there, complete with their revolvers,' he said. 'Let's leave by the other door. Have you got it?' 'Yes,' said Fernande, happy and appeased. He took the box, looked at it. 'The princess had better look after it. She has a big handbag.' I understood that they were afraid of being picked up. Opium smokers are not brave. I didn't want to make a fuss because I'm fond of all of them, Jean and these two – I'm sorry for them, too – so I slid the drug into my bag as inconspicuously as possible. Whereupon they began to run – to run much more nimbly than I would ever have expected; I had a hard time keeping up. They hailed a taxi, plunged into it. I caught up, they pulled me in, the taxi drove off. 'Ouf!' went Fernande. 'Ouf!' went Sacha. We drove past the cops who didn't notice us. Perhaps they never had. 'Quick, Liane, hand over my box.' She snatched it, looked at it lovingly, squeezed it between her hands with a tender delight that I have sometimes seen in lovers. She explained: 'Jean's stuff is very good, light, quite old. The older the better, with opium. In China princes and emperors use an opium covered with mould that's hundreds of years old, and it's beyond compare.' – 'Oh poor Jean, poor Jean,' I said, obsessed by that painful image of decay and intoxication. Emaciated, tormented little Jean, whom I used to know when he was twenty. His talent, a gift from heaven; his poor mother, so beautiful with her white hair; he was trampling all that under foot, and for what! When Mayol spoke about him the other day he told me: 'Cocteau comes to my open-air theatre on Sunday evenings. *He wears badly.*' With those words he was trying to say it all.

This morning I was in the garden watching the household's children doing their gymnastics in the fresh air and sunlight, when I heard: 'Liane! Hey, Liane!' It was Fernande and Sacha. I went up to them. Fernande told me, 'We went back to Toulon yesterday evening. Coming out of the cinema we met a very pretty gentleman with big dreamy eyes, a little beard, a cane, spats, a dancing step – guess who!' – 'The cat has got my tongue.' – 'It was your beloved Reynaldo! He was coming out of a frightful bar called the Oasis, with a boy. They parted with a lot of simpering and just as the boy was leaving Reynaldo gave him an affectionate tap on the shoulder with his cane, then he started peering through the windows of the neighbouring cafés, looking for someone or something.' It really pained me . . . Jean, Reynaldo . . . 'And then,' said Sacha, 'a little further on we met Pierre Meyer with his coat-collar turned up and his hat pulled down over his nose, and an enormous flower in his buttonhole. He tried to avoid us. What he looks for is middle-aged men, rather pot-bellied.'

Jean, Reynaldo, Pierre! I left them with my hands over my ears, arguing with myself, clamping down on so many things to keep them from hurting me too much. To have adored Reynaldo for thirty-five years, perhaps more, only to hear this about him! Of course I told myself: but I knew that he was that way inclined. He works better after he has given way to animality, his music becomes more beautiful, he is purified. He is all ideals! But it hurt me, all the same. I overcame the pain, the disgust – I laughed a little: yes, I laughed, to drive away the tears.

September 24. Lunch with my dear good Mayol. Family, hospitality, exquisite food. A feast worthy of a bishop, and excellent coffee on the terrace. Mayol reminds me of Napoleon, surrounded as he is by his family who owe him everything. He has four engagements to sing, but he can't make up his mind to leave his beloved home, his people, his sun, his fruits and his flowers. I think I can understand. He retired on the crest of the wave. He didn't watch his star grow pale. He is still in a position to refuse to make a gift of his singing. In this way he will be spared the cruelties of dwindling fame. He lives among his own vines, in his own house, with his family, in his own country, on his well-earned gains. His green theatre is a plaything, echo-memory-habit. When he puts on a show it's for his good works. To the town of Toulon he has give a Rugby stadium; to his family he has given abundance. A happy man who bestows happiness: it is a comforting thing to see.

I shall preserve this memory carefully so that it can blot out a few others: the memory of a great artiste who has known how to run his life and remains happy with his lot until the end.

September 27. Cabanel, the lioness of Paris, fashion-setter, model and arbiter of elegance, the one they whisper about as she passes, the one they admire and copy; yesterday, as she was preparing her little pipe with graceful care, she said to me: 'Liane, I've got another year left, and if by then I haven't found my dream companion, husband or lover, I don't care about that – if I haven't found him I shall kill myself.' These demoralizing, though I suppose plucky, words made me feel terrible. I was sadly oppressed all the evening –

an evening dimmed by the eclipse of the moon which was almost entirely hidden by a brown mist except for a thumbnail segment which kept its brightness.

What poor things we women are, condemned to love! Cabanel is beautiful, strange, elegant, rare. Up till now she has been in control of events. She takes advantage of artificial paradises. As for me, I have a confused glimpse of a peace that may never come!

September 28. Telegram forwarded by Maître Collet's office: 'Will arrive Paris Sunday (that's yesterday) Love. Georges Ghika.' I am afraid the poor boy is deceiving himself. He thinks that I am in Paris and doesn't doubt for a moment that he is going to see me again, possess me again, that everything will go on as usual until the next escapade! I am not worrying, God, I put myself in Your hands, I submit in advance to Your decision whatever it may be. I am here, and here I shall stay quietly as long as You allow it. If You want my frightful misery to begin again – all right, Georges will turn up one day and I will welcome him. If not, he will become resigned to my absence, will make a corner for himself somewhere, will give himself over to his pleasures in his own way – and I shall continue to wander alone and abandoned to the very end.

....

September 30. .... It has been announced in *le Figaro* that the great poet Jean Cocteau, who has been spending his holidays at Toulon for the last few years, has just been admitted to a nursing-home there, very ill with typhoid! . . .

....

October 11. The director of Claridge's (in Paris) will let me have a room with a bathroom at a big reduction (for forty francs a day). He asks me to keep it a secret and he seems anxious to see me there. I am in no hurry to do anything. At the moment I'm trailing around in this beautiful weather with a monstrous depression. Letters keep on arriving from my husband, disconcerting, demoralizing, unworthy of me, unworthy of a man. Worthy of him. He is abject and irresponsible. Enough of that. I have still got some good friends in my twilight; but friends come and friends go. One ends up alone. I feel as though I were in a prison: grief and solitude. Oh to find God! My God, still beyond my reach, accept my piercing, deep and overwhelming sorrow.

I have just been with Cabanel and her little Xanaris. All they want is luxury and they smoke opium. At present they are out of money. Clothes, keeping up appearances, making a show – it's hard on their poor little incomes. She is looking for a rich man to dazzle; the boy will go back to his family in Greece. She's going to find herself penniless and without her companion. She is beautiful, her elegance is unusual and daring, hers and hers alone. Knowing how to dress like that is a sign of intelligence; it surpasses good taste and becomes art.

When I left them just now I said: 'Go on, find your little happiness. Enjoy yourselves for a while, put on your rose-coloured glasses! As for me, I am going to throw myself on my bed, bury my face in my hands and talk to God, no doubt it will do me good.' – 'To each his own drug,' murmured Xanaris as he kissed my hand.

I have made a feminine conquest this year. Women do usually like me and come after me. One can go on attracting them for a remarkably long time – I have often noticed that in others. In spite of their haggard faces and their puffy flesh, the old veterans of lesbian love go on inspiring real passions almost into their seventies! I suppose the enamoured young have times when they need a refuge from masculine brutality and inconstancy . . . They want to be liked by their elders, to attract them by the sweet tenderness of a loving friendship. There too, alas, one finds weeping and gnashing of teeth, betrayal and lies . . .

November 24. Things have been happening. I took to my bed with a slight pulmonary congestion. I had a high temperature and I spat blood – pretty pink, frothy blood. When I saw that I thought I had better call in a doctor. The Monets, our landlords, produced theirs: Doctor Jules Regnault, formerly of the navy, a crafty and rather bizarre Norman who has his fads and uses a lot of electricity, shocks and all kinds of little gadgets. His treatment exhausted me, laid me really and painfully low, and at the end of two weeks my congestion, which had been arrested too soon and too abruptly, came back in the form of a terribly violent bronchitis. This time I refused to cut it short. I let it develop and take its course, while I coughed and spat and sweated. Now I have been up for three days, feeling light and free and disintoxicated. In other words: never cut bronchitis short, the illness stays inside you, building up, and then explodes.

Meanwhile Georges Ghika arrived. On Sunday the 25th my door

opened and there was my husband, delighted to see me again, prancing about like a puppy, loaded with presents, as irresponsible as can be – and ill, too. What adventures and misadventures he'd been having! In June he developed a tumour under his upper lip. Because it might become awkward they lanced it, and since then it has spread. Georges doesn't appear to be worrying, except that he no longer dares to kiss me. So here I am at last, delivered from those desolating loveless embraces! I called in Doctor Regnault, who gave my husband a very thorough examination. The word 'syphilis' was uttered. Is that the truth? And is it to spare my sensibilities that the word 'hereditary' was added? It is always preferable to blame one's ancestors, less distressing and indecent. So the verdict has been pronounced: my husband becomes a syphilitic by inheritance. Nothing worries me, nothing upsets me. I am reassuringly here. He is not drinking any more, is smoking less and has not yet blasphemed. He looks dreadful. On my side the ordeal is lessened if I feel I can comfort and help him. I am not reproaching him; I am not questioning him; I repress. He admits nothing and confides nothing; he represses. He tells me about his stricken mother's terrible conditon of incurable infirmity.

November 25. .... The crisis! Nothing but the crisis! Lolo (Margot de La Bigne's lover) has lost half his fortune, perhaps more. Max is anxious. As for us, we remain calm. My sensations of distress have been focused on other causes, stirred up by other circumstances. To be short of money, to make do without a lot of things – I don't give a damn.

....

December 7. This morning I went for a walk by myself in the grey, in the mist, in the warm wind which foretells a storm. I felt so good, alone in the universe, dreaming, cut loose. I no longer knew where I came from, I had no idea where I was going. Yesterday my chapter from the *Imitation* was about solitude and silence. I have just been granted an experience of it. I felt the sweetness of it. A great peace, a great calm and serenity flowed into me with the air I breathed.

December 15. Georges has jaundice! It declared itself unequivocally twenty-four hours ago. Doctor Regnault has been: he has ordered broth, Vichy water, orange juice and yoghurt. Georges looks frightful. He feels sick all the time. I am looking after him to the best of my ability. He is depressed, exhausted, aching, cross. All this makes it difficult for me. I daren't try to manage him too much; I have a hard time carrying out the doctor's orders because Georges jibs, Georges has his own theories, Georges belongs to Georges. Come what may, Georges alone is the master of Georges's destiny.

1932

Mourillon – Le Prieuré, January 1 to April 14

January 1. A door opening on the unknown prospect of a new road. This morning my husband came in to kiss me at about half-past one, then gave me a charming letter. Mayol sent me his brother and his secretary with two bottles of Cap Corse Muscadet, his kisses and his good wishes. I took my lunch in my husband's bedroom. I drank champagne and a cup of coffee too – complete orgy!

January 4. Gabrielle Chanel has sent five thousand francs to my little invalids at Saint Agnes'. So generous, particularly considering the general crisis. If it continues, how are we going to provide them with coal and warmth?

January 23. This might be entitled 'Confession'.

Yesterday evening I was feeling gay, light-hearted, friendly and affectionate towards all of poor humankind. I sang to myself: 'I am the happiest woman in the world.' I thanked God, I said some prayers, I thought about my parents.

Then, quite suddenly, I felt within me, against me, a flood of bitter reproach. The flood rose, submerged me, all of my life was hurled at me like stones, all of my sins like mud. It became a delirium, tears poured from my eyes, I accused myself, I asked pardon, I had become nothing but repentance and desolation. I said to myself: 'What have you done since your birth, and now that you are approaching death's door, what have you done with your life? Spoilt child, stupid egotist, indifferent pupil, you made a cold first communion without piety, faith or love. Your parents lived for you and you broke their hearts. Your brothers were brave and honourable officers and you brought shame on them. You dragged your family's name in the mud. You were a torment to your husband

and an overwhelmingly heavy moral burden to your son. You had mercy on no one! Not one of those who came near you found grace in your eyes. You never loved even the most magnificent of your lovers. Kings, great financiers, poets, children, old men, scholars – they all clustered round you and you deceived them all. You sold yourself – '

Then during the night I cried out: 'Yes, all that is true and still worse, still worse!' I admitted all my sins, my crimes against life . . . I said to myself: 'Is it possible that *that* was my role on this earth?' Then at last I stared at myself as though in a cruel and faithful mirror. I loved love, never a lover; I hunted for love down evil ways. I was a deranged little Messalina, cerebral, woefully vain. My suffering was true and immense. I want no excuses. I could have pleaded this or that reason – my youth, my foolishness, temptation, my poverty! I was a shameful creature, I had the face of a completely pure virgin and the banal, idiotic vanity of a simpering, talentless dancer prancing like a circus horse to the sound of the orchestra . . . 'And you will write this tomorrow,' I ordered myself. 'You will write down your brutal and abominable confession. Your memory will be accursed and you will be buried like a pauper in a common grave.' Oh! To submit entirely, to expiate – But Georges Ghika is my saviour! He redeems me! And I have dared to complain, to find ways of making people feel sorry for me! I am a monster of heartlessness and idiotic pride! How, how did it happen? Life is now starting up again. I have made great resolutions: no more self-pity, no more complaining, to do my duty at whatever cost, with Heaven's help to understand what it is and accomplish it. Not to think of myself any more, to give way, to bow down and to do so willingly, cheerfully, with enthusiasm even if my self feels pain and wants to rebel. In fact, to renounce myself completely, without making a show of it, for God – for forgiveness!

January 24. After yesterday's confession I felt completely broken. I slept well. This morning my exaltation had ebbed and I was able to think about it very coldly. I take back nothing. Yet I am what people call a charming woman.

February 7. Yesterday Reynaldo's surgeon came to examine Georges. 'At present you couldn't stand surgery,' he said after his questions and the examination. 'Your liver is enormous: hypertrophic cirrhosis of the liver. It's serious. You would be taking a great risk if you moved to Paris just now. A cold, influenza, over-fatigue – anything could make you turn up your toes.' He used that expression again as I was seeing him out, meaning 'to die'. Surgical jargon, no doubt!

February 8. Gilles is very ill. Tomorrow morning we are going to the radiographer. He has frequent sweats and faintness, and I'm none too solid myself. I'm sleeping badly, lying awake in spite of myself, out of worry.

February 9. My husband has jaundice: my niece is suffering from another stomach ulcer; Margot de La Bigne is fading away in nursing-homes after a series of operations; my mother-in-law has been dying for almost a year after a stroke which has paralysed the whole of one side. Help me, oh Lord, to accept, to serve, to love, to bear, to be pleasing in Your eyes through suffering. Increasingly I renounce self. I no longer love myself, I ask nothing for myself. I seek God. I may not have tried to find Him when I was surrounded by pathetic earthly joys, but I hope that I will do so in this distressful accumulation of sorrow.

I would like this notebook to contain no complaint of any kind. This is what I would like to promise God: no complaining, no lying, a plain account of facts, a complete submission to whatever may prove to be my lot. But I shall not be able to attain that kind of perfection without His help. I have already been tart and disagreeable this very morning at the radiographer's, because Georges was cold and so was I. Oh what a lot I have to do about myself before I can even begin to think of judging others!

February 17. Appalling news about my niece.

Several evenings running I have read the following words in my *Imitation*: 'You must separate yourself from your acquaintances and from your friends and wean your spirit from every kind of earthly consolation', and 'to become truly spiritual it is necessary to renounce those nearest to you as though they were strangers, and to beware of no one more than of oneself.' It seems to me that God is speaking to me and guiding me. I put myself in His hands.

February 19. . . . . I adore nougat, I have laid in a stock of it and I eat it every day. When I open my cupboard I am unable to restrain myself, I start chewing greedily. I will give up my nougat until Aimée's [her niece's] operation is over.

February 21. They operate on my child tomorrow. I am waiting in agony. She no longer seems to me to belong to this world – I may be wrong; they are keeping the truth from me. They are sparing me. I know that it is terribly serious.

My husband is confined to his bed. He is miserably weak physically. He is sharing my anxiety, he is trying to be less dry, less hard, less difficult. Dear God, sustain me through this ordeal. Help us, and help my child.

March 2. They are sending me telegrams saying that my little Aimée is going from strength to strength, that the doctor and the surgeon are very pleased . . . and I know the truth. There is no hope for her. Let us accept what we must accept, stiffen our resolution and do the best we can.

....

March 16. My husband's doctor called this morning and found him much improved, but he didn't hide the fact that half the liver is ruined. I am very worried, so distressed for him and at the thought of what might happen to him, particularly if he leaves me. Villechaise made it clear: a cold, flu, exertion, over-tiredness, excess, one drop of alcohol . . .

March 23. Clouds hide the sun, wind drives the clouds away, there's a gleam of sunshine – and life is just like that. One must love the beautiful clouds and beautiful sorrows, make the best of little gleams of fugitive happiness.

Dear God, listen in this holy Passion week to the voice of the least of your servants, give her her daily bread, faith in You, hope in You, love of You. Accept and warm the numbness of your poor Marie Chassaigne, Marie-Anne who comes to you broken, worn out, footsore from the long road she has travelled, frantic with grief in the throes of remorse and despair of having too often offended against You.

April 1. I have been neglecting my notebook. The Easter holidays brought us visitors from Paris: my good old friend Lewis who brought me a magnificent basket; Madeleine Vionnet who came three days earlier with her handsome Russian husband Netchvolodoff – a retired naval officer, tall, slim, elegant, with a stubborn, discontented, beaten look. He is hard on Madeleine, deceives her and spends all her money. As for her, it's quite simple: she loves him and finds it natural to put up with everything, forgive everything and work for him. She gave me five thousand francs for Saint Agnes. That was the pretext for her visit, but the real reason was to amuse Netch by showing him Liane and Prince Ghika. Madeleine is unhappy and she knows that I have been unhappy in the same way. Our sorrows make sisters of us.........

Aimée has been at Roscoff for the last two days, lying in bed with her window open on the sea. She is full of plans. I say yes to everything.

April 5. The Prior of Saint Maximin came to see us. My husband asked him lots of questions in a gentle voice but with, perhaps, rather impertinent intentions. The Father sat beside the invalid's bed, answering him simply and seriously. He stayed for about an hour and I had a few moments with him in my room where he blessed me and we had quite an edifying little exchange. I made a small contribution.

April 9. We have decided to leave on the evening of the 18th. Georges's brother will meet him in Paris and take him straight to Cautru's nursing-home, the Villa Borghèse in Neuilly. He will be quieter and warmer there, the air will be fresher, the diet will be more varied. I shall stay in rue Saussure for three days to pick up threads again and put everything in order.........

My god-daughter Margot de La Bigne spent Monday evening with me. She left on Tuesday morning to join a cruise on the *Paris*. She was so delighted to be going off like that, all on her own, to rest and breathe all that fresh and invigorating air. The poor girl spent eight months in bed after her operation. It was moving to meet again after all our disasters. She has written me a charming letter from Palma, Majorca: 'I thought you were looking well, Godmother, strong and decisive, and your face looked rested; but in spite of yourself your eyes, your beautiful face, were marked by distress and unhappiness.'

This morning I dropped my little pocket looking-glass when I was in the chemist's and it broke. I didn't care for that!

April 10. Spring is here, hot in the sun, cold at night and in the shade. Georges Ghika is braver about going out. He is preparing himself for the journey, a turning in the road, something new.

. . . .

Neuilly – Villa Borghèse, April 29 to June 7

. . . .

May 10. Aimée is here, shrunken, frail, delicate, but fresh and cheerful at having got rid of her aches and pains and believing herself to be well on the way to recovery. Aimée is here, weak and pretty and incredibly young – she hardly looks twenty-five and she is rising thirty-seven. Aimée is here, affectionate and happy. We meet again after so much sorrow, once again we have survived, and our time together is sweet. Thank You, God, and may Your will be fully and piously done since everything we have is lent to us by You.

Yesterday my friend and master Salomon Reinach sent his car for us. I saw him lying on a sofa, depressed, unhappy, his fine prophet's face scarred with pain. When I came into the room he could hardly restrain his tears. The room to which he is confined is handsome, spacious, tidy, fresh and sunny in spite of walls lined with books kept in the perfect order characteristic of a good library. His poor legs, covered with a woollen rug, refuse to work for him any more. Will his condition improve? One wants to believe it so much, one refuses to consider it hopeless. Salomon is following a frightfully strict regime. Professor Marcel Labbé is in charge of his treatment. He is in despair at being so inactive and can't resign himself to not writing and to reading much less than he used to. He could not prevent a few groans and complaints from escaping. We chatted. He told us about his condition in so far as he can judge of it, and we spoke about the President's death. Madame Reinach kindly came to join us. She is the affectionate companion who watches over everything and remains unmoved by outbursts of irritability. Being a doctor, she is valuable and beneficent at all times and in any circumstances. When I got back into the car she laid a beautiful sheaf of lilac and tulips in my lap.

Today the President of the Republic was elected. It is Albert Lebrun.

May 15. The other day I made my Easter devotions at six in the morning at a little wooden chapel in the rue de Chézy belonging to a clinic run by nuns. Georges Ghika waited for me outside in the street, in the rain, all through the service. The officiating priest was the one who confessed me. At the moment of communion I approached the holy table together with the sisters. They made a place for me by drawing aside their full skirts with such a charming movement of pious fraternity. And I was so far from feeling their fervour! Dear Lord, will you never grant me that grace?

I left the chapel very much moved, but upset. Meanwhile Georges Ghika had been alarming a lady who ran a bakery. He had been strolling up and down and she had been watching him. She opened her shutters and peered at him, whereupon she became so alarmed that she locked up her shop! If a crime had been committed in Neuilly that day, she would surely have reported my husband – 'He must be a Russian!' – and the police would have taken him in and interrogated him. I had a good laugh.

My Aimée left yesterday. The pretences and subterfuges held firm! I managed to seem credulous and stupid.

May 16. Max Jacob came to see us the other evening with a handsome set of false teeth 'which cost eleven thousand francs', said he with pride. They made him look younger, and also more diabolic than ever. He is busy trying to sell some paintings and place an article and some poems. He is very pleased with himself and is still living at the Hotel Nollet – on credit, so he says, while he waits for the result of the case he brought against the insurance company after his bad motor accident three years ago. The Nollet is expensive; they like artists there, and exploit them. Max paid for his teeth with seven thousand francs, one painting and two drawings. He is seeing a lot of Nathalie Barney and told us in a heavily meaningful way that she had forced 1,700 francs into his hands, saying: 'I have heard that you are in want, take this, you can pay me back later.' He had sent her a parcel of his manuscripts.

May 21. Yesterday evening my niece's surgeon, Doctor Bergeret, came to see me. He confirmed verbally that there is no hope. Judging by his experience, he gives her a year perhaps, or eighteen months.

May 30. .... A note from Salomon. I do so miss my drives with him! Paris, Saint-Germain, Paris, our talk, his generous affection, his lectures, our silly quarrels, the companionship . . . everything is disintegrating around me. He encouraged me to put up with things and do my duty. He made me write honestly in these notebooks – which he is sorry that he can no longer read.

June 7. We have been married twenty-two years! Gilles has written me two letters, one celebrating this anniversary, the other asking me to go with him to Roumania. I asked him for this second letter. Being face to face with me cramps his style, I thought that this way he would be more convincing. Well, he was not. I told him: 'Don't worry, I won't come with you. I have weighed the pros and cons. I ought to stay here so that is what I'll do.' He produced reasonable arguments. I shall not go. 'We will be so pleased to see each other again afterwards,' I told him. 'All I ask is that you don't do yourself too much harm.' If he had written: 'My wife, I love you, come with me, I shall be unhappy without you,' I might have been disarmed, or at any rate mollified. Nevertheless I think it was prudent from every point of view to decide not to go to Roumania in the midst of all those Ghikas and their satellites, knowing what it would be like.

While my husband is away I think I shall go to visit my dear asylum near Grenoble, then take a holiday with my old friend Lewis. He will soon be here to pick me up and take me to a charity tea at the George V, at which Yvette Guilbert will be singing. Old memories . . .

Paris – July 6 to December 29

July 6. We have been back in the flat for almost a month. A great deal of cleaning and tidying to be done, and one of my former maids, re-employed, to train. My husband leaves for Roumania tomorrow. He wants to see his mother before he and I set off on a seventy-day cruise on the *Washington* which will take us to Vancouver and back. I shall be getting ready for it. I lack the moral and physical strength to go to Roumania with him.

Because life has become so difficult Colette – whom I admire and like to see from time to time – has opened a shop selling beauty products in the rue Miromesnil. I went to the opening and she exclaimed: 'My fortune is made – here is Liane, beautiful Liane!', and she threw herself into my arms. I reeled – she is no mean weight – and let her sell me everything she wanted. A few friends approve of what she is doing, but most people blame her: 'With her talent, selling make-up!' No work is disreputable, and one thing will advance the other.

They have buried Gyp, Comtesse de Martel – eighty two years old, I believe. She once wrote to a friend: 'Dying is slow and difficult.' I already think the same.

July 12. Two notes and two telegrams from my husband. I feel more cheerful, more relaxed, full of self-confidence. Gilles is difficult in so many ways. The first time he left I thought I would die. The second time I was indignant, annoyed. This time it's all in the day's work. I have nothing left to regret, I have nothing more to expect, so let's adapt ourselves smoothly to this inevitable solitude.

Mother Marie-Xavier was here, upright and accessible, smiling with pleasure at seeing me again. Everything draws me towards her. I do so love that poor moving shelter-for-all-suffering. I foresee that it may become a refuge when I have truly succeeded in renouncing my self.

July 17. Alone . . . sad. Yes, it is sad to be alone towards the end of one's life, even though life with my husband has become a perpetual distress. I breathe more easily when we are apart, but still . . .

December 11. I am beginning this notebook on my return from a long sea voyage. I shall spread myself with pleasure on the details of this journey on board the steamer *Wisconsin.* It took us on board at Le Havre on September 12, carried us to Vancouver, and deposited us at Le Havre on November 27. I went on this cruise for the sake of my husband's health and to take his mind off his worries: his grief at seeing his mother so terribly crippled and at seeing me ageing so sadly because of his fault! Is it really because of his fault? And anyway, is it really so sad? As for him, he was anxious to give me the pleasure of this lovely cruise. But today I can only think of the great sorrow which greeted me when we got back; the death of my master and friend, Salomon Reinach. I can't bring myself to believe that I will never see him again. My friend, my matchless friend, I want to express here my inconsolable heart's emptiness and pain. I place the two last letters I had from him between these pages with pious emotion. The last of them reached me while I was on my first visit to San Francisco, then there was silence . . . he was no more. I no longer have the strength to go on, and tears are useless.

December 29. On the 24th we had a visit from Antoine Greffier, our Captain on the *Wisconsin.* We took him to a matinée at the Arts Theatre to see a play by Bernard Shaw, *Too True to be Good.* He was delighted and my husband was full of enthusiasm. I found it interesting but lacking in freshness and youth, dry and drying, the work of an old man; in short, very fine in its way, but demoralizing and conveying no impulse towards anything.

1933

Paris – January 1 to April 14

January 1. I have known since yesterday that my little Aimée will soon be dead. The disease has recurred. It is implacably there and nothing more can be done. Her anguish is apparent in spite of all her efforts – she is very brave. My God, I offer You this year which will be a cruel one for me. Grant us all your blessing, help us to do our duty, give me strength, light and a greater faith.

January 4. When I got back from having lunch with my good Lewis, I saw in my *Figaro* that Georges Menier, husband of the most beautiful, the best, the most charming of wives, has died. On the same obituary page I found an announcement of the death of Manon Thiébaut, the woman who carried off my husband in 1926! She did us – particularly him – much harm. When I believe in God and have a heart full of that grace which is Heaven's best gift, I can bring myself to forgive her . . . During my bad times it is another matter! This evening I even tried to pray for her. . . . .

January 6. They are burying Manon Thiébaut this morning. I have not yet said anything to my husband. What point is there in stirring up those stupid abominations which laid our existence waste? Nothing can ever change what happened.

January 14. The other day we went to see Madame Salomon Reinach. Sad and pious pilgrimage. We found her shrunken and reduced, tears poured from her eyes. We wanted to see the lift which Salomon had longed for. He didn't have the time, alas, to use it much.

January 19. Madame Salomon Reinach died yesterday. I do not know the details. I am shattered. It seems to me that my pure, wise, matchless friend has now died twice over.

March 17. My little Aimée died at five in the morning on March 14. I have no child, no refuge left. I was able to help her and cherish her and surround her with affection for more than six weeks. The memory is simultaneously comforting and agonizing, because I watched her suffering, shrinking, changing. She was very brave, kept going and endured everything elegantly, even. She laughed, went out with me, seemed to enjoy her food while she could still eat. My husband was a great help and support; he was loving, generous and intelligent in what he did for Aimée.

She has been in her grave since yesterday, next to her father and her mother who were carried off by the same disease. Her death leaves me very much alone. Life passes . . . Aimée has gone and I – I! – am still here.

Good Friday, April 14. During this past week I have been rereading Perroy's beautiful book *la Montée au Calvaire*. In the two years since Mother Louise Tourbiez (one of my childhood friends) introduced me to this magnificent book I have followed our Saviour's passion in this way, page by page. As I read I experience inexpressible emotions.

It is a month today since my little Aimée died. That is a nail driven into my flesh that I can offer You, God the redeemer!

My husband and I went to spend two days at Bourges. I wanted to pray on the tomb which bears the names of my brother and his wife. That of Aimée is not yet there. I saw the two children; Christiane is not yet thirteen. Since her mother's death she has grown up a great deal. I have been appointed their deputy guardian. I accepted because I am the only one left of Aimée's father's family.

Good Friday: fast, prayers, retreat. A man appeared on earth two thousand years ago and that man was the son of God. Oh Jesus, my Jesus, You who are still concealed from me, I give You my torn, calloused heart, so cold and indifferent, do with it what You will. The example of Your passion and that of the admirable devotion of my beloved sisters at the Asylum of Saint Agnes inspires me with the courage to give up everything. I am ashamed of my frivolity and triviality. I feel low and ridiculous, humiliated at never having accomplished anything big, strong or beautiful.

How could I have done that when I have never been able to conquer myself even in little things!

Toulon – le Prieuré, August 7 to October 3

August 7. I return to this notebook which I abandoned several months ago. Shattered by my niece's death and suffering from colitis, I had to rest and follow a course of treatment. It was all very trying. My organism is too old to react properly. In the midst of all that my husband thought fit to announce one day that he was off to spend two months with his mother in Roumania. On July 30 he put me on the *Train Bleu* and that same night he took off for his native land in an aeroplane. I am a bit depressed, my last years really are being rather pathetic, but it is a relief to be alone.........

August 8. There was a splendid party on June 5th. I was dressed divinely for it by Lanvin. The preceding day I had a visit from my nephew, I began to tell him about this invitation, this little pleasure to come – and suddenly I stopped in the middle of a sentence, stabbed by our cruel grief, stammering: 'Oh Louis, how frightful! I ought not to have accepted, it's not three months since our Aimée was buried. I shan't go, I'll cancel the whole thing, forgive me!' Whereupon dear Louis began to urge me not to lose this chance to escape from the sadness of my fireside and my everyday life. He went further; 'I'll take you there myself!' he said, and he did. He took me to Fouquet's where we were all to meet and form a procession of period vehicles in which we drove to la Cascade. On arrival I made a sensation. Gaby Morlay, Trébor, Madeleine Carlier, Parysis all greeted me with cheers. Someone cried out: 'Oh how beautiful Princess Ghika is, she looks just like Liane de Pougy!' Laughter. An unknown lady looked me over, shrugged and said: 'She's a very good-looking woman, but how can you compare her with Liane de Pougy!' – 'But it *is* Liane,' someone explained. 'Oh go on with you!' said the lady. 'Liane de Pougy must be as old as the hills.'

My husband writes that his mother is worse, he found her much changed. The poor woman speaks about me with affection. She admired my last photo and the one of me with him done by Piaz which she had framed and put where she can see it from her bed.

August 11. Cabanel arrived yesterday evening, thinner, pretty, glad to be back in her lovely room at the Prieuré and to see me again. The dream won't last long: her neighbours – a naval officer and his wife – have already complained about the smell coming from her room since she has been there, the smell of opium. I went in to say good morning to her. She was lying there smoking with her little incandescent stove beside her, beautiful, calm and smiling.

The Sacha Guitrys have broken up. Yvonne Printemps has run off with Fresnay, rather a pretty little actor who is married to Berthe Bovy of the Comédie-Française. Sacha has been dreadfully unhappy; Bovy has made several suicide attempts. Yvonne says that she is happy. Can one be happy when others are in despair? ....

August 14. My saint's day tomorrow. I am alone, no family near me, no intimate friends, just my memories. Memories of vanished people and silenced voices. My husband sent me a telegram and a registered letter with his wishes.........

Cabanel went through a bad time yesterday: out of opium. Frantic to the point of loss of control. She was told of a couple who smoke so much that they have had to be put up somewhere else because of the smell. Cabanel spent a marvellous evening with them, her nerves were calmed. Today my Fernande is gay, energetic, taking things easily. Why are people so very hard on this vice when they say nothing against alcoholics who fritter away their wits, their teeth, their hair, their wisdom, their happiness and their family's happiness – and bring damaged children into the world? My poor Gilles with his dentures, his irresponsibility, his sparse grey hairs, his madman's maunderings; I saw the effects of alcohol on him when he came back from his flight with that girl seven years ago, and again two years ago when he got back from Roumania: three attacks of jaundice, incurable cirrhosis of the liver, and the existence we are condemned to lead at each other's sides.

August 16. My saint's day went off rather well: letters, chocolates from my nephew, telegrams. My own present to myself was Mayol's concert. There I found my dear old pal who sang me everything I asked for, rather naughty in the way he pointed me out to the public. Two ravishing little girls of twelve and thirteen did an exquisite dance. When it was over Mayol came on stage to sing. He laughed and said: 'My two little girls are a bit of all right, aren't they?

They're my daughters. I had them with Liane de Pougy!' And everyone laughed and looked at me.

August 22. Georges writes that malaria is rampant on the maternal estates. Now that my mother-in-law has had it herself she admits its presence in the neighbourhood, but she insists that it's only since the floods. In addition there is a plague of snakes, a collapsing house with no one to repair it, an unsaleable harvest. What a holiday! I believe my charming husband is bored to death, is seeing only the dreary side of life, is missing me and would like my state of health to provide him with an excuse for coming back sooner. I shall say nothing. He has almost no money. His journey cost eight thousand francs, kindly supplied by Aunt Jeanne.

August 24. The mistral has been blowing for two days without a break. It makes one tired and irritable, but there really is something magnificent simply in the privilege of feeling the wind and watching the raging sea. The prior of Saint Maximin has moved to Toulouse. The new prior has asked me if he can take his place. I am going to thank him and tell him to pray for me because my spiritual life is difficult.

....

September 6. Henri de Rothschild has just published a book describing his youth before he got married. He refers to me in rather insulting terms that I might well have deserved but it happens not to be the truth. I met him at Angèle de Varenne's house. I can still hear Angèle saying: 'I like Liane, she's so straight that she doesn't even flutter an eyelash at our little Rothschild.' That wasn't always the case between friends. I never liked to be treacherous; I can't remember a time when I did that – flirted with a friend's lover or husband. I always waited for people to come to me, to love me, to tell me so, to prove it. Sometimes I let myself be won. And often – very often – I couldn't make up my mind: there were many occasions when I refused to give myself. They reproached me for being cold, they said I was made of ice. There were some men – and some women too, yes – who were never able to melt that ice. What I really did was love Love for Love's sake; and once my head had been won over, my body took great delight in giving itself. There were also a good many times when I was a little intoxicated animal with irresistible appetites . . . Then Georges Ghika came by, what a benefactor he was! He took me and placed me where, at my age, I ought to be.

Henri has been definitely unfair to Liane de Pougy and more than caddish to Princess Ghika. I sent him a letter, reproachful but in as nice a way as possible, ending like this: 'I forgive you, it was a mistake, wasn't it? But it was a mistake which wounded me, Henri, so for that you must send me a contribution towards buying coal for the patients in the Asylum of Saint Agnes, which you have already helped.' The cad hasn't even answered.

September 12. .... There was a picture in the paper of Célimène, Sacha and – I think – Gillaume de Ségur ('When Célimène rehearsed music-hall . . . with Sacha Guitry'). Sacha was the only one I could recognize. Sorel has had her nose done and her face lifted so often that she has ended with a different face. She is still pretty through it all, but one wonders who it is. I wrote to ask if she – she who is favoured so highly, so publicly, so universally – would make a little contribution to my asylum of Saint Agnes, and she never answered. She has no time, she forgot, perhaps she didn't even get my letter. What I expected from my long-ago comrade Célimène was some gesture as light and graceful as the flirting of a fan, something in the nature of a friendly and charming smile. Silence has reigned and I dare not disturb it.

....

September 19. Read a rather nice article about Lucie Delarue-formerly-Mardrus. She is adorable, childlike, yes – she gazes at you with ardour and amazement out of huge, wide-open eyes. She is not designed to cope with the practical side of life, but still she manages very well thanks to the talent which makes her independent, and her love of work. She is human in the best sense of the word, has been able to surround herself with a good deal of devotion and has the gift of making those who are dedicated and devoted to her perfectly happy. She publishes three novels a year, first in serial form, then as books. You think that she's off giving lectures somewhere in central Europe and then you learn that she's been having a great success in Barcelona. She sculpts, rides horses, loves first one woman, then another, then yet another. Luckily she was able to escape from her husband, and since that experience she has never thought of marrying again, nor of winning the heart of any other man.

I was given a very affectionate welcome by her after my husband had left me. She played the violin for me and read me beautiful passages from her poems to distract me from my grief. At that time she was often close to me – very close, within touching distance – gazing at me with meaningful looks, gentle and silent. She seemed to be waiting for me to make some move, to give way to some impetuous impulse. There is still something charming about the thought of that time.

September 21. Found an article in the *Mercure de France* about the great Sappho, high priestess of lesbian love. It summed up pretty well all that can be said about that legendary and fabulous woman. Miss Barney – the Flossie of my *Idylle saphique* – loved to tell me about her in her own, idealizing way. We began a one-act play in blank verse about Sappho on her island, a happy, flowery island where all the women loved each other like very tender sisters served by almost invisible slaves, nimble, quick and devoted . . . sisters with a natural disposition to every kind of caress. I do not want to expand here on lesbianism, having already said all that I think about it in that same *Idylle saphique* – all, and more. Yes, having been witness to some distressing sights, some sinister results of the practice of that vice, I wanted to drive home my opinion rather fiercely. And anyway it was necessary to do so in those days, in order to find a publisher who would consent to bring out a book on the subject. I made it lyrical and sometimes slightly realistic. That was in the days of the Amazon's youth, and of my own. We were passionate, rebels against a woman's lot, voluptuous and cerebral little apostles, rather poetical, full of illusions and dreams. We loved long hair, pretty breasts, pouts, simpers, charm, grace; not boyishness. 'Why try to resemble our enemies?' Nathalie-Flossie used to murmur in her little nasal voice.

September 25. Yesterday evening Georges Ghika arrived from Marseilles, where an aeroplane had deposited him after a trip to Athens and Corfu. He comes to me in fairly good condition except for the tip of his nose which is deformed by two boils. He has brought me some charming presents: exquisite Roumanian chocolate, excellent cigarettes, and a magnificent bright blue silk dress embroidered with gold and silver which he bought in Corfu – a traditional dress opening like a coat – picture post cards of the Acropolis, toilet water. All this is very nice, but his nose – oh his nose! . . . and in addition to that he has skinned the knuckles of his left hand. 'Clumsiness – stumbled on a tramline in Athens,' he tells me. What a fine husband to get back!

The sea is rough. If it is still rough on Friday I shan't go. I shall send them off, Netch (Madeleine Vionnet's husband) and Georges to spend four days in the Balearics, and wait their return in peace and quiet. The Mediterranean has always been particularly unkind to me. I remember with horror those crossings from Marseilles to Algiers. They were one long agony and used to send me to bed for a whole week afterwards, my liver totally capsized.

September 26. I see in *Figaro* that the Germans are getting ready to attack us. They will invade through Switzerland by way of Geneva, there will be 'The Battle of Lyon'. So much for disarmament, our victory, all that spilt blood and the work of the League of Nations!

I am packing this journal; I will get it out again in the Balearics. Grant us your protection, dear God, on this little journey which will give so much pleasure to my old bad hat.

Paris – October 12 to 15

October 12. As it turned out, God did not want us to have the Balearics and everything conspired against us getting there. Being French I didn't need a visa; being Roumanian, my husband did – very complicated, with guarantees from two Spaniards who must be resident in Spain. The Spanish consul wanted nothing to do with the matter. In vain did Georges Ghika show his papers and declare himself to be the son of the diplomat Grégoire Ghika, the cousin of the minister Demetrius Ghika, the nephew of Queen Natalie of Serbia – nothing doing. We betook ourselves to the Roumanian consul in Marseilles, one Jean Fraissinet, a rich ship-owner. There our defeat was total: he didn't even see us, made us appear before an old grey-beard who drove us mad by gabbling endless arguments . . . imagine it! The boat just about to leave, our cabin booked, and this unscalable wall! Since no one could be better equipped than I am to do it, I have just written him four pages of fury from Paris. It has made me feel a little better.

October 15. When we got to Marseilles I went down with flu. While

I was in bed I had the joy of seeing my beloved Reynaldo's triumph reported in the papers. He wrote the music for an operetta, *O mon bel inconnu*, for which Sacha wrote the book. I was not able to go to the opening which took place just when I was feeling at my worst. Reynaldo gave me a little occupation. I piled up glowing articles about his music and his rare and precious gifts, I took up my pen with heartfelt joy, I congratulated him.........

Great agitation in Europe since yesterday. Germany has withdrawn from the League of Nations and refused control of armaments. What comment can one make on this crushing news? Thanks to Hitler, that is that: nothing for it but to wait for the war and prepare on our side.

1934

Toulon – le Prieuré, August 7 to October 3

August 7. We complain, we rail, we rage, we swear that never again . . . and here we all are, back at the Prieuré with its ideal position, whimsical ways and almost perfect comfort. I have been back here since July 30 when my husband put me onto the *Train Bleu.* I have come back as I do each summer to live my little calvary of solitude.

Georges Ghika has gone to Roumania: he wants to see his poor mother, who is still crippled: he also wants – I think – to be away from me; he wants a change and some amusement; he wants to assert his independence. I have become a little old thing, a very charming little old thing, I must say. I am amazed at the extent to which I can still be charming in my face, figure, style and character. My walk has become rather heavier, that I do notice. My husband has grown older, too, in the eyes of other people. For my part I don't really notice it; I still see the rather ponderous and profound adolescent in his beautiful eyes.

August 8. We have had the revolution, the beginning! Rioting and massacres on the evening of February 6. They brought back Doumergue, the dear old boy smiled at his good Parisians who had been clamouring for a king and wanting to hang corrupt politicans, whereupon they accepted the latter just as Doumergue wished. The Stravisky affair, the death of Counsellor Prince, etc, all forgotten. They made a start, they attempted a protest, but they fell back in the same place, submitted to the same manipulation. On February 7 I went to tea at the Ritz. My husband insisted on coming to fetch me. The two of us were in the Boulevard des Capucines at about 6.30 when an army of demonstrators went by, a long procession of men walking at least ten abreast. They were grave, orderly, heads up, eyes fixed on the horizon. They were singing. One felt that they were ready to endure anything, and also to do anything. They were marching straight towards their goal, invincible. I turned to Georges Ghika and murmured: 'How beautiful they are, how I love them!' Impelled by I know not what, I moved in amongst them without fear, with sympathy and confidence. They didn't even see us, so intent were they on their goal and all the risks it involved. I shall never forget that sensation. A newspaper-seller was shutting up her kiosk as fast as she could. She said: 'Yesterday they were burning kiosks.' Yes, but it was not these men; it is the mob which follows in their wake which does the looting and stealing. Oh no, it was not *these* men!

Soon after that I went to Bandol, empty this year. The few people on the beach looked sad. The whole of France is experiencing a profound uneasiness. Everyone is wondering what is going to happen: war? revolution? perhaps both, the one bringing on the other.

Yesterday they showed Lyautey's funeral at the cinema, then that of Dollfuss. Hitler is going to be appointed supreme commander. What will he do? They say he is a visionary. Oh my God, grant us a being who is pure and strong, powerful like Mussolini. He one can only admire; everyone likes him.

August 9. I simply must make a mention here of the most fabulous, the most marvellous theatrical event of the year, unexampled, unique, incredible! The descent on the music hall of Cécile Sorel of the Comédie-Française. I saw Cécile close up at Armenonville in July. She was presiding over the competition for the prettiest hands in Paris, I was on the jury. She is fairly frightening, her body delicate, supple, quite fashionable, her face tortured, the eyes sunken and too wide open. They say that she has had her eyelids lifted and that now it's impossible for her to shut them completely. The day I saw her she had just come from the prison in which her husband, Comte Guillaume de Ségur, has been shut up for killing a woman in the street. He took fright and drove on, leaving his victim there, tried to snub the police, denied everything – succeeded in complicating his case which started out simply as that of a drunk who had been unlucky. Now he is locked up. He is not a bad fellow – a man about town without much to keep him busy, who lost his head. Naturally they asked me to perform; Varna, the director of the Palace, was very insistent. I refused. I no longer expect anything from life; I seek God with all the strength which remains to me.

August 18. Something extraordinary happened today. I had gone to Toulon to buy some silk thread. As I came out of the shop a silhouette very familiar to me was coming in, I glimpsed a half-ironic, half-amused smile: Nathalie! As soon as our eyes met I began almost to run away, making for the Café de la Rade. There I felt safe, lost in the crowd, alone at my table. I was beautiful: white pyjamas, long white crêpe de chine jacket with a navy blue belt. I haven't set eyes on Nathalie for eight years. Will that really turn out to be the last look?

August 20. Mussolini has won all hearts, including mine. His standard is that of order and peace, for the good of beautiful Italy. That corner of Europe has stopped suffering and bleeding, its wounds are healing. Let us hope that the Führer – now a dictator – will do the same thing. Let us hope that France too will find a man strong enough, steadfast enough, wise and pure enough to bring her back into the light and rediscover the strength and grandeur she has lost.

....

September 11. I have just written a long letter to Max Jacob. I tell him that the only real earthly happiness I can now envisage is doing the washing-up for my invalid children, escaping from the ignoble sewer in which I have lived and in which my old age is bogged down. I tell Max: 'I know that you will understand and that you will love my wish to do their washing-up. Would I be worthy of the task? Would it not be too good for me? *Without rubber gloves*! And doing it cheerfully, singing old songs even if only "The atmospheric lobster" ' (which Max's mother used to sing him to sleep with when he was a baby – and which Max taught us at Roscoff, with roars of laughter). Max is predestined. If Jesus remains on His cross till the end of the world, Max will be there beside him, insulted, crucified, whipped, tortured, carrying his heavy cross with a bleeding heart. He does, of course, have instincts which are hard to overcome, his share of human baseness, but what grandeur and nobility there is in his incessant poverty, in the persistence of his efforts, in his impulses of love, in his inexhaustible and always alert charity!

October 3. Georges Ghika is with me again. He doesn't look too bad. He arrived with his trunks full of presents, an affectionate smile on his face, full of solicitude and all the details of his journey. He wanted to find out about Mussolini's work, so he visited Sabaudia and Littoria. He broke his journey at Rome and made an excursion as far as Ostia, to see the *autostrada*. He found everything magnificent. The Pontine marshes drained, two comfortable and charming townships built for ex-service men. Land has been allotted, farms built. Everything is governed and directed by a spirit of openness, clarity, precision and practicality. Georges was filled with admiration. Bravo! That is what patriotism ought to mean! At present Mussolini is my idol.

Arcachon – November 14 to November 19

November 14. Big hotel, half shut, half heated. Good food, and the people are charming and attentive, glad to have us here to provide them with something to do. We have covered the neighbourhood in every direction in spite of rain, thunder, wind, hail and cold. I put on my big rubber boots and my raincoat and off we go along the jetties, the beaches, the streets, window-shopping, buying warm underclothes and woollies, equipping ourselves for the weather.

November 17. Doumergue is now back at Tournefeuille. Why is France governed by old fogeys, so unlike the leaders of the other Powers? How envious I am of Italy with her Mussolini! Our leaders are old, white-haired, flabby, sly, selfish. They intrigue, they talk drivel. Yet France is so beautiful, so majestic, so magnificent. We ought to have a young King, a dictator, a president, a man of energy, open in his dealings, a saviour, a child of France entirely dedicated to reviving and renewing the sickening, stagnant, crumbling government which is at present preparing the darkest pages in our history!

....

1935

Le Havre – July 8 to August 20

July 8. My husband left me here a week ago – it is pure luck that the hotel people happen to be charming – and has gone off as he does every summer to play the naughty boy and the infamous husband. His excuse, as usual, is his mother's continuing illness. Who could argue with such an excuse?

I return to my blue notebook yet again, and start with some very sad news. The day I left Paris, skimming my *Figaro*, I saw that Frédéric de Madrazzo, perhaps my most intimate and dearest friend, was dead. His health was always very delicate in all kinds of way. He lost his mother when he was very small. While he was still a little boy his father's imperious love for Mademoiselle Hahn (Reynaldo's sister) gave him an amiably indifferent step-mother.

Today he is the only thing I want to talk about. I am unhappy – unhappy for my own sake, not his. Frédéric was extremely musical – but he was brought up very close to Reynaldo and Reynaldo wanted to be a musician, so Jou-jou made way for him, remembered that his father was a painter and turned his energies in that direction. He always obliterated himself before the friend of his infancy whom he loved wildly and completely until the end – Reynaldo hardly let himself love – Frédéric so ugly, Reynaldo so beautiful, prodigiously beautiful, a dream of beauty, beautiful with so many beauties, beauty of mind, of mystery, of the finest culture, of sensibility.

One day when I was about twenty-four I fell ill, became anaemic, every day that spring I was made to drink the sharp green juice of three bunches of cress. This cure restored me, but it gave me a crop of big red pimples which completely disfigured me. Frédéric came to see me. I didn't mind showing myself to him. He thought that I was ruined for ever and he found words, gestures . . . how well I remember. He knelt down beside my bed, kissed my hands and said: 'Look after yourself, I will go to work, I will give you all the money you need. I, at any rate, will always be here, whatever the others do. You mustn't be unhappy, you mustn't worry. Have courage!' He came to lull me to sleep every evening, lying at the end of my bed. He played with my feet, my lovely feet (size 37 – that's small considering that I am tall: one metre 68) with their long toes which the pedicurists used to say were beyond compare and which now hurt me so much! So Frédéric played with my feet, his nervous, sensitive hands started to roam higher. I laughed, he told me stories, then became strange, incoherent. How could this emotion be concealed from our gay, quick youth? I could not hold out against it. He gazed at me with wild eyes, paused, then blankets flew in every direction and he fell on me, crazy, quite out of control, sobbing and weeping. Alas – he was too nervous, too excited, all he could do was devour me so passionately that I almost fainted and he spent himself. He was soaking, my sheets were wringing wet. We never tried again, we hardly even referred to it. He was more or less an invert, his love of beauty led him towards handsome men. Reynaldo represented his first meeting with beauty. Freud could explain it better than I can.

July 9. My husband wrote to me on June 8th, the day of our jubilee – our silver wedding. And I had a nice poem in English from the dear boy, as well. Distance is already having its effect. I get a fond and charming letter every day – the little holiday (!) task. He is at Florence staying with his Aunt Jeanne and sends me magnificent postcards of the Duce, who fascinates me. Pleasant habits which have survived catastrophe.

July 11. When my god-daughter Margot lost her mother she came on a bundle of letters addressed to her grandmother, Valtesse de La Bigne; twenty-four of them were from me. She put them in an auction! My twenty-four letters fetched sixty francs. Indecent treachery! Nothing on earth would surprise me now.

July 12. Mother Saint-Anselme writes to give me news of Mother Marie-Xavier. Alas, I know that she is very ill, quite worn out and without strength, and that she cannot take the absolutely indispensable rest which she ought to take. I beg her, I advise her, I send her the means for it; for one reason or another all she will consent to are half-measures. I know, I can feel that quite soon this friend is going to leave me, leave me even more broken, even more desolate. God wants me to be alone – and it is moving and splendid to be able to hear those three words in my soul: God wants me!

July 14. A touching note from Yvonne de Bray. I haven't seen her: she lives most of the time in a Neuilly nursing-home the name of which is not divulged. She takes a cure, returns to life, relapses. Last spring she attempted to go on tour with a series of sketches; the first stop was Brussels; they had to bring down the curtain and return the money. She is an incurable dipsomaniac, drinking everything she can lay hands on, even her eau de cologne. She will never get another engagement and will lose all her friends. It is appallingly cruel to see that mind foundering in madness. Have pity on her God, You endowed her with such gifts.

July 15. Anniversary of the day on which I got married and on which, with one thrust which quite deprived me of breath, I lost my virginity.

July 17. Heaven has sent me a friend in my moral solitude: François Siraudrey who writes me beautiful pious letters, tells me what books to read, and at the end of the month sends me twenty-five francs for coal for Saint Agnes. He is punctual, he is good, his thought is elevated and he wants mine to be the same. I answer his letters and follow his advice to the best of my ability. He also sends me pictures with beautiful prayers printed on the back. It compensates a little for all the blasphemy I hear, all the irony heaped on me. I find it rather comforting to think that somewhere there is a good and pious man who is thinking of me, prays for me, takes the trouble to send me advice. He has given me a guardian angel, Pauline Leroy, a pious young woman who has just died of tuberculosis at the age of thirty-three. She suffered a great deal, and a few days before her death she promised him that she would be my good angel in heaven and would watch over me. I feel all this, I am moved by it, but I have not earned the marvellous boon of an absolute faith. Brother François is poor, he works and deprives himself for the sake of Saint Agnes and in order to write to me and make me read this or that. I am lukewarm, he wants to drive me on to apostleship! Alas, I am a very long way from that. He doesn't realize – can't even imagine – my conditon and my sad surroundings.

....

August 12. Have been reading some odd little childish songs – our poets go in for them at times. There was this by Cocteau: 'Am-stram-gram-bouret-bour-et-ratatam', and readers roared with delight. Between each couplet of one of his songs, Max Jacob had the line: 'I-want-to-make-pipi-and-I'm-going-to-make-it-here.' I don't really understand the artistic value of this kind of thing, or what is funny about it.

August 18. Benjy arrived at six o'clock in the morning and I had him without interruption until half-past nine in the evening. I was exhausted: talking English all day – an effort; talking loudly because of his deafness – an effort. What a dear thing he is! I am pretty sure that several times during the day he made little passes at me – little amorous wheedlings. He brought me some of what used to be my favourite scent, and he had ordered me a magnificent pot of hydrangeas – flowers that frighten me, but how could I tell him that? I accepted them – grinning like someone whose toes are being trampled!

August 19. Georges arrives the day after tomorrow: back to our accustomed ways, back to hearing cynicism and blasphemy, back to the pain which comes from lack of tenderness. My Benjy, on the other hand, heaps me with it, takes me in his arms, kisses me. But I cannot and will not surrender. He leaves this evening on the Southampton boat which sails at eleven o'clock. I am rather tired from talking so much English; but these signs of affection, this desire, these offered arms and lips have cheered me up. And he is eighty years old! Men, poor fellows, never give up. Alfred! Eternally loving, unable to see my wrinkles – or else liking them – melting with tenderness at the sight of me.

August 20. Alfred left yesterday evening. He was tender, cheerful, generous, he even managed to make a display of passion – in vain. My virtue triumphed over his pressing advances. At times I really had to put up quite a struggle. This surfacing of youthful love is beautiful. Soon I shall have nothing to envy Ninon de Lenclos. It has all been quite transfiguring – a woman needs to feel loved.

1936

Le Havre – August 1 to December 26

August 1. I return to these notebooks after a year's interruption. In the last few months some serious things have happened. My mother-in-law died in Bucharest on December 19. When they received news of her attack, my husband and his brother left by train in order to pay her their last respects and be invested with their estates – big words for what in fact came to them.

France has had a decisive election and is now in the hands of Léon Blum and his set. I once had a slight acquaintance with Léon Blum, in Henry Bernstein's set. He is a cultivated man who carries weight, a thinker, a decent man. He seemed to me to be afraid of responsibilities – it is now his fate to have them forced on him by circumstances. There have been strikes, first one, then another, finally general: a sure and silent method without cruelty or bloodshed, but still implacable.

Cécile Sorel is singing and dancing at the Alcazar with her husband, Guillaume de Ségur, grandson of the famous countess. They need the money. That sort of thing proves how the times have changed. Mistinguett is making a film at the age of sixty-six, and she will be good in it. Her talent is human, comic, full of feeling. Child of the Paris streets that she is, she is so French! One feels rather sorry for Sorel, but one marvels at Mistinguett.

Colette is a commander [of the Legion of Honour]. She has had to shut up her beauty shop, but she keeps a little back-door ajar for favoured customers.

And now we come to the bloody days of the Spanish revolution, which takes precedence over everything else at the moment. Churches burnt down, streets turned into fields of battle. No more respect for anything, butchery. Those who can escape the flood of destruction by emigrating are lucky. They are pouring into the south of our own tormented country.

As for us, we are here in this dear, charming little hotel with its ravishing view of the harbour and its boats, surrounded by greenery, flowers and birdsong. Down there they are killing each other, lying in wait, burning; here we have the usual antiquated music of the merry-go-rounds and the coming and going of many coloured cars. Here we will wait for what is to come, for what they will tell us. Leaving my France in such a condition will make me unhappy; but at my age, at the end of my life, what else can I do? I will try to find some peace and quiet in England. I shall retire there, and then my God I shall pray to You every hour of every day to have pity on my country; yes, I shall spend my exile in prayer, and no sacrifice will seem too hard in my attempts to reach and move You, oh my Lord God, thou who are also our Father.

August 5. A Saint Anne's day letter from Max Jacob. He never forgets. These are hard days for the old poet, the great artist in his decline. I thanked him and he sent us a copy of the new edition of his *Saint-Matorel*, which can be considered as his masterpiece. He spoke of how much he missed our summers at Roscoff, saying: 'Roscoff, our Paradise lost.'

Rather worrying letter from our old friend Alfred Benjamin. He is over eighty. I am afraid he is ill. I want to see him again, to go to England, which may become our refuge one of these days whether we like it or not, as it did for our ancestors. And two days ago, as though destiny were bent on fulfilling my wish, I open a newspaper and see an advertisement for an excursion to England: August 21 to August 24, leaving on the *Ile-de-France* and returning on the *Normandie*. Once in London, of course, all we shall want to do is see Benjy, so we will dump the rest of the group. Georges went to see the Company; we were enrolled; they even told him that because we had been the Company's clients and spoilt children in the past, they would put a very good cabin at my disposal – the members of this little cruise are only allowed to use one particular deck.

....

August 27. Here we are, back again, tired, dazzled, enchanted. It all went off quite beautifully.

We set off – rather moved – on the *Ile-de-France* at three o'clock on the 21st. The ship stopped off Southampton and we left her hospitable decks for an ugly little tender. Then nearly two hours crossing the wide, calm bay, the night air brisk, stars, lights. We saw the Isle of Wight and great luminous ships gliding past, unreal and silent. The special train was waiting for us when we disembarked and we reached Waterloo at 1.20 in the morning, two hours late. I was sure my dear Benjy would have gone away, but no sooner had I set foot on the platform than I saw him romping towards us, laughing and waving. We went off in a magnificent Daimler, as fine in its way as the *Ile-de-France*. A room was waiting for us at the Grosvenor Hotel, a big bunch of lilies of the valley on the table between our beds, my favourite English scent on the dressing-table, pink crystals for my bath, chocolates, excellent cigarettes – every kind of spoiling, in fact. We gazed at each other fondly over supper. It was a lovely, friendly, joyful occasion, our confident and tender youth was there within us and around us.

August 28. All of Saturday was devoted to Alfred. He gave me a magnificent red and white scarf to wear over my head when on deck, which is the fashion at the moment. This beautiful scarf was signed 'Rodier' – long live French taste and those who appreciate it! We lunched at the Savoy, still quite elegant for the summer, cosmopolitan, the food exquisite. After lunch a little walk and a good siesta, then we dressed for dinner and a cabaret – at the Savoy again. I wore a pretty dinner suit of black satin with a big white flower on the lapel and another magnificent new scarf made of black cashmere round my neck. Good dinner, elegant, quiet people, dancing, cabaret acts. I was tired to death but felt happy and spoilt, plunged back into the atmosphere of my youth when I was pleased with myself and people loved me.

August 30. On the Sunday I told Alfred to order the Grosvenor's famous 'grilled bones'. They were exquisite. We went to rest, I packed my case, and after tea Alfred took us to catch the train at Waterloo. The suburbs, then a little of that radiant English country-side, meadows, trees, heather – carpets of mauve heather sur-rounded by the world's most beautiful greenery. On board the *Normandie* the purser had us conducted to 'Mont Saint Michel', a ravishing suite: luxurious and pretty dinging-room, bedroom decorated in pale lemon yellow, the beds covered in pink satin, bathroom, showers, a vestibule with closets. At one-thirty they came to lay a lovely table for our lunch. It didn't last long, but it was a fairy tale!

The other day Georges bought a copy of the Popular Front newspaper from a young red who brandished it under our noses. He was enchanted when the young man said 'Thanks, comrade'. He's such a child – hard to put up with – laying down the law about everything, sarcastic, unsociable, looking down his nose at poor human nature and reacting against anything that's established. At his best he is not a bad little chap. My pity for him is so affectionate that I can no longer get angry.

....

September 4. Letter from dear Benjy. As he says so nicely, how pleasant for me that my last days are brightened by such a solid and loving affection!

Georges enjoys the news from Spain as though he were watching some horrible ballet. He is going on about how sorry he is that we didn't go to Pau instead of coming here, because on the frontier he could have had a near view of the disaster, been able to hear the sound of battle, machine-guns, aeroplanes, bombs. I said to him: 'How bored you would be in Heaven.'

....

November 16. 'What does he know, who has never been tested?' I read that fine line in yesterday's chapter of the *Imitation of Jesus Christ*. It is true that a satisfied, full-fed person who has been successful almost without a struggle is never sensitive or interesting. 'Who knows himself who has not suffered?' said the poet. Suffering is good, it purifies, sanctifies, enlarges, elevates. We must tell ourselves all that in order to comfort ourselves and make it more bearable. Joy is only for little children – yet how well they know how to cry from their earliest days! ....

November 18. And now there has been a strike at my Ritz! To think that an institution of the Ritz's elegance should be touched by such a manifestation of modernity! Some guests have left, others haven't come. I am going to send my condolences to our charming and faithful Olivier, so sincere and devoted, his affection mingled with his strict sense of etiquette; Olivier, friend and confidant of Marcel Proust whose invalid's existence made him depend greatly on gossip and tittle-tattle.

....

December 4. The papers are full of the adventures of King Edward VIII who is madly in love with a charming American and wants to marry her. The clergy, severe and cold, have expressed their displeasure. They allege that coronation is a sacrament, that a king's wife must be a queen, and that because Mrs Simpson has been divorced she can't possibly fulfil the conditions. Give way, or abdicate. The King does not want to give way; the Duke of York is getting ready to take his place. What a beautiful love story! The people of England are quite crestfallen. They seem to be very fond of their king, who on his side has lent himself to the job's innumerable demands with great good will and much style.

December 5. More articles about Edward VIII and Mrs Simpson. Everyone is thrilled: a king carried away by love, ready to renounce his throne! Young English people have been demonstrating in his favour outside Buckingham Palace. It really is the apotheosis of love. Imagine Georges Ghika renouncing his Liane, twenty-eight years ago!

December 9. My old Benjy thinks the King is wrong. He himself has always put snobbery and material success before love, so he has no experience of the great disturbances which make life worth living.

December 11. Edward VIII has just abdicated. He has sacrificed his crown for love of a woman. He did not give way; that is royal. He has left everything for the one he loves: he is a marvellous and courageous lover. The story is a larger version of my own. I was rather younger than Mrs Simpson at the time of my marriage to Georges Ghika who was many years younger than I was but who was very serious, basically very serious and didn't often laugh.

December 26. A mildly happy Christmas; spoiling by Georges, traditional lunch.

Charming, affectionate, optimistic letter from Max Jacob. A pity we are so far apart! He wishes us a share of his peace – that day's peace, or that hour's, or even that moment's, given how unstable, tumultuous and capricious he is, as changeable as the sea or the wind! He veers between genius and absurdity, love and hate, gentleness and rage, kindness and cruelty, but he is not able to be ungenerous. Dear Max, dear Max, my new-year's heart wishes him so much good!

1937

Le Havre – January 3 to March 10

January 3. Farewell to a tragic year, and may 1937 prove to be assuagement, balm, convalescence, renewal! The war in Spain continues, it is no longer a civil or guerrilla war but a European war, a war between the parties. Reds of every nationality are taking part and coming to the rescue. Europe is a chess-board, whites against reds. Alas, when all are brothers . . .

January 9. The year began in an almost symbolic fog; there is no brightness in sad European life.

We are getting ready to spend a few days in Paris during the coming week. It is an event, and I realize sadly that my strength is failing and the least thing exhausts me.

I saw something at the cinema which broke my heart. The film described a day in the hard life of the miners of Charleroi. We were spared nothing, not even the sight of unhappy children of fourteen or fifteen with blackened faces. How can we go on laughing, amusing ourselves, breathing fresh air, gorging ourselves, when our brothers are bent under the weight of their work in a hell such as that! How those people must hate us! I understand, yes I understand the hate in the air these days. It is only a few people, and always the same ones, who enjoy the blessings of civilization. We ourselves are the real barbarians, the real tyrants. I don't know; I no longer know what is good and what is bad. You have made the earth so beautiful, God, and this is how we use it. From now on I understand revolt and protest, I understand why brothers kill each other.

January 11. I have calmed down. That is the trouble: we calm down, we accept, and everything goes on as before. I am packing bit by bit, a woman fussing over herself and avoiding fatigue – and those other people down there in the depths of the mines, continue as before. I try not to forget anything which might contribute to our comfort – and those people down there . . . Yes, I do work for Saint Agnes – that has fallen to my lot – I do what I can for it. In spite of all the difficulties and worries, in spite of people's becoming poorer, we do still manage to find charitable and generous benefactors.

January 27. We are back in Paris where we spent ten days at the Hôtel de Castille . . . where Jean Cocteau has been staying. So Jean was a neighbour, still bouncy, sparkling, dazzling, smoking his opium at fixed times.

February 8. . . . . Are we going to South America or to Switzerland? Nothing has been decided yet. To be undecided is to dream a little.

My husband has just gone out: a little shopping, a letter to post. I often stand by the window to watch him leaving. He always looks up, we smile and throw kisses. The people going by and the taxi-drivers on the rank watch us and must say to themselves: 'How those two do love each other.' At bottom they are right. I would detest him so much if I were not fond of him!

February 16. Georges was quite determined to persuade me into a wonderful cruise to Buenos Aires, Rio, Montevideo, etc, and had found a ship which met all our conditions: date of departure, price, comfort. And now we read in this morning's *le Petit Havre* that there have been outbreaks of trouble on board, scenes at the various ports, and that it would not be possible to disembark and see all those lovely unknown countries, which would be the purpose of the voyage. It would be pointless to go in those conditions. We agree about this and have told Aunt Jeanne and our close friends, and now we are looking for some other dream. It will probably be Switzerland, beautiful, stodgy, grand, slow. Perhaps it will win me over by being peaceful and welcoming? I like obeying fate's mysterious decrees. Heaven no longer wants to grant me another lovely cruise.

Mother Marie-Xavier has written me a letter which ends like this: 'We have lost Nathalie, the dwarf who used to hit herself when she was happy. Her death was holy. Ten minutes before her last breath, having received extreme unction, she said to me: "I give my life to dear God so that he will let you keep yours a very long time.* Thank you, Mother, and all the sisters." ' I was moved to tears. How beautiful and peaceful it is, that little nook of suffering so remote from wars, slaughter, lies – that little dream-nook.

Articles on 'The Beauties of the Past'. I am in good company (Cavalieri, Cléo de Mérode), but how ugly the photos are, and the style of the captions is as out of date as we are!

March 1. The first day of the month in which we will leave Le Havre. Yet another stage finished. We were here waiting to go on a cruise. Cruises seem to be done with. It will be Paris – transit – then Grenoble, that corner of Heaven, and finally Switzerland. We have a 'pretext' – I can't say a 'reason' – which is to take Georges to his Aunt Jeanne. And I feel within me a strong desire to live in peace, quietly, in that beautiful landscape where the air is freshened by snow. It is an egotistical desire, but my strength has run out: it is a rather mad desire. How can it be anything but mad, to long for peace in any place where there are men? It is at Grenoble that I want to end my days. Will that be given me? Will I be allowed one day to wash dishes for my invalids and the holy sisters, their poor dishes of chipped enamel? To obey the rule, within hearing of the convent bell; to play a part in that shelter of suffering – of suffering, yes, but also of devotion, piety, goodness, renunciation? There I could have opened my hands and let everything go. Am I capable of that? To be capable of it would be to be worthy of it. Lord, speak just one word . . .

. . . .

Paris – Hôtel de Castille, March 18 to April 10

March 18. We have been here since yesterday evening, with an enormous amount of luggage.

We left the Grand Hotel, or rather its proprietors, without much regret, their helpfulness and friendliness faded out in the course of our long stay. Nevertheless, sickly and unbalanced Madame cried when the time came to say goodbye, and gave me two roses to pin to my mink. May Heaven bless them.

* Mother Marie-Xavier died in 1956 at the age of ninety.

March 19. Cécile Sorel has tried to poison herself. Her husband Guillaume de Ségur had left her; he has gone off with quite a young girl. Jean Cocteau, who came by yesterday, told us all about it. I suddenly noticed a shadow of embarrassment in his look, a hesitation in his voice. He was remembering that I had been abandoned, and how distressed I was. He exclaimed: 'I've simply got to have an hour's sleep, I'm absolutely exhausted!' and disappeared.

March 22. .... We went for a drive round the lakes in the Bois, to Neuilly and to Boulogne. There I saw a brand new plaque bearing the name of Salomon Reinach. I shut my eyes, I saw the master's dear handsome face, the indulgent, reflective look he kept specially for me, his rather reserved smile, the characteristic serenity of his expression, even at the very end. So then I wanted to go slowly past his house. I saw the shady enclosure which used to protect him, the wide bay-window behind which stood his big desk; behind the desk was the chaise-longue on which he lay for several months, his whole body in pain, his mind so alive. We went to see him there. I took him flowers, and when I was leaving, just as I was disappearing through the door, he very quickly blew me a pert little kiss off the tips of his fingers, with a delightful smile. Salomon . . . I feel brimming with tenderness and dreams, I loved him so much. I often used to disturb him. I knew that, I rather made a game of it for my own amusement. I used to tease him, I often made him cross. I abused the deep and affectionate interest he took in me. How badly I needed his purity, his friendship, the support he gave me, and his knowledge too.

April 10. We leave tomorrow. I have had a great deal to do. I went to rue Saussure to collect the last of the things we will need. I shut it all up, said farewell to my dear family portraits and my family mementos. Will I ever see them again? Since then I have had an aching heart and the sorrowful and tormented feelings of an emigré. There are a lot of rumours, one meets a great many anxious people. Now the forty-hour week is a fact the big stores all shut on Mondays. They say the Exhibition will open on May 3rd and that nothing is ready. The building sites are often deserted. Foreigners are doubtful about coming – announce that they will, then postpone or cancel. I am leaving my Paris with a heavy heart.

My friends have been exquisitely attentive, competing with each other to spoil me.

I have seen a friend of Max's, Sauguet the musician, who had been staying at Saint-Benoît. He says Max is well, and working, that he dresses like a peasant, that he gets physical strength from the fresh calm air of the Loire valley and moral strength from his solitude.

Vevey – April 22 and 23

April 22. We have been in this magical, peaceful place since yesterday, in a quiet, comfortable hotel on the lake-shore. Our ground-floor room is huge and blue, with a pretty bathroom. There is a stream of cars going past the hotel, which is on a street corner, but no hooting to be heard: the cars pass silently, slow up at the cross-roads, glide furtively away. An impression of gentleness and peace struck me the moment I got out of the train at Geneva yesterday. I shall describe my ten days at Grenoble and my agonizing visits to the asylum tomorrow. Mother Marie-Xavier's affection gave me plenty of moral courage, but I was very weak physically, panting for the calm restfulness of a lakeside resort, for the cleanliness, neatness and delicious slowness which Switzerland provides.

The sky is grey, the clouds are low, the mountain is shrouded, the sea-gulls have disappeared, it's the time of day for melancholy thoughts . . . I want to turn mine to my marvellous saint, to her life of sacrifice, to that illumination which radiates from her, throwing light and warmth. Oh how badly my emigré's soul needs her, and how I bless You, dear God, for giving her to me.

April 23. To go back to Grenoble. Having arrived very early in the morning, I did not send a message to Mother Marie-Xavier because I knew she was not well and the last thing I wanted to do was tire her. We booked the best room in the Hôtel de l'Europe – oh dear, poor France! Forty-five francs a day, beds which didn't match (one of them simply a frame and a mattress on the floor), two windows opening onto an incessantly noisy street, trams, hysterical hooting, bells, the lot. No curtains in the windows, just thin blinds with makeshift cords which wouldn't work . . . every morning the night's dirty linen piled in the hall. We were as good as gold and didn't murmur. After all, we had before us the most marvellous example of sacrifice and renunciation: Mother Marie-Xavier. As soon as I had unpacked and rested a little, I could wait no longer; towards the end of the first day I sent her a message by telephone saying that I was there – at last! – and had come in order to see her. The next day my holy Mother came to the hotel, together with the little Polish sister, Sister Saint Augustine. We were much moved, very happy. Mother Marie-Xavier looked well, better than I had expected after three years of bad health. Oh how sweet and good it was to see her and listen to her. She wanted to have us to lunch the next day, and the day after that as well. I accepted. The sister had prepared us a delicious feast, and sat down with us although she didn't eat – that is the rule. I gave her a small sum of money from us both, necessary for the purchase of some water rights which she wanted badly and for which she was being charged far too much. We had bought sweets and apple turnovers for the children and gave them a party: sausages and brioches for the little ones, cheese for the big ones. Oh how appalling it was when we went in to see this agonizing spectacle. We had forgotten. There were a hundred and ten of them, and worse – yes, worse. Faces tortured and convulsed, eyes anguished, hunted, crazy or blank. Surrounded by these poor creatures, I thought I would fail, I wanted to push my way to the door, to flee. I looked at my holy Mother and I held firm, I made the rounds, I saw everything, I talked to them in so far as I could, stomach quaking, nostrils pinched, sustained by her splendid example. There is one child which has lived in a wicker cradle for six years without stirring, horrifying, the hands of a new-born infant, a long serious face, heavy eyebrows, a woman's eyes, an atrophied body. She was surrounded by the howling, twitching crowd. Some of them wept, some jigged, they slobbered, wrung their hands, threw themselves on the floor. Some of them came up to us and touched us, babbling incomprehensibly, their wet mouths grinning from ear to ear. All of them gave off a frightful smell in spite of the incessant care which Gabrielle Chanel's generosity has made possible.

Afterwards we were horrified, broken. For the first time I said to myself: 'They ought to be put to sleep for ever.' When I accused myself of this rebellion to Mother Marie-Xavier she said: 'They are being cared for; that is enough, our task is not useless.' It is all immense, magnificent, sublime. Faced with such sanctity, it is I, I who am and who feel myself to be the poorest creature on earth. Sanctity of the stricken, of pitiless suffering; sanctity of devotion. I tell myself: these are the Lord's beloved. What, on either hand, are they expiating?

We went back the next day; then a third time, when they sang me two songs. One of the least afflicted read us a little speech with great emotion. We pressed a great many poor little damp, misshapen hands. We promised that we would come back . . .

I am too much moved to be able to express myself properly. You who are reading what I say – go to see them, spend just five minutes with them and you will never again be able to complain of anything.

1940

Lausanne – Clinique de Bois-Cerf, October 15 to October 21

October 15, the Feast of Saint Teresa of Avila. Praise the Lord, o my soul; inspire me, o Holy Spirit, to express God's goodness towards His poor, misguided, sinful creature. Great Saint Teresa who burnt with love of Him, awaken my poor heart which would be broken, bruised, bleeding if it had not been – by God's marvellous grace – recovered.

It is on my knees that I ought to be writing these lines; it is on my knees that I think, that I prepare them, that I attempt to co-ordinate my thoughts. I never succeed. Cries break out, outbursts of feeling throw my whole being into such a turmoil that I am quite unable to write methodically about the extraordinary events which brought me here to the dear Trinitarian Ladies of Bois-Cerf, to their example, their faith and their devotion.

It was God who willed it, God who guided me. The sinner has disappeared, Liane de Pougy of the forty blue notebooks full of iniquity and scandal, lightness, frivolity, intrigue and lies – Liane de Pougy is no more. 'My God, my suffering at having offended You is extreme.'

October 16. 'The sight of the Lord is beyond compare.'

First movement of divine grace towards me, June 8, 1910, my marriage with Prince Georges Ghika, ending my dizzy descent into disorder and sin. After my little Georges's act of – say it! – so much courage as well as of love, I completely changed my life. Wedding at the town hall, wedding according to my religion, after obtaining dispensation, at Saint-Philippe-de-Roule. Confession, which I thought of as a necessary formality and dispatched quite lightly. Not wanting to hide anything or to lie, but being unable all the same to give the details of my interminable list of sins, I settled for saying: 'Father, I have lived a very free life. Apart from killing and stealing I have done everything.' I came away with a load off my mind, believing that I had amply fulfilled my duty and thinking that I could put myself right with God like that. I went on living the life of an elegant woman, pagan, free in language even if careful in behaviour, frivolous, egoistical, whimsical. All my whims were highly approved of by Georges, Georges the atheist, the free-thinker who believed in nothing – which never ceases to stab me.

October 17. .... My dream would be to shut myself away and see no one but our dear Trinitarian Ladies who have really become everything to me now, family and friends. Their example is beautiful: it has won me over and carried me along with it. I hope I can stay here, can die here. I am not free of fear; events follow each other violently, explode, scatter us, as God wills.

To go back to my story . . . After my marriage my conduct improved, but no faith, no prayer; absolute aridity: a more or less graceful, more or less charming animal drawn back into the herd by adequate emotions.

The war of 1914: our house in Saint-Germain turned into a dressing-station, devotion to the motherland, yes, but it was an unthinking sort of excitement; Marco's departure when he volunteered with Gilbert Garros; his death . . . I fell victim to an indescribable despair, a grief made far worse by remorse at not having been a good mother, at not having loved that child enough, at having preferred Georges – that is to say myself – to my son. I became very ill, a nervous disease, food and space phobia. I learnt the cruelties of nursing-homes. During this physical collapse I came to perceive the fact that I had a soul which had woken up under the pressure of suffering, a soul which was looking for the light, which was looking for something which cannot be found on earth. I began to pray to my good and powerful patron Saint Anne, mother of Mary – Mary who was so pure that my unworthiness dared not turn towards her. I could no longer remember my prayers very well; I dug down into my memory; it was painful and difficult. I spoke to Saint Anne often, asking for forgiveness and help. In that way, bit by bit, I contrived a sort of fervent piety, a religion all my own, still very remote from the true way, but taking me – with God's help – in the right direction. Some undesirable friendships were not able to hold me back; gradually I was able to sacrifice them. Some of them chose to leave me. I began to resist my own inclinations and their passions. I began to go into churches. Not daring to go in further than the holy-water stoup, I stammered prayers, was present during parts of masses, spoke to God, glimpsed Jesus on His cross, and at last I made my confession to good Abbé Duchemin at Saint-Germain. I told him everything that came into my mind and I made my act of contrition with all my heart, but I was still very far from the 'extreme suffering' which I feel today when the weight of my sins crushes me to the point of feeling dizzy as I ask how could I, how could I, when I didn't even have the excuse of liking that frivolous life of so-called pleasure.

The Jesuit Father Pierre Charles tells us that while we must certainly repent of our sins and rid ourselves of them, we should at the same time see them as a means of proving God's loving-kindness and the miraculous forgiveness he grants us. I was advised to read his book last spring, by Father Sanson who stayed a short while at Bois-Cerf, and my dear Sister Marguerite who runs the clinic and looks after all bodily matters as well as those of the soul, when the need arises. This book made me better able to trust in God, to give myself over to His will, and to conduct my life in such a way as to be close to God every hour of the day. I had made a beginning – very imperfectly – when an old Superior of the Faithful Company of Jesus (the convent of my childhood) – who is still at their house in Amiens and who had maintained a pious correspondence with me – advised me to read *The Road to Calvary* during Lent. It overwhelmed me. That book awoke the love for Jesus that had been sleeping in my heart.

Sister Marguerite also gave me several pamphlets, one of them about the Mass. I had remained impervious to these rites and our beliefs. I was ignorant, I didn't understand or want to understand. I rejected whatever might have shown me the way.

October 18. There was the death of my son . . .

There was my husband's flight one July morning in 1926. That quite crushed me. That violent blow changed me completely, stripped me. Then, when my husband came back, cynical and dissolute, a wild horse trampling everything underfoot, sickly and ill – that was cruel. I took him back, I love him.

I try to set him a good example, I pray for him. There is no visible sign yet, except perhaps for a change in his language. Blasphemy, obscene words and sacrilegious irony have gradually disappeared. He is fond of the sisters and they are fond of him. He is charming to them, gentle, friendly, doing whatever he can to please them and doing it willingly. He enjoys arranging the flowers in their pretty chapel, takes me there twice a day and waits for me near the door, in the garden. Grant me, o God, the conversion of my husband Georges, my friend, my devoted companion, my unhappy child.

And then there was the appearance in our life of the reverend Father Rzewuski.

October 19. We had met him in Paris, remarkably handsome, young, attractive, full of the joy of life, much in demand, much liked. We had lunch with him in the rue de Lubeck at the house of Madame Mac Cormick, whose portrait he was painting. Impossible to forget him.

Last December 24 Georges and I were waiting for Sister Marguerite in the hall at Bois-Cerf when we beheld a most striking apparition in the person of a Dominican father in his white habit, with his black cape slung over his shoulder. He was going up the main staircase, upright, erect, illuminated as though he were going up to heaven itself. His eyes swept over us. I was disturbed, and said to Georges: 'Don't you think he's very like that young Polish artist we met at Madame Mac Cormick's?' A few weeks later, when we were installed here, we were lunching in the dining-room when Georges said to me: 'Look, there's the Dominican father.' He was dressed soberly in black, and to his natural elegance and innate charm there was added a sort of extra grace. At about five o'clock that evening Georges came in and said: 'Guess who spoke to me – the Dominican father! I met him in the garden on my way back from Aunt Jeanne.' And it was indeed him! And Father Rzewuski came . . . and he became our friend, my counsellor and my support. In him I confide the inevitable scruples which sometimes nag me, my fears, my ordeals. For instance, during one of our first meetings I said to him: 'Oh Father, how I envy you for not having been, as I am, a last-minute recruit.' – 'Alas,' he said, 'but neither was I one of the early ones. It is only twelve years since I took refuge in Saint-Maximin, leaving everything in order to find everything!' – 'Who or what pushed you towards God? What event brought about this vocation, your conversion? Some great sorrow, some insurmountable disgust?' He looked at me gravely: 'Neither sorrow nor disgust, but an immense inner emptiness which only the love of God and of my neighbour could fill.' How happy I was to hear those words addressed to myself, so simply. Since then our friendship in Jesus has become closer. Father Rzewuski's visits are one of my holy pleasures. I have talked to him about my remorse, about my often despairing repentance. He has always restored my courage; he has always found the right words. I have told him how much I envy him for having had so many beautiful things to sacrifice to God: he was handsome, young, intelligent, clever, well-born and he had his art. He laid everything at the feet of God; he became, as he says, a beggar. Magnificent beggar who always gives a thousand times more than he receives! And what have I to offer to my God? I no longer have youth, beauty or strength.

October 21. We were staying in a nearby hotel and both of us were suffering physically as well as morally. Occasionally I came to Bois-Cerf to confess and take communion – perhaps three times a year. One day I met a severe little almoner who told me: 'But Madame, you have to go to mass every Sunday, on pain of mortal sin.' I made excuses, pleading my age and my unbelieving husband, who made everything difficult. He was insistent. I almost lost my temper and we were very cross with each other. But his words tormented me. With God's grace they worked in me and brought about a change in me. Now I go to the six-forty-five mass every Sunday; I pray with all my heart, I take communion and I would not miss it for anything in the world.

So then I began to want very much to move to the Bois-Cerf clinic. There were difficulties which Sister Marguerite smoothed out to the best of her ability, but there was still the problem of leaving the Carlton, the hotel chosen for us by Aunt Jeanne where we had been staying for eighteen months. Moving was quite a problem with all that baggage. Family pictures, rugs, little pieces of furniture – we had brought with us everything we most loved. The proprietors thought we were installed there for ever. I prayed to God, begging Him with all my heart to lead us to Bois-Cerf. One morning I woke up (here comes the miracle!) covered all over with red blotches. I thought of measles, of scarletina. I sent for the doctor who pronounced firmly: food poisoning. The proprietor, very vexed, said I should consult a specialist. I saw Professor Ramel: 'Food poisoning'. They made a great fuss but I remained unmoved and three weeks later we arrived at Bois-Cerf! It was at least two months before I got rid of those blotches; I almost loved them.

Here I became a new creature in a new life. Bois-Cerf is a wonderful place for serving, loving and feeling God. Bois-Cerf is a wonderful place for suffering. I have seen my country betrayed, conquered, crushed, and the sisters suffered with me, we prayed together and offered it up to God. We work for the poor. Here I have every sort of example, every sort of courage. Bois-Cerf is my little paradise on earth. I love to feel myself enclosed within its walls; I want never to leave it. I love my dear Trinitarian Ladies, so pure, so dignified, so devoted, so agreeable. I love their life of work and abnegation. I have thrown myself into prayer, into the way of sacrifice and into pious meditation. Such discoveries! Such marvels!

I have just been rereading this. I am ashamed at expressing myself so badly. I would have liked to compose a beautiful canticle of grace-inspired acts. I accept my mediocrity, my depressing twaddle – my age, I expect, I'm a very old lady! – but it hurts me to think that I am here, before God, with empty hands: it is sin which has turned aside from me, not me from sin. What have I got to give? My loneliness, my losses, my exile, my country in tatters, other people's sorrows which tear my heart, vague fears for a future which may never be mine, a few trivial acts of charity, a few sacrifices. Prayers, yes, whole-hearted prayers. I recite them in obedience, I compose them in great outbursts.

1941

January. This book will be given to Father Rzewuski. All the other notebooks have been desposited at my behest with the Dominicans at Estavayer, Monsignor Besson has given permission. I close them, I put them away, safe in this pious place. If anyone thinks that they ought to be destroyed, I approve. If anyone wants to publish them, make a selection of these memories which crush my repentant heart – if their publication either with impurities removed or in all their horror might benefit some straying soul, I approve.

But I ask above all that the presence of the divine mercy in these notebooks should be emphasized; that it should be recognized as being there, hidden for a long time between the lines as it was between the hours of my sad existence; that I repent of that existence, that I am ashamed of it, that I find it a humiliation to think today that these frightful confidences will be made public, and that it is ONLY in the spirit of humiliation that I offer them.

Last night, half awake, I had such a lovely dream. I was looking at my big family Christ which hangs opposite my bed, and Jesus's body faded out, disappeared gradually and gave way – right in the middle of the cross – to the head of the infant Jesus, the little Jesus of the crèches. I was moved and happy.

This morning I went to kneel before the crèche in our chapel.

Prayer is an important part of my life: it is my strength and my support. Kneeling is my way of resting. I pray for France, for Georges, for all the victims of this war, for our leaders spiritual and otherwise, for my family dead and alive, for the Trinitarian Ladies, for Father Rzewuski, for the people I offended and led into sin. I pray very fast, at great length, with passion, with all the strength of my soul. My prayer often brings me little miracles; instead of becoming weary I draw genuine physical strength from it. Sometimes I go through hours of despair and discouragement; that is the test. I pray, I resist, I do all that I can, how little that is! What could come out of me without your merits, oh Jesus? From month to month, from day to day, from prayer to prayer, I feel my soul's spiritual life affirming my conversion and yet I am only at the beginning of the way.

My God, I believe in You, I hope in You and I love You. May Your will be done.

Anne-Marie Ghika

May those who read this say a prayer for the last of the last: A-M.G.

INDEX

CONTENTS

Degrees of Nonsense

Introduction

The nature and role of university education has been contested as long as such institutions have existed. Debates concerning their place in relation to economic and industrial, so called "modern", society, date to the early nineteenth century and their rehearsal belongs elsewhere.

This volume has its origin in the troubling developments occurring in Ireland where universities are increasingly underfunded; conceptualised almost entirely as a means of preparation for the workplace; promoted as the most appropriate destination for every Leaving Certificate student; diversifying into a multitude of areas, some of which sit uneasily within higher education as historically understood; required to react immediately to the whirling weather-vane of political and economic imperative or whim; bedevilled by micro-management and preposterous metrics and, perhaps most troubling, subject to European and domestic principles of financing and regulation that are invasive and often deeply unsympathetic to scholarly work as traditionally understood. These and many other issues are tackled by the contributors in this volume. They do not always agree on the nature or extent of the challenges facing universities or on the solutions and this is as it should be; such is the dynamic of scholarly discourse. However, it is hoped that amidst the heat there is some light and that this volume helps to generate, what I believe is, a long overdue and crucial discussion on the nature and purpose of education in Ireland. I am deeply grateful to each of them for their thought provoking and compelling contributions.

For all the challenges, working with students and colleagues within the university community is a remarkably rewarding experience. For some of us it hardly requires the designation "work" because much that constitutes our personal and working lives would, in any event, include those things we do as academics. It is because of our dedication to this work, to the institution and to the great potential of higher learning for individuals and society, that we have written this book.

This volume also includes contributions by Professor Dennis O'Keefe of the University of Birmingham and Emeritus Professor of Higher Education at the Institute of Education, London, Professor Ronald Barnett. I asked Dennis and Ron to contribute as they are working in the UK where dramatic changes in the relationship between government and the universities have done much to alter the work of scholars and institutions there. It seems to us that the worst excesses of interference in the UK and Northern Ireland are now casting a long shadow over Ireland's institutions. Their insights have minded me to look further afield to our European colleagues........perhaps in another volume.

I would like to express my personal thanks to Professor Roger Scruton for agreeing to pen the Foreword to this volume. I have long admired his work, agreeing or disagreeing with it often in equal measure but always impressed by his preparedness to defend what should be valued, regardless of the consequences.

Dr. Brendan Walsh
School of Education Studies
Dublin City University
Ireland
January 2011

CHAPTER 1
FOREWORD

Prof. Roger Scruton

Although modern European universities claim descent from the Academy of Plato, they owe their core curriculum to a process of reflection that began in medieval Europe and culminated in the German Enlightenment. And they owe their funding to Government. Increasingly tensions have arisen between the historically defined curriculum and the Governments that pay for it. Governments dispose of money that they have taken from taxpayers, and one way or another the taxpayers demand an account. It seems that taxpayers don't mind government spending if it is in the cause of 'economic growth'; but they do mind government spending in order to support a privileged class of recipients at the taxpayer's expense. The resulting tension is leading, not just in Britain and Ireland, but all over Europe, to a growing suspicion of state institutions, of welfare provisions, and of educational systems that do not prepare children for life in the world to which they are destined. This timely book, assembling reflections on the situation from important thinkers with first-hand knowledge of the crisis in higher education, initiates a much-needed debate, not only in Ireland, but also in Britain. How should universities account for the money that they receive?

The utilitarian answer – that universities constitute an 'investment', and that the money spent on them is justified by the long-term returns – has a natural appeal, since it makes universities look like businesses. But utilitarian reasoning has a corrosive effect, as many contributors to this volume point out. It encourages us to calculate cost and benefit, and to approach every subject in the curriculum as a means to profit. But, as the contributors make clear, the curriculum of our universities arose from the conviction that knowledge is not a means but an end in itself, and that there are subjects worth studying for their own sake, which it is the duty of universities to perpetuate. Of course, in the long run, this perpetuation of the useless is useful. But how do you explain that complex thought to people who have not had a university education – or even, in the modern world, to people who have had one, but in one of those subjects like business studies or media studies that arose from the mistaken view that utility is what it is all about?

Contributors are by no means united in their diagnosis or their suggestions for a cure. Some see the problems faced by universities as a result of 'market' thinking, and the universities themselves as a place of refuge from the 'neo-liberalism' that has infected the political culture. Others – and notably Dennis O'Keeffe in a powerful and no-holds-barred defence of Hayekian principles – see the problem as an effect of public ownership, which creates a 'rent-seeking' class determined to hold on to its privileges, regardless of the educational goal. For O'Keeffe there is only one way forward, which is privatisation, and the introduction into the British Isles of the 'liberal arts' tradition that has rescued the university curriculum in America. Others hope for a change of heart within the existing system: a return to the university as a 'space of reasons' (Ronald Barnett), or a counter-insurgency against the anti-intellectualism of the 'yakademy' (Brendan Walsh). Some believe with Aidan Seery that the whole concept of knowledge has been put in question by recent thinking (notably by Foucault, whom O'Keeffe dismisses, however, as a nihilist). Others, like John Hughes, believe that the problem arises because we have not redefined the place of universities in our emerging 'knowledge society', which a cynic would describe as an 'opinion' society cut loose from genuine knowledge.

All in all the contributors manage to place the problem of the university before the reader in all its complexity and without concealing the fact that they are united only in one thing, which is their belief that the university has entered a state of crisis. This crisis is not economic only, but concerns the identity and self-definition of the university in the emerging social order. Maybe universities are destined to disappear. Maybe they will have to change entirely if they are to safeguard their precious legacy of knowledge and culture. Maybe the present process, whereby subjects requiring serious study and hard work – music, oriental languages, Latin and Greek, Chemistry, mathematics – are one by one dropped from the curriculum to be replaced by the soft options, will continue to the point where universities are widely regarded as places for wasting time. But then, would this not in its own way be a triumph of the useless? How do you argue that the difficult study of useless things like Sanskrit and Egyptian Hieroglyphs is in some deeper way useful, while the study of superficially useful things like football and cartoons is, in a deeper way, entirely useless? That, to me, defines the intellectual question. And I am grateful to the authors of these essays for encouraging me to pose it in its true and enigmatic form.

Scrutopia, February 2012.

CHAPTER 2
REASONING THE UNIVERSITY: MAKING SENSE IN A NON-REASONABLE WORLD

Ronald Barnett
Emeritus Professor of Higher Education at the Institute of Education, London

Introduction

'Things fall apart; the centre cannot hold;
Mere anarchy is loosed upon the world, ...
The best lack all conviction, while the worst
Are full of passionate intensity.'
(W B Yeats, 1865-1939, The Second Coming)

Two considerations may set us off on this inquiry, one empirical, and the other more reflective. The first consideration may be opened up by a question: how many universities, if any, include the concept of reason in their self-descriptions, in their mission statements or their 'corporate strategies'? Rather few, I suspect. If this is the case, how might we account for this situation? Is the university no longer to be associated with the idea of reason? Are universities not self-consciously to strive to be sites of reason?

Our second consideration also can be opened up by a question, but somewhat more speculative. In a world that is marked by a falling-short in its reasoning powers, what implications if any befall the university? Does not a dual role open up for the university as being itself transparently a centre of reason in society and of displaying that reason to society? But there are many difficulties associated with carrying through such a project. Firstly, 'the principle of reason', as Heidegger (1996) observed, is itself problematic. It is by no means clear that secure conditions of reasonable reason – as we might term it –

can be identified. Secondly, it is unclear how any such conditions can be taken on and exemplified in the university of the twenty-first century, in which its destiny seems to lie in some amalgam of the entrepreneurial university, the corporate university and the bureaucratic university. Thirdly, the university's own knowing efforts seem largely to lack the reflective capacities that surely should accompany the development of such a university. And lastly, it is by no means clear as to how any such reasonable university can itself engage with the wider world so as to demonstrate its reasoning credentials or if the world would even notice if it did so.

The reasonable university, accordingly, seems a distance prospect. However, gloominess need not be the only attitude here; perhaps there are grounds for a little optimism.

An Absence of Reason

If the idea of reason is falling, or has fallen, out of the university's self-understanding, that occurrence is hardly surprising. The past half century or so has seen a performative turn in the stance of the university. The university has retained a close connection with knowledge but the nature of that connection has changed. An interest has come to be invested in the academy's knowledge, as the knowledge society has taken off. Here was a society in which sophisticated knowledge played a crucial and particular part. Now, the university's formal knowledge's made possible advances in all manner of social developments – in medicine and pharmaceuticals, transport, military matters, food technology, building technologies, household consumables, utilities, communications and even clothing. So knowledge was put to work and became the basis of work. Knowledge was now to display its performative capacities. This knowledge had to be doubly performative: it both had to have a demonstrable impact on the wider society and had to help to generate income for the university. This 'academic capitalism' (Slaughter and Leslie, 1997) or 'cognitive capitalism' (Peters and Bulut, 2011) went hand-in-hand with the formation of the entrepreneurial university.

In such a situation, the university is prey to losing any interest it might have had in reason as such. Its attention is now diverted towards the wider world rather than in the character of the communicative processes out of which knowledge is borne. That those processes might be in part constructed by reason, reasoning and reasonableness was not its concern. Its concerns now lay elsewhere, in financial and performance management, in societal impact, in return on investment (explicitly so in the case of the 'spin-out' companies that it created) and in its income flows, not least increasingly from students who now exert their claims as customers of the university.

So the horizons of the university shift. Perhaps just one indication of this shift is to be found in the terms 'scholar' and 'scholarship', for they have become awkward terms. They seem to imply slow rhythms of academic life and an inwardness at that. After all, what is a scholar if not one who loves existing texts and coming to a deep understanding of such texts. Where, in such resonances, are there the necessary present claims of outwardness, of performativity and of impact on the wider world?

In turn, the mode of reasoning associated with being a scholar is now passé. For that reasoning was concerned with the reasonableness of the texts in question. It examined those texts in some detail and critically so. It sought to identify their weaknesses and their strengths and then to move on, adding to the conversation of generations. The past layers of academic and textual life might be now jettisoned but only by implicitly acknowledging that they were part of the conversation. In exposing their limitations, contemporary scholarship paid homage to those past texts. Now, such historicity embedded in the academic life is given short change. Is there here, perhaps, one explanation of the apparent blankness with which the humanities and the more scholarly social sciences are nowadays met, an incomprehension as to their validity? For now, the urge is always to look into the future, to bring the future into the present and not to be overly concerned with the past. The temporal horizons of 'scholarship' seem out of kilter with a forward-looking age, and an age in which the academic life is called upon manifestly and materially to assist the onward development of the wider society.

A Space of Reason

Recently, David Bakhurst (2011) has explored the idea of a 'space of reasons', which was 'first introduced by Wilfred Sellars' (p99). In Bakhurst's explorations, this idea of a space of reasons points to a logical space in which reasoning is possible and encouraged. At its essence lies the further idea of the giving of reasons and of justifying one's knowledge claims. Bakhurst looks at the views of other philosophers who have also taken up the idea of the space of reasons and brings out differences in their positions: for example, McDowell holds the view that the space of reasons is inhabited by persons and the justifications that they might bring forward to back up their assertions, whereas Brandom points to the social character of the space of reasons (ch 5) in which the norms of reasoning lie in the contextual practical activities and attitudes serving those activities. Drawing on Ilyenkov, Bakhurst himself goes on to argue for the space of reasons 'as a normative space, with which we engage in a dialectic of recognition and transformation'. In turn, he goes on to draw some educational implications from this point of view, focusing on the space of reasons as a 'site of the game of giving and asking for reasons'. (p115)

I have entitled this section 'a space of reason'. I do so because I want to keep as close as possible to the phrase 'a space of reasons'. However, in the apparently very small move from the plural 'reasons' to the singular 'reason', something significant happens. In that move, we turn from a focus on individual persons making claims such that they are able and/or willing to give them backing with 'reasons' to a focus on the space itself in which that reasoning takes place. This move is necessary when we turn to consider an entity such as a university, for a university is a social institution in which persons – hopefully reasoning persons – are conducting their activities. In other words, once we turn our gaze from (reasoning) persons to the university as a site in which such reasoning takes place, the relationship of reasoning persons and the social context of their reasoning and their attendant social interactions is inverted. Now, we focus on the university as a possible site of a space of reason as such.

In this perspective, in which the university comes well into the horizon of our gaze, the key questions are these: what might it be for a university to be a site in which it serves as a space of reason? What might it be for a university self-consciously to develop for itself 'a culture of intellectual encouragement'? (Myerson, 1994: 151)

Such questions open out a sense, perhaps a renewed sense, of an association of the idea of the university with the idea of reason. Over the past fifty years or so, around the world, such an association has surely been neglected as universities have been encouraged, if not required, to integrate themselves with the wider society. In the process, they have also implicitly been encouraged to avoid any undue concern with their internal character for any such inwardness was liable to evoke repudiation (of living in 'an ivory tower' and not 'living in the real world'). But this more external orientation may have unwittingly had as one of its effects that of diminishing the university as a space of reason. For the contemporary university has had to develop a competitiveness, a concern with income flows, and transparent demonstrations of its 'performance'. All of these developments run against the idea of the university as a space of reason.

In the context of considerations such as these, the term 'reasoning' prompts itself in a particular way, namely the university as a site of reasoning. For reasoning calls for reciprocity, for give and take, for mutuality, for a focus on the argument and the evidence and the inferential moves being made. These are aspects of the processes of reasoning. And the university came to be, since its mediaeval inception, an institution that nurtured such reasoning processes. The university may not be the only institution in a democratic society that can identified with reasoning in this way; the legal institution may be another such institution. But, still, the idea of the university and its practices came to be unintelligible apart from a sense that it offered and nurtured a space of reasoning.

Return to Reason

Return to Reason is the title of a (2001) book by Stephen Toulmin. In his book, Toulmin distinguishes between reasonableness and rationality. He argues that with the development of rationality over the past three centuries or so has come an eclipse of reasonableness. Academic disciplines, as the embodiment of modern forms of rationality, seek to establish universal truths and are insufficiently sensitive to both local situations and to the varieties of human experience. Their methods of inquiry, too, are unduly limited in just the same ways. Accordingly, we need to find ways of attending more sensitively to the local, to the immediate, to the fine-grained nature of the present (as does an occupational therapist with her patient – which is one of Toulmin's examples). Reasonableness is, accordingly, a larger concept than rationality. It includes rationality but goes beyond it, calling for judgement in complex situations. It also acknowledges its own problematic nature: 'all scientific knowledge is a balance of the theoretical with the practical, the verbal with the non-verbal'. Reasonableness, accordingly, is sensitive to such tacit aspects of the way we might come to know the world and is characterised as much by judgement as by attempts to form universally true propositions.

Toulmin's targets do not primarily include the academic world as such but he comments, in keeping with his argument, that:

> 'The organization of late twentieth century universities has encouraged a narrowness of preoccupation that has

> ended by rewarding participants who remain closest to the middle of their chosen intellectual road.'
>
> (*Return to Reason*, 151)

I take Toulmin, across the course of his book, to be arguing that universities should embrace reasonableness, which is to say that they should open themselves up fully to a life of reason. This in turn is to suggest that universities should be sensitive to there being different valid forms of reasoning and (going on from Toulmin) that they should allow for debate as to what is to count as reason itself. And this in turn leads to the idea that the life of reason itself, including the processes that are to count as reasoning processes, should themselves be kept in view, if not under review within the academy. All such concepts as reason, dialogue, communication, criticality, and rationality are each problematic and deserve and require continuing attention and reflection.

This all may seem straightforward but that is far from the case, and for three large reasons. Firstly, to return to earlier reflections, arguably the forms of legitimate reasoning in universities may even be narrowing, even if in some ways they are also widening. We noted that Toulmin refers to occupational therapy but in the new para-medical areas (of which occupational therapy is but one) we are witnessing fields of understanding that should be in large part influenced by the idea of 'care' (in the Heiddegarian sense, namely of 'concern'). These health oriented fields are finding themselves dominated by scientistic and positivistic modes of reasoning: they have become all too rational and too little reasonable. Such tendencies, initiated firstly by the dominance of science within the academy, are now being exacerbated as the state gives its explicit backing to the sciences and technological and mathematical fields (in the UK, to the so-called STEM disciplines). There is in play, therefore, a kind of politics of reasonableness.

Secondly, the academy lacks – and has always lacked – an infrastructure for its own reflexivity through which it could monitor and interrogate its own collective capacities for reasoning. Until now, that has hardly mattered; or so it seemed. The academy was left in peace to attend to its processes of inquiring into the world, and its processes of reasoning and dialogue that accompanied those processes. Now, however, that wider world is taking an ever-closer interest in the character of its epistemological positioning. It is saying to the university that, as remarked, it favours certain knowledge fields (the STEM disciplines) and, by extension, it has lesser interest in the humanities and the social sciences. It is also looking to the processes of inquiry having an impact on the wider society and so those knowledge fields that have overt demonstrable effects are likely to gain more legitimacy than those whose effects – such as benefiting the culture of society and its reflective processes – are less tangible. Accordingly, the university's capacities for understanding its own processes, directions and forms of inquiry and their relationships with the wider world now assume an entirely new significance. However, as stated, the academy has no infrastructure for conducting such self-reflective processes.

There is a bizarre implication of this situation. Over the past fifteen years or so, a new sub-field of knowledge management has grown up in universities, mainly directed at the ways in which research-intensive corporations in the private sector manage their own knowledge systems. That such a field might have something to say to universities is barely countenanced. Consequently, that senior managers in universities might understand their role in part to be that of managing the knowledge fields and systems of universities is hardly recognized. To my knowledge, the various workshops and courses now available to institutional leaders and would-be leaders show a distinct lacuna in this respect. Knowledge management is not an overt concern in the leadership and management of universities.

Thirdly, and perhaps most significantly (and as implied), what is to count as reason is itself problematic. That very reflection is to open up significant philosophical debates and perspectives over hundreds of years, which has seen both attempts on the one hand to identify criteria of bona fide propositions, that could then be held to be instances of reason (which characteristically came to see scientific propositions as the embodiment of reason, with their legitimation as representative of the world in the correspondence theory of truth backed by the verification principle and then by the falsification principle) and, on the other hand, a critique of that whole enterprise, through Kant and Nietszche through (the quite different perspectives of) Rorty, Lyotard, Feyerabend and the Frankfurt School of Critical Theory, in which the pretentiousness of science was undermined. At best, science and its attendant theories of truth (as correspondence) could only be seen as one form of rationality. More critically still, all reason was held to be saturated with interests and unduly limited in its scope and might even harbour nihilistic tendencies of some kind. That complex of jostling perspectives and critiques led, in turn, to much more of a concern with the character of debate and argument rather than its substance. Habermas (1989; 1991) was – and is – perhaps the dominant presence here, focusing on the 'validity claims' that, for him, underpin any claim to significance beyond itself; but others have also offered accounts of reason that stood apart from any substantive form of reason.

Insofar as it can be used with any comfort, reason is seen as occupying a conceptual space together with a number of other concepts such as communication, argument, truthfulness and dialogue. In the remarkable book, *A Thousand Plateaus,* by Deleuze and Guattari (1987), such a clustering of ideas leads to concerns with being and, more importantly, to becoming, within a space of multiplicities. In a liquid world, in a decentred age, being is a matter of perpetual becoming or, rather, surely we should say becomings. An institution, especially a complex entity such as the university, has open to it at any one time, a multitude of potential 'lines of flight' (1987: 23 et seq). Deleuze and Guattari make much of the metaphor of the rhizome, an organic entity but without an obvious centre and so developing in manifold directions. Perhaps, though, the university-as-squid might be a more apt metaphor, for the university does have momentum, mobility and reach, not to mention possible agility and speed for all its apparent lethargy. And it even has a quite hard crust, making it difficult – though not impossible – for would-be predators to penetrate it.

Reason and Culture

Do reason and culture inhabit the same universe or are they profoundly different? Is reason tacitly an attack on culture, declaring culture to be at best non-rational and at worst mired in dogma and superstition? Or can the idea of reason only make full sense in the context of a culture of reason? That is, to say, perhaps reason can come supplied with, and even armed with, its own culture.

In his (1992) book, *Reason and Culture,* Ernest Culture traverses just these issues. Ranging widely in his characteristically magisterial style, across long traditions of philosophical and sociological thought, Gellner weaves between many large debates. Reason has brought itself to attack reason, reason is unable to vindicate itself, culture remains impervious to reason much as it might embrace it, we cannot free ourselves from culture but yet we can legitimately and should also opt for the life of reason: these are just some of the stopping-off points in the ground that Gellner traverses.

Key to our theme here, though, is Gellner's observation that reason places culture on trial (1992: 169). No cognitive assumptions, and especially those inherent in cultures, can justifiably be taken on trust; they can be hauled before the court of reason. Of course, reason itself can be put on trial, and has been for some time and continues to be put on trial continually. Critical Theory, deconstructionalism and postmodernism all did just this. In their and other such critiques, it came to be felt that irrationalism always threatens to break out. But rationality can evade its critics to a large extent: it is not entirely self-justifying for it can point to successes beyond itself (even if there are failures to be clocked up too). 'Cognition continues to function admirably, even given the absence of any such guarantee' (Gellner, 1992:181). Through its 'rational' procedures, knowledge can shore up itself. In other words, rationality comes armed with its own powerful culture, a culture of criticality, through which demonstrably (at least in some domains) 'knowledge can grow'. This rationality is, as Alvin Goulder, once termed it, a 'culture of critical discourse' (1979: 28 et seq).

This rationality, this culture, can never get sufficiently outside of itself fully to ground itself. Part of the reason for this state of affairs lies in so-called reason being itself a complex, and a complex that becomes increasingly more complex. To the complexities of proliferating fields of knowledge and their sub-disciplines has been added both fuzziness and new claimants for membership of the domain of rationality. Is morality a site of rationality, or religion, or politics, or professional life in general? Does the internet expand rationality or diminish it? Can knowledge be tacit, or interest-laden, or theory-laden, or processual, or community-based (just some of its aspects that are alleged to constitute its features)? In a globalised and networked age, forms of and communicative processes escalate: global geo-politics reveal starkly the challenges of securing 'rational' debate and consensus.

As we saw earlier, Deleuze and Guattari (1987) call up the rhizome, a decentred complex, as a metaphor of being. Becoming here is a matter of potential 'lines of flight', chosen amid 'multiplicities'. Rationality cannot easily be confined to any particular formation. A moment's reflection supports the point. Tacit reasoning, the reasoning embedded in professional action, the reasoning characteristic of large-scale interdisciplinary projects, poetic reason, the reasoning embodied in the creative arts, the arts of political reasoning: all these have their own characteristic forms of reasoning and it not obvious that there should be any connecting tissue running across them.

The university of the twenty-first century, it seems, can neither be cashed out through the idea of reason and yet nor can we sensibly separate the idea of the university from the idea of reason. Can the university unpin itself from the horns of this dilemma? Does not an increasingly a-rational world desperately need the university as a site of reason in its midst? Does the university have any substance unless it can anchor itself in some way on the idea of reason? The idea of culture, at least in the idea of the culture of critical discourse, may seem an attractive way out, but we still seem to be left with an infinite regress of trying to cash out the criteria of such a culture. Everytime the matter is pressed can sensibly come the retort 'and what are your grounds for such an idea?' It seems to be impossible rationally to ground the university in the idea of rationality.

The University Of Reason

We started this chapter with a famous quotation from Yeats' poem, The Second Coming. Perhaps overlooked in the stanza – surrounded by allusions to anarchy (being 'loosed upon the world'), fragmentation ('things fall apart') and passionate intensity – is the observation that 'the best lack all conviction'. Why might the best lack all conviction? Is it not that the best are supremely rational and can see various angles on an issue, and know that whichever position is taken up, it can be critiqued? The best, in other words, are paralysed by their own rationality; they can identify too many contending reasons, such that it is far from obvious that any one move could command unassailable support.

An important word in that phrase is 'all': 'the best lack all conviction'. An implication, presumably, is that some conviction might just be defensible. But how might this be? Is not conviction precisely non-rational? Where, if anywhere, might there be a place for conviction amid rationality? This is a serious matter in attempting to give some grounding to the university. Is it a purely rational institution or might it also be legitimately imbued with conviction?

We should return to one of our starting points and recall that Heidegger observed that the principle of reason cannot itself rely on principles; or, at least, not on the principle of reason itself. Ultimately, the principle of reason is not about reason but about being itself: 'the principle of reason is ... not a statement about reason, but about beings, insofar as there are beings.' (1966: 44) In other words, life can opt for reason, being can opt for reason; and then two things follow. Firstly, opting for reason is not itself an entirely rational act but is a matter, as we may say, of will; and secondly, rationality is not all there is of value in life. In turn, there is a third related point, too: that the full exercise of reason is a creative and imaginative process and the imagination is, again, not an entirely rational process. We reason with words but, as Peter Murphy has recently incisively put it: 'Words come after the fact of creation.' (Murphy, 2010: 44).

The university, then, has the potential to be regarded as a much-needed site of reason in a largely a-rational world but it should not pretend that its opting for reason is itself either a fully rational matter or that its processes of reasoning are themselves fully rational. To the contrary: conviction enters at both levels. The university has to opt for a life of reason: it has to will the life of reason. And this will is surprisingly fragile. In a neo-liberal age, where money and income streams count, reason is easily set aside (as the acceptance of donations from dubious sources testifies: a university therein prejudices not just its reputation on such occasions but its integrity as a site of reason). But the very processes of reason, too, are themselves not without conviction. Reasoning processes are imbued with a will to press on, to press through, to engage with critical comments, to communicate even to multiple audiences. Reason requires commitment. A university of reason, therefore, is a university for reason: it opts for reason.

Such a university for reason may not be imperilled in today's world but it is in constant difficulty. Overt causes of this difficulty are readily to hand: they include increasing demands for 'accountability' and for meeting the expectations of external stakeholders, the sheer busy-ness of universities and academic life (being called upon to do more and more within limited resource horizons), and the need to generate income and to survive in knowledge and learning markets (not to mention the competitiveness wrought thereby). Each of these phenomena are not themselves intent on impinging on the zone of rationality within which the university has had its being but they each have that unwitting consequence. For their interests do not lie in rationality as such but elsewhere – in customer responsiveness, in overt performance, in efficiency and in economy. Their latent effect is to tilt the university in those directions and away from a primary interest in the life of reason.

There is, however, a more insidious force at work that underlies those phenomena. It is connected with time. It is a commonplace to suggest that, in a world characterised by speed, time itself has quickened. Academic work has itself become a kind of fast work. There is point to such readings. But the contrary position can be put, namely, that in the fast world of the academy, time has been occluded. Where everything is fast, or at least evaluated by fast metrics, slow time disappears from view; but then time itself disappears in a way. The sense of the university having its being amid long expanses of time, even in eternity, of contributing to the voices and narratives of 'la longue durée' of ever-lasting generations has now been punctured if not entirely extinguished. Or again, the further counter argument can be put that the metaphysical university was timeless. Its truth-telling had a timelessness about it. Now, its truth-telling has to have an impact, and a fairly immediate impact at that: time, this time, is of the essence in the contemporary university.

These are complex matters and deserve a more careful, indeed a longer and time-full examination (and they are matters that, in their more general aspects, Heidegger, Ricoeur, Bachelard and more recently Nowotny and Hassan have explored). What can be said here is that our sense of time affects our sense of reasonableness. Where the world – or here, the university – crowds in with its pressing expectations of being productive, efficient, performative and accountable in short time horizons, reason itself changes. Conviction is still present but its character changes. Reason takes a pragmatic turn, being placed against a horizon of utility (understood certainly in broad terms) in fast time. Reason takes on an urgency; different kinds of argumentative moves are made; different kinds of concept and theorisation come into view. Reason has to perform in the here-and-now.

And there is a phenomenology of time at work here, too, as Bachelard made clear: 'There is ... above lived time, thought time. This thought time is more aerial and free, more easily disrupted too ...' (Bachelard, 2000: 37). Dare an academic be seen reading a book in his or her room on campus? Would that not be seen as downtime – as the Director of Estates conducts his or her round, during the annual (or more frequent) assessment of space usage? After all, the room is not – as it is seen – the academic's room, but simply an expensive space of the University in question for which the cost-benefit analysis for different activities has to be conducted. So reasoning requiring lengthy periods of gestation, with slow rhythms, comes to be repudiated. The conviction that links reasoning to generations if not to eternity gives way to a species – if not a malformation – of reasoning that links conviction to immediacy and financial solvency. It is a mathematised form of conviction.

The Lure of Pragmatism

How is a university to respond in the wake of considerations such as those we have encountered? Is reason to be abandoned as a watchword? Could any university without embarrassment enter the term 'reason' or 'rationality' or 'reasonableness' into its self-description on its web-site? Is the university now too far removed from the idea of reason to claim any allegiance to it? Not at all. The university contains the possibility of reasonableness within itself, in the lecture, in the seminar. These remain as spaces for reasonableness, if not always of reasonableness. Especially in the seminar, but even in the lecture too, a space opens for public debate. I use 'public' here in the sense advanced by Masschelein and Simons. Masschelein and Simons (2012) trace various senses in which the university has been a public institution, from its invention of the written text as a pedagogical device (available as a book-text for public study (p168)), through the development of public reasoning (identified by Kant as a public use of one's own reason, and potentially 'the entire reading public'), through the formation of a public sphere of learning, to the institutionalisation of the 'public' lecture. By 'public' here, Masschelein and Simons want to draw attention to the way in which the university's characteristic activities – of lectures and seminars – make reasoning public and call forth a public, in the sense that the reasoning is on trial in a public space.

What these insights prompt, I think, is the following question: does the twenty-first century call forth, if not demand, of the university that it find a new public, or a wider public, space for its reasoning? Can the university expand the horizon of its reasoning, of its space of reason, to dwell more fully in the world? In the same volume, Michael Peters and his associates, Garett Gietzen and David J Ondercin (2012), implicitly answer a very clear 'yes' to these questions.

In their paper – the last chapter of the volume, as it happens, and so one that especially looks ahead – an idea of 'intellectual commons and openness in the university' is opened. That phrase is actually the sub-title of their chapter, the main title of which is 'Knowledge Socialism'. Dwelling on the theme of openness, Peters and his colleagues point to the ways in which technology has brought successive waves of, and possibilities precisely for, the university to be increasingly open. From the Open University through to universities placing their research and their course material on open access to emerging technologies that facilitate interaction and independent production of texts, the story is traced of a possible knowledge socialism. In this latest incarnation of openness, 'education is placed at the centre of global society and human rights', accompanied by a 'recognition that knowledge and its value are ultimately rooted in social relations'. In this sociality of knowledge - of knowledge socialism – is provided 'mechanisms for a truly free exchange of ideas'. (pp198-99).

It should be acknowledged that, in their closing remarks, Peters and his colleagues admit that their scenario may be somewhat unrealistic, given the corporate interests driving the contemporary neo-liberal university. There are also more reflective critiques to be brought to bear on what might be called the virtual university. At the fore lies the critique of Paul Virilio who has recently (2010) drawn attention to the 'university of disaster'. Building on his past oeuvre of works engaging with the interlinked themes of speed, communications, technology, time and space, the matter of the university comes to Virilio's attention. In a world of instantaneity, we face 'a new absolute of a century which ... will ...turn its back on the 'Enlightenment', degenerating instead into a dark age ...' (p9) Charting complex interconnections between knowledge (especially 'big science'), globalisation and the instantaneity of digital communications, Virilio sees apocalyptic consequences. And the university is implicated in all of this; hence the coming of 'the university of disaster'.

In fact, Virilio, close to the end of his book, reaches not far from Peters' position for he points to the 'necessity of a more democratic approach to research and to scientific and technological development' (121), even if his text seems highly doubtful of such a prospect materialising. But this, it seems to me, makes the kind of theorising of Michael Peters particularly necessary and (to use a term of Leavis) urgent. For what Michael Peters offers us is a kind of feasible utopia, as we might term it (Barnett, 2011). That is to say, he – and rare thinking such as his – is pointing to possibilities that are most unlikely to come about but yet are shown to be feasible. They really could come about in the best of all possible worlds. At the same time they both are utopian and are feasible.

Conclusions

The world is not just complex – that is already an outworn commonplace – but it is dynamically so complex that it may be beyond the capacities of the human race to steer it in rational ways. Not least amid the challenges of this situation is that we hardly have either a consensus on the significant aspects of the world's complexity (whether it be risk, or digital frenzy, or ecological mayhem, or epistemic runaway, or discursive incomprehension across cultures or yet other aspects) nor do we have an adequate meta-language for describing the world that we are in. The university is doubly implicated in all of this. Firstly, it has been a significant player in contributing to this state of affairs, through its expanding languages, perspectives and modes of apprehension. Secondly, it is one of the key institutions in society that has a responsibility to address the state of affairs so identified and examine and determine its roles against that horizon.

A key matter in all of this has to be that of reason: the matter of reason. Reason matters. This has been, of course, a long running theme in the work of Jurgen Habermas, at least since his book *The Rational Society* some forty years ago. As is well known, Habermas has sought to establish a more rational society through its remembering and rediscovering the rationality deep in its own discourses. Seriously to engage in a rational discussion is implicitly to commit oneself to certain 'validity claims' embedded in such a discourse. Habermas, too, has seen a role for the university as an institution in living up to the ideals – of sincerity, truthfulness, appropriateness – that are reflected in those validity claims.

This is certainly a start in drawing out the possibilities for the university in the twenty-first century but we surely need to go further, for the challenges in front of the world – and of universities – are not only matter of discourse but of systems, ecologies, and turbulence of many kinds. This is not to open the way to apocalyptic or dystopian stances; on the contrary, the university has new spaces and new possibilities open to it, even if it may seem that its room for manoeuvre is heavily circumscribed (and it is). Still, there are spaces for imagination, and an imagination that might identify feasible utopias at that. This is not easy work, since feasibility points to real practical (and therefore) political possibilities in a context of large powerful forces which are fearful of such thinking. But in a world that is now one of continuing turbulence, to draw back from such a task would be to avoid the responsibilities of being a university in an arational world.

Bibliography

Bachelard, G (2000/ 1950) *The Dialectic of Duration*. Manchester: Clinamen.

Bakhurst, D (2011) *The Formation of Reason*. Malden, MA: Wiley-Blackwell.

Barnett, R (2011) *Being a University*. Abingdon: Routledge.

Barnett, R (2012) (ed) *The Future University: Ideas and Possibilities*. New York: Routledge.

Deleuze, G and Guattari, F (1987/ 1980) *A Thousand Plateaus*. London: Continuum.

Gellner, E (1992) *Reason and Culture*. Oxford: Blackwell.

Gouldner, A W (1979) T*he Future of Intellectuals and the Rise of the New Class*. London: Macmillan.

Habermas, J (1972) *Towards a Rational Society*. London: Heinemann.

Habermas, J (1989/ 1981) *The Theory of Communicative Action (Volume Two): The Critique of Functionalist Reason*. Cambridge: Polity.

Heidegger, M (1996/1957) *The Principle of Reason*. Bloomington: Indiana Press.

Masschelein, J and Simons, M (2012) *'The University: A Public Issue'*, in R Barnett, op cit.

Murphy, P (2010) 'Imagination', ch 1 in P Murphy, Michael A Peters, and Simon Marginson, *Imagination: Three Models of Imagination in the Age of the Knowledge Economy*. New York: Peter Lang.

Myerson, G (1994) *Rhetoric, Reason and Society*: Rationality as Dialogue. London: Sage.

Peters, M and Bulut, E (eds) (2011) *Cognitive Capitalism, Education and Digital Labour*. New York: Peter Lang.

Peters, M, Gietzen, G and Ondercin, D J (2012) *'Knowledge Socialism: Intellectual Commons and Openness in the University'* in R Barnett, op cit.

Slaughter, S and Leslie, L L (1997) *Academic Capitalism: Politics, Policies, and the Entrepreneurial University.*
Toulmin, S (2001) *Return to Reason.* Cambridge, MA: Harvard University.
Virilio, P (2010) *The University of Disaster.* Cambridge: Polity.

CHAPTER 3
THE CONTEMPORARY UNIVERSITY AND ITS CULTURED DESPISERS

Gerard Casey
Associate Professor in the School of Philosophy at University College Dublin

> Caroline Bingley: *I should like balls infinitely better...if they were carried on in a different manner....It would be much more rational if conversation instead of dancing made the order of the day.*
>
> Charles Bingley: *Much more rational, my dear Caroline, I dare say, but it would not be near so much like a ball.*
>
> —Jane Austen

Introduction

Once upon a time, not so long ago, there were no universities. You could travel wherever your fancy took you and stumble upon kings and courts, soldiers, churches (some with little schools attached), towns, merchants, farmers, in fact, all manner of things—but no universities. Then, in a very short period of time and in different places—Paris, Bologna, Oxford—and no one knows quite how or why, the university appeared; chaotically, anarchically, without any grand plan or design, with its subsequent organisation by authorities merely tidying up a pre-existent emergent order (see Knowles 1962).

If there was a time at which universities did not exist; there may come a time when they cease to exist. The unimaginable is only unimaginable because of the limits of our imagination. I know of no law which states that the world as we know it would come to a crashing halt if universities were to disappear. Like many other things in our mutable world, the university is radically contingent, its apparent solidity being just that, apparent. Institutions are essentially functional entities. If they cease to perform the function they emerged to serve then they either cease to exist, exist as a kind of mummified relic (as do many churches in Europe) or find another function to serve (as constitutional monarchs have done).

The University and the State

The university is the second-oldest surviving institution in the Western world. Only the Catholic Church is of greater longevity. The university predates most of the forces that today seek to control, re-model or, in extreme cases, to re-engineer it, in particular, the modern state which traces its origin back to the Peace of Westphalia. An institution of such an age can only exist if, throughout its long life, it answered and continues to answer some need or set of needs in the changing social and political circumstances in which it exists. And it can answer changing needs only if it itself adaptable. Such linkage as the university has had with the State has been historically contingent and was not and is not in any way necessary to its being or its operation; and while such association may have been of material assistance to the university, it has also carried a cost—the shrinking, sometimes to the point of invisibility, of the university's autonomy and the imperilling of its function.

Over the centuries since universities began, several different models have emerged: the Newmanian University which prioritises the educational experience of the student, the Humboldt University which places research at the university's core, and that strange, peculiarly contemporary institution that has been called by Clark Kerr, the Multiversity (Kerr 2001), whose essence, like that of the Sartrean man, is apparently to have no essence. This Multiversity is not "based upon a clear and identifiable historical 'idea'. It [is] rather a collection of ideas competing with one another. It [is] messy and chaotic" (Rothblatt 2006, p. 26). From the British model to the German model to the model of the new, entrepreneurial university (or multiversity) whose job it is to "seek research contracts from industrial, pharmaceutical and military concerns, and encourage their members to act as consultants to outside business" (Thomas 2010, p. 14). The multiversity is comprised of "a pluralist amalgam of different functions, serving different constituencies and lacking any single purpose" (Thomas 2010, p. 14). The forms of government appropriate to either the English or German model, it would appear, are no longer suitable to the new multiversity. The multiversity is to be governed (or, rather, managed) by a "managerial class, led by vice-chancellors" who see themselves as "thrusting business executives rather than self-effacing ancillaries" and who pay themselves accordingly, "typically three or four times as much as a professor" (Thomas 2010, p. 14).

There are ever increasing demands on universities: more and more students, more and more courses or modules (especially if they are 'relevant') together with either the same or declining numbers of academic staff and diminishing financial resources.

Knowledge-based enterprises in the economy and society create an expanding and rapidly changing professional labour market for which universities are expected to provide competent graduates. Governments expect universities to do much more for society in solving economic and social problems, but at the same time they back and fill in their financial support and become unreliable patrons. "Pushed and pulled by enlarging, interacting streams of demand, universities are pressured to change their curricula, alter their faculties, and modernize their increasingly expensive physical plant and equipment—and to do so more rapidly than ever. Some more traditional fields of study are bypassed, others fall into disarray. With the humanities now highly vulnerable, critics contend that universities do not know where they are going, even that they have lost their souls (Clark 2007, pp. xiii-xiv).

Other commentators broadly agree with Kerr. Slaughter and Leslie claim that "the structure of academic work is changing in response to the emergence of global markets" and that "...the globalization of the political economy at the end of the twentieth century is destabilizing patterns of university professional work developed over the past hundred years" (Slaughter and Leslie 1997, p. 209). All that being said, there is nothing inherently unreasonable in requiring that universities make some contribution to society at large. That is what universities have always done and, as long as they persist, it is what they will continue to do. Universities, from their very beginning, have not only had a broad general education remit but have had a vocational element, originally in the fields of law, medicine or theology, later in engineering and technology. The earliest universities were closely tied to the rational exploration of Christianity. Within a short space of time, the dynamic political structure of Europe required a functioning bureaucracy and the university (for example, the University of Naples and the University of Bologna) began to serve the function of producing an educated and well-trained proto-civil service. The English idea of the university took as its principal purpose the provision of the appropriate kind of educational training of an intellectual and social elite, in its decadent phase concentrating almost entirely on the social side. On this model, the advancement of learning through research could scarcely be a primary function of the university and, indeed, the principal intellectual advances in Britain tended to be made for the most part outside the influence of the universities. The German, or Humboldt model, by contrast, placed a premium on the notion of original research. The influence of this model spread widely from its beginnings in the early nineteenth century so that by the start of the twentieth century, even English universities were expected to engage in scholarship and to advance knowledge as well as to train young minds in a largely non-vocational way. The history of the university, then, is the history of a dynamic institution which has had among its goals the advancement of the Christian religion, the education of a governing elite, the advancement of knowledge and, now, the provision of mass education for citizens of democracies. Where next?

How much change can an institution undergo and still remain essentially the same? Not all change is mere development; some change is transformative so that the outer shell of social institutions remain the same while their interiors are extensively, even radically, remodelled. For example, Augustus and his imperial successors maintained the republican forms of Rome for hundreds of years after Rome had effectively been transformed into an empire. Is the modern university a hollow-shell, capable of being internally colonised by some new and transfigurative set of purposes? Is the multiversity a university? In particular, has the ever-increasing entanglement of state and university via funding and explicit control changed the fundamental nature of the university?

It is possible to overstate the case and to draw the contrasts between the past and the present too starkly. We must beware of romanticising the past and thinking that we have declined from some patrician past into a plebeian present. Gordon Graham writes: "There is to my mind a dangerous romanticism in thinking that once upon a time British universities were suitably Newmanesque until the arrival of utilitarian Philistines...." (Graham 2002, p. 2). Universities, at least those in Great Britain and Ireland, have always had a relation to the state and have always, to some extent, been under its control. What is new, however, is the almost total reliance of universities on government funding. One very unwelcome result of this funding reliance has been an increasing micro-control by the state and its agencies of universities and their activities. In the UK, the Higher Education Funding Council introduced funding initiatives, then the Research Assessment Exercise (RAE). Graham remarks that, willy nilly, the universities "had been forged into a state 'system' largely paid for by the state and subject to extensive central control" (Graham 2002, p. 14).
He who pays the piper calls the tune and increasing the state has been telling the universities what tune to play. There is no absolute necessity for universities to be state funded. They originated without state funding and have operated without state funding for most of their history. There are a number of

possibilities. We can have: either no state funding and no state control; or state funding and state control; or declining and/or inadequate state funding and increasing state control. Of these, the latter is the least satisfactory option and it is the option we increasingly have. Slaughter and Leslie write "If the state share of public university funding continues to decline, at some point the universities will become de facto independent or private, if they are not already" (Slaughter & Leslie 1997, p. 239). This judgement may be too sanguine as the state appears to be unwilling to relinquish the control is has acquired through funding even when the funding is declining. In the words of the bumper sticker, universities have become accustomed to doing so much with so little for so long that soon they will be required to do everything with nothing—still under government control.

Government interference reaches into the very heart of the university. Under funding pressure from government, universities are persuaded to change their curricula, close what are deemed to be irrelevant subject areas (even, in some cases, core but expensive subject areas such as chemistry), develop closer links with business and commerce and become ever more relevant. This being so, you would think there is every reason for universities to get out from under the increasingly intrusive hand of the state and to recover some sense of what it is that they are supposed to be. "Universities then need greater self-consciousness on where they draw the line between what they are willing to do and not do to meet these demands" (Kerr 2001, p. 140).

Just as state dependence has been bad for the Christian Churches in the past, so too is it bad for the university. But if universities are not funded by the state, where will they derive their income from? The answer is reasonably obvious and it is a mystery as to why it should be thought obscure. Those who provide goods and services normally derive their income from those to whom the goods and services are provided or from those willing to subsidise such beneficiaries. The university is a service provider and so its funding will have to be raised from those who benefit directly from the university's core activities;

the students who are taught and those who are willing to fund or to pay for the university's research. There is nothing revolutionary about this sentiment. It is not so very long ago that much of the cost of university education fell in whole or in large part on students or on their parents. Then free university education was instituted as part of a programme of universal access in which tax revenue was used to provide benefits to some at a cost to others; "free" doesn't really mean free, it simply means that someone other than the immediate beneficiary pays for it. The 'free fees' regime in Ireland introduced by a Labour minister in the 1990s is a case in point. It was intended to facilitate access to the universities by previously under-represented groups ('under-represented' being code for 'working-class' or 'poor') but instead of being targeted to the social groups deemed to be excluded from university by financial considerations it was made a general entitlement. Furthermore, it neglected to address the more fundamental problems limiting the access of those groups, namely, a paucity of social capital and deficiencies in second level education. Not only did it not achieve its stated aim of improving the number of students from poor backgrounds at university, it removed a source of independent funding from the university and tied the university hand and foot to government funding. From a financial perspective, this might have been all well and good in times of plentiful tax revenues (though even then the level of funding was not particularly generous) but in times of fiscal austerity, the results have been productive of cutbacks and staff shortages.

Graham notes that using "substantial amounts of tax revenue to support [higher education] can mean, and in practice often does mean, that the preferences and choices of some are being paid for at the expense of others, and that the relatively rich are being subsidised by the relatively poor" (Graham 2002, p. 110). Whatever about the ideological aspects of the aspiration of universal access, financially it was possible only when the cohort of the population attending university was relatively small. "The fact that tax revenues are necessarily limited means no government can support a system of funding, whether of health, social security, defence, legal aid or education, which requires virtually unlimited expenditure" (Graham 2002, p. 102). The situation is now changing in the UK where universities have recently been given permission to charge fees that bear some real relation to actual costs. In Ireland, we delude ourselves that university education is still free to all, ignoring the fact that the rapidly escalating Registration Charge is a fee by another name; a totally inadequate fee but a fee nonetheless.

There are other costs that are borne by those attending university even if they don't have to meet the direct expenditure required, namely the opportunity cost of the time spent at the university that could have been put to use in remunerative employment elsewhere. In the past, this opportunity cost was thought to be compensated for by the higher earnings that would eventually accrue to the graduate but this is no longer the case and hasn't been for quite some time. A degree is worth very little as a distinguishing factor on the job market now that virtually half to two thirds of the population has one. For those who advocate a university education primarily as a means to career advancement, the rapidly declining "job-value" of the first degree should cause them to reconsider the wisdom of advocating a policy of tax-funded universal access. Peter Thiel, co-founder of Pay Pal, caused a bit of a storm in May 2011 when he offered twenty fellowships of $100,000 each to students to pursue innovative scientific and technical projects, learn entrepreneurship, and start to build the technology companies of the future. The proviso is that the recipients of these fellowships have to stay out of college (see National Public Radio 2011).

There are those who would fear that the independence of the university would be compromised if it were to become dependent on fee-paying students. Whatever dangers fee-paying students might represent to the autonomy of the university, it couldn't conceivably be more destructive that the danger represented by a government motivated by ideological and financial considerations. "The government middleman........

threatens academic, and more importantly intellectual independence far more than the fee bearing student would do" (Graham 2002, p. 117). As the writer of an article in The Economist pointed out some years ago, in a fee-paying culture, the university would be beholden to nobody and it would decrease or eliminate dependence on government funding, thereby promoting genuine university autonomy. It would also, incidentally, increase student motivation. A dependable fee income would free universities from domination by government and government agencies and would require universities to provide an education that meets the requirements of value as determined by those individuals who stand to benefit from its services.

As it happens, not only are some (but not all) private universities surviving, new ones are emerging, driven primarily by market considerations. One of the largest of these, the University of Phoenix, has 280,000 students concentrating largely on business and technology subjects. As well as the University of Phoenix, we have Strayer University, Concord Law School and Cardean University. These all make extensive use of the internet. The emergence of these universities is happening at a time when the state is increasingly disengaging, at least financially, from the university so that we might describe the disengagement process, as one university president is alleged to have done, as a shift from the university as state institution, to state-supported institution, to state-assisted institution, to state-located institution, to state-annoyed institution.

When it comes right down to it, then, there are two and only two ways to get the funds to run a university: either get your money from fees, donations, investments, and so on, or get your money from the government, which is to say, from the taxpayer. Be self-financed and determine your own fate, or be state-financed and state-run.

State funding carries a lot of extra baggage with it. Universities are expected to do things that are not explicitly their business. Apart from the requirement to educate (or at least to certify) increasing numbers of students, social engineering comes high on the government's priorities.

> Universities can indeed give the disadvantaged a leg-up—but they will do it much better if the state stands back. Micro-managing university admissions, as the British government has been trying to do on grounds of class, with targets, quotas, fines and strictures, risks the same consequences as similar American experiences based on racial preference. It humiliates the talented but disadvantaged, whose success is then devalued; it infuriates the talented who are not deemed under-privileged enough and who feel their merits ignored, and it makes universities do a job they are bound to do badly (Anon. 2004, p. 11).

The problem with so-called under-representation of some social groups is best addressed elsewhere, in improving the quality of second-level schooling or in addressing the question of the destruction of social capital cause, in large part, by state interference in familial structures.

The universities, nominally private, are in fact controlled by the state with a life threatening stranglehold. As MacCabe puts it, "The government is the problem. Its laudable desire to increase, for economic reasons, the number of students attending university; to increase, for social reason, the number of students from poorer homes at university; and to make sure that the government is getting value for money, all turn out, on examination, to be either misguided in themselves or actively counter-productive" (MacCabe 2005).

There are other assumptions about the state's promotion of university education that must be questioned. One of these is "the utilitarian notion that universities' main merit is their economic usefulness. Amid much blather about the 'knowledge economy', the core of this belief is that more higher education means higher productivity and more wealth" (Anon. 2004). This presupposition is deeply flawed as a causal connection between a prosperous economy and a university system catering to a large section of the population has yet to be scientifically established.

In a way, the matter of state support of the university systems in the UK and Ireland has already been decided. The present rate of rapidly reducing levels of state support will not continue but will reduce even further. Cuts will continue to be made and those subjects that are considered central to the economy (the so-called STEM subjects: Science, Technology, Engineering, Mathematics) will be prioritised. If your subject doesn't attract large numbers of students or, worse still, doesn't attract research grants, you're vulnerable. Consider this Orwellian excerpt contained in a memorandum from a senior administrator at King's College London which tells us blandly that it is necessary to "create financially viable academic activity by disinvesting from areas that are at sub-critical level" (Thomas 2010). The language is as unlovely as the sentiment is disingenuous.

Do we need universities? If so, what do we need them for? The current upheavals in tertiary education have given the question of the nature, status, role and function of the university more point than it has had for quite some time. "The causes of the media's sniping at the University are not individual resentments but a more general uncertainty as to the role of the University and the very nature of the standards by which it should be judged as an institution....It is no longer clear what the place of the University is within society nor what the exact nature of that society is, and the changing institutional form of the University is something that intellectuals cannot afford to ignore" (Readings 1996, pp. 1-2). He connects the current uncertainty about the nature and role of the university with the decline of the national state. In his view, the modern university existed to provide the cultural underpinnings of such states and, with their decline, the universities are left without a defining role. I think he is correct in his identification of the uncertainty of nature and purpose that lies at the heart of the contemporary university; however, I think he is profoundly wrong in his location of that problem in the decline of the modern nation state.

In the age of the internet and immediately accessible information, has the university's raison d'être disappeared? If there is still a need for the university, what should this university do or be? Is there some one thing a university must be in order to be a university; is there, to use Newman's words, an 'idea' of a university or are universities infinitely malleable? As evidenced by its longevity the university is a remarkably flexible and adaptable institution but it is not infinitely flexible. There are many things it can be and do and still be recognisably the same institution but there are some things it cannot be and do or do and be without ceasing to be a university. The education of students, their intellectual formation, their acquisition of intellectual skills and independence of thought together with, where appropriate, professional training is at the very heart of what it is for something to be a university. Unless it is educating students, a university is not a university but, at best, a research institute.

I remarked earlier that universities, from their very beginning, have not only had a broad general education remit but have had a vocational element, originally in the fields of law, medicine or theology, later in engineering and technology. While education in such areas has a practical dimension, it is "radically incomplete if it remains at the level of the technical or even technological" (Graham 2002, p. 44). Graham believes that those in various professions need an understanding of the significance of their professions. The aim of these vocational subjects is the attainment of a certain kind of practical mastery but these subjects, if they are to be liberal and not merely technical, must be able to give an account of themselves.
Academics working in the humanities are tempted to defend what they do on the grounds that their students come to acquire what are known as 'transferable skills.' This is a tactical mistake based on a conceptual misunderstanding. As Graham notes, "...justification [of the humanities] in terms of transferable skills offers no support whatever for the content of these subjects" and

he points out that "The error in the appeal to transferable skills does not lie in its falsehood, but in the fact that it attempts to explain value in terms of use....The protagonists of classics, philosophy, Egyptology, Sanskrit or art history who adopt the language of transferable skills need to think again" (Graham 2002, pp. 24-25). The conceptual error that those erstwhile defenders of the humanities make is to accept a commonplace, nonetheless false for being commonplace, that education is valuable only inasmuch as it contributes more or less directly to material enrichment. In saying this, we needn't go to the other extreme and embrace the view that a liberal education enables one to despise the wealth it prevents one from acquiring. Nonetheless, education is not purely instrumental. It is an end in itself.

For Newman, education brings about an enlargement of the mind and this thought is as true today as when Newman had it. The human mind is not a passive instrument. It does not simply wait around for information to impress itself upon it but, rather, it engages in an "energetic and simultaneous action upon and towards and among those new ideas, which are rushing in upon it. It is the action of a formative power, reduction to order and meaning the matter of our acquirement." In a robust physical image, Newman compares it to "making the objects of our knowledge subjectively our own...a digestion of what we receive into the substance of our previous state of thought..." (Newman 1889, p. 134). Education is a matter of intellectual character formation; a permanent dispositional change.

Thus characterised, isn't education useless? Yes, in the same sense that children are useless, that music is useless, that friendship is useless, that conversation is useless, that anything which is an end in itself is useless. That is to say that the concept of the useful has no application here. To think that anything and everything can be judged to be useful is precisely not to be educated.

The ends of education are not extrinsic to the process, as if by being educated we become able to do something we could not otherwise do. The ends of education are intrinsic to the process; education makes us not so much able to do things (though it does do that), it makes us able to be something we otherwise would not be.

Education is the process by which our basic capacities (both intellectual and moral) are more-or-less permanently modified. These modified capacities (sometimes called somewhat misleadingly, habits (hexeis)) constitute a kind of moral or intellectual capital. They enable us to know and to do easily and accurately what would otherwise be known or done intermittently and with difficulty. Their acquisition, like all capital acquisition, is achieved by restriction, by saving, by abstention from the immediate gratification of natural pleasures. Learning is the formation of intellectual and moral capital, and education is the process by which such capital is formed.

All this being said, it is a valid question to ask how education is provided for in the university. The traditional method of instruction has been the lecture. In a time when scholars alone had 'the book' and when in most areas, whether of philosophy, law, theology there were accepted authorities, it made sense for the mode of instruction to be a reading by the lecturer of that book to the students, together with associated comments and glosses. In the age of the internet, when raw information is widely and easily available and anyone with a computer and broadband has access to a wealth of data (good and bad) that previous generations could only dream of, the informational transfer role of the university has receded. This is not something that all academics appreciate. Lectures encourage the 'assimilate and regurgitate' mentality which is at odds with university education. Now, more than ever, when the lecture is not the only or even the primary mode of information delivery, the contact between academic and student must be interactive—i.e. seminar, tutorial, workshop, etc.

"But," it might be objected, "hasn't the internet made the university redundant?" The market suggests not. Fathom, an internet venture supported by Columbia University and 13 other universities closed after a few years; Caliber, which was an e-partner of Wharton, went bankrupt, and Temple University ditched its Virtual Temple with indecent haste. NYU Online also closed.

What, in the 21st century, is the added value of the university? Some things can be taught by straight information delivery; others cannot. Here, the process is part of the content, and that process is interactional, human, live and irreplaceable. This has consequences for the 'normal' university which must examine traditional teaching methods, particularly the lecture, and ask whether they are, in all circumstances, fit for purpose. When all have access to the basic information, the lecture re-telling this material again is not a good idea. Students are cutting classes with a vengeance now that the lecture notes are online. The lecture originated in a context where only the lecturer had the book and so had to read to the students. There is no justification for making the lecture the primary mode of information delivery in the 21st century. Contact time between students should, whenever possible, be used interactively to explore, evaluate, and practise the knowledge and information already easily available.

One negative development in university teaching over recent years has been the introduction of modularisation. Superficially, this innovation seems perfectly in order. Surely, the student is a consumer and should be free to choose what he wants from an educational menu. In one sense, yes. A student can choose to study philosophy or music or engineering. At this level, choice is just fine. However, within a discipline, a student is not in a position to judge what it is that he should learn—that's why he's a student. Whatever about its success from a marketing point of view, educationally, modularisation is nonsense. It fragments disciplines and sticks their dismembered remains to pin boards. Modularisation appears to be designed to put the student at the centre of the education process—but it should be disciplines not students that occupy the centre. When students come to university they begin a trek into the world of scholarship in which their guides are those already engaged in that task.

The notion of modularisation is modelled on the idea that the student is a customer. In the commercial world customers are kings; producers are not in any position to dictate to customers what they should or shouldn't want. Customers want what they want and that's the end of the matter. This is not the relationship between student and professor. The object of education is not to fill some sharply determined and particular need but rather to change and indeed to change in some more or less radical way what it is that the students wants and is. The relationship between student and professor is much more like that of inexpert to expert than it is to customer and provider. The expert music teacher induces the requisite practical skill in his students and, even more to the point, elicits, modifies and moulds the music student's taste. It doesn't matter whether students like what they are learning or not, at least not in the beginning. Very often, they don't like it at all. However, the test of whether or not they have been educated is whether they have acquired the skill or skills and also whether their tastes and preferences have been permanently modified (see Graham 2002, p. 48f.).

Modularisation is an attack on this attempted distinction between the student as customer and the student as inexpert. "University students are not only enabled, but encouraged, to pick and choose between the academic courses on offer as one chooses between the goods in a supermarket. The question is this: Is this to their benefit? Or more precisely: is this to the benefit of their education?" (Graham 2002, p. 52) Graham thinks the answer to these questions is no. "...modularization may have brought advantages....it is nevertheless the case that in large measure [it relies on] and strengthens presuppositions about university education that, upon no very close examination, can be shown to be conceptually confused" (Graham 2002, p. 53).
What we have here is a conflation of two kinds of choice. Most certainly, a student has the right to choose what discipline, if any, he will follow. However, it is quite another thing to assert that an erstwhile student has the right to be taught, in an institutional setting, how he will be inducted into that discipline.

That is a task, a task that can be performed well or badly, by those who are the acknowledged experts in a given discipline.

The University and its Managers

Throughout most of its history, the usual mode of university governance has been collegial. Deans, proctors, and masters did not act as if they were employers of a workforce but were primus inter pares, academics who oversaw the work of other academics and the running of the university in its various modes of self-organisation. Whether modelled on Bologna or Paris, universities were autonomous self-governing corporations (reflecting the structure of the medieval guild) electing their own officials and organising their own assemblies. "At the time of their greatest independence the universities lived in the interstices of medieval society, taking advantage of its decentralization and the balance of its conflicting powers to further their own corporate interests" (Hofstadter 1996, p. 7). Today, by contrast, our university presidents, provosts and registrars like to think of themselves as chief executives or managing directors. This bizarre self-conception is revealed in their adoption of business speak with its mission statements, strategic plans, logos and corporate images. In Ireland, some years ago, we witnessed the spectacle of our university presidents attempting to justify their extraordinary salaries by comparing themselves to the managers of large multi-national corporations and demanding to be recompensed for their emotional intelligence, an attribute, the presence of which is rendered dubious by the very making of the claim. Talking about the rise of managerialism in the university, Malcolm Saunders describes as 'academic feudalism' a system that rewards "obedience, conformity and quiescence, and punishes non-compliance, eccentricity and dissent. Academic feudalism breeds fear, cowardice, cynicism and sycophancy..." (Saunders 2006,p. 11). Another point well made by Saunders is that universities are nowadays more often concerned with research money than with research. Research that doesn't cost money is less valued. "Money is not pursued to allow research, research is pursued to attract or acquire money" (p. 12). Whatever the norm was in the past, university administrators today are no longer recruited by temporary secondment from among the academic staff but are full-time administrators who may once have been academics but are so no longer. Once they have gone through the apotheosis from a mere mortal academic to the divine status of what is revealing termed 'Senior Management' our new gods rarely deign to condescend to return to the academic ranks whence they came.

Accusations that those who control the universities are not real academics are nothing new. As early as 1909, John. J. Chapman remarked that "the men who control Harvard today are very little else than businessmen, running a large department store which dispenses education to millions" (Chapman 1909, p. 40). Others have pointed out a distinction that you would have thought would have been obvious to all but apparently isn't, namely, that not all who work in a university are academics, an egregious error endemic in reports in the Irish press which suggests that the reporters are under the that impression (Caws 1970, p. 98).

"UCD [University College Dublin] staff top survey for Ireland's highest paid educators" is the headline over a front-page piece in UCD's student newspaper (University Observer). Inside the paper, a companion piece, titled 'The Wages of Fear' tells us that a recent Irish Times report reveal that "UCD's academic staff are among the highest paid in the country". This would be interesting if true. Is it? That depends on what one means by the terms educator and academic. Lots of people who work in University College Dublin and in other universities are not academics: grounds-keepers, restaurant staff, technicians, school administrators, and personnel officers, Vice-Presidents for this, that and the other, Registrars, Provosts and Presidents. However important the work they do, it's not education and it's not academic and they are neither educators nor academics. Some of these workers may have been academics in the past but they are not academics now.

The top 10 of the Irish Times list ["The top 100 best-paid in education" (note, not 'educators')] contains five people from UCD: the Vice-President for Research, the Dean of the School of Business, the Principal of the College of Engineering, the President, and the Vice-President for Staff (Flynn and McGuire 2010). When you continue through this list you discover that virtually everybody on that list is a non-academic. You will have no difficulty finding University Presidents and Provosts, IT Presidents, Vice-Presidents and Vice-Provosts; Deans, Directors, Bursars, Principals, Registrars, the Secretary General of the Department of Education and Skills, the Minister for Education, the Director Generals of FAS, of the Institute of Public Administration, of Science Foundation Ireland, the Director of the ESRI, the Chief Executive of the State Examination Commission, the Chief Executive of the National Qualifications Authority of Ireland, the Chief Executive of the Higher Education Authority, and so on, ad nauseam, on the list but you'll need a Hubble telescope to detect any genuine full-time academics there. In the end, what is truly remarkable about the Irish Times list is the glaring absence of academic staff and educators from the ranks of the most highly paid people who work in the education sector. University administrators are no more academics than are the university's cleaning staff or its restaurant workers. Like the cleaners or the cooks, university administrators are ancillary staff—much more highly paid than the cleaners of the cooks but still ancillary.

One defensible explanation for the shift in university governance from self-governance to managerialism lies in changes in the size of universities in the recent past. Collegial self-governance is relatively unproblematic when universities are small, with few students, fewer academics and small budgets. With increasing size comes an incentive to move from self-governance by academics to government by management. Until comparatively recently, the number of students in universities was a small proportion of the relevant cohort: 2%, 5%, or 7%. Now it can approach or exceed 50-60%! To get some idea of the effect of numbers, let's look at the growth of the higher education section in the USA. In 1939 there were 1,708 institutions with a total enrolment of 1,494,203 whereas in 2003 there were 4,168 institutions with a total enrolment of 15, 927,987. The number of academic staff in the same period went from 146,929 in 1939 to 1,173,000 in 2003 (see Schuster and Finkelstein 2006, p. 39). In that 64 year period, the institutions increased by almost 150%, academic staff by almost 700% and students by almost 1,000%. Considerations such as these lend support to the managerialism imperative. The proper response, of course, to this perverse incentive is for universities to become smaller until they can once again be governed by academics.

With the shift from collegial self-governance to managerialism, university bosses are less concerned to defend and protect ordinary academics. Indeed, as we saw above in the media attacks on academics and their high salaries, university administrators by their extravagance often open the academic profession as a whole to unjustified attack. The pressure coming from government, the principal funding agency of many of the universities, is enormous and university administrators, instead of resisting those pressures and defending their staff, are in effect collaborating with the enemy in a quisling-like manner, outdoing each other to show that they can do more with less, which typically means that their academic staff will be forced to do more with less of everything except, unfortunately, less of those who are increasingly telling them what to do. Of the making of managers or senior administrators there is, alas, no end. The cost of administration is constantly rising as a proportion of the amount of money actually spent in universities until, in some institutions, it exceeds 50% of the budget. If one were to add on the costs of Government Departments and government agencies charged with the supervision of the universities, the administrative overheads would appear to eat up much of the entire budget.

A standard political ploy when one wants to attack a certain social group is first to demonise it, then the attack will have public support; one thinks of Jews in Nazi Germany and the monks and their lands in Tudor England or the kulaks in the early days of the Soviet Union. One now commonly hears it said of academic staff that they can do whatever they please at the public's expense, thanks to the twin safeguards of academic freedom and tenure. Academics are the new medieval monks, the new kulaks. Derek Bok, former President of Harvard, characterises this cartoonish caricature of academic workers as representing the belief that academics "remain at home most of the day tending their garden or enjoying their hobbies without much fear of detection. So long as they meet their scheduled classes and refrain from criminal acts or other grossly improper behaviour, they can stay happily in their jobs until they retire" (Bok 2003, p. 21). Bok notes that, despite this apparently anarchic situation, the universities (American, that is) are unusually successful in what they do. Perhaps the universities are successful not 'despite' the apparently anarchy but rather because of it.

Currently (May 2011) under discussion by academics in Ireland is a take-it-or-leave-it document emanating from the Department of Education which is imbued throughout with the language of managerialism and which evinces throughout its provisions a suspicion that if academics are not constantly watched, monitored and managed, they will spend all their time gardening, double-jobbing or taking never-ending coffee breaks. This document "Application of the Public Service Agreement in the Universities" (APSAU) requires academics to work one extra hour per week at the discretion of management, blithely ignoring the fact that an unknown quantity plus one is still an unknown quantity. It requires academics to implement workload models "to aid the transparent and equitable distribution of work within the university community." Management (again!) is to be given the authority to vary the proportion of an academic's teaching, research, scholarly activity and contributions to administration. Academics are required under the APSAU to cooperate with what is called Full Economic Costing (FEC) by completing an Academic Activity Profile and to participate in the university's Performance

Management and Development System (PMDS). If this isn't redolent of 1984 and Big Brother, it's hard to know what is.

How much do academics actually work? Between 1972 and 1998, a period of just over twenty five years, the average hours worked across the range of third level institutions went from 42.9 to 48.6, an increase of just over 13% with the biggest increase and the largest number of hours considered absolutely (50.6) being worked in universities granting graduate degrees (see Schuster and Finkelstein 2006, p. 79). In the approximate 30 year period between 1969 and 1998, the publication rate in all parts of the university sector have increased substantially. The percentage of those who had not published in the previous two years in universities granting graduate degrees dropped from 28.8% to 14%; the percentage of those who had published 5 or more pieces in the previous two years in the same class of institutions went from 19.4% to 40.9%. The same movements down and up, albeit less startling, can be found in the 4-year institutions and the two-year colleges (see Schuster and Finkelstein 2006, p. 100). The evidence, such as it is, suggests that academics on the whole work longer hours than their compeers in other employment sectors and have increased their hours of work and their publication output over the period measured.

According to Slaughter & Leslie, in the times and circumstances in which we live, the idea of the university as a community of scholars will continue to disintegrate further and management will continue to replace governance. University managers will relate best to those parts of the university that generate money. Those academics in those areas, particularly those that generate large amounts of research income, will have relative freedom but academics in other areas can expect to find themselves increasingly hamstrung: "...administrators will assert greater control over departments, beginning by managing the large contingents of part-timers. Regents and trustees concerned with rising institutional costs will encourage administrators to take over more and more planning, until administrators rather than faculty decide which fields will grow and which will not" (Slaughter and Leslie 1997, p. 243).

In this atmosphere of the assimilation of the university to the world of business, it should come as no surprise that the many and varied schemes that have been proposed for the rejuvenation and reconstruction of business eventually trickle down to the academy. Among the army of acronyms by which these schemes are known to the cognoscenti, we can find PPBS, MBO, ZBB, TQM/CQI and BPR, which stand, respectively, for Planning Programming Budgeting System, Management By Objectives, Zero-Base Budgeting, Total Quality Management/ Continuous Quality Improvement and Business Process Reengineering (see Casey 2006). Two additional non-acronymised schemes are Strategic Planning and Benchmarking. The hulks of such schemes litter the shorelines of academia. Some unkind person, possible a failed philosophy student, remarked that there is no theory so foolish that some philosopher has not adopted it; likewise, none of our acrynomic schemes is so foolish, bankrupt or inappropriate that it has not been adopted by the academy, usually about the time when its defects had become manifest in business, a point established at some length by Robert Birnbaum (2001).

The most radical of such schemes, surely the most audacious, is Business Process Reengineering. Its thesis is simple. Whatever you've been doing up to now is wrong. Stop doing it! Wipe out all existing structures and start again from scratch! "In business reengineering," Birnbaum remarks "old job titles and old organizational arrangements—departments, divisions, groups, and so on—cease to matter" (Birnbaum 2001, p. 109). It is, of course a romantic illusion to believe that there was some golden age when universities were like the Garden of Eden before the slithering arrival of the serpents of block grants, accountability, FTEs and Resource Allocation Models. It is, however, an equally dangerous romantic illusion to imagine (as Graham has noted) that the university is a kind of Rousseauian lump of clay that, as in the dreams of Business Process Reengineering and the nightmares of everyone else, can be modelled according to the will of those momentarily in control of it. At its best, such voluntaristic hubris is a harmless distraction; at its worst, it can result in an outbreak of African Map Syndrome, named after those 19th century Colonial Office officials who thought that what they had to do to sort out African affairs was simply to sharpen up their pencils, get out the map of the Dark Continent, draw nice neat lines on it and then retire for drinks to the Senior Conservative with the satisfying feeling that their duty had been done.

Less intrinsically malign to institutional integrity than Business Process Reengineering but with its own destructive potential is Strategic Planning. This is almost certain to be the case if Strategic Planning becomes Central Planning. The political shortcomings of central planning were graphically demonstrated in the 20th century in China, the former Soviet Union and its Eastern European satellites, in Kampuchea, and elsewhere. Economically, the 'calculation debate' has shown convincingly that central planning not only does not work but that it cannot work. The situation is little different in academia. Plans indeed there must be if we are not to be complacent, or flounder from one crisis to another but the plans must respect that balance between the old and the new, the top and the bottom, the essential and the ephemeral that Confucius so eloquently expressed.

In commencement speeches and graduations and other formal occasions, Newman and his idea of a university is mentioned reverentially. Alas, that those who mention Newman in these contexts seem to be innocent of any of his thought other than the title of his book. One author has written that

> If Newman had really been profoundly and consistently influential, we would not have much of the machinery of administration, the structure and content of courses, the huge array of rules and regulations, the debates over access, over SAT scores in the US and A-levels and Highers in England and Scotland. We wouldn't be talking bureaucratically

> about 'seat time,' 'enrollment (sic) targets,' interactive teaching technologies, modular systems of instruction. Newman's vocabulary and conceptualization would not have led us to discuss quality control mechanisms, student transfer, the relationship of further education to higher education, contract research, funding, loan policies, pension schemes for academics (Rothblatt 2006, p. 5).

Similarly, Gordon Graham remarks,

> The universities of Britain have been blown hither and thither by modularisation, semesterization, academic audit, quality assurance, staff appraisal, resource allocation modelling, on-line management, student evaluation, research assessment and countless other 'initiatives'." All this might seem like a nostalgic longing for the return of the 'good old days' but, since there never were such days, we cannot return to them. Critically, Gordon concludes that "What [the universities] have not done is to deploy their own intellectual resources to take critical stock of these changes. Consequently, they have not exhibited that very critical independence which must lie at the heart of their rationale (p. 17).

The RAE (now the REF—Research Excellence Framework) was devised as an instrument for measuring the extent to which academics were contributing to the advance of knowledge and understanding. This is a crude and counter-productive instrument. One of its presuppositions is that continuous publication is a sign of academic well-being with an accompanying prioritisation of research at the expense of teaching. This system encourages academics "to spend as little time as possible on teaching by applying for research leave, negotiating reductions in their lecturing and tutorial hours, and competing for research fellowships and professorships to free them from students altogether" (Graham 2002, p. 14). Research (and publication) has always been assessed by academics on behalf of the academic community; what is new is the formalisation (and mechanisation) of the process by the use of standard indicators on behalf of so-called management. "RAE has the nature of a race in which no one believes, but in which everyone has to take part, and to do so vigorously and with the appearance of enthusiasm" (Graham 2002, p. 76). Unfortunately, as every academic knows, acceptance by a reputable journal isn't conclusive evidence of value; nor is rejection, conclusive evidence of worthlessness and citation indices are intrinsically bizarre inasmuch as merely counting citations is entirely indiscriminate—you may be cited because you are good, or because you are bad!

Quality Assessment (and Quality Enhancement) are yet more bureaucratic tools of management that measure the insignificant and fail to measure the significant. The entire Quality Assessment exercise is radically misconceived. The examiners appear to be selected for their lack of knowledge and their distrust of what it is that universities do. The exercises themselves are a waste of time and money, time perhaps more than money. Preparation for the Quality Assessment carries a huge opportunity cost taking up valuable time that could have been put to other good uses, distracting the members of the Department being assessed from what it is that they are really supposed to be doing. It is important to realise that these exercises are not just harmless but are actually positively harmful in that "...the need to produce a paper trail mean that huge amounts of time were spent on doing so, with the ironic result that teaching was reduced in order to allow to prepare for 'the QAA'" (Graham 2002, p. 59). A mordant comment on the futility of both the Research Assessment and Teaching Quality assessment comes from Alan Ryan, who writes

The Teaching Quality Assessment system rewards departments which waste the time of two faculty members for a year to assemble the paperwork that will get the department a perfect score. The Research Assessment Exercise (RAE) is a flat-footed five-yearly form of peer evaluation; in the US, informal but continuous peer competition and peer evaluation produce widely accepted rank orders that anyone funding research would go along with. Princeton has a Nobel prize-winning physics department because it is always looking over its shoulder at its rivals, not fidgeting about the RAE (p. 29).

The universities came into being to fulfil certain felt needs in society at a particular place and particular time; they are historically contingent institutions, not eternal verities. Over the years, they have adapted themselves to the changing requirements of their circumstances without abandoning their original calling. If they are to survive, let alone, flourish, then they will need financial independence to free them from the malign and heavy hand of government, the enemy without, and a return to a robust form of self-governance to free them from the inept hand of academic managers, the enemy within. In 2012, the prospect of attaining either of these goals in any meaningful way in the near future appears remote.

References

Anon. 2004. *"Pay or decay."* The Economist, 24 January.

Birnbaum, Robert. 2001. *Management fads in higher education.* San Francisco: Jossey-Bass.

Bok, Derek. 2003. *Universities in the marketplace: the commercialization of higher education.* Princeton, NJ: Princeton University Press.

Casey, Gerard. *"Reengineering the academy: a response to Professor Rothblatt."* In Lavan (ed.), pp. 31-34.

Caws, Peter. 1970. *"Design for a university."* Daedalus (Winter) (cited in Bok).

Chapman, John J. 1909. *"The Harvard Classics and Harvard."* Science 30 (cited in Bok).

Clark, Burton R. 2007. *Creating entrepreneurial universities: organizational pathways of transformation.* Bingley, UK: Emerald Group Publishing.

Flynn, Sean & Peter McGuire. (2010). *"The top 100 best-paid in education."* The Irish Times. 9 November.

Graham, Gordon. 2002. *Universities: the recovery of an idea*. Thorverton, Essex: Imprint Academic.

Hofstadter, Richard. 1996. *Academic freedom in the age of the college*. New Brunswick, New Jersey: Transaction.

Kerr, Clark. 2001. *The uses of the university*. Cambridge, MA: Harvard University Press.

Knowles, David. 1962. *The evolution of medieval thought*. London: Longman.

Lavan, Ann. (ed.) 2006. *The university and society: from Newman to the market*. Dublin: UCD College of Human Sciences.

MacCabe, Colin. 2005. *"Set our universities free."* The Observer, 13 March.

National Public Radio. 2011. *"New fellowship pays for college kids to drop out."* http://www.npr.org/2011/05/26/136690533/new-fellowship-pays-for-college-kids-to-drop-out

Newman, John Henry. 1889. *The idea of a university*. 9th ed. London: Longmans, Green, and Co.

Rothblatt, Sheldon. 2006. *"Loss and gain: John Henry Newman in 2005."* In Lavan (ed.) pp. 15-29.

Readings, Bill. 1996. *The university in ruins*. Cambridge, MA: Harvard University Press.

Ryan, Alan. 1999. *"The American way."* Prospect (August/September), pp. 24-28.

Saunders, Malcolm. 2006. *"The madness and malady of managerialism."* Quadrant (March 2006): pp. 9-17

Schuster, Jack H. and Martin J. Finkelstein. 2006. *The American faculty: the restructuring of academic work and careers*. Baltimore, MD: The Johns Hopkins University Press.

Slaughter, Sheila & Larry L. Leslie. 1997. *Academic capitalism: politics, policies and the entrepreneurial university*. Baltimore, MD: The Johns Hopkins University Press.

Thomas, Keith. 2010. *"What are universities for?"* Times Literary Supplement, 7 May 2010.

The University Observer (University College Dublin). 2010. *"UCD staff top survey for Ireland's highest paid educators."* 16th November.

CHAPTER 4
THE IMPORTANCE OF VALUES-BASED LEADERSHIP IN THE MODERN UNIVERSITY

John G. Hughes
Vice-Chancellor of Bangor University

Introduction

In recent years a wave of Philistinism has beleaguered the university system in many countries, including Ireland, led by politicians and civil servants with little understanding of the principles and values of university education. We have been told that we should be more utilitarian, organs of economic development, servants of the State and that we should be run in a more business-like fashion, focused on efficiency and on economic return. Such calls have often been coupled with attempts to limit university autonomy using funding levers or other forms of government control. When university leaders respond enthusiastically to such pressures, considerable damage can be done to scholarship and to the quality of university education.

However, the tension between utility and traditional academic values is often exaggerated and, with appropriate leadership, both can be accommodated successfully within a modern university environment. Universities are key elements of our economy and must play their part effectively and enthusiastically. More broadly however, universities are vital contributors to public policy, to improving civic life, to creating a fairer and more inclusive society, to our cultural and artistic life and to how people perceive us in the world community. The keys to accommodating traditional values with utility are informed by values-based leadership, academic freedom and a spirit of openness and collegiality.

In this paper I address three issues, based on my experience of university leadership in both Britain and Ireland:

1. The importance of effective but sympathetic leadership and the qualities required of a leader in the modern university.
2. Universities in the knowledge society and the tension between utility and academic values.
3. The factors that I believe will determine the future direction and effectiveness of the university system.

Leadership

In recent years many universities have experienced major transformations, usually initiated by an enthusiastic, newly appointed president. However, it has been my experience that radical transformations are more often driven by presidential vanity and zeal, rather than the wellbeing of the institution. In particular, many institutional reforms are driven through without appropriate consultation or indeed regard for the views of staff. It is expected that staff will be compliant and that behaviour change will take place across the institution on the whims of senior administrators, who often have no experience of academic life. In fact, long-standing experience from across the world demonstrates that changes in behaviour are unlikely to become embedded unless there is a change in underlying values. That is, leaders need to work on the hearts and minds of their staff and unless this occurs, changes in structure and procedures will have only a limited impact on their behaviour. Therefore, because organisational change will only take effect if there is a change in values, true behavioural change takes a long time to occur. While leaders are important in creating the springboard for change, the importance of values is central to the process. In addition, within universities it is vitally important that effective change is integrated successfully into the existing institutional culture and history. Presidents must not lose touch with core historical values and indeed should make those values central to their words and deeds. Indeed, changes introduced by a culturally sensitive leader may be seen either as constructive developments of historic themes or as manifestations of a desirable new stage in institutional evolution.

As a result of a large number of surveys of the kinds of leadership that work best for most people, Kouzes and Posner (2003) came up with five factors which I have found to be particularly effective in a university context. These are:

- Modelling the way– leading by example in a manner that is consistent with the leader's stated values; recognizing and indeed celebrating 'small wins' that signify achievements by staff consistent with them and dismantling barriers to their realisation.
- Inspiring a shared vision– developing a compelling but realistic and achievable vision of the future and enlisting the commitment of staff.
- Challenging the process– being on the lookout for opportunities to improve the organization, especially within the service functions of the university, and being prepared to experiment and take calculated risks.
- Enabling others to act: promoting collaborative working; delegating authority and empowering others; building trust.
- Encouraging the heart: recognising individuals' contributions; celebrating accomplishments; being supportive and protective of staff, their jobs and their positions within the organization.

In universities where independence of thought is treasured and collective governance is highly valued, the challenges of leadership are very different from those in business. University leadership requires not only the creation and articulation of vision and values but also a willingness to engage ones colleagues in the process. For all the time, effort and compromise that consultation and collaboration may involve, in a university environment failure to adopt this value often leads to less robust ideas and almost always to resistance to implementation. This is not advocating management by committee but rather the implementation of change through honest and open dialogue and the retention of those most valuable assets of a university - good will and collegiality.

Recent studies of leadership in higher education (Bryman, 2009) support this view by demonstrating that there are a number of qualities of leaders that are particularly valued by academic staff. These are:

- Honesty and integrity
- A consultative approach
- Values
- A sense of direction
- Supportive and protective of staff

These are very much consistent with the five factors for effectiveness listed above. It may be surprising to some, but academics expect that their leader be someone who is trusted and who has personal integrity. In this respect we may differ from those in banking or high finance! Indeed, a lack of honesty or personal integrity in the leader of an educational institution can very quickly reflect very negatively on the whole institution. Not only can it destroy morale internally, but also it will lead other institutions and external organisations to view the university with deep suspicion and mistrust, avoiding opportunities for collaboration. The damage that this can bring to a university can be considerable.

Another aspect of leader behaviour in higher education that is particularly significant is that effective leaders protect their staff. This is often linked to the notion of the value of autonomy, in that effective leaders are seen by academic staff as protecting them so that they can get on with their work relatively unhampered. One feature that is striking about the qualities listed above is the absence of forms of leader behaviour associated with the 'new' leadership approach, such as transformational or 'so-called' charismatic leadership, or leadership based on managerialism.

What lies at the heart of this discussion on university leadership is the need for a leader to create an environment for academics and others to fulfill their potential and maintain their pride and interest in their work. There is no clear blueprint for such leadership but there are clear indications of how not to lead in a university context. Failing to consult, not respecting existing values, actions that undermine collegiality, not promoting the interests of those for whom the leader is responsible, being uninvolved in the life of the institution, undermining autonomy, and allowing the institution to drift are all likely to cause damage. These may seem, in many respects, common sense things to avoid but it is surprising how frequently in recent years some academic institutions have failed to respect these values.

Of course a leader's influence and effectiveness may be undermined by outside intrusion, particularly from government. The erosion of autonomy that has taken place in Irish universities in recent years has severely limited the ability of presidents to provide the kind of supportive environment that is so essential. Staff autonomy has been almost entirely eroded by the rigorous imposition of the Employment Control Framework (ECF). While universities cannot be immune from the fiscal austerity measures implemented by successive Irish governments, it must be recognized that universities, unlike the civil service, operate in a globally competitive market when it comes to attracting and retaining staff. Denying universities the ability to appoint, promote or reward staff, as they see fit within their tightly constrained budgets, will soon cause such damage to the system as to erase all of the advances that were made during the so-called 'Celtic Tiger' years. The ECF has introduced Soviet-style control and micromanagement of staffing in the universities to a level that does not exist anywhere in the developed world. One of the most disappointing aspects of the ECF has been the enthusiasm with which the Higher Education Authority has embraced it and rigorously enforced it, despite the fact that they must be fully aware of the incalculable damage that it is doing to the system.

Universities in the Knowledge Society

There is now a general consensus in Ireland that we have to build our economy on knowledge because we cannot compete with other areas of the world on low cost manufacturing or rely on inward investment. A fundamental economic shift is taking place in Ireland. The principle that knowledge, innovation and creativity are the foundations on which our new economy will be built has been widely accepted. We have also begun to recognize that our universities, as important knowledge generators, have a central role to play in the new Ireland and this has put higher education at the heart of economic development policy.

However, for many in academia, the proposition that universities should operate in a marketplace or service context is often not enthusiastically received. My own view is that this tension between utility and traditional academic values is more imagined than real. Academics should not feel threatened by this debate, for an honest discussion about the aims and functions of the university is not only a healthy sign of academic freedom but has been a part of the tradition of universities since their founding in the middle ages. Universities are key elements of our economy and we must play our part effectively and enthusiastically. More broadly, universities are vital contributors to public policy, to improving civic participation, to creating a fairer and more inclusive Ireland, to our cultural and artistic life and to how people perceive Ireland in the wider global community.

Our goal must be to create a knowledge society where learning, understanding, creativity and ideas add value to almost every aspect of society, not just to the economy. The OECD Review of Higher Education in Ireland (2004) supported this view. The report recognised that increased investment in universities 'is a critical element in achieving and sustaining a knowledge society with a high capacity for innovation which is at the centre of Ireland's strategy for economic development'. It is unfortunate that the emphasis of this report on economic development led to charges that it was utilitarian. In fact, the report clearly stated that 'The importance of tertiary education to Ireland's economic and social development should not obscure its role in the intellectual and artistic life of the nation and the contribution it makes to citizenship and the civil society'. I believe that the OECD report offered the best chance for a generation to set a strategic direction for higher education in Ireland. Together with partners in Government, in industry, in the community, we needed, at that time, a strategy to build a knowledge society with higher education at its heart. Unfortunately the opportunity was missed.

Our vision of a knowledge economy must be an ambitious one. A fully developed knowledge economy must have a creative, well funded and internationally competitive higher education research base providing new and innovative processes and products. Universities must be better enabled to take these opportunities to market, but industry must be engaged with universities in the joint development of promising ideas and technologies. Higher education must be in a continual and increasingly productive dialogue with industry, professional and statutory bodies, and companies from both Ireland and abroad must routinely tap into the knowledge resources of universities to develop products and processes and to add value to all of their activities. Universities need to provide ease of access to their technologies and their resources and people should be able to move flexibly between industry and academia with a good understanding of each other's purposes. Meanwhile, the workforce will continually learn new skills in a higher education sector geared up to delivering more continuing professional development. The result will be a more prosperous Ireland with a more robust economy built on highly skilled, well-paid jobs.

Much of the current debate about science in Ireland links it to the commercialization agenda. In this context, it is important to remember that the core purpose of higher education is to create knowledge and to pass it on through teaching and research. Commercialization is an important part of our role and one that we take very seriously, but commercialization opportunities emerge from basic research in a wide variety of disciplines, including the arts, and if we do not support these or if we distort these activities there will be no knowledge or technology to commercialize. The economic role of science is important, but we must also value its other roles – in understanding our world and our environment, in improving health and our quality of life, in informing our decisions and in inspiring people. This is also important to correct the often poor perception and distrust of science among the public, to attract young people into the study of science, and to revitalize science at school level.

A longer term, more stable funding horizon which is less risk-averse could remove the pressure on universities to make short-term gains from their intellectual property at the expense of a potentially more effective long-term approach. Universities could do more to embed an ethos of innovation, which could mean everything from better dialogue and the sharing of resources between institutions to training in entrepreneurship for students and academics. We also need to engage more with the business and finance communities to ensure that the appropriate skills and resources are available to make the best of our opportunities.

If an analysis of Ireland's strengths, weaknesses, opportunities and threats was undertaken, our strong tradition of education and learning would be seen as a real strength and a great opportunity. Our higher education sector represents an enviable asset for a country of our size, but any asset is only as effective as the use that is made of it.

The Future

No small nation in history has prospered without a thriving university sector helping to lead the way. The higher education sector in Ireland is experiencing a crucial transition that will see the landscape of the sector change radically in the coming years. Universities have made some historic and deep-seated changes. We have witnessed a clear determination to make the changes needed to deliver economic renewal, to putting students first and to widening access to people traditionally excluded from the advantages of a higher education. Much more needs to be done

We are in an era of global higher education where student flows are growing worldwide and where businesses pick the best partners for their collaborative research regardless of geographical location. Though the challenges of such an environment are great, the rewards can be just as big. A substantial amount is contributed to the Irish economy each year by the international and EU students studying in the country and thousands of jobs are sustained by the presence of students from overseas. Positive experiences of our universities contribute to a higher international profile for Ireland and the input of academic staff from overseas helps to enrich our research base. Over the past decade, many of our academics and researchers have come from the international community - this in turn helps develop the knowledge networks required for our economic renewal. As universities we must be deeply engaged in our localities, contribute to the social and economic life nationally and be high flying internationally. These three roles are essential and complementary aspects of the core mission of Irish universities.

Research and innovation is one key area where Irish universities have shifted gear. We will only prosper as a nation in an increasingly competitive global economy if we have a comparative advantage in the innovation exchanged between universities and industry and in the skill levels and talent of our people. Though Ireland, along with many other countries, is currently in a difficult place economically, this position can be turned around through a concerted effort between universities, government and industry.

Investment in university research is far from cheap. For various reasons, public investment in research and innovation in Ireland - including at universities - has fallen short of the investment made in other parts of the world, particularly the Far East. A major push on science and research in Ireland will require sustained levels of investment from the government if it is to help us catch up in the ever faster 'race to the top'.

This is far from an 'elitist' agenda – it is grounded in a firm commitment to social justice, or 'inclusive growth' as the European Union's 2020 strategy calls it. Continuing to widen access to universities in Ireland is vital where higher education has always been an important springboard to better living standards for individuals and families. In an economic context, where having low skills means a declining chance of getting on the career ladder, this is even more important. Specialist postgraduate skills are now increasingly demanded by employers in the burgeoning 'knowledge economy' – and we are not doing as well as our economic competitors (Singapore, China) in ensuring that we are generating a home-grown workforce with the highest levels of skills. In a context where China will graduate two million higher education students this year –almost as large as the total size of the Irish labour force - the challenge is stark.

Just as important as upskilling is the life-enhancing and horizon-broadening experience that university gives to students. Helping and watching students develop over their period at university is one of the most satisfying aspects of the work of any academic. That is why we must proactively attract students from social backgrounds that have not traditionally reached university. The latest performance indicators show that Irish universities have continued to perform well in widening access to groups with no experience of higher education. The figures underline the effort that Irish universities put into raising aspirations within our communities and in creating new pathways to higher education for those who may not have otherwise considered it an option.

Despite this, society is still stalked by the continuing scandal of educational inequality, which means that a child's social background is a major predictor of whether they will get a chance to benefit from a university education. This is a challenge for us all: for parents in setting a child's sights high, for schools in preparing pupils for higher learning, and for universities in supporting both parents and schools in recognising the potential of children in our most deprived communities. Some progress has been made in recent years, but every university has a key role to play in addressing this problem, including by expanding part-time learning opportunities for adults.

Funding

Most academics accept the need for reform in Irish universities but are concerned that such reform should retain ideas central to university education – academic freedom, autonomy, openness and collegiality. Substantial reforms have been implemented in recent years, which, according to some, have improved the efficiency and effectiveness of the universities whilst providing students with a broader choice and greater intellectual challenge.

I believe that some Irish universities are sensitive to these issues but are implementing reform in the face of a massive decline in core funding in recent years. The crucial condition in securing our vision of a flourishing and internationally competitive university sector is the provision of appropriate funding. Sustained and adequate funding is essential to all activities in a university: attracting and motivating the best staff, equipping laboratories with the latest equipment and providing students with the best environment for learning. Irish universities are using the resources available to them in an effective and efficient way and cannot be expected to do much more unless they are resourced more generously. Indeed few other sectors in the country can match the remarkable record of financial integrity and probity that has been a consistent feature of the Irish university sector for many years. As a nation, Ireland spends less on tertiary education per student, less as a proportion of GDP and less as a proportion of total public expenditure than all of our major competitors. Some countries are above us due to higher levels of public funding while others have more to spend by also requiring a much higher contribution from students. There are also cultural differences which affect resources – for example in the US where corporate and alumni donations are on a much greater scale.

Irish universities are learning lessons where they can, and most institutions have greatly increased their attempts to bring in funding from alumni, industry and from overseas students. But without the introduction of tuition fees in Ireland and despite a significant amount of 'blue sky' thinking on where resources might come from, no realistic alternative to increased direct contributions from students has been identified. Higher education cannot function without a proper infrastructure, and that infrastructure is, in places, threadbare. Teaching and research relies on basic facilities such as libraries, lecture halls and laboratories. In addition, modern teaching and cutting-edge research also rely on new and innovative infrastructure, particularly up-to-date IT and laboratory equipment. There is also a rise in costs caused by increased expectations. Students rightly expect to have access to the latest technology and other facilities, but keeping pace with these is expensive.

Of course, universities must be held fully accountable for how they use public money, but this must be balanced with the need to enable them to act in innovative and entrepreneurial ways. We need agile institutions that are prudent but not risk averse. In this regard it is instructive to return to the issue of autonomy. A recent study of university autonomy in Europe by Estermann et al. (2011) shows that while Irish universities have a high level of academic autonomy, they fall much further down the league tables when it comes to financial autonomy and staffing autonomy. Extensive studies have shown that universities with high levels of autonomy are the most successful, have the highest international reputations and are the most entrepreneurial in all of their activities. Universities in

Ireland must lose the shackles of government interference and control if they are ever to achieve the international standing that they crave.

In summary, universities are striving to radically improve their contribution to society across the board. Ireland will get the university sector it truly deserves when all the key players come together to address our varied higher education challenges. Higher education is a key asset in any advanced society. We have all to play for as the opportunities (and threats) of globalisation become ever clearer.

References

Bryman, A. (2009) *Effective Leadership in Higher Education*. London: Leadership Foundation for Higher Education.

Estermann, T., Nokkala, T. and Steinel, M. (2011) *University Autonomy in Europe II.* Brussels: European Universities Association.

Kouzes, J.M. and Posner, B.Z. (2003) *The Leadership Challenge*. New York: Jossey Bass Wiley.

Organisation for Economic Cooperation and Development (OECD) (2004) *Review of National Policies for Education: Review of Higher Education in Ireland,* EDU/EC. Paris: OECD.

CHAPTER 5
A CONFEDERACY OF DUNCES: THE ASSAULT ON HIGHER EDUCATION IN IRELAND

Tom Garvin
Professor Emeritus of Politics at University College, Dublin

The Death of Rhetoric

In 2004, University College Dublin's new president, Dr. Hugh Brady, spoke noisily if not eloquently to a mildly bemused academic staff about a thing called synergy. The word comes from two Greek words meaning "work together". He complained that UCD academics didn't engage in interdisciplinary work or talk to each other. This was news to most academics, being generally a talkative lot who do a lot of cooperative work with each other. The next thing that happened was the internal phone book ceased to be issued annually, and UCD became possibly the first university in the English-speaking world not to have a hard-copy internal telephone directory. The annual staff listings also ceased to appear, as did the annual President's Report. The faculties, with their internal representative structures, were closed down and replaced with Soviet-style top-down "councils" which passively received instructions from on high. Attendance levels at these kangaroo parliaments were very low. Every effort was made to discourage communication inside the college, which is why academics were eventually forced to resort to the letters pages of the newspapers. Departments were separated from each other and amalgamated with others with little intellectual connection being established; Engineering was wrecked, and what was the best engineering school in Ireland ceased to exist. There ceased to be any relationship between what the management of the university said and what they actually did. A thick layer of non-academic management grew up, and eight years later non-academic staff at UCD far outnumbered academic staff. UCD, even more than other Irish universities, became enshrouded in "management-speak" and a brown tide of nonsense on stilts, purveyed by overpaid and underqualified vice-presidents of everything, including football fields and non-subjects such as "Teaching and Learning". A grey philistinism increasingly characterised the public culture of the college, and a hideous management-speak drowned out all coherent communication. An indescribable vulgarity characterised the new regime. Professor Gerard Casey of UCD's School of Philosophy put it marvellously in 2006:

> At present there are those who ask: "Why can't the university be more like business?" (Oddly enough, not many ask the equally pertinent question why businesses can't be more like universities!) In this atmosphere it should come as no surprise that the many and varied schemes that have been proposed for the rejuvenation of business eventually trickle down to the academy. Among the army of acronyms are known by the cognoscenti, we can find PPBS, MBO, ZBB, TQM/CQI and BPR, which stand, respectively, for Planning Programming Budgeting System, Management by Objectives, Zero-Base Budgeting, Total Quality Management/Continuous Quality Improvement and Business Process Re-engineering. Two additional non-acronymised schemes are Strategic Planning and Benchmarking. The hulks of such schemes litter the shorelines of academia (Casey in Lavan, 2006, 32).

We all know that benchmarking in the Irish public service was a huge con-job, fed by the Celtic Tiger, to rationalise giving inflated wage increases to already highly paid officials and workers, explained away as rewarding an increased productivity that was mainly non-existent. Similarly, in the newly governmentalised academy, an obsession with money and a peculiarly half-witted form of benchmarking usually referred to pejoratively as "box-ticking" replaced any real concern with scholarship and blue-sky research. Third level education in Ireland went, in sixty years, from an assumption that education had nothing to do with economic development to an equally absurd assumption that education was about nothing else: from one barbarism to another. The higher acronymic nonsense uttered by university senior administrators is designed to camouflage this deliberately engineered intellectual tragedy.

As often happens, this cultural collapse was foreseen by science fiction. Ray Bradbury's *Fahrenheit 451* prophesied a television-fed future in which books are illegal and are burned by the fire brigade. Things haven't quite got that bad, but this new barbarism takes various forms in modern societies. Some time ago the well-known British commentator, Bryan Appleyard, in the course of a book review of the well-known American philosopher Harry Frankfurt's rant *On Bullshit* commented "we are all drowning beneath a tide of, not to put too fine a point on it, bullshit." According to Frankfurt's entertaining little book the true essence of bullshit is that the bullshitter neither believes that what he is saying is true nor does he believe it is not true; he is indifferent to the truth or falsity of what he is saying. The only purpose of bullshit is to lower the intellectual content of the conversation, spread confusion, and allow the speaker get away with something. "It is just this lack of connection to a concern with truth – this indifference to how things really are – that I regard as of the essence of bullshit" (Frankfurt, 33-34). George Orwell had a politer term for the same phenomenon in his 1949 science-fiction satirical nightmare, *Nineteen Eighty-Four*. He called it Duckspeak, a particularly refined form of the official language of Oceania, Newspeak. A good duckspeaker could change his party line in mid-sentence and be *quite unaware* that the second half of the sentence contradicted everything in the first half. This ability was highly prized by the Party. Newspeak was designed to eliminate independent thought, and was essentially a radically impoverished version of the English language:

> Quite apart from the suppression of definitely heretical words, reduction of vocabulary was regarded as an end in itself, and no word that could be dispensed with was allowed to survive. Newspeak was designed not to extend but to *diminish* the range of thought, and this purpose was indirectly assisted by cutting the choice of words down to a minimum (Orwell, 1984, 313).

Democratic politicians have always used Duckspeak, as have conmen, agents of totalitarian governments, bad philosophers, unscrupulous academics and journalists everywhere. Irish university presidents have recently joined the ranks of the purveyors of Duckspeak. This particular cultural act of treason is part of a wider political revolution. Eighty years ago, the political style of fascist Europe was best described as a diseased romanticism, and best represented by failed artists and second-rate intellectuals in power. Nowadays, the continent's political style is easiest to describe as a diseased meritocracy, best represented by failed students and second-rate academics in power. The rhetoric of the thirties was one of demonisation of the Other, the rhetoric of nowadays is the higher nonsense. In Ireland, this authoritative nonsense on stilts combined with a deep unawareness of the difference between truth and falsity is best represented by the public utterances of Bertie Aherne, Taoiseach of the Republic between 1997 and 2008. One sample of Bertiespeak suffices, when he confused the Provisional IRA with the Northern Ireland police force in 2004:

> They believe that a number of operations which took place during 2004, not just the Northern Bank Robbery, were the work of the PSNI and would have had the sanction of the Army Council and be known to the political leadership (Mangan, 2009).

This is the man who presided over the wrecking of the Irish economy and subsequently denied that he had ever been warned about the property bubble or the banking fiasco. The fact is he shouted down the academics who warned of the coming crash, and subsequently his party, Fianna Fail, orchestrated a vilification campaign against university lecturers, alleging that they were lazy people living high on the hog at the taxpayers' expense. What was really operating here was a fear of electoral defeat combined with a hatred of intelligence and free speech. In 2011, the Soldiers of Destiny transformed itself into the Lemmings of Destiny and found the cliff it had been unconsciously looking for. The party got the electoral thrashing it so richly deserved, and its remnants relapsed into the intellectual vacuity which had led to its misfortunes.

The Uselessness of Free Inquiry

Andreas Hess of University College Dublin wrote with some eloquence in 2009 about a central problem in modern universities, particularly in the English-speaking world. I agreed with much of what he had to say in a piece in 2010 (see *Irish Times*, 16.2.09 & 1.5.10)[1]. Both of us wrote, in rather different ways, about a recent commerce-driven loss of respect for what is termed "blue sky research" or, more cheekily, the idle curiosity of trained minds. One of the human race's greatest inventions, the university, has at its core the free exercise of trained curiosity by intelligent and well-trained people with the secular equivalent of a vocation to the work. Since the takeover of many universities by commercially-minded presidents with extraordinarily narrow intellectual outlooks, the pressure to engage in applied, intellectually derivative and financially profitable research at the expense of free inquiry has intensified[2]. Intellectual derivativeness is a symptom of provincialism. Great universities, almost by definition, do not have this problem, but more humble, but worthy, universities that are being pushed into intellectual provincialism do. Researchers are being required by bureaucrats to specify what they are going to discover before the money to do the research is made available. Pablo Picasso's famous comment, "if I knew what I was going to do, what would be the point of doing it?" is apposite. In a devastating little article, Sean Duke pointed out in December 2010 that the Irish attempt to use scientists to produce commercially viable products and techniques betrays a complete official incomprehension of the nature of scientific research. He describes, by way of contrast, Israeli scientific research, which is far more successful than its Irish counterpart, as simply funding "the best researchers and [giving] them what they need. The Israeli authorities do not impose 'conditions' on researchers by demanding to know, in advance, how they will produce commercial results. The research is at the heart of what is done, but there is a far more clear-sighted approach by the Israeli government:

> The greatest scientific discoveries come by funding the best people, not by trying to wedge people into categories that bureaucrats have decided might produce an economic return. Penicillin was discovered by Alexander Fleming when he failed to disinfect cultures of bacteria and returned to find the bacteria dead and contaminated with penicillin moulds. *This is how science works. It is not linear and cannot be controlled.* Our policy [in Ireland] should be to support the best scientists, be they in a "trendy" area or not. Great discoveries are often made from obscure work' (*Sunday Times*, 12.12. 10, "There's no Magic Pill for Science", emphasis added).

The essential idea that knowledge is an end in itself has become alien to much of elite opinion in Ireland. Greed and utilitarianism have threatened to cretinise intellectual inquiry. There are powerful people in our country who dislike free research and would like to strangle it. People who have never written a scholarly book and who possibly have never read a scholarly book, sometimes openly despise books but are in charge of the national third-level education system. One of them recently laboured under the apparent notion that Einstein concocted the theory of evolution; presumably she also believed that Darwin discovered relativity. Real research and the writing of books are seen as self-indulgent and pointless; some observers, including this writer, would describe their minds as darkened. Having half succeeded in killing free research off, they find themselves being advised by fewer competent people than might otherwise be the case. Knowledge being an end in itself is despised and the further *central idea* that having an appetite for knowledge is *a public good in itself* is lost. The further proposition that free research encourages detached and penetrating thinking about very practical matters is also being lost. The real cost of this anti-intellectualism has been immense, because the result is a loss of wisdom. This entails the growth of silliness and the destruction of imagination. I believe our present crisis is directly due to this growth of public silliness. Contempt for intelligence and free debate transformed Fianna Fail ("Soldiers of Destiny"), once an extraordinarily successful political party run by relatively intelligent and well-informed men and women, into Ali Baba and the Forty Thieves and thence into the Lemmings of Destiny.

Micromanagement of the Intelligent by the Unintelligent

Naturally some people despise it, but the idea that the appetite for knowledge and understanding is a good in itself has always existed in Ireland, despite some hostility from governmental, commercial and clerical sources. The Gaelic proverb "The Scholar's life is beautiful" says it all. The connected idea that intellectual leadership should be in the hands of the most accomplished is also being flung away by universities. The universities' leaders claim they are abolishing self-indulgence and mediocrity, but they are actually blowing out their own brains. We are treated to the spectacle of experts in mathematics, engineering, economics, history, political science, modern languages or Celtic studies being told how to do their teaching, research and publication by means which are sometimes wildly inappropriate to their disciplines. These half-educated and extremely authoritarian frauds ensconced in power in some of the best universities in the country also commonly despise undergraduate teaching, a fact which was immediately spotted by the more alert undergraduates. Many of these people despise good academics because they are not intelligent enough to have an inferiority complex toward them. Academics have a horrible habit of answering back, sometimes in an irrefutable way.

The old Faculty of Arts in UCD ran a magnificent broad-based Bachelor of Arts degree programme, offering two dozen different subjects as a three-year degree programme ranging from pure mathematics through archaeology to philosophy. It was easily the best and most varied such programme on the island. It has been comprehensively damaged by these people. Among other sins, by insensitive introduction of modularisation, the administration of the college effectively fragmented the subjects and made them well nigh impossible to study in a stepped and ordered fashion. The "reforms" also distracted students in other faculties. In late 2010, a Fourth Year UCD medical student wrote eloquently about her catastrophic experience of UCD's much vaunted "Horizons" programme, designed to give access to the Arts curriculum to undergraduates from the physical sciences.

> As Christmas exams loom and a new semester beckons outside the realms of UCD, venturing into full-time clinical education in UCD's teaching hospitals, I feel this is my opportunity, on behalf of many medical students, to voice our frustration at the Horizons elective programme
>
> In short, the entire Horizons elective programme is a farce, especially in career-oriented degrees such as medicine and veterinary medicine. In medicine, for example, we must do an elective every semester to stage 3. In stage 4, we are granted some respite as we must enrol in one for the first semester.

> The elective module counts as five credits but our five other medicinal core modules which actually form our degree programme are also worth only five credits. Now naturally anyone with an iota of intelligence will deliberately choose to subscribe to an easy elective module because when faced with five other complex and study-intensive subjects, the last thing anyone wants is to be weighed down with work from a completely unrelated subject to their degree programme.
>
> There is absolutely no way that a stage 1 elective module such as French Stage 1, Massage or Health across the Lifespan can be equated with a Stage 4 Haematology and Immunosupression core module, however, judging from the repertoire of modules undertaken by my classmates … this is a common occurrence. There are complete disparities between module credit weightings in different courses.
>
> While the argument may be that the aim of Horizons is to broaden our horizons, I would rather channel my studying into my core modules than study some futile module just to notch up those five credits. In the case of degree programmes which lead directly to a career path most students are aware from the day they fill out their CAO, they are embarking on a more refined learning experience. Why pester them with this nuisance Horizons programme?

Prior to the introduction of UCD Horizons Elective Programme in 2005, students from every faculty managed perfectly fine without any broadening of horizons.

> The entire Horizons elective programme needs to be reviewed – either rehauled [sic] to stop the credit-weighted disparities or dropped altogether in the case of direct career-path degrees like medicine. We have enough work to do without the added stresses of

> Japanese homework, politics essays and juvenile poster-making, which serve only to overwhelm the already exhausted medical student (*University Observer*, 30.11.10).

The then Registrar, Dr. Philip Nolan, in designing Horizons, apparently misunderstood some American prototype. US medical students commonly have already done a complete four-year Arts degree which is broad-based and includes Arts, Social Science and Science courses at undergraduate level. Only then are they permitted to start a minimum five year degree programme in medicine. They do not experience this weird amalgamation of unrelated subjects at different levels at undergraduate level. On top of all this expensive idiocy, the UCD administration commenced in 2010 to abolish the teaching of foreign languages by language laboratory. Such teaching, a worthy activity initially financed specially by the Higher Education Authority (HEA), apparently cost too much. The money is eventually to be diverted to bioscience, the salaries of vice-presidents and those of the President's many half-educated courtiers. What's left can be diverted to build roads to nowhere in particular on the campus, concrete being the rhetoric of the inarticulate. Anyway, who needs French or German? During the economic crash of 2008, the first move towards economy was to freeze the purchase of books for the UCD Library. UCD Archives, truly a jewel in the university's crown, had its budget cut by fifty per cent. On the 16th October 2009, bang in the midst of the financial crisis, a glossy magazine extolling the glories of UCD was given away free with the *Irish Times*, that well-known bastion of Irish intellectual enlightenment. It was apparently modelled loosely and intellectually on *Hello!* Magazine, and cost enough to provide for ten postgraduate scholars for a year. *Hello!* epitomises accurately the mentality of those ensconced in power in Irish universities by Irish government.

The Burning of the Books

In the new university, books will be abolished, echoing various attempts, ranging from ancient China to Nazi Germany, to annihilate the past and start again in a Brave New World. The Vice-President for Research in UCD, has declared in my hearing that books are obsolete and that in future historical research will be carried out by teams of researchers, the results being published in refereed journals after peer review. On being informed politely that historians actually did not work like that, he declared that "we scientists" would show historians "the way". He had no idea whatsoever what he was talking about. The idea that research in the humanities or the social sciences should be carried out by teams has a very limited application indeed. Generally, researchers in these areas work individually or in very small groups, but form part of an "invisible college" spread around the international intellectual community. They are not "lone scholars" at all. The vehicle of communication may be the article in a peer-reviewed journal, but in the case of a mature practitioner, commonly it becomes the book. This is particularly true of discursive subjects such as philosophy, history, political science, sociology, parts of psychology and even economics. The book is also the most synergistic vehicle of academic publishing. An economist is very unlikely to dip into a political science journal, but will be fairly likely to peek into a book by a political scientist.

Imposing a model derived from some of the physical sciences on these subjects stultifies research in languages, history, political science, sociology and the policy sciences in general. This includes economics, the subject which the Irish government rather pathetically hoped would get us all out of the hole which a deeply anti-intellectual silliness got us into. The intellectual incoherence of the UCD administration is quite surreal; having abolished the teaching of Arabic and Hebrew, it then immediately decided to extend international recruitment of students to the Middle Eastern area. Between 2004 and 2007 there was a sustained assault on the Taught Master's degree in Arts and the social sciences on the grounds that it was not a "research degree" and therefore did not generate brownie points on some international ranking system. This was an unconscious attempt to drive the university back to the 1950s. This assault was only called off when it dawned on some idiot that the MA, unlike the BA, was income generating. The fact that it was also a degree that actually *prepared young students for research* was not known, and is still not known, to the university's rulers.

Bureaucratisation reached grotesque levels. Professor Michael Laffan informed President Brady publicly at Academic Council in February 2010

> ...We [academic staff] are throttled by a system in which ever-more managers and bureaucrats are appointed, some of whom seem to do little except hinder us academics from getting on with our teaching and research.[3]

At least twelve million euro has been spent on plans for a mad "Gateway" project at Belfield, involving acres of concrete, a hotel, a multiple-storey car park, a string of lakes, a "hospitality centre", a "beltway road" and God knows how many other non-academic irrelevancies; it is a very, very expensive fantasy, reflecting only the vanity of its originators. The hotel is planned to be sited within a stone's throw of the now closed Montrose Hotel. Maybe the Brady Bunch knows something that Doyle Hotels do not. It is patently obvious that Gateway will never happen, and that its legacy will be a well-appointed and silent builders' yard in the middle of the Belfield campus. UCD and its fellow bankrupt Trinity College Dublin are joining hands; they propose a "knowledge corridor" of science institutes along the 10 bus route which connects the two campuses. Dublin Bus has accordingly abolished the 10 bus which was to connect them, in a well-coordinated move straight out of Myles na gCopaleen. Engineering was torn to pieces under this extraordinary UCD regime, and is now being put back together again, much like

Humpty Dumpty. Mathematics, regarded by President Brady as the Jewel in the University's crown, is actually being *moved off campus*, in a move weird even by the standards of this regime. During my last years in UCD (2004-2008) it felt occasionally that the university was being ruled by mad spectres left over from Celtic mythology: Crom Cruach and His Sub-Gods Twelve, perhaps.[4]

The role model put forward by these new barbarians was the Chinese university system, a system created by one of the most hideous regimes running a major country in this century. Chinese universities are best known for their fondness for plagiarism, academic feudalism and their hatred of free speech. The government of China is famed for its cruelty and corruption. In 2010 a famous Chinese dissident, Liu Xiaobo, imprisoned for eleven years for speaking his mind, won the Nobel Peace Prize for his political courage. An enraged Chinese government had a hissy fit, immediately locked up his wife in their own house and prevented any member of his family or any of his friends leaving the country to go to Oslo to accept something which was a national honour for China, although not for its government. The Chinese government habitually disobeys its own laws while accusing peaceful protestors of disobeying Chinese law. The Chinese Embassy in Dublin has threateningly advised Irish citizens not to attend meetings held in sympathy with the Falun Gong, a harmless organisation disliked by Beijing. In a normal country, the Chinese ambassador would be rebuked or even thrown out. UCD has yet to protest, but don't hold your breath.

As even the casual reader will notice, I have concentrated mainly on the university I know best, but this kind of thing has been going on in other Irish third-level colleges as well. In Trinity College Dublin, an ambitious restructuring project carried out at great expense and waste of human effort has been declared a complete failure. A similar exercise in Cork ended up with the retiring president half-apologising for its failure and for wasting everybody's time. This attempted top-down barbarisation of Irish universities is labelled "Americanisation".

This is an insult to American higher education. American universities are generally managed skilfully and the better schools, of which there are many, are among the most civilised and intellectually strong in the world. I have worked in five American universities and one research institute, and none of them bears the slightest resemblance to the "new" UCD. The American administrations understand that the academic's intellectual output in the form of teaching, research, argument and publication is the university's product, and they know that the morale of the academic is essential to the quality of that product. They respect both the academic and the product, and know that the quality of undergraduate teaching depends on the ability and morale of faculty. They have reverence for the Humanities, and liberal arts degrees are in huge demand in the United States and Canada. The Humanities are not subjected to the illiterate denigration they are continually subjected to in Ireland, often from university senior officials who should, but do not, know better. By contrast with the United States, UCD, this once well-known and well-respected Irish university, resembles one of the lesser English provincial colleges, run on authoritarian top-down lines, profligate financially and profoundly anti-intellectual. UCD, the largest university in the country, is in the hands of ex-academics masquerading as businessmen (they're nearly all men, by the way; welcome to 1961 and *Mad Men*). They claim proudly and accurately that they are no longer academics. Actually they are failed academics. They have re-invented themselves as practitioners of non-subjects such as "Managerialism", "Teaching and Learning", and "Studies" of various kinds. As the great Liam de Paor once said to me, if it's got the word "Studies" in it it's probably no good. On top of all this, the system foisted on UCD and TCD is fantastically wasteful. UCD's once-efficient top administration increasingly resembles the Irish Health Service: terrific at the bottom, a shambles higher up. As Colm McCarthy has put it with characteristic bluntness, senior university administration in Ireland is looking *more and more like a racket than a profession*. Sean Barrett, a Trinity economist trained at the "old" UCD, in a brilliant paper published in 2006, gave a horrific survey of what was happening to our universities:

> The benefit sought [by the new rulers of the universities] is an improved research performance in international league tables and the means are the downgrading of arts and social science departments and faculties, the combination of academic staff in groups of at least fifty, the downgrading of undergraduate lecturing, the replacement of academic officers by managerial staff, the apportionment of fixed university budget shares to restructuring and research and the allocation of university resources according to strategic managerial criteria rather than on the basis of either consumer preference or cost. Restructuring risks increasing costs per student, lower academic standards, lower earnings for graduates, higher central managerial and administration costs, continuing mismatch between courses provided and consumer preference and continuing lack of knowledge of course costs in universities (Barrett, 43-44).

Invasion of the Box-Tickers

By judicious fiddling, Irish universities were promoted within three years of these people's ascension to power from being in the top 500 in the world to being safely within the top 200, a world total of about 6,000 universities being considered. Entering a notional top 100 was also done quite easily, by hiring in a few part-time international stars at huge salaries, mostly "earned" *in absentia*. Another ruse was even simpler: give more places to foreign students and the university looks more "international" in the almost meaningless ranking systems run by the University of Shanghai (China again) and *The Times Higher Education Supplement*. A further, even simpler, trick is to force academic staff to publish in certain highly rated journals regardless of intellectual appropriateness. Yet another fiddle is to count non-staff postgraduate temporary workers (tutors and demonstrators) as full members of staff, thereby mightily inflating the staff-student ratios. To put it simply, modern Irish university senior management is openly and increasingly fraudulent. Furthermore, all this is increasingly known internationally. In early 2009, the Irish Labour Court condemned attempts at TCD to limit intellectual freedom and research choices among lecturers and professors in favour of commercial considerations. *The Times Higher Education Supplement,* in an uncharacteristic moment of enlightenment, described it as a decision which would "echo around the world" (*Times Higher Education Supplement,* 13.3.09).

There has been a substitution of ranking for one's own informed intellectual judgement in senior management. The fact that this has taken place demonstrates that the rulers of Irish universities are dimly aware of their own very considerable intellectual limitations and try, mainly out of intellectual laziness, to get mechanical processes to do their thinking for them. The results are worthy of Swift's Academy of Projectors in the Third Book of *Gulliver's Travels*. It has been proposed, in effect, that three articles in some unread "learned" journal controlled by some self-appointed clique should be worth more than Keith Thomas's magisterial *Religion and the Decline of Magic* or Jared Diamond's classic *Guns, Germs and Steel. Nature,* a journal embroiled in several intellectual frauds, is extolled. Einstein wouldn't get hired as professor of physics by this confederacy of dunces. The London *Times* commented on the British equivalent of this kind of exercise in 2009:

> Government adores its faulty league tables of schools, universities, hospitals and local authority services. Instead of intelligent inspection and help, billions of pounds and years of effort are poured into lists and tables that serve little purpose. They demoralise some, make others smug, and condition thousands of

> managers to work to targets that skew and corrupt their core mission.[5]

This government-driven assault on Irish intellectual life, apparently initiated by Fianna Fail politicians at the instigation of uninformed officials in the Department of Education, has been met with deafening silence on the part of Irish journalists. Why? For some reason, possibly the intellectual and moral bankruptcy of the Fianna Fail party, it is open season lately on Irish academics. The spin is we are lazy, work only five hours a week, are no good and are widely believed, quite inaccurately, to have huge pay packets. In my experience, most Irish academics are enthusiastic, love their subjects, enjoy their teaching and strive to increase their research and understanding. Brady and company boast that our universities rank highly internationally. Our rulers cannot have it both ways: either Irish academics are so terrific that they can get us into the top 100 without effort, or they actually work pretty hard and to some effect. Alternatively, the rankings system is essentially meaningless.

I suspect academics were attacked so as to divert public attention from the stupidity, greed and corruption of Fianna Fail's political leaders. My further belief is that academics, particularly in the more humanist and discursive subjects, are envied and resented by failed academics and authoritarian power-holders who dislike being answered back or being laughed at by intelligent people. This insecurity is derived from two things. The first is the inarticulate character of some people unfamiliar with humanist education. This is combined with the conspicuous freedom of speech which Irish academics possess in a society which has never fully accepted the right to speak truth to power, otherwise known as the right and the duty to answer back.

Back in 2009, Professor John Kelly urged that the government should assert its authority over higher education (*Irish Times*, 16.4.09). He pointed, quite rightly, to the anti-intellectualism of the university's rulers, but was very certainly chanting at the wrong spook. *Government* in the form of the Higher Education Authority and a camouflaged Department of Education, led in the 1990s by its Secretary, is behind this cultural catastrophe. All of this assault on intellectual life is being financed by our taxes, and it should by now have dawned on our government that one of its most important assets, the third-level education system, has been taken over by non-academic forces, and that this is very definitely not a good thing. The universities and their products are our collective brains, and contempt for them is both stupid and deeply unpatriotic. The people who nowadays "run" Irish universities pretend to be businessmen running efficient commercial enterprises. They also pretend that their support for the more scientific and applied activities of universities is going to bring about greater economic growth. This is false, and there is evidence that education beyond second level has no obvious immediate connection with growth; this holds particularly for small countries with a local capacity to import higher education. While education in general does indeed correlate with wealth, *there is no correlation by subject*; Latin correlates as well as does physics. Both are trace variables for elite intelligence and enlightenment, little more. Elaine Byrne, in an interesting reaction to my *Irish Times* piece remarked on its ranting about anti-intellectualism:

> It goes to the heart of the malaise that is now affecting the country. I worked in the bank in the 1970s and 1980s and witnessed the change in policy when profit became the only game in town and the customer suddenly became a target. Anything could be justified in the name of profit and growth. Anyone who challenged this belief was sidelined. The frontline staff along with the customer became the enemy. In this new philosophy, efficiency meant cost-efficiency, nothing else. The staff's social skills in understanding the customers and their needs were no longer required as the customers' needs were surplus to requirements.

> Members of staff who complied were promoted and given a bonus each year. The same failed business model is being pushed through the public sector at the moment. Cost-efficiency is the only requirement and members of the frontline staff are now the enemy. Impossible targets are used for measurement. There has been a build-up in middle management and all they seem to do is measure what the frontline staff do and go to meetings to talk about it. The selected few receive a bonus for the cost-efficiencies they have achieved in reducing the frontline staff to a skeleton service. Research has shown that the most profitable companies are the ones that do not focus on profit solely but take the wider view… (*Irish Times*, 5.5.10).[6]

The rulers of Irish universities nowadays often seem to have no idea what universities are for and are sometimes aggressively incompetent. They have commonly no sensitivity to the great variety and complexity of any good university. Their top-heavy administrations are expensive, obstructive and uncomprehending, as well as being ludicrously expensive. The vulgarity of the advertising spin is obvious, and the overall effect suggests children being given the keys to BMWs at age twelve. Staff morale in Irish universities is at an all-time low, a fact that students immediately sense and which provokes high levels of student absenteeism. Anti-intellectualism automatically leads to the glorification of ignorance, and this country is well on the way from the former to the latter.[7] Professor Tom Dunne, in a gentle warning, comments in his extraordinary memoir *Rebellions*, that the "reforms" in the universities directly threaten his own subject, history, and even Irish collective historical memory. An anti-intellectual and pseudo-commercial bullying has attempted to replace academic freedom, a freedom which the nation itself desperately needs, whether or not it realises it:

> … fudging of the more abrasive and unpleasant aspects of our past … chimed with the new prosperity and

> philistinism of the Celtic Tiger era, which accelerated the erosion of the memory of the Troubles and transformed our universities on business lines. Academics are increasingly expected to acquiesce in what is proposed by 'executive' presidents and their 'Management Teams'; the independent academic voice is heard less and less. Promotion and sabbatical entitlement can nowadays be rewards for conformity. Thus, raising awkward questions, whether about academic policy or interpretations of the Irish past, can pose new cultural and psychological challenges for young – and not so young – academic historians...The professional academic historian is a privileged public servant, with a clear duty to the wider community, not to tell it what it, or its political class, wants to hear, but to challenge it to engage with the past in all its complexity, and on the basis of all the evidence, including that for appalling deeds committed by its own people. Academic freedom, if it means anything, guarantees the historian's independence to do that... (Dunne, 299-300).

"University reform" has proven to be an existential intellectual threat to the country. This threat is to Irish intellectual life in general. Irish third-level institutions produce our political leaders, journalists, scientists, doctors, engineers, architects and other brain workers of every sort, and historically they have done so for a cost roughly half that of the United Kingdom per head. They are very good value for money, and we are very lucky to have them. Universities in Ireland are microcosms of the nation, not isolated and self-absorbed ivory towers as their many detractors claim. The fiscal and financial disaster that this country is going through was prefigured by the wanton assault by powerful forces on our universities and colleges in the first decade of this century in the era of Aherne. A cultural disaster preceded the economic disaster. Duckspeak finally took over not just little old UCD, but the entire country. The cow used to be the national animal of Ireland. It is now replaced by the bull, and Ireland, for the third time in sixty years, is in danger of collapsing in cultural and psychological defeat. The irony is that the danger is, yet again, almost completely self-inflicted, and the remedies are in our own hands.

Back in 1957, a well-known Irish-American academic, J. V. Kelleher, spotted this enduring characteristic of Irish political culture. He argued that a lack of intellectualism among Irish leaders, combined with an emigration-generated apathy among the general population, was almost literally killing the country. The evident official hatred of intellectual and psychological freedom was a real threat to the entire project of Irish nationhood. He sketched a little country living on the memory of real and imagined past wrongs, continually making excuses for itself, while the solutions to her problems were in her own hands: "I can ... imagine that Ireland may do what no other nation has ever done, and perish by sudden implosion on a central vacuity." (Kelleher, 495). *Plus ca change, plus c'est la meme chose.*

Academic freedom must be reasserted, and the attempt to commercialise Irish universities brought to an immediate close. Apologies from the "reformers" would be nice, but their resignations would be preferred. Staff morale must be restored. The management of Irish universities must be immediately put back into the hands of academics, and the internal structure of the colleges should be democratised so that the universities are informed by the academics and their students. Universities produce knowledge, and their governance must be informed by that knowledge. The entire destructive set of doctrines and practices enjoined by the monstrous pseudo-science of Managerialism should be shed publicly and immediately. Strangely, the financial impoverishment of Irish third level education which is following the downturn and the crash of Fianna Fail just might lead to the abolition of this particular brand of modern snake oil. The alternative is a bureaucratised vacuity worthy of the Soviet Union or J. V Kelleher's Ireland of the fifties.

Notes:

1. See also Stefan Collini, Times Literary Supplement, 13 November, 2009 on the similarly idiotic government-led assault on British university education.
2. Here I flatter Irish university presidents; some of them have no intellectual outlook whatsoever.
3. Professor Michael Laffan, Academic Council UCD, 18 February, 2010.
4. See Irish Times, 23 March, 2010 for a wonderful piece of technocratic Duckspeak nonsense which gave an appropriately meaningless expression to the purposes of the presidents of UCD and TCD.
5. See Libby Purves' hilarious and devastating lampoon on this administrative fad, "List Mania is the Besetting Folly of Our Age", Times, 14 December, 2009
6. This is not Dr. Elaine Byrne of the Department of Political Science, TCD.
7. For a comparative perspective, see similar developments in the United States: Susan Jacoby, The Age of American Unreason, London: Random House, 2008.

References

Sean D. Barrett, "The Economics of Restructuring Irish Universities", *Administration*, vol. 54, no. 2 (2006)

Casey, Gerard "Response to Professor Rothblatt: Re-engineering the Academy" in Ann Lavan (ed.) *The University and Society: from Newman to the Market*, Dublin: UCD College of Human Sciences, 2006

Tom Dunne, *Rebellions*, Dublin: Lilliput, 2010

Harry G. Frankfurt, *On Bullshit*, Princeton: University Press, 2005.

Irish Times, 16 April, 2009.

Mangan, J. D., *The Little Book of Irish Bullshit*, Dublin: Kenilworth, 2009.

George Orwell, *Nineteen Eighty-Four*, London: Penguin, 1990 (first published 1949)

Times Higher Education Supplement, 13 March, 2009.

J. V. Kelleher, "Ireland … and Where Does She Stand?", *Foreign Affairs*, 1957, 485-95, quote from 495.

University Observer, 30 November, 2010 (UCD student newspaper).

Times Higher Education Supplement, 13 March, 2009.

Irish Times, 16 April, 2009.

CHAPTER 6
THE GODS OF THE MARKET TUMBLE: AGAINST NEO-LIBERALISM, FOR INTELLECTUALISM AND TOWARDS NEW UNIVERSITIES IN IRELAND

David Limond
Professor at Trinity College Dublin

As I pass through my incarnations in every age and race,
I make my proper prostrations to the Gods of the Market Place.
Peering through reverent fingers I watch them flourish and fall,
And the Gods of the Copybook Headings, I notice, outlast them all.
… …
But we found them lacking Uplift, Vision and Breadth of Mind,
So we left them to teach the Gorillas while we followed the March of Mankind.
… …
But they always caught up with our progress, and presently word would come
That a tribe had been wiped off its icefield, or the lights had gone out in Rome.
… …
In the Carboniferous Epoch we were promised abundance for all,
By robbing selected Peter to pay for collective Paul;
But, though we had plenty of money, there was nothing our money could buy,
And the Gods of the Copybook Headings said: '*If you don't work you die*'.

Then the Gods of the Market tumbled, and their smooth-tongued wizards withdrew
And the hearts of the meanest were humbled and began to believe it was true
… …
As surely as Water will wet us, as surely as Fire will burn,
The Gods of the Copybook Headings with terror and slaughter return!

Rudyard Kipling, 1865-1936.

Introduction

Of course Kipling did not mean what I am making him seem to mean. As an arch-conservative, he was hardly against capitalism and he and I disagree on much. Broadly I do rather favour 'robbing selected Peter to pay for collective Paul'. At least I oppose excesses of personal wealth that are harmful to others' liberty and to general social cohesion, and corrosive of the souls of those more possessed by than possessing the wealth, if that means the same thing. I would also prefer to say that it is human to be humane and deplore his sometimes mean-spirited sanctimoniousness, as when, elsewhere in the poem, he condemns any kind of welfare as '[paying] all men [*sic*]... for existing' He valued patriotism, socio-sexual respectability and devil-take-the-hindmost individualism. In his worldview any society that did *not* value these was doomed. The poem vindicates this view, or claims it to be vindicated. For Kipling, the copybooks' stark nostrums are always right. In the end, the lights *do* go out in successive versions of decadent fifth-century Rome when these lessons are again forgotten.

Thus when he spoke of the marketplace and the ideas it spawned he did not have in mind anything specifically economic. His marketplace is simply the public square, the venue where people meet to agree on the certainties of their age; his Gods of the Market Place are the fashionable orthodoxies of any epoch: seemingly insightful, but wrongheaded. By contrast his Gods of the Copybook Headings bring a gospel that is banal but profound. They preach simple truths: eternal verities, fundamental things that endure as time goes by. Although each age's sophistical 'smooth-tongued wizards' piously tout the fashionable doctrines in the short-term, terror and slaughter result from ignoring the commonsensical propositions of the copybooks.

I have manipulated his words, though I have only done so to the extent of noting what seems to me undeniably true: the Gods of the Market Place in our age *are* the gods of the market. The babble of claim and counterclaim in the marketplace of ideas of the early twenty-first century is almost invariably silenced by a portentous voice of authority intoning: 'Where's your business plan?' or, perhaps more significantly when education is involved, 'How does that relate to the world of work?' (see, for example: Caesar 2009). If children today still learned cursive, copperplate hand by copying supposedly improving texts ('If you don't work, you die' and the like), the phrases they used might be:

> 'Thou shalt be profitable';
> 'Thou shalt be business-like';
> 'Thou shalt covet thy neighbour's goods and be entrepreneurial enough to get more than thy neighbour'.

I do not share Kipling's view of the folly of seeking progress and am optimistic enough to believe that modernity confers benefits: 'Uplift, Vision and Breadth of Mind'. But while all progress requires change, not all change constitutes progress. Hence this much might be agreed both by social conservatives and those of a more radical bent. The fashionable gods of today *are* the fetishes of wealth, avarice and consumption and one previously sacrosanct space these idols now occupy is the university quad.[1] Consequently, far-reaching, ill-considered and detrimental change is underway.

Of course nothing is ever entirely new. Fifty years ago an American author noted that some people looked at US universities 'not as if they were engaged in a nonprofits enterprise, but as if they were failing to make a profit' (Barzun 1959/1961, 203). If this was so during a period of relatively genteel capitalism, the 1950s, then how much greater is that malaise against the background of an aggressive, modern or neo-liberal capitalism drunk on its own apparent post-Cold War success? Rather than being thought of as constituting a separate sphere of human activity (a sphere that had to be served by, not serve, others because there was something irreducibly and ineluctably *good* about its endeavours) university education is now increasingly seen only as an aspect of the pursuit of material wealth, collective and personal. Preparing for the busyness of business increasingly supplants the acquisition of learning, and some laud this (*Economist* 2005).

Specifics

This chapter, taken as a whole, is not supposed to be a dirge, a lament for what has been lost, a keening over the tumbled stones of the Academy's portico. It is supposed to be a positive piece about alternatives: redoubts of intellectual values in which and from which it could be possible to build again. However I have to spend a little time describing what I oppose before I can point towards alternatives. Hence I must render in more concrete terms some examples of intrusions into academic life. Thus, if I speak of a hijack of universities by assumptions and practices imported from business I have in mind particularly the assumptions of quality assurance [QA] and the practices of Taylorism.

Libraries have been written (alas) on the subject of QA. Essentially, whether in the context of university education or not, it refers to an extreme proceduralism aimed at achieving predictable outcomes. But its very name is a subtle trick. For, if I oppose QA then, surely, I am opposed to quality? And if I am opposed to quality, then I have either misunderstood the word or I am some sort of dangerous lunatic. Akin to the bibbed 'chugger' on the street who asks 'Have you time for [insert charity's name]... ?', the person who invokes QA has won the rhetorical battle before I can speak. Of what variety of stone would my heart be made that I could say simply, 'No'? But suppose I have thought about the matters involved and, as a result, prefer not to donate to the group named? 'Yes, I'm very concerned about [insert issue's name]... but I have doubts over the methods of the organisation you represent' is rather a mouthful. The compromise can thus tend to involve feigning some pressing engagement and bustling apologetically past.

Similarly it can be tiresome always to find oneself pointing out that we do not assure quality by embracing something called QA and that the *true* assurance of quality lies in a clear conscience before, during and after teaching, supervising or assessing students. QA-ist proceduralism infantilises all concerned and makes for legalistic defensiveness and superficial conformity at best and outright deceitfulness at worst as people struggle to maintain impossibly many and complicated records so that, in the end, trust dies (O'Neill 2002). If simply opposing QA looks deranged, explaining *why* one opposes it takes time Hence, slouching along in a spirit of acquiescence with it all becomes the norm.

I have also suggested that Taylorism, named after Frederick Winslow Taylor [1856-1915], is an unwelcome import into the world of education. Simply put Taylorism amounts to the attempt to regulate work for greater productivity through constant measurement. In one way, obviously, it represents the culmination of complicated processes of change that began in the period of the Industrial Revolution, or even earlier, when amateur science and nascent mass manufacturing converged in the north Atlantic world. Just as the military/political imperialists of the age colonised other continents, so the techno-capitalist imperialists first colonised the night (making round-the-clock working possible in factories) then, gradually, they colonised most or all aspects of workers' lives, measuring and regulating every conceivable thing.

Understood in this way, Taylorism is, of course, about more than Taylor himself. But if, for convenience, he is seen as the quintessential proponent and architect of such developments then there is a perverse irony concerning Taylorism and education. Not long before he died, Taylor told an official hearing that he had been inspired to seek maximum productivity in the work of others through relentless scrutiny by a teacher whom he had known half a century before who had used a stopwatch to calculate how many problems a pupil could reasonably be expected to solve in a specific time and had then used this knowledge to ensure that his pupils would always face two hours of maths homework (Kanigel 1997, 215).

The circle turns full and Taylorism now haunts the university, under the guise of metrics: *pseudo*-scientific measurements of academics' efforts used in an attempt to show who is slacking and who is not. Heaven knows I would like to be more prolific but I have few problems that could not be solved by being *brilliant* and none that will be solved by being timed and measured in everything that I do, or taken to task over everything that I do not. Yet if it is protested that academics are paid so that they *may* research/write, not paid *to* do so and that not all forms of labour can be subject to the metronomic tyranny of the time-clock (even assuming that any should), the bloody shroud of students'/tax-payers' money being wasted is waved and debate is silenced. (These issues have been discussed in many places already and I shall not prolong the agony for those who are familiar with such developments by discussing them further at this juncture. However, amongst much else on these topics, see: Fleischmann and Halliday 1996; Muller 1996; Readings 1996; Henkel and Little 1999; Duryea 2000; Jarvis 2001; Sörtlin and Vessuri 2007. In the Irish context, see for example: Hoey-Heffron and Heffron 2001; Hogan 2005; Limond 2005; McDonagh 2005; Scientific, Industrial Professional and Technical Trade Union 2007; Garvin 2010; Hess 2011).

Some History

Regrettably there has always been a degree of cupidity and laziness on the part of some people in academia. The tale is told of a Provost of Trinity College, John Hely-Hutchinson [1724-1794], who once went to Dublin Castle on an errand. Before he spoke, however, the Lord Lieutenant of the time hurriedly bestowed an office on the inveterate sinecure-seeker to get rid of him quickly. The bemused Provost found himself gazetted a major in the cavalry when it was still possible to sell such commissions; which he promptly did (Foster 1988/1989, 229-230). Conversely a contemporary of Hely-Hutchinson, Edward Gibbon [1737-1794], left Oxford to *seek* an education because, as he later complained in his autobiography, he was 'never summoned to attend even the ceremony of a lecture' (Gibbon 1966, 10).

Equally there has been sclerotic intransigence in the face of change that goes beyond anything rational, as in the case of John

Sparrow [1906-1992], Warden of All Souls College, Oxford in the 1960s. Sparrow 'used every art to defeat attempts by others to change the college' and supposedly even vetoed some suggested reforms solely out of personal spite towards Max Beloff [1913-1999], later to be instrumental in founding the independent/private Buckingham University (Annan 1999/2000, 201). But if a culture deserves to be judged by the best that it can produce, not the worst, then have not the dominant traditions of UK/Irish universities, as they have emerged over centuries, without the dubious benefits of either QA or Taylorist management, more often been of intellectual rigour, dedicated scholarship, disinterested pursuit of truth, self-government according to *academic* norms and an ascetic frugality?

Today

Now the presumption is of guilt without even the formality of trial. Lacking QA, you academics would mark students with random abandon, lose their work or do who knows what. Without managers overseeing your work, you would probably not work at all and hide behind the tattered gown of tradition to forestall any reasonable modernisation. And in my saying all of this, it should be remembered that I write from within the stout iron railings of Trinity College where the encroachment of this so-called 'new public management' is less advanced than elsewhere, though even there traditions are threatened (*Times Higher Education* 2011).

Newman or Davie?

The memory of John Henry Newman [1808-1891] sits heavily on the shoulders of those who inhabit universities and, all the more so, on the shoulders of those who would debate the university's nature, meaning, function[s] and future. *The idea of a university*, complete with (overly emphatic?) definite article, sets the agenda for much debate in and around universities We are especially fond of Newman in Ireland. We tell ourselves that as his famous discourses on universities were devised and delivered when he resided in mid-nineteenth-century Dublin, so, in a certain way, they belong to us (Gallagher 2005). True, Newman *did* deliver his discourses while managing the ill-starred Catholic University (later re-founded as University College, Dublin). However it can be instructive for the Irish person tempted toward such an appropriation to remember that the plaque commemorating his association with the Birmingham Oratory does not acknowledge the interruption in his life/work there that saw him go on secondment to the Dublin institution. And if the realities of his ideas were better known (for example, that he wrote: 'a loyal Catholic spirit… in the scientific inquirer, [demands] a due fear of giving scandal… [and] keeps in mind the moral weakness and the intellectual confusion of the majority' [Newman 1996, 233]) he might be less of a secular saint in some left/liberal quarters.

Overall there is often a sense that we are following Newman's lead, if only to disagree with him. Newman's idea of the university has been variously: recovered, renewed, changed, eulogistically mourned for and confidently repudiated (Graham 2002; Maskell and Robinson 2001; Smith 1999; Seery 2010; Cunningham 2005, respectively). To put it otherwise, we routinely dance to his tune or, at least, feel we must explain why we are *not* dancing to it. One way or another, Newman is rarely ignored in discussions such as this. Am I simply saying 'Come back John Henry and save us'? In other words, do I hope that merely by repeating some formula to the effect that universities *really ought* to be places of lofty contemplation into which non-intellectuals should not intrude all will somehow be again as once it was? Well, no. Being a cantankerous Scot (is there any other kind?) I prefer to take my lead from George Elder Davie [1912-2007] and the ideal of the democratic intellect, not from the supposedly liberal Newmanesque university.

Davie, by his own admission a philosopher turned historian, hypothesised that by the mid-nineteenth century the Scottish universities had come to be characterised by their promotion of what he called democratic intellectualism, borrowing from the Scottish Conservative politician Walter Elliot [1888-1958] who had originally coined the term. Roughly speaking, Davie suggested that, before they became Anglicised in the latter part of the century, tending more towards desiccated specialism in classics/mathematics, the Scottish universities promoted a culture of enquiry that was broad, humane and philosophical (Davie 1961/1982; 1986; 1993). This thesis has occasioned much enthusiastic support in Scotland (see, for example: Walker 1994). However some have been moved to suggest that Davie was a better philosopher than historian. In other words, he may have been guilty of wishful thinking, projecting back onto the Scottish universities in a certain period what he wanted to find. But leaving that aside, we might allow that he could have hit on an almost perfect account of how universities *ought* to be and the kind of person they ought to form. If the contemporary university is under attack, as it seems to be, then at least the values so astutely summed up as the democratic intellect/democratic intellectualism could be revived elsewhere. Values can be tenacious.

Intellectualism

Up to this point I have repeatedly used the words intellectual and intellectualism and, sooner or later, somebody will charge me with failing to define these rather vague terms. But being aware that others have blunted their own intellects in the attempt to do so I shall not even try, beyond the following, somewhat random, observations. Some may contend that intellectualism simply involves being very well informed, ideally about aspects of what is called culture Those who know and understand most culturally are society's intellectuals: a refined, patrician aristocracy of the mind, primarily distinguished academics. However I have already aligned myself not just with intellectualism but with *democratic* intellectualism and, for my purposes at least, this kind of patrician intellectualism looks suspiciously like the self-satisfied piling up of knowledge and understanding for no end. Further, intellectualism is certainly not tantamount to educational/academic success, nor is it tantamount to one kind of work as opposed to some others. Though it pains me to admit it, because I hate to let the old varsity side down, I have known all too many academics who were very far from being intellectuals. Fortunately I have met many other people who were much more intellectual than most academics.

To my mind, being an intellectual is to have a howling void of inadequacy at the heart of one's life. Intellectualism causes a state of constant unhappiness, verging on despair; despair at never quite knowing or understanding enough. However in my conception intellectuals must always be seeking knowledge for a *moral* purpose. Thus intellectualism is, for want of a more elegant way of putting it, the discontented mind in pursuit of a better world.[2] Patently it is possible to be a decent person without being thoughtful in the intellectual sense and, equally obviously, seemingly clever people can be morally blind, after the manner of Professor Moriarty. But it must be some kind of ideal to have an informed and active mind and to employ it in the service of good. Thus when I say that I have met many 'other people' who are more truly intellectual than most academics (and I very much have myself in mind when I say 'most academics') what I mean is that I have often met people who think more profoundly about the improvement of life than those whom society tends to *designate* intellectuals.

Without entering the quagmire of definition again surely intellectuals, in whatever walk of life and recognised as such or not, are those earnestly thinking about fundamental issues rather than being content to make the best of existing arrangements for personal gain? However this does not mean that I am making intellectualism equivalent to political activism. Much of the latter may be thoroughly self-interested (not so much the pursuit of the better world, as pursuit of a better place for oneself in the world). An intellectual can (must?) be beset by doubt as to how exactly to proceed in trying to improve the world and, in consequence, eschew politics. Intellectuals are thus sometimes seen as being more interested in problems than solutions. Consequently this condition (of almost crippling uncertainty) is often thought of as the essence of intellectualism. This, I shall simply assert, this should *not* lead to moral relativism but intellectualism *is* incompatible with/precludes the false certainties of political/religious fanaticism and probably requires a rejection of conventional forms of politics.

It could seem that the only way to defend intellectualism is to win back the universities, but understood in my sense, as a moral ideal, intellectualism never was the unique preserve of the university scholar and it *has* thrived in other ways/places, both in Ireland and elsewhere (Rose 2001). Indeed, if I am right, universities as presently constituted may have something of an unhelpful stranglehold on our imagination.

Alternatives

No doubt to be present at a great clash of ideas would be thrilling: the nature of virtue debated in the ancient Athenian agora; the future constitution of England in the Church of St Mary, Putney in August 1647; the origin of species in a sweltering Tennessee courtroom. But, ultimately, the cause of intellectualism is *better* served when lively debate does not seem exceptional. The kind of ferment there may have been around a British Army Educational Corps class *c*1945 would do as a model. However I am not suggesting that book groups and earnest conversations (important as these may be) will entirely compensate us for the demise of the conventional university as a site of intellectual values. Furthermore, *pace* the techno-futurists' hopes (*Economist* Intelligence Unit 2008), I rather doubt that internet discussion boards can do the job through some digital magic that will make all knowledge instantly available to all in, as it were, a cloud of knowing. Although this is, I admit, an unverifiable empirical claim and may simply reflect my prejudices.[3] In addition to a diffuse *background* of intellectualism there may well always be a need for what might be called *sites* of intellectualism and, roughly speaking, sites of intellectualism is what universities have historically been.

With these points in mind, I describe below three intellectual sites/institutions of specifically Irish provenance: the Catholic Workers' College, the Free University of Ireland and the People's College [CWC, FUI and PC, respectively]. The examples I give are of institutions *like* universities in certain ways (indeed, one is actually styled a university by those associated with it, though it is not recognised as such by the Irish state). And my point is that these, and/or others, could be universities-in-waiting: embryos from which credible replacements for the increasingly discredited conventional universities may yet come.

The CWC was founded in 1951, initially at the behest of the then head of the Jesuits in Ireland, Thomas Byrne [1904-1978]. It was largely associated, especially in its early years, with two other Jesuits: Edward Joseph Coyne [1896-1958] and Edmond Kent [1915-1999]. It operated as the CWC until 1966 when it became the College (later National College) of Industrial Relations, before being subsumed into other another institution in 1998, becoming the National College of Ireland [NCI]. In 2011 the School of Community Studies in the NCI, the *de facto* heir of the traditions of the original CWC, was slated for closure and this story is, in some ways, a cautionary tale, reminding us that there will be dead ends and casualties on the way to a revived intellectualism and new universities.

The CWC drew on models and sources of inspiration as diverse as the moderate social activism of the English Catholic Social Guild (founded by Charles Dominic Plater [1875-1921] and Henry Parkinson [1852-1924] in 1909) and the rather more radical anarcho-communism of Dorothy Day [1897-1980], founder of the *Catholic Worker* newspaper and, with Peter Maurin [1877-1949], the movement of the same name in Depression-era America. The CWC specialised in equipping trade union officials to play informed (Catholic?) roles in industrial relations issues, a fact reflected in its subsequent name changes, and did not deal, strictly speaking, in liberal or general education. But it was a place where people came together to think, read and talk about ideas and their application: discontented minds in pursuit of a better world.

In the CWC's early days many lecturers worked for free. In similar vein, the FUI, which came into being in 1986, created by a coalition of retired and serving academics and adult educators to fill a perceived gap in the provision of liberal learning for mature students in Ireland's capital, receives no state funding, managing to survive largely on the goodwill of volunteers and through charging students modest fees. It affects the trappings of a university, though it is not recognised as such under the terms of the 1997 Universities Act, and occupies a site of some faded grandeur, the former City Arms Hotel on Prussia Street.

The PC was founded in 1948 under the auspices of the then Irish Trade Union Congress (itself founded in 1894 and merged with a rival body in 1959 to form the current Irish Congress of Trade Unions). It operates from premises in Dublin's Parnell Square and offers an eclectic mix of adult education classes.

Laid out like this, the bare details of the CWC, the FUI and the PC may not seem like much. Each is/was tiny; one does not meaningfully exist anymore; none could handle sciences (and it would be a romantically dilettantish fantasy, or the product of superstitious Taliban-like *anti*-intellectualism, to imagine that we can dispense with scientific knowledge in a future university). But I submit that they are, or point towards, the sources from which new universities might yet spring. Indeed, in some respects, these rag-tag arrangements may stake a better claim to being the heirs of the often-impecunious medieval European universities than institutions that *are* their heirs.[4]

In other words, the modern university in Ireland has evolved as a state-controlled enterprise, and like the modern state, increasingly does the dirty work of business. (For further discussion of the development of Irish higher education in the latter half of the twentieth century, setting this claim in context, see: White 2001). However, there have been and still are alternatives wholly or largely free of state/business involvement. Small and marginal they may be, but the alternatives I have described work (or, in the case of the CWC, worked) because of a commitment to the pursuit of knowledge for personal and mutual moral/intellectual improvement amongst those involved in them. In other words, they are/have been animated by a spirit of intellectualism that may be increasingly absent from Ireland's contemporary universities. If I am correct in saying these things, then it follows that such institutions may yet be the seeds of, or models for, a new university project that both springs from and increases a general, or democratic, intellectualism.

Objections

At this point it can be objected that it is naïvely utopian to hope for such a thing because, whatever their medieval origins, universities do not now come into being without significant state funding or, increasingly, commercial backing.[5] Effectively, only one private but not-for-profit university (Buckingham) has really been founded in the UK or Ireland in modern times. But precedent from elsewhere shows that those who are sufficiently determined to do so may be able to found viable institutions, even if they have only modest means.

Cobbled together in ramshackle accommodation, initially including former railway wagons, on the wind-swept Canadian prairies in 1927 by a dynamic Catholic priest to educate locals who might otherwise have had to abandon their communities or simply have gone untutored beyond school, what is now styled Athol Murray College of Notre Dame (in honour of Athol Murray [1892-1975]) functions as a university in every conventional sense. Of course, whatever may have been the intellectual/communitarian aspirations of its eponymous founder it too may now be touched by neo-liberalism, both in teaching 'what employers want' as the modern rallying cry often has it and by conducting its affairs generally in a business-like way. But even if this is so (and I have not researched the matter sufficiently to be able to say one way or another) the fact remains: significant institutions *have* grown from modest beginnings even recently.

A more basic objection might be that no state today allows any university to come into being without some sort of registration process contingent on adopting the values/practices of QA, Taylorism and the like. Indeed, in 2011 this was the stated position on the creation of a proposed new Irish technological university (Marginson 2011). Thus let us suppose that those behind the FUI decided to increase its size considerably, teaching more students/subjects, and sought university designation from the state. Legislation exists that would require the expanded FUI to become like the existing Irish universities: QA-fetish, Taylorist metrics, management practices and all.[6] While it would be unfortunate if events did unfold in that way, all I can do is point out that laws *may* change and, more importantly, inspiring examples *do* change socio-political landscapes.

Buckingham University, founded by Beloff and others as a university college but styled a university since 1983, has always had strong links to the Institute of Economic Affairs, itself established to lobby for the adoption of neo-liberal socio-economic policies (Ferns 1969/2009). Yet, much as, despite their political differences, Eric Blair/George Orwell [1903-1950] found it possible to admire Kipling simply as a writer and poet (Orwell 1942/1965), I have some grudging respect for the Buckingham founders' contrarian tendencies. And Beloff later noted that creating a new university proved to be remarkably easy, once one got over what might be called the conceptual threshold of imagining such a thing (Beloff 1977).

In the end, as one who is fundamentally an anarchist, I am not especially interested in matters of legal recognition for some sort of new university. Nothing in the human world is ever true until it is made so. I am as sure as Kipling was that moral values are absolute and eternal, though I have very different ideas as to their nature, but there were *no* social institutions until they were invented: no states, no universities. Social institutions are contingent, they are created or evolve and what is true now has not always been true, nor need it necessarily always be true. It must at least be *possible to imagine* a future in which those who care about intellectualism take matters into their own hands and, perhaps building from some institution[s] already extant, do something along the lines I have suggested.

Conclusion

Ultimately, my point is simple. Even if universities are further denuded of it, intellectualism might still thrive in other institutions and, more importantly, in enduring habits of mind and dispositions.[7] As long as these habits/dispositions exist, ways can be found to create new universities. Kipling elsewhere wrote 'Cities and Thrones and Powers/Stand in Time's eye/Almost as long as flowers'. But, more optimistically, he added: 'Cities arise again'. The now dominant Thrones and Powers, those who decree that academics should be 'line-managed' and universities should be 'customer-focused', will *not* always endure. The city of knowledge *will* rise again and it may yet be from the redoubts of intellectualism I have described - small, unglamorous, often voluntarist institutions, surviving despite the orgiastic worship of the market - that a few intellectuals emerge who topple the marketplace gods of neo-liberalism with a terrible slaughter of their own.

Notes

1. I am not especially interested in the ontological niceties of what counts as a university. Much of what I have to say applies to higher education as a whole and, indeed, concerns the very idea of education itself. However, as a matter of convenience I shall refer primarily to universities and I simply assume that we all more or less recognise what this term means.
2. I am no moral relativist and I am also certain that there are objective standards of rationality. Thus, although it would take too long to make the case against the relativist/postmodernist errors, I take it that those whose ideas are immoral or irrational are ruled out of contention as intellectuals. Bettering the world might be understood in many different ways but I am going to assume that twenty-first-century views on respecting/furthering human rights broadly apply, so the proposed reintroduction of slavery, say, would be deemed

immoral and people whose ideas are simply *mad* can be ignored for present purposes.

3. However I am not entirely technophobic. In January 2011 a group (and associated website) came into being, styled Dublintellectual [*sic*]. Its founders' aim is to bring issues and debates in the arts/humanities to popular attention in Ireland. The founders have links to established universities/colleges but the group is apparently independent. During 2011 it organised several public lectures and similar events. Such a body may yet have a significant part to play by acting as a broker, providing links between various institutions and interested parties. (http://www.dublintellectual.ie/#/history/4549176518, accessed 18 October 2011).
4. I have pointed to the CWC, FUI and PC only as examples that are suitable for my purposes. This does not constitute my unequivocal endorsement of any of them. Were I to found some sort of new Irish university it would not resemble any of these. The CWC was created to promote an explicitly Catholic philosophy of social order to which I do not subscribe. Similarly, although my politics are avowedly of the left I am by no manner of means wholly enamoured of the union-dominated PC. Further, none of these institutions is/was set up for meaningful scientific work and, as I have said, that is a deficiency. My conception of the intellectual is certainly not intended to perpetuate the tired two cultures, arts and sciences feud (Snow 1959/1962) However, I am ecumenical and prepared to be inspired by various organisations. Overall, if I have a preferred model it is the FUI, but many comparable establishments/groups might be mentioned, in Dublin and elsewhere (Ó Buachalla 1978).
5. The *for-profit* university is the perfect expression of neo-liberal values in higher education, in that such an institution both teaches business skills and is a business For-profit universities are the antithesis of everything that interests me. (For further discussion see, for example: Kinser and Levy 2005; Limond 2010).
6. The NCI could be said to be a not-for-profit, private/independent university in miniature already.
7. However, labour ennobles and I do not suggest *vocational* learning is undignified or in some sense less worthy than academic learning. Both are necessary, neither sufficient. The important issues lie in the striking of a correct balance between the two and in how we ensure that everything, even the most seemingly humdrum piece of work,

can be undertaken in a spirit of intellectualism. This is only possible if we first believe that intellectualism is not precluded for anyone, promoting it accordingly.

References

Annan, Noel. 1999/2000. *The dons: Mentors, eccentrics and geniuses*. London: HarperCollins.

Barzun, Jacques. 1959/1961. *The house of intellect*. London: Secker & Warburg.

Beloff, Max. 1977. The University College at Buckingham. In *Black paper 1977*, eds, Charles Brian Cox and Rhodes Boyson, 114-117. London: Maurice Temple Smith.

Caesar, Ed. 2009. Nice little earners – Q: Which subject will get you the best job? A: English Literature B: Golf Studies. *Sunday Times: Magazine*, September 13: 21-27.

Cunningham, Patrick. 2005. Higher education sector must do better: Newman saw university as a community of scholars, but for an elite. *Irish Times*, July 25: 14.

Davie, George Elder. 1961/1982. *The democratic intellect: Scotland and her universities in the nineteenth century*. Edinburgh: Edinburgh University Press.

Davie, George Elder. 1986. *The crisis of the democratic intellect: The problem of generalism and specialism in twentieth-century Scotland*. Edinburgh: Polygon/Edinburgh University Press.

Davie, George Elder. 1993. In defence of the ordinary MA. *Edinburgh Review*, 90: 61-69.

Duryea, Edwin. 2000. *The academic corporation: A history of college and university governing bodies*. New York, NY: Falmer.

Economist. 2005. Higher education, free degrees to fly. *Economist*, February 26: 63-65.

Economist Intelligence Unit. 2008. *The future of higher education: How technology will shape learning*. London: *Economist* Intelligence Unit/New Media Consortium.

Ferns, Henry Stanley. 1969/2009. Towards an independent university. In *Major themes in education: The history of higher education, volume 3*, ed. Roy Lowe, 211-227. London: Routledge.

Fleischmann, Otakar and Halliday, Jo. Eds. 1996. *The university in a liberal state*. Aldershot: Avebury-Ashgate.

Foster, Roy. 1988/1989. *Modern Ireland: 1600-1972*. Harmondsworth: Penguin.

Gallagher, Michael Paul. 2005. John Henry Newman. In *The UCD aesthetic: Celebrating 150 years of UCD writers*, ed. Anthony Roche, 11-21. Dublin: New Island.

Garvin, Tom. 2010. Grey philistines taking over our universities. *Irish Times*, May 1: 16.

Gibbon, Edward. 1966. *The decline and fall of the Roman empire and other selections from the writings of Edward Gibbon*. Edited and abridged by Hugh Trevor-Roper. London: New English Library. (Orig. pub. 1776-1796.)

Graham, Gordon. 2002. *Universities: The recovery of an idea*. Thorverton: Imprint Academic.

Henkel, Mary and Little, Brenda. Eds. 1999. *Changing relationships between higher education and the state*. London: Jessica Kingsley.

Hess, Andreas. 2011. Universities must safeguard intellectual vitality. *Irish Times*, February 10: 13.

Hoey-Heffron, Angela and Heffron, James. Eds. 2001. *Beyond the ivory tower: The university in the new millennium*. Cork: Mercier Press/National University of Ireland Convocation.

Hogan, Pádraig. 2005. Report threatens third-level values. *Irish Times: Working in Education Supplement*, March 11: 12.

Jarvis, Peter. 2001. *Universities and corporate universities: The higher education learning industry in global society*. London: Kogan Page.

Kanigel, Robert. 1997. *The one best way: Frederick Winslow Taylor and the enigma of efficiency*. London: Little, Brown.

Kinser, Kevin and Levy, Daniel. 2005. *The for-profit sector: US patterns and international echoes in higher education*. Albany, NY: Program for Research on Private Higher Education.

Limond, David. 2005. Marketspeak and malaise in our universities. *Studies*, 376: 407-414.

Limond, David. 2010. Towards a for-profit university in Dublin: Another brick in the wall of neo-liberalism? *Higher Education Review*, 43/1: 38-56.

Marginson, Simon. 2011. Criteria for technological university designation. Unpublished memorandum. Dublin: Higher Education Authority.

Maskell, Duke and Robinson, Ian. 2001. *The new idea of a university*. London: Haven.

Muller, Steven. Ed. 1996. *Universities in the twenty-first century*. Providence, RI: Berghahn Books.

McDonagh, Enda. 2005. Make or break time for Irish universities. *Village*, January 22-28: 22-24.

Newman, John Henry. 1996. *The idea of a university*. Text and accompanying essays edited by Frank Miller Turner. New Haven, CT: Yale University Press. (Orig. pub. 1852-1858.)

ÓBuachalla, Seamus. 1978. Non-traditional forms of higher education in west Ireland: A case study. *Paedagogica Europaea*. 13/3: 107-154.

O'Neill, Onora. 2002. *A question of trust*. Cambridge: Cambridge University Press.

Orwell, George. 1942/1965. Rudyard Kipling. In *Decline of the English murder and other essays*, 45-62. Harmondsworth: Penguin.

Readings, Bill. 1996. *The university in ruins*. Cambridge, Mass: Harvard University Press.

Rose, Jonathan. 2001. *The intellectual life of the British working class*. New Haven, CT: Yale University Press.

Seery, Aidan. 2010. Knowledge and the idea of the university: Val Rice and John Henry Cardinal Newman. In *Essays in tribute to J. Valentine Rice, 1935-2006*, ed. Aidan Seery, 182-191. Dublin: Lilliput.

Services, Industrial, Professional and Technical Union Education Branch. 2007. *Universities or knowledge factories?* Dublin: Services, Industrial, Professional and Technical Union.

Smith, David. 1999. The changing idea of a university. In *The idea of a university*, eds, David Smith and Anne Karin Langscow, 148-174. London: Jessica Kingsley.

Snow, Charles Percy. 1959/1962. *The two cultures and The two cultures: A second look*. Cambridge: Cambridge University Press.

Sörtlin, Sverker and Vessuri, Hebe. Eds. 2007. *Knowledge society vs knowledge economy: Knowledge, power and politics*. London: Palgrave Macmillan.

Times Higher Education. 2011. Clash of the centuries: Trinity College Dublin staff follow ancient traditions in the election of their head. *Times Higher Education*, April 14: 36.

Walker, Andrew Lockhart. 1994. *The revival of the democratic intellect*. Edinburgh: Polygon/Edinburgh University Press.

White, Tony. 2001. *Investing in people: Higher education in Ireland from 1960 to 2000*. Dublin: Institute of Public Administration.

CHAPTER 7
UNIVERSITIES AND PUBLIC FINANCE: THE SUBVERSION OF BRITISH HIGHER EDUCATION

Dennis O'Keeffe
Professor of Social Science at the University of Buckingham and Senior Research Fellow in Education at the Institute of Economic Affairs

British Education: The Key Defects

Two closely connected defects above all others mark the recent history of British education in general and higher education in particular. First, the system overall is excessively reliant on public finance. This has kept the universities in virtually permanent crisis for decades. There are obvious limits to the taxation citizens are prepared to accept. Indeed, government, scholars and public alike, all seem increasingly aware today that if we are to have more university students, more funds will have to come from private sources.[1] One straightforward explanation for this over-reliance on public finance, however, is the passionate support for it in some quarters. Although British universities are formally private and independent, most are overwhelmingly dependent on public funding. There are only two private *British* universities, although there are quite a few outposts in Britain of private American ones.

Since the Second World War, overall educational policy in this country has been driven by an administrative elite united in its doctrinal commitment to public finance. Indeed, for this elite, public funds seem to possess a kind of intrinsic purity and virtue.

Secondly, British education is highly centralised, from infant teaching to post-graduate university work. In all free societies, this is typical of public sector organisation, whose leading personnel always try to achieve such centralisation. Naturally they pursue income and power as well. Of the latter, senior civil servants, for example, have a great deal, manifestly possessing the ability to frustrate or modify political initiatives they have been instructed to introduce. The elaborate "National Curriculum" ushered in by the 1988 Education Act is a case in point, and one pregnant with implications for the university sector today. Margaret Thatcher, understanding the dismal cognitive standards in British schools, had wanted to improve things by means of simple English and Mathematics tests.

In the hands of the administrative elite, however, her straightforward plans became the now familiar, and unsuccessful, giant bureaucracy, the National Curriculum. Its aim was to plan the entire framework of intellectual life in our primary and secondary schools, from the *political centre*, a kind of Soviet-style conceit, doomed to failure, as anyone with an elementary knowledge of Hayek could have predicted. It is apparent that today the elite would like a similar confining structure to shackle at least the majority of non-elite universities. This is largely what the Quality Assurance Agency (QAA) seeks to do. Its website proclaims its interest in improving the quality of British higher education. Its activities verge on stultification. There is a gross emphasis on *measurement of outcomes* and on a depersonalising bureaucracy. For example, supervisors of higher degrees are now forbidden to use friends and former colleagues as external examiners.[2]

The British journalist, Simon Heffer, opined in *The Daily Telegraph* of February 16th 2011, that two of the Liberal Democrats of the present coalition government, Mr Nick Clegg and Dr Vince Cable, are planning the *Sovietisation* of our universities, as one might expect from ardent supporters of the EU Leviathan.

Centralisation permits the intensification of elite power. Central control facilitates the creation of barriers to entry in particular areas of production and thus maintains that power. In the educational case, central control is used to define what counts as a qualified teacher, what is regarded as acceptable teaching at all levels, and what constitutes adequate appraisal of the work done by students. These three: curriculum, pedagogy and appraisal, are the main constituents of educational transmission. Effectively, monopoly powers in education accrue to the elite bureaucrats and politicos who control this transmission.

Education in modern free societies

Modern societies under civilised governance, a group to which Great Britain and the Irish Republic belong, are rightly seen as possessing more self-knowledge than un-free polities. This does not mean that their populations do not make mistakes in education. On the contrary, their educational errors are legion. Since, however, our knowledge and especially our *self*-knowledge are crucial conditions, first as cause and later as consequence, of the evolution of freedom itself, our intellectual arrangements must include sound education. And a sound education system must include universities.

Do we have such a system? Up to a point, yes. This essay sets out to see what is wrong with our overall arrangements. Students, teachers, civil servants and taxpayers all make mistakes. They also make many *correct* decisions; the survival of modern civilisation entailing populations which bequeath to their children a decent education system. If the universities are wrong they will poison and enfeeble the whole structure.

The overall sanity of the life of universities is maintained, in an at least semi-decent condition, by the weight of a successful educational tradition and perhaps even more by the enormous pressure of the occupational structure. Most people demand literacy, numeracy, moral training and employment qualifications for themselves and their children. These pressures rein back the worst effects of shortcomings in the system at all levels.

The nature of education

Education is a philosophical activity, compendiously defined as "the pursuit of things which are true, or beautiful or morally binding on us". This definition holds at all levels, notwithstanding the necessary early *instrumental* emphasis on the tools of learning. As Kenneth Minogue asserts, "philosophy provides the core perspectives of the academic realm". By definition education is *not* fundamentally about politics or economics or employment, although these issues are legitimate *subject matter* for educational activity.

Economics and politics are not only legitimate subjects for education but crucial ones too. Learning can operate only on a very limited basis *outside* an economic context, that is to say, without consuming scarce economic resources. Nation-wide education is evidently called for and it inevitably makes very large calls on the nation's wealth. Universities in particular are very expensive. Education is therefore a key sector of the economic realm. Both its costs and its output must be carefully monitored. It seems very probable that higher education might function better if it were to turn more on *private* rather than *public* funding. Private finance is always more cautiously and prudently deployed than state funds. Its effects are not only more efficient; they are also more popular.

Education, public finance and socialism

Education in advanced economies inevitably involves massive financing. No highly developed economy has thus far plumped for general private funding of learning. This means we have a heavy quotient of the public variety. Yet the stark fact, still not widely recognised, is that in free societies public finance is a very problematic way of organising certain key activities, especially intellectual ones. The public finance of education in the advanced societies is *not* a matter of economic logic but rather of lazy habituation.

Public finance is *not* a neutral medium of economic transactions, as good or as bad as the institutions which employ it. Public finance greatly empowers and legitimates those who manage it. Very often it actively *shapes* the institutions in which it pays the bills, in the educational case subverting and displacing proven useful practices and methods.[3] Under certain common circumstances, public finance of education leads to unsound standards in education, with especially marked effects in the case of higher education, which effects are then relayed down to lower levels of the system. Over time, a kind of circular stasis builds up, in which the faults of primary and secondary education interact mutually with those of higher education. Many pupils pass from primary to secondary school without mastery of the basics. Many reasonably intelligent children are ill-equipped for university education when they leave secondary school.

Under public finance, perhaps especially in the case of free societies, certain kinds of political and intellectual conceit, can adversely modify, and even radically corrupt, both teaching and learning, at every level of the system. In Britain as in most advanced societies, schools and universities connect intimately with socialism in both its principal forms, that is to say both with *institutional* socialism and *ideological* socialism.

The two socialisms of education: the institutional and the ideological

Institutional socialism in education involves public finance of the running costs of schools and colleges. Similarly, the capital assets of the system are in public *ownership*. In place of private owners, characterising private enterprise production, sectoral socialism generates a non-owning managerial class. Their *ideological* socialism is characterised by a pervasive belief in egalitarian policies and practices, backed up by other socialist ideologies such as scientific "planning and management" of education.

"Progressive Education" as an Example

The patterns of our education at all levels are greatly affected by their financial arrangements. Publicly financed production of any kind is very subject to "producer-capture" – the take-over of aims and purposes by the suppliers. In the British instance there was no public demand in the primary or secondary sectors for "progressive education", with its abolition or modification of streaming, its deliberate downgrading of spelling, and of the reciting of times-tables and its hostility to factual learning in general. These ideas descended on schools from higher education, from Colleges of Teacher Education and University Institutes and Departments of Education. The case for "progressive education" has now been shown wanting on an enormous international scale. It connects in Britain with distressingly large welfare dependency, often trans-generational.

Education and the Advent of Public Finance

The American scholar Andrew Coulson has shown that all successful education systems in history have been privately financed.[4] Many of the problems of modern education in the advanced free societies stem from the *socialist institutional structure* in which teaching and learning are encased, a context in which *ideological socialism* has thrived. Variations on the theme of public finance have since the *first* example of state monopoly in late eighteenth century Prussia, gradually become the norm in the "advanced world". First the Prussians and then, in the second decade of the nineteenth century, the French, adopted a kind of institutional socialism, i.e. public finance, for the purposes of mass education. From the late nineteenth century the British followed suit, although their recent educational history, had they understood it, would have warned them off such a course.

We cannot outright condemn what seems now a catastrophic policy error. In the early years of the British economic transformation, in the late eighteenth and early nineteenth centuries, the British themselves did not *know* that what we now call "industrialisation" was happening, let alone understand the intellectual nicety that its cognitive requirements were being spontaneously, *privately and voluntarily,* financed. In the late nineteenth century the magnitude of change in British society was blindingly obvious. Yet even then no one seems to have been hugely impressed that the cognitive learning crucial to these changes had been secured with *neither public finance nor compulsory attendance at school*. The British political management thus chose to follow Prussian and French example, and plumped for the now familiar mix of government money and compulsory school. This dire combination now holds sway in all advanced societies, in the British case the steering of the system being operated by the Civil Service elite, with the help of the more prestigious universities. In the United States there is a far larger, genuinely private university sector than in Britain. This probably helps to compensate for pre-university education in America's being even worse intellectually than its British equivalent. Overall British performance is much helped, on the other hand, by a stronger – although very much minority – presence of private education at primary and secondary level. Even allowing for differences of size, on the other hand, the American higher education system is superior to the British, mostly because the contribution of private finance is so much more significant.

Three kinds of expenditure: consumption, investment and waste.

We must now discuss some of the basic dynamics of the public finance *vis à vis* intellectual transmission. All economic life involves three basic types of expenditure, which between them cover all possibilities. An expenditure can first of all be *consumption*, motivated by the pleasure/utility the consumer gets. It may alternatively be an investment. This means it is future orientated and it may lead or be intended to lead, to increased future consumption. Lastly, an expenditure may be merely a matter of wasted resources. One suspects that Media

Studies and Marxist Sociology in British universities largely fit into this category.

Public finance effects a change in the calculus of scarcity and choice, because the economic actors are operating with the taxpayers' money. Students and their families are not paying directly out of their own disposable incomes. The administrative elite of education, too, are not working with resources for whose sound use they must account, but with those of taxpayers. This induces a damaging frivolity both in demand and supply. The suppliers exercise, like all socialist elites, the immemorial prerogative of the harlot: power without responsibility. They are not like capitalists who must efficiently manage the funds they own and/or answer to others for funds entrusted to them. They do not want *ownership* but control *without ownership*.

All three kinds of expenditure – consumption, investment and waste – happen in education, as they invariably do everywhere. Some educational expenditures are only or mainly consumption – as in the case of the media studies and sociology mentioned above – others are only or mainly investment, e.g. accountancy. Yet others are largely a waste of resources, such as money spent in Britain on wrong methods of teaching reading or a similarly faulty teaching of mathematics. The effects of these errors – bad English and Mathematics teaching are probably the worst – are seen in the form of illiteracy and innumeracy, and catastrophic levels of truancy from school.[5]

They also affect university entrance. Many students, whose natural ability would get them into college under good teaching, fail to do so. Others who do get in are simply unprepared for the pace and they drop out. Universities feel the pinch when their undergraduates in science and arts are gravely underprepared for college. The percentage of wastage in the case of university courses is truly dramatic, conditioned as university teaching is by the shortcomings further down the system. Under public finance money is raised from taxpayers and distributed, administratively, to the participants in the educational process. There are no proper educational markets. All this is better known and understood in Post-Communist societies than in countries like Britain. Socialism lacks a proper "scarcity map" of the kind generated by private enterprise. This scarcity map is an informal structure providing individuals with information about prices, types of goods and services, delivery times and so forth. Many British people know all this on the level of reflex with regard to their supermarkets, indeed most purchases, but it is not something the entire adult population understands in relation to education. People in the former Communist countries may be advantaged, having experienced widely and deeply the sorrows of those who live generally without markets and the price information they generate.

The socialist educational arrangements of advanced free societies affect the three categories of expenditure. For some people intellectual consumption is encouraged. The middle classes in Britain contain a very large socialist minority who are very powerful in the media and in education. They dominate, we have seen, the administrative educational elite. It is their influence, sometimes theirs and their children's influence, which drives the system. They largely control education, at all three levels, whichever political party is in power. They wasted our time for decades on the now discredited cause of "multiculturalism".[6] They predominate in primary schooling, in secondary schooling and in university teaching. The more perverse aspects of the curricular composition reflect their influence; and the pedagogy is even more their creature. They were the authors of "progressive" teaching and they have maintained it long after its proven failure as a method.

Educational production is greatly affected by the financial methods which obtain

People make different economic choices in life in terms of who is paying for those choices. In school or university, students who know they and their families are not paying directly, may go for choices they would not entertain if they had to pay themselves. They go for easy subjects like Sociology or Media Studies. All this supplies some of the explanation of the now grossly inadequate overall British performance in mathematics, science and foreign languages. These failings, of course, make a stark contrast with the brilliant performance of the upper British academic elite.

The collapse of the formal socialist vision and the lingering, residual suspicion in its wake

True, the formal espousal of the socialist vision has mostly been abandoned, not only in the Soviet homeland but in our societies too. The Marxist version of this vision was the most influential socialist afflatus of all time, a veritable mania in the first seventy years of the twentieth century. The mania has today totally collapsed, in the sense that almost no one in Britain would now propose general socialism as a cure for our problems.

Evidently, the West has learned some useful lessons from the Communist experience. Marxism is dead as a political and economic prospectus or educational vision. Sad to say, the other side of Marxism, the sour and suspicious disposition which Marx also inspired, remains very strong in the former Communist countries. Decades of lies and brutal policing explain this. Our Western version of such suspicion, in the form of widespread moral relativism, popularised with the help of French nihilists like Foucault and Derrida, remains strong in *our* universities and colleges, teacher training institutions, and even some schools. This is the terrible suspicion of the world to which so many modern intellectuals subscribe. For them everything is woe, oppression, sexual exploitation, racial bigotry, and cultural imperialism. Gripped by their own largely manufactured sadness, they want to impose their own guilt and anxiety on our school-children and university students.

The hermeneutics of suspicion: propaganda and economic inefficiency

For example, the intellectuals who dominate many British university departments believe that the British disdain societies less wealthy than theirs and where other cultures predominate. These intellectuals – better called ideologues – are deeply suspicious of their fellow citizens, indeed of everything they encounter in the world. They are dominated by what the French philosopher Paul Ricoeur called "the hermeneutics of suspicion". Their interpretation of everything they experience is passed through a kind of suspicion filter, designed to cast the world in the most adverse light possible.

That many university teachers believe these sinister ideas and are able to influence lots of other minds, often young ones, is just as much an example of economic inefficiency as a high incidence of illiteracy or innumeracy. If school resources are efficiently employed then the teaching they finance will flourish and only people of very low abilities will be found unable to read or calculate. Similarly, if there is rigorous instruction running up through the primary curriculum on through the secondary and ultimately into the university curriculum, there will not be large numbers of people professing absurd beliefs.

Economic inefficiency is a law of socialism

British universities are adversely constrained by the lower levels of education. That British education does not function very efficiently is merely the British version of a universally operational law: socialism is a very inadequate economic system. In a free society, with a socialist education system, education will be among the least effective economic agencies, despite the overall success of the economic system. In Communist societies, by contrast, mass instruction was the most successful part of the whole economy, the whole, of course, being spectacularly unsuccessful. Communist schooling was better at least at mass instruction than is the case with schooling in most free societies. Obviously a system predicated on Marxism was not engaged in education. It was good at mass instruction, nevertheless, because the leadership prevented the adoption of Western style "progressive" notions and a ruthless competition was maintained so that the cleverest children could be identified and suborned by the nomenklatura.

In advanced Western societies, including Britain, many of the presiding intellectual elite loathe what they paradoxically call "elitist" competition. In the private schools, however, competition is the dominant imperative. This explains the vast achievement gulf between private and state schooling in the United Kingdom and the astounding dominance of the products of the former in the elite universities. The aim and the claim of excellence in British education are alike contradicted above all by this hatred of intellectual competition. It hurts the whole society because it hurts the mainstream. Its worst effects, however, are reserved, as always with socialist arrangements, for the poor and the weak.

Thus in the historical background to higher education one can see distinct advantages for the former European socialist societies. Are Poles surprised by the claim that Poland's universities are perhaps in better shape than those in Britain? That claim simply reflects the differences between the intellectual histories of our two countries. Poles are rightly suspicious of the State. Accordingly, Poland has much greater trust in private higher education than one finds in Britain. Above all Polish academics are urbane. One cannot imagine any Polish university, for example, insulting Margaret Thatcher as the University of Oxford insulted her, in 1985, by refusing her an honorary degree. Colleagues may know that at about the same time, the University of Cambridge bestowed exactly such an honorary degree on the late Jacques Derrida, an intellectual charlatan of the kind France has long specialized in producing. French conservatives refer to such writers as "Marxisant", meaning that while they have abandoned the Communist fantasy, they have retained the terrible suspicion of the world and intellectual intolerance which were the real Marxist message.[7] Of course we have plenty of British nonsense too. In the British case at all levels, from nursery schooling to Post-

Graduate research, the education system is shot through with intellectual errors. Thus we cannot understand what is wrong with British Universities, unless we know what is wrong with British primary and secondary education.

The controlling elite and their mistakes

The entrenched mistakes of British education constantly impede economic optimality. Proper education is subverted by the contradictory goals of those who control the system: senior civil servants, teachers' unions; powerful educationalists with socialist opinions. Time does not permit much detail, but the central point is the emphasis on equality at the expense of excellence. The elite do not want high standards; they have resisted decades of attempts by governments, Conservative and Labour, to raise them. It may be doubted by this juncture whether any large-scale improvement can occur without a very large switch into *private finance at all levels of the system.* This change would meet with huge opposition from strong vested interests.

In free societies, the government does not have untrammelled control over the public sector. Control is inevitably exercised by the leading personnel of state activities, because under public finance the contributing public are mostly cut off from the levers of influence. In the British case there is much public anger and discontent at the schools which the leadership have provided. Because of their low standards, primary and secondary schools are often regarded with deep hostility by much of the population; most families claim that they would prefer private education if they could afford it.

Too few, however, seem willing or able to make the requisite financial effort and move their children to private schools. Meanwhile, government attempts at improving standards fail monotonously year after year. The system is caught in a stasis, a kind of paralysis, where nothing much changes, despite the discontent. Many teachers are demoralised; some, however, are able to increase their incomes with lots of private tuition. This serves to hide the extremely poor overall performance to some extent. The private work of British teachers, whose official work is within the public sector, is economically analogous to the old Soviet resort to buying grain from outside when the harvest was poor.

Education in the older democracies is "institutionally" socialist

Let us repeat – repetition being of the essence of education – that in Britain, as in all advanced societies, education, and especially higher education, there being so few private universities, relies heavily on public finance. Costs have been borne overwhelmingly by taxpayers. There has, in recent years, been a marked and proper transfer of some of the financial burden onto users of the universities. Almost all the property of the system, the buildings and facilities, is state-financed. There is no real educational bourgeoisie. There are, sad to say, few entrepreneurs trying to satisfy the public's demand for education.

The system as a whole responds only sluggishly to the preferences of parents and other interested parties. There *are* pressures for excellence and improvement but these are largely frustrated by production rigidities. The good teachers, school or university, are praised and rewarded but *not sufficiently*. Bad teachers and schools are despised but *insufficiently* corrected. The key fact in the lower sectors is that exit from the system is frustrated. This militates against those improvements in school standards which would benefit universities. Parents can often neither get their children out of bad schools nor into good ones. Either they do not have the resources or think they do not. Indeed, know-how is the most crucial resource of all. Compare the educational paralysis with shopping. If we do not like a particular shop, we go to another one. It is the threat of bankruptcy which keeps private shops responsive. Socialist education in free societies, by contrast, is subject to what economists call "producer-capture" – control lies with suppliers.

All efficient production, however, in all eras, is demand-led. Indeed, the American scholar, Andrew Coulson, has shown, incontrovertibly, that throughout history all good education systems have been private.[8] *Education is, in practice, effectively run on Communist lines in the older democracies.* The mental life of the schools, too, is socialist, quite simply because the controlling elite in the universities and educational civil service, is socialist. Education is regulated by the same destructive ideologies of equality and the same pseudo-scientific cults of human management – attempts at comprehensive planning such as the National Curriculum, Key Stages and so on – which obtained in Communist societies. In our socialist education systems there is a *tendency* to downward convergence in intellectual standards of the same kind which prevailed in the patterns of income distribution and social stratification under Communism, although the system also generates one of the world's most brilliant intellectual elites. It has to be said, however, that if the whole economy were to mimic the methods employed by the education system in carrying out its allotted tasks, Britain would be a "third world" society.

An important admission: the forces of educational sanity are, and have to be, stronger than the forces of educational socialism

Even so, of course, a real source of educational salvation in countries like Britain lies in the surrounding market economy and the rule of law. There are benign outside pressures on schools and universities. Indeed, these favourable influences, especially the ceaseless demands of the division of labour, are in overall terms stronger than the adverse ones. They have to be, since there would be mass rebellion from the majority of the public were this not so. As a result, most people do all right at school; most learn to read and write and so on. Moreover, the other side of the coin of mediocrity and failure I have described is the intellectual brilliance to be found in the United Kingdom, the USA and Australia. Their best secondary schools are the world's best. Their best universities are matchless. In the twentieth century, one university, Cambridge, has earned 83 Nobel Prizes and one single Cambridge College, Trinity, 32. These countries evolved, moreover, mostly by educational selection from the working-classes, the huge middle class which is the real social genius of the market economy, which has largely eliminated class warfare, permitting a consensual, un-coerced system of social control.

Communism, like feudalism and slavery, had a permanent problem in the legitimation of its governance, because of the dichotomous social structure it generated. Where the middle class is huge, as in developed free enterprise economies, there is no such dichotomy needing to be legitimated. The adverse output effects in the overall education system are, nevertheless, still very severe. The intellectual elite is smaller than it should be; the middle class, though by far the biggest group in the society, is nevertheless smaller than it ought to be, and the stratum of educational underachievers much larger. Millions leave school illiterate and innumerate. In Britain and America and other similar countries this last group are demoralised, widely criminalised and welfarised. They are a permanent drain on their fellow citizens.

Educational production is qualitatively inferior under socialist management

Such, in broad outline, are the outcomes of socialist institutions and ideologies in the education systems of the older free societies. The reality is a Manichean battle now waged for some three quarters of a century between straight thinking and corrosive ideology. How, though, are the forces of socialist decay made operative? The educational life of the free society is not extinguished – far from it – but it is profoundly impaired by the reiterated presence of a socialist "interrupter system".[9] The overall inefficiency is driven by the intrinsic qualitative inferiority of production under public finance, especially in free societies.

What keeps the system in permanent semi-crisis? My answer may surprise. Socialist education in free societies is obviously in some ways like *education* in socialist/Communist societies. This is not, however, the most useful comparison. It is actually more useful to say that Western state education resembles the overall Communist system. It has much the same *rulers versus ruled* structure. The administrative education elite in Britain are the equivalent of the Communist Party. By contrast, most participants in the education system constitute the counterpart of the population constrained to live under Communism. Just as happened under Communism, the lucky ones prosper. The words of the best-known educational trades unionist in America, the late Albert Shanker, are very revealing here. Shanker was till late in the day virtually a Marxist. He must have recanted, however, for he said, quite baldly, late in his life, that the American school-system:

> …operates like a planned economy…it's no surprise our school system doesn't improve…it resembles the Communist economy.[10]

The cult of skills and the absence thereof

Shanker would seem to be right, insofar as it was also the case under the Communist system that the mistakes kept repeating themselves. There is, for example, a recurring cult of skills in British education, some educationalists maintaining that skills are the key to everything. This is very odd. The skill cult is an error as bad in its way as the neglect of skills. It is very damaging to the educability of children. Education is about understanding. Children need skills in order to engage in the *deeper* activity of understanding. Moreover, the oddest thing about the cult of skills is that it occurs in education systems which chronically neglect such skills. Millions of people in Britain (and in America, Australia, France to name but a few) cannot read or write or calculate or understand and conform to the moral order. At the University of North London, where I worked for many years, the undergraduates were taught learning skills. There were even "Access" courses designed to make up for the students' deficits, without its ever being acknowledged that it was London primary schools and secondary schools which had produced these students and their terrible intellectual deficiencies. This is common in all the older Western free societies. I absolutely refused to take part in what was really an outrageous obfuscation, an attempt at cover-up.

The cult of happiness

In Britain it is also widely and destructively believed that the purpose of primary schools is to produce the happy development of children. This folly is often continued at the secondary level and university levels. Like the errors of Communist dogma it is blind to the evidence. Since many children are happy being idle, they have fulfilled this false ideal of human happiness by emerging illiterate and innumerate and without much moral understanding, after eleven years of school [six years of primary school and five compulsory years in secondary school]. And of course, the three levels – primary, secondary and tertiary – are connected, as much by the links of failure as by those of success. Secondary schools have to deal with the unschooled products of primary schools, and universities have to try to teach students what they should have learned at secondary school. Many teachers, at all levels, embrace the view that education is fundamentally a philosophical endeavour; but they have to battle against the institutionalised errors which have bit by bit invaded educational practice in Great Britain and elsewhere since the advent of public finance.

It is true that no one is totally immune to error: at the same time the level of immunity is much higher in post-Communist Poland, for example, than it is in Britain. This is a direct result of Poland's long historical travails, but especially of those she endured in the twentieth century. The most encouraging aspect of higher education in Poland is, indeed, that so many Poles have done precisely what needs to be done with respect to education everywhere – they have embraced free enterprise, not only in consumer goods and engineering, but in intellectual life too. They are reading the historical runes correctly. The next phase of civilisation will surely require a much closer nexus between education and private monies.

Education's suspicion-mongers have to fight an unequal battle, thank the Gods. To win they would have to overthrow the rule of law and reverse the order of private property. They have thrown up barriers against the spreading of free ideas. The erection of a socialist education system is their masterpiece. The fundamental problem they have landed us with – and the problem is much the same in the other advanced free societies – is, we repeat, that the participants, namely teachers, pupils, students and civil servants, are not in the main operating with their own financial resources.

While it is a commonplace among economists that public finance causes inefficient use of scarce resources, it is much less well understood that in the educational instance this inefficiency is mediated through the effects of such finance on the core activities of education: on curriculum, pedagogy and evaluation. Public finance of education in free societies does not merely result in given material being less well taught, it also results in different and sometimes very dubious educational practices. Until these perverse dynamics are more generally realised and better understood, the imperatives for genuine reform will remain muted and actual attempts at reform will be frustrated. There is, moreover, a tendency among senior personnel, to pursue private goals to the exclusion or diminution of their official public functions. The relatively new branch of Economics called "Public Choice" theory is predicated on this substitution. For example, a civil servant who is supposed to be facilitating teaching and learning, but whose real aim is to promote a more equal society, is effectively substituting his pleasure in political equality for his duty to advance education, understood as the quest for knowledge and moral goodness.

In truth, education is intrinsically elitist

Civil servants may pursue income and power as well. Of the latter, senior civil servants have a great deal. They manifestly possess the ability to frustrate or modify political initiatives they have been instructed to bring into operation. They also strike Utopian attitudes, some writers even advancing the lofty proposition that everyone should receive or be offered "excellent education", on egalitarian/democratic grounds.[11] This is an illegitimate political intrusion. The idea of education has no *direct* connection with the concepts "equality" or democracy, despite the long decades of agitation to which the egalitarians have subjected us. Indeed, quite the opposite is true. Elitism more *typifies* education and its various processes than do equality or democracy. Intellectual advance consists in the search for the best learning that can be achieved. This means that rigorous subject hierarchies must be established, that is to say *elite* subjects must be identified and pursued by the ablest men and women available.

Moreover, clever children should be brought in touch with superior intellectual subject matter as early as possible. Such adults and such children *are* the intellectual elite. They are not *qua* scholars superior human beings. They are superior only as scholars. Given that there are huge variations in the distribution of talent, education is in fact an intrinsically *elitist* process, from which some pupils profit enormously more than others in many ways. This may be because they are cleverer than most, more hardworking and devoted than most, or have more gifted or richer parents than most, or for all these reasons. Elitism is no more than an objective search for the proper registration of the way things really are. If excellence is a key educational concept and equality at best only a marginal one in educational considerations, then excellence should trump equality at most points. Above all we must insist that the very idea of a university is an *elitist* idea.

Economic rationality and intellectual coherence are cognate phenomena

If the philosophical character of education were more widely recognised, a superior curriculum could develop and the scarce resources available to education could be more optimally employed. In other words, *educational and economic efficiency are the same thing*. Our ancestors knew that education is philosophical. This is why research degrees carry the title "Doctor of Philosophy". Above all, elitism often wears a very ordinary face. Education policy should be guided, not by Utopian fantasies, but by the simple but traditional and commanding notion that "everything is what it is and not some other thing". Such notions are part of the intellectual apparatus which has made the nations which speak English so dominant in the life of the mind

Notes

1. Such a development could increase the productive capacity of the British economy.
2. I would wryly observe that friendship is an essential element in intellectual activity.
3. The introduction of progressive education in the late 1950s is the classic example. The headmaster of the Secondary Modern, where I taught English in the early 1960s, told me that the feeder primary schools from which he drew his intake, suddenly, in the late 1950s, began to send him a large minority of boys who could not read or write and did not know their tables. The sinister ghost of Rousseau was now stalking our classrooms, having recently gained access to teacher education institutions.
4. Andrew J. Coulson, *Market Education: The Unknown History*, Transaction, 1999.
5. Truancy is on an enormous scale in the free societies, a point which my own research has shown in the case of England and Wales. Despite the attempts by the educational management to blame the parents, the evidence is overwhelming that truancy is largely a curricular and pedagogic phenomenon, according to the students themselves. See D.J. O'Keeffe, *Truancy in English*

Secondary Schools, Her Majesty's Stationary Office, April, 1994. The key thing in truancy research, is to ask the students, confidentially. I did this.

6. They also wasted huge resources fulminating about "racism" and "sexism", seemingly unaware that modern market economies are functionally indifferent to the race or sex of their various economic agents.
7. Incidentally, many British and American academics will believe any nonsense provided it was originally written in French.
8. *Market Education: The Unknown History*, New Brunswick: Transaction Press, 1999.
9. The idea of an "Interrupter System" in education came first from Basil Bernstein, although that talented but deeply ambivalent scholar did not seem to deplore the interruption in question as one might have wished.
10. Albert Shanker, late President of the American Federation of Teachers, is alleged to have said: "It's time to admit that public education operates like a planned economy.... It more resembles the communist economy than our own market economy".
11. This was the line commonly taken during the 1970s at the influential Institute of Education of the University of London.

CHAPTER 8
KNOWLEDGE AND THE UNIVERSITY

Dr. Aidan Seery
School of Education, Trinity College Dublin

It has been well acknowledged for some time now that the university as institution, but also individual universities in their self-understanding and identities, have experienced a crisis that has impacted significantly the historical relationship between the university and knowledge (Barnett, 1997; Blackmore, 2001; Kogan & Hanney, 1999; Millar, 1998; Smith & Langslow, 1999). A number of mostly external factors have been invoked to explain this critical change; the massification of education, globalisation, the knowledge society and information technology all have been identified and analysed as factors in the literature of the early years of the millennium. In more recent times, and particularly in the case of Ireland, it is possible to identify a further factor in the financial crisis that has engulfed not only Ireland but Europe more generally that can be read as also having an effect on the changing relationship between knowledge and the university.

However, despite all talk of crises in the contemporary university and many other institutes of higher education, they continue to identify themselves as places of knowledge generation, dissemination and evaluation. This claim can be read, in the first instance, as descriptive of activity and offering at least an analogous sense of "productivity" for those who need the language of industry to describe the work of universities, even though it has become clear that the university no longer has a monopoly on this kind of activity. A second way of reading this continued identification of the university with knowledge is as the expression of an enduring need to retain some communal normative idea to hold the academic community of teachers, researchers and students together and to give the institution some shared substantive identity rather than a conventional one based, for instance, on rights (Hamlyn, 1996). In what follows, it is the latter, normative sense of the relationship of the university and knowledge that is of interest.

One reason for the attachment of universities to their identity with the generation and transmission of knowledge, despite a loss of authority in the field is, I suggest, the lack of other shared normative understandings of the nature of the university and higher education, coupled with a residual harking back to a time when this authority was uncontested. The medieval university could rely on a communal understanding of academic life and work as the shared endeavour to promote and demonstrate the "unity of knowledge". This unity, traditionally, was interpreted in at least two ways. In a first sense, it was a unity of knowledge guaranteed by a fundamental ontological or better metaphysical assumption that everything can be considered to be constituted to one kind of "thing", or, "type of stuff", for instance, "matter" or "being". In its more modern version, this unity of all knowledge and science is manifest in a reductionist programme of explaining and constructing all knowledge on that of physics rather than metaphysics. A second possibility for constructing a unity of knowledge lies in the adoption in all disciplines of similar methodologies. Thus, the demand in all disciplinary knowledge for evidence, openness to critical scrutiny, explanatory power in theory and an economy of assumptions, could be seen to provide the basis for a methodological unity of knowledge. In the event, neither of these possibilities, the ontological or the methodological, are ultimately successful in the history of philosophy of securing a communal normative idea for the university. With regard to the founding of the unity of knowledge in a singular metaphysics, the critique of Nietzsche in particular, put paid to that idea for most philosophers of education. The possibility of a foundation on methodological grounds, on the other hand, did not survive the schism between the natural sciences and the human sciences which led to the declaration of independence on the part of the human sciences for their own models of knowledge based on the purpose of understanding rather than explanation. Thus, it would seem, the project to construct an identity and shared understanding for higher education based on the "unity of knowledge", at least, is a failed one.

Historically, in the wake of this loss of identity for the university, a similar crisis to the one declared today ensued. The search for a new self-understanding began and culminates in the nineteenth century notion that the university forges its identity in the communal involvement of all members of an academic community in the formation of "the cultivated human being". This is the notion of *Bildung*, the defining idea of the Humboldtian university, and by extension of the mainland European university of the nineteenth and most of the twentieth century. However, this foundational idea collapses, in turn, under the critiques of Adorno and Lyotard, but more significantly under the weight of the new social, political and economic demands made on higher education. As a result, the university is plunged into an identity crisis once again, but one this time that cannot be resolved by philosophical reflection on the nature of education.

Against this background of a twice lost identity, the question arises whether the university can find either a new identity and self-understanding, or whether it might be possible to re-construct itself out of the remains of either of its former selves. Given the nature of the institution, the manner in which it still constitutes itself and re-generates itself from within, coupled with a strong sense of self-preservation, it is unlikely that the university is going to be able to construct a totally new identity for itself. As a result, the effort of most thinkers concerned with the nature of higher education seems to be concentrated in a re-construction based on either the idea of "knowledge" or that of "Bildung".

In this chapter, it is the first possibility that is pursued a little further by first examining more closely the nature of some of the challenges to such a re-construction and how a re-modelling might address these. Therefore, the initial section takes up a number of themes that have been well-rehearsed but worthy of a renewed view, while the second part attempts to make one or two suggestions on a possible re-modelling of the knowledge-university relationship.

A key challenge to a revival of the idea of knowledge providing a unifying and defining feature of the university lies in the way in which a changed and changing concept of knowledge does not provide the necessary conceptual stability for the task and thus eliminates itself as a candidate feature. The classical enlightenment idea that knowledge is associated with the stable notions of universality, reason, truth and progress no longer holds in the university. And this shift has not gone unnoticed in wider society. Ironically perhaps, because this enlightenment view of knowledge has slightly more currency in wider society than in the academic world, some critics of the university from the public perspective are known to point to the "fact" that the university is no longer producing knowledge in the sense of universal, justified truth and that in many fields and academic departments the classical division between doxa (opinion) and true knowledge (episteme) has been blurred. Observers on the outside have little difficulty in finding examples of academic publications and new teaching programmes that are regarded as self-centred, self-referential and self-serving indulgences lacking in any universality or wider utility. Even among the traditional disciplines, the singular failure on the part of academic economists to be able to foresee the present fiscal calamity can be cited as an example of the failure of university to produce the kinds of knowledge that not only an economy but a society needs and demands from it. Thus, from the outside at least, the case for the university as seat of knowledge has been weakened to the extent that for some commentators, universities are indeed producing nonsense rather than knowledge.

Within the academy, and not only in the arts, humanities and social sciences, it is much easier to see why the enlightenment notion of universal, reliable knowledge has been challenged and, in many quarters, rejected. For one, the now widely accepted link between knowledge and power, associated most obviously with the work of Foucault, has raised awareness that knowledge is rarely, if ever, a neutral, disinterested search for truth. Enlightenment knowledge is charged as being reductive, all too rational and even "masculine". The development of new fields of learning and new types of knowledge is thus regarded as a necessary counterbalance to this reductionism or as a means of asserting power by groups and interests that have previously not had a "voice" in the academy and have declared their intent to unmask the hidden male subjectivity of traditional knowledge. The rejection of what is seen to be an oppressive and narrow view of knowledge is heralded as a liberation that has led to the development of new research approaches and instruments, new ways of understanding social and personal phenomena and news ways of disseminating this new knowledge. The now classic example of a concerted challenge to the traditional view of knowledge is that mounted by feminist thinkers. The view that all knowledge reflects the "position" of the knower in society in a matrix of historical and cultural forces has gained considerable acceptance particularly in the social sciences but has been argued in a most striking and convincing manner in the case of the position of women, though the significance of a knower's standpoint (within social class) was, of course, known already to Marx and Mannheim. The result of challenges such as these to the traditional idea of knowledge has led to the formulation of what are known as "new and diverse epistemologies" and often violent and divisive arguments about what counts as knowledge (Horsthemke, 2010), what counts as evidence for knowledge claims, and whether, in these new worlds, it is possible to construct principles of "warrantable assertability" and so on. In the extreme, some of the efforts to construct "new knowledges" seem to have indeed tipped over into nonsense as seen in the infamous case of the Sokal hoax (Sokal, 1996) in which it appears that he demonstrated that social constructivist knowledge is no more than post-structuralist rubbish (though he may merely have demonstrated a case of appallingly poor review and editorial work). However, for our purposes here, the effect of these debates has been internal strife within universities that seems to have dispelled for ever any hope of finding any shared normative idea in knowledge that could serve to construct a distinctive identity for the contemporary university. A second consequence is, of course, that such internal fighting and bickering does little for the status of the university in society, though it is possible to salvage some important features of a view of knowledge that is broader than objectivist truth-seeking.

There would seem to be an increasing realisation and demand in the public sphere, at least, that academic knowledge, including scholarly and scientific knowledge is, or should be, connected to human interests, culture and history, social organisation and power. That this is the case with "ordinary" knowledge; tacit knowledge, knowledge from experience and practical knowledge would seem obvious. However, universities have not been successful in demonstrating the continuity between ordinary knowledge and scientific or academic knowledge to the extent that those outside of universities are convinced of this possible and valuable continuity. This provides a clue perhaps to the best opportunity for the re-definition of university identity on the basis of an understanding of knowledge and this idea will be pursued further later in the chapter.

A second key challenge to the re-instating of knowledge at the centre of an understanding of the university is the economic and social demand that the knowledge generated and transmitted be connected with commercial, vocational and instrumental ends. This challenge is particularly pertinent at a time in which economic pressures have resulted in greatly reduced public exchequer support for universities and when such support is contingent on higher education acceptance of government economic priorities. This has led to pressure being exerted on universities to re-define themselves in the light of what is seen as corporate aims; as "enterprise universities"(Marginson &

Considine, 2000). This particular pressure is more keenly felt in some sections of the university than in others and has the effect of possibly splitting the university community between, on the one hand, those for whom this demand is accepted and can be met and those for whom this demand means an almost complete de-legitimisation of their field. Thus, the demand for a more vocational focus made to a School of Law, Nursing or Education elicits a less passionate negative response than perhaps from a School of History, Cultural Studies or Philosophy. Consequently, the assumption is made, and not without warrant, that the arts, humanities and social sciences are not going to make in any way, the same contribution to future economic growth as the knowledge fields associated with the STEM [Science, Technology, Engineering and Mathematics] disciplines. However, it is worth noting that, in the context of a university, the kinds of knowledge generated even in the sciences do not always align closely with economic or narrow practical utility. As Berube points out "some endeavours in pure mathematics or cosmology contribute no more than does the study of medieval tapestry to the economic or physical well-being of the general citizenry"(Berube, 2003, p. 26).

A result of this particular pressure is the construction of a new hierarchy of knowledge, based not even on the grounds of broad human interest taking precedence over disinterested inquiry, but forced by exigencies of funding that privilege certain fields rather than others. The prospect in these circumstances is that many of the new ways of knowing outlined above that were born of the breaking open of the bind of enlightenment knowledge will not survive, not as a result of epistemological debate or even on the basis of societal acceptance but of funding starvation. No amount of protestation about the noble pursuit of higher things than skills and competencies is likely to be able to reverse this seemingly irreversible movement to servicing an economy.

Of course, the practice of categorising types of knowledge and the privileging of certain kinds of knowledge over others is not new. In the 1790s, for instance, Kant describes the division of faculties of the university into "higher" and "lower" with theology, law and medicine in the higher category and the arts humanities and social sciences (or their rough equivalents at the time) in the lower ranks (D. Evans, 2008). Here it is perhaps interesting to note that the three higher disciplines are all associated with vocational and professional ends but also reflect what Kant sees as at the core of the relationship between the state and university. Viewed from his perspective, the state has a concern for the physical well-being of citizens, their security and the condition of their souls. The three higher faculties reflect these concerns because of their engagement with these human and political interests!

The contemporary disquiet, on the other hand however, about a hierarchy of kinds of knowledge based primarily on arguments of utility, is reflective more of an appreciation of Habermas' taxonomy of analytical, hermeneutical and critical knowledge that are generated in the natural sciences, the humanities and social sciences, and the philosophical and political sciences (Habermas, 1978). Those who argue that knowledge is becoming more narrowly focussed on technical interests employ Habermas' work to highlight that other kinds of knowledge are neglected by this reduction. In particular, it is pointed out that the emancipatory interest, that is the motor for critical knowledge, is crucially missing from this conception of knowledge and that this kind of knowledge is of particular significance for the university and could form the basis of its distinctive role in the generation and dissemination of knowledge.

Central to the claim that universities should be places of critical and emancipatory knowledge is the understanding that it is necessary to interrogate the ideological nature of traditional forms of knowledge [including the sciences], of the rhetoric of policy and, especially, of the "commonsenseness" of political and economic imperatives. In the case of the argument for utility and relevance in knowledge, for instance, it is difficult to say anything to the claim that the university is situated in the "real" world, is funded by tax-payers, and therefore must make its contribution to the good of society. This is a matter of such obvious commonsense that it is extremely difficult to engage in debate, particularly outside the university, on the "normalisation of the real"; the way in which the "real" is invoked in a particular manner that excludes interpretations other than that constructed in politics and the media. The very attempt to construct such a critique by academics, and to teach in a way that promotes this type of critique, is regarded as a further example of how far removed the university is from the ordinary lives of citizens lived in the obviousness of the real (Barrow, 2010; M. Evans, 2010)). Thus the satisfaction of possibly finding a new identity in the relationship with a special kind of knowledge that is distinct to the learning and teaching of a university is dashed in the face of the impossibility of communicating this identity to a society which considers the message nonsense, not commonsense.

These then are just some of the not inconsiderable challenges to re-formulating the relationship between the university and knowledge in a way that might provide a shared identity in a community of scholars and students. The prospect of a new relationship, however, is not without a future. Two ideas that seem worthy of consideration in the construction of a new relationship lie in the overcoming of what might be termed "postmodern fundamentalism" and the second is suggested in a radical acceptance of a pragmatic notion of knowledge.

With regard to the first, it would seem timely to bring to an end the isolationism that has been the feature of the relationship between the sciences and the humanities for too long now. This could be achieved through efforts on two fronts in parallel. Both in the sciences and in the disciplines of the arts, humanities and social sciences there is need for a fundamental engagement with theoretical underpinnings and ontological commitments to reveal, and perhaps accept, ambiguities, uncertainties and the provisional nature of all knowledge. Generations of scientists, medics, technologists and engineers seem to have received an education and induction into their fields of endeavour without any introduction to the epistemological and ontological foundations of their disciplines. Science students, for instance, even on completion of Masters' degrees have often not heard the names of philosophers of science such as Popper, Kuhn or Feyerabend. They have rarely, if ever engaged in a critique of the positivism that they are unwittingly accused of by fellow academics in the humanities. Social scientists, on the other hand, trained in many institutions almost exclusively in qualitative research methods, if aware of the particularity and contextuality of their knowledge, often overcompensate by declaring this to be a pure virtue. In this case too, it would seem that the engagement with epistemology and fundamental theory is short-circuited on the way to taking a "position" from which to view the world from a high epistemic ground. If it is the case that students and young researchers rarely engage with the epistemology of their own fields, it is an even more rare event that they would have any knowledge of the other's. This leaves a situation in which social scientists and humanities scholars depict their scientist colleagues as guilty of crude and naive positivism and the scientists regard their humanities colleagues as relativists contributing little to the world of objective knowledge.

And yet, it is clear that within the university there are theoretical physicists, mathematicians, biologists and others who are engaged in research that is quite remote from the caricature of positivist utility. It is based on imaginative speculation that requires the construction of new languages and modes of inquiry that resemble the most creative interpretations of text and situations to be found in any of the humanities or social sciences. On the other side, it is possible to find academics keenly aware of the way in which literature, art, history and education can contribute usefully to aspects of lives that are of shared interest with health specialists, architects and engineers. What is required is an understanding that forms or "bodies" of knowledge do not require a metaphysical commitment to the unity of knowledge nor of methodological uniformity in order to enter into dialogue. From a philosophical perspective, it is possible to be an ontological realist and, at the same time, an epistemological non-realist. Perspectives in knowledge can provide complementary, diverse, mutually-enriching models for understanding the multiplicity and ambiguity of the world.

An engagement with epistemological questions within academic fields will, however, not be sufficient to bring about any new relationship to knowledge within the university unless there is engagement between the fields. This type of engagement required would go beyond the invitation to seminars and beyond the construction of task-specific inter-disciplinary research teams. It would demand open forums of debate on epistemological and foundational issues in the arts, humanities, social sciences and natural sciences. It would require that students initiated into specific, academic disciplines would also receive an introduction to epistemological ideas and questions in other fields. This would be possible only with a reform of traditional undergraduate studies in English and Irish universities to include this kind of study. A consequence would be the marking out of a distinctive programme of studies that would distinguish university studies from those in other third level institutions focussed solely on single disciplinary programmes but this would be possible only if there were infra-structural efforts made to enable this kind of curriculum planning(Barnett, 2000).

The second suggestion, not unconnected to the first, regards a conceptual re-orientation of the kinds of knowledge distinctive to a university that entails a radical acceptance and extension of the demand for the "real" of utility. Rather than attempting to defend notions of knowledge by reviving or re-stating the argument for the importance of the noble destiny of disinterestedness and knowledge for its own sake, the public university should seek to accept the idea of generating and transmitting "real" knowledge but in a way that takes the concept of the "real" to its very limits. This should be done by extending the notion of utility beyond the economic demands of a market economy to the equally real and demanding questions that challenge human society more generally and the relationship between humanity and nature. It includes asking about the values that inform socio-economic change and what are the real pressing human interests and concerns that our knowledge must address (Perry, 2006). This suggestion is not radically new and has been made using a slightly different argument with regard to the place of wisdom in the university (Barnett & Maxwell, 2008). The work of Maxwell, over nearly four decades, has called for a radical review and even revolution in the aims of academic knowledge. However, to build on this work, the choice of line of argument in the current political and economic situation is crucial. It is not likely that political and economic power-holders will be swayed by arguments that universities should be permitted to become "centres of wisdom" in a process of internal transformation, important as that dimension of knowledge might be acknowledged to be from outside the university. It is much more the case that the university must mount a social and political argument for being centres of talent and engagement in pursuit of answers to pressing human concerns in a way that engages with the different discourses of politics, economics and society generally. In this engagement universities must demonstrate that they have unique properties and characteristics, not possessed by any other institutions of knowledge and learning, to carry out this task.

Some of these unique features include a tradition and a culture in many universities of academics and researchers working not for personal economic return but for either some imagining of the common good, or of the development of a body of knowledge without specific utility but with the historical recognition that some knowledge finds its application only many years after its development and in fields not envisaged by the developers. This traditional attitude to knowledge can make possible a broader view of potential solutions; one that is not restricted by a narrow instrumental rationality or pressure group concerns.

Linked with this feature is that of a culture of criticality in universities that permits academics and researchers to assess solutions to problems and to consider alternative solutions (Maxwell, 2008). The imperative to find quick solutions to narrowly defined problems in order to gain a commercial or economic advantage from research and knowledge generation militates against an attitude of careful critique. However, universities must show that deeper and more considered solutions are ultimately of greater value and do not run the risk of paralysing self-analysis and subjectivization of research.

Thirdly, universities have a particular asset in the manner in which academic international collaborations are commonly structured. These, for the most part, are open and collegial structures that are often not bound by national interests or exploitation of patentable knowledge. They have the potential to bring the best talent in the world together in ways that permit the free transfer and sharing of knowledge but not in the manner of an unregulated market of self-interested forces. This, of course, relies on the generous attitude and sense of the common good previously mentioned. These international inter-disciplinary groups have already existing funding mechanisms and channels of communication that cannot easily be found in the commercial sector bound as it is by sectoral interests.

There does exist, then, a possibility of re-constructing the relationship between the university and knowledge but only, it has been argued, on the basis of a real engagement with society on determining the kinds of knowledge that are needed for humanity to address its most pressing concerns followed by a re-orientation of academic and research work to reflect these new purposes. The determination of the greatest challenges to be addressed is not a straightforward task. Some agreement might be found concerning the problems of human health, conflict and poverty, but these agreements will not be without the operation of power-relations and interest groups. At the level of solutions, the ability to achieve agreement will be even more difficult. However, these difficulties will have to be met. A new engagement with new knowledge will also require change in curricula and the infra-structural support to do this. The possible reward is a distinct identity for the university in its relationship with deep, real-world knowledge. At risk is the future of the university as a place of knowledge-making and assessing and the reduction of its activities to vocational teaching along with all of the other, often cheaper and more efficient, "providers". There is the opportunity for degrees of rich, human sense but the danger also of a multiplicity of degrees of nonsense.

References

Barnett, R. (1997). *Higher Education: A Critical Business*. Buckingham: Open University Press.

Barnett, R. (2000). Thinking the Unversity, Again. *Educational Philosophy and Theory, 32*(3), 319-326.

Barnett, R., & Maxwell, N. (Eds.). (2008). *Wisdom in the University*. London: Routledge.

Barrow, C. W. (2010). The Rationality Crisis in US Higher Education. *New Political Science, 32*(3), 317-344.

Berube, M. (2003). The Utility of the Arts and Humanities. *Arts and Humanities in Higher Education, 2*(1), 23-40.

Blackmore, J. (2001). Universities in Crisis? Knowledge Economies, emancipatory pedagogies and the critical intellectual. *Educational Theory, 51*(3), 353-371.

Evans, D. (2008). The Conflict of the Faculties and the Knowledge Industry: Kant's Diagnosis, in his Time and Ours. *Philosophy, 83*(04), 483.

Evans, M. (2010). The Universities and the Challenge of Realism. *Arts and Humanities in Higher Education, 9*(1), 13-21.

Habermas, J. (1978). *Knowledge and Human Interests* (J. J. Shapiro, Trans.). London: Heinemann.

Hamlyn, D. W. (1996). The Concept of a University *Philosophy, 276*, 205-218.

Horsthemke, K. (2010). 'Diverse Epistemologies', Truth and Archaeology: In Defence of Realism. *Science and Engineering Ethics, 17*(2), 321-334.

Kogan, M., & Hanney, S. (1999). *Reforming Higher Education*. London: Jessica Kingsley Publishers.

Marginson, S., & Considine, M. (2000). *The enterprise university : power, governance,and reinvention in Australia*. Cambridge: Cambridge University Press.

Maxwell, N. (2008). From Knowledge to Wisdom: the Need for an Academic Revolution. In R. Barnett & N. Maxwell (Eds.), *Wisdom in the University* (pp. 1-19). London: Routledge.

Millar, R. (1998). *As if Learning Mattered: Reforming Higher Education*. Ithaca, NY: Cornell University Press.

Perry, B. (2006). Science, Society and the University: A Paradox of Values. *Social Epistemology, 20*(3-4), 201-219.

Smith, D., & Langslow, A. (Eds.). (1999). *The Idea of a University*. London: Jessica Kingson Publishers.

CHAPTER 9
IRISH UNIVERSITIES IN THE EARLY 21ST CENTURY: A VIEW FROM SCIENCE

Dr. Paul Van Kampen
School of Physical Science, Dublin City University

> He sat writing in the room with the deadly statistical clock, proving something no doubt — probably, in the main, that the Good Samaritan was a Bad Economist.
>
> Charles Dickens, *Hard Times* (1854)

In this chapter, I discuss the many changes that have taken place in the Irish university system since 1998, with an emphasis on the area of science, in which I work. I have taken the year 1998 as a reference point for a number of reasons. Of course any cut-off is arbitrary, and I might equally well have chosen 1995, the generally acknowledged birth year of the now deceased Celtic Tiger. The year 1998 has threefold significance. It is the year that the first call of the Irish government's Program for Research in Third Level Institutions (PRTLI) was issued (HEA 2011). It is, not unrelatedly, the year I started to work in Irish academia, albeit as a postdoctoral researcher for the first two years. Entirely coincidentally, it also happens to be 13 years ago – and whether it has been a lucky or unlucky thirteen is worth discussing.

Science in Universities

There seems to be more or less general agreement that universities play a dual role: they exist to educate, and to carry out research. Where the balance should lie, and what constitutes a good education and suitable research, on the other hand, is a matter of much, often heated, debate. In this chapter, I discuss some of these issues from the viewpoint of somebody who was educated as a scientist, and is now plying his trade in the area of science education.

Science has always had a special status in the education system, for better or for worse. This is not an observation by a man blinded by his own enthusiasm, but a conclusion drawn from studying the history of science as part of the curriculum. Science was introduced into the curriculum in the nineteenth century, partly for utilitarian reasons: science was seen as a way to promote progress, industrialization, or capitalism (choose the terms that match your political views most closely). Educational arguments led to a competition between the view of science as a body of knowledge acquired over more than 2000 years, and the several processes that science engages in. In the nineteenth century, the idea of "developing the faculties" supported introducing the inductive reasoning that is found in science to complement the deductive reasoning of maths that was already embedded in the curriculum (deBoer 1991, Solomon 1998). Nowadays, cultural and democratic arguments are also brought to bear on the importance of science in the curriculum.

All of these views of science education have their merits. They also apply, more or less unaltered, to research in science. The intrinsic value of research in science is worded beautifully by Poincaré (1908, 22):

> The scientist does not study nature because it is useful; he studies it because he delights in it, and he delights in it because it is beautiful. If nature were not beautiful, it would not be worth knowing, and if nature were not worth knowing, life would not be worth living. I am not speaking, of course, of the beauty which strikes the senses, of the beauty of qualities and appearances. I am far from despising this, but it has nothing to do with science. What I mean is that more intimate beauty which comes from the harmonious order of its parts, and which a pure intelligence can grasp.

Other aspects of science research, and the complexity of their interplay, are illustrated by a famous exchange (Fermilab 1969) that took place in 1969 between Robert Wilson, looking for $250 million funding to build a machine called the bevatron to carry out fundamental particle physics research, and Senator Pastore of the Congressional Joint Committee on Atomic Energy. To avoid confusion: Pastore is supportive of the proposal, and aims to add arguments to the case he will make with the Senate. I will first discuss the following exchange:

Wilson:	[...] Because of the kind of research that we are now starting, men will eventually be able to enjoy a richer life, in an intellectual and spiritual sense certainly, but also in their physical well-being.
Pastore:	Is there anything connected in the hopes of this accelerator that in any way involves the security of this country?
Wilson:	No sir; I do not believe so.
Pastore:	Nothing at all?
Wilson:	Nothing at all.
Pastore:	It has no value in that respect?
Wilson:	It only has to do with the respect with which we regard one another, the dignity of men, our love of culture. It has to do with those things. It has nothing to do with the military, I am sorry.
Pastore:	Don't be sorry for it.
Wilson:	I am not, but I cannot in honesty say it has any such application.
Pastore:	Is there anything here that projects us in a position of being competitive with the Russians, with regard to this race?
Wilson:	Only from a long-range point of view, of a developing technology. Otherwise, it has to do with: Are we good painters, good sculptors, great poets? I mean all the things

> that we really venerate and honor in our country and are patriotic about. In that sense, this new knowledge has all to do with honor and country but it has nothing to do directly with defending our country, except to make it worth defending.

Note that the justification *du jour* for policy makers at the time was the aim to pull ahead in the arms race with the Soviet Union. One can rejoice in Wilson not attempting to justify his proposal in military terms, and in the lofty ideals on display that many non-scientists could happily embrace. However, this is not all. Just before the celebrated passage quoted above, Wilson also argues:

> One can see the possibility now of using nuclear forces for controlling our environment better than ever, or digging canals, or for preventing pollution. For example, I live in Chicago, and the more nuclear plants that are built near Chicago, the more bearable is the air that I breathe there. I can see a direct effect of nuclear energy in decreasing pollution. We will also see a decrease in the cost of electricity, for all men, especially as time goes on.

It is not just out of idealism that I like the "make the country worth defending" argument better. I accept that the statement was made before Three Mile Island accident and the Chernobyl and Fukushima disasters; the 1957 Kyshtym disaster was still under tight wraps and probably not known to Wilson. I also accept that the arguments he makes, as applied to the field of nuclear physics, are true today: electricity from nuclear power stations is cheaper than burning oil or coal, and leaves the air cleaner. Of course, nowadays we are much more keenly aware of problems with nuclear waste and core meltdowns.

Even if we are willing to excuse Wilson from not knowing or foreseeing these downsides to the use of nuclear power plants, I argue that he should not have made the argument in the first place. Wilson makes the argument for past generations of particle accelerators, and appears to leave it as an implication that future particle accelerators will have the same benefits. However, given the parameters for the bevatron, the knowledge that was going to be gained from it was unlikely to be of relevance to nuclear power plants; any impact in that regard would have been utterly unexpected. Moreover, apart from any objections one might raise concerning the disingenuity of the energy argument, subsequent developments illustrate how dangerous it can be to play games with the true motivation for a research project. In November 2011, the German parliament voted to close down all nuclear plants by 2022 and discard nuclear energy as a power source. Presumably, as a corollary it would also have stopped funding particle physics research, if providing cheaper, cleaner electricity had been accepted as the only reason for the undertaking. In a sense, Wilson's argument is a contortion not very different from trying to make a case for the bevatron in terms of the arms race.

It is not my intention to excoriate Wilson for "stooping so low"; I imagine a lot of people would reluctantly betray their principles somewhat and make a utilitarian argument to obtain funding for worthy curiosity-driven research. To illustrate the complexity of the point further, consider an exchange later in the hearing:

Pastore: Essentially, the major purpose of this bevatron is for fundamental high-energy physics research, which is an educational and academic process, is it not?

Wilson: And a cultural process, yes, but with the firm expectation that technological developments will come. Directly, but after a very long time; from the results of the research will come new technology.

> However, there will be a bonus that will come indirectly but very soon, through the technological inventions, that is "Spin-off," that results whenever such work is done.

Wilson's argument here is neither disingenuous nor exaggerated. Many scientific projects or engineering research indeed have the potential to generate income and technological spin-offs, directly or indirectly. I am not against research with these potential benefits – it would be a futile objection in any case, and they do add to the story – but am wary that inevitably they will be conflated with the intrinsic value of research, and become the driver. The bevatron was built for curiosity-driven research; and so, in a sense, the spin-off argument muddies the waters for the general case for curiosity-driven academic research. I have chosen these examples to illustrate the complexity and richness of science as a human endeavour. It is precisely this complexity that provides science with many opportunities, but also many threats.

My View of Academia, Pre-PRTLI

When I started in academia, in 1998, funding levels for science were increasing but still low. By and large, academic staff had a clear expectation of what their role was: they would teach as outlined by their head of school, and carry out research besides. While these roles were embraced with different levels of enthusiasm, the expectation was more or less universal. Postgraduate funding was by no means guaranteed, and many postgraduate students made ends meet by being paid for tutoring duties and one-on-one tutorials ("grinds"). Postdoctoral researchers preparing for a career in academia taught labs and lecture modules to gain experience needed to boost their chances of joining the academic ranks. This is my own story, and I know it was a common one.

There is little doubt that the ability to teach well was certainly a factor in recruitment or promotion, but that one's research was of greater importance. Recruitment was typically open to all fields of research, or targeted to replace an academic or strengthen a group in an existing research area; within these constraints, it was by and large the intrinsic value of research that mattered. Promotions were based largely on research indicators such as peer-reviewed publications and postgraduate students supervised. Requirements on the teaching side were much less stringent. In support of this statement, let me point out that there were and are many senior academic staff who have never read, let alone written, a single paper on teaching a topic in their field, while there are none I have heard of who have never read or written a paper in their own area of research.

The Intervening Years

In what follows, I will argue that a number of changes have taken place in academia in the last thirteen years or so, and I will discuss their impact. Firstly, there has been a drive across the board for quantification of almost all aspects of university life, under various guises: for example, in quality assessment and quality control of teaching and learning, and in research assessments, at the cost of a significant increase of the administrative load. Secondly, increased funding for research has shifted the relative importance away from undergraduate teaching and towards research. Thirdly, the development of the so-called fourth-level of postgraduate education. (This development is still in its infancy, and I will not consider it in this chapter.) Fourthly, increasingly oriented research has distorted the fabric of academia.

Sometime in this period, the invidious notion that universities must be run as a business seems to have taken root. This is of course a locution so vague that it can mean anything. Unfortunately, it does not seem to mean a concern for sustaining intellectual powerhouses while preserving trusted drivers for undergraduate education and basic and applied research, but a shift towards generating capital[1] as the main driver in academia. The business model that was to be adopted has never been defined in a way that I could understand, but it appears to involve the introduction of additional horizontal and vertical layers of management and focus on evaluation and commercialisation. My observation that nobody seems able to support the premise with any data has never been popular. When the economy was booming, I was urged to stop being an ivory tower academic and accept the realities of life; now that the economy is bust, I am apparently only scoring cheap points by pointing out that business models do not always seem to work out so well – whether there was really a coherent model for the economic boom and subsequent bust as a whole, let alone for universities in particular, is a question I will leave for others to discuss.

At a more practical level, it has always seemed clear to me that one aspect of the business model, the drive for the generation of Intellectual Property (IP), could not fit easily with the university as a disburser of knowledge. A recent example shows how the two can clash. For the sake of non-attributability, I have left out the specifics; but the general features will suffice to make the point.

Some time ago, I attended an informal seminar. A really nice application of a certain physical principle was shown, and a slightly modified version of part of the talk would be a beautiful addition to a first or second year module, illustrating a difficult concept in physics and at the same time showcasing some state-of-the-art research taking place at an Irish university. When after the talk I asked the speaker for the slides, the rather sheepish and very apologetic answer was: sorry, there are IP issues, I cannot help you here. I did not ask, but understood that I was expected not to make my own slides from memory. To me this is a powerful argument against the drive for university-generated IP: the university should be a place where knowledge is not only generated but also transmitted, and not obscured for financial gain.

The Quantification Fallacy

There are many reasonable questions that are hard to answer. To list a few that are germane to this book: What is a good university? What is a good student? What is good research? What is a good academic? What is the role of a university?

Almost inevitably, it seems, once it has been accepted that these questions are hard to answer, mankind tries to find an answer by making some sort of measurement. No doubt these measurements often capture one or more aspect of the question, and no doubt when the measurement is first devised, the limitations are made explicit. However, soon after, the caveats are marginalised if not forgotten. "What is a good university?" becomes "What is the university's ranking?" on some list or other; "What is a good student?" becomes "Did the student obtain a first class honours degree?"; "What is good research?" becomes "What is the impact factor of the journal you published the results in?"; "What is a good academic?" becomes "What is your h-index?". Perhaps most deplorably, "What is the role of a university?" becomes "What is the short-term socio-economic impact of universities?", or "How much capital does the university generate?"

These proxy questions have the advantage of the original questions by virtue of the numerical scales they introduce. Numerical answers allow for rankings, and their evolution can easily be tracked. They also lend an air of objectivity to the answer. The main problem is of course whether the proxy questions encapsulate the original questions adequately, and whether somebody is prepared to rely completely on the quantified data. In my experience, not many people will claim that they do, but many are prepared to jump to the defence of at least some of the proxy questions, often in the form of a question like "Well, I agree it's not perfect, but how would you do it in a way that is fair?" I admit that there are instances where it is hard not to have some sympathy for a desire to use numbers to soften a blow. If by consensus there are eleven people deserving of promotion, but there is only money for five promotions, how do you tell the other six that a committee "had the impression that, on balance, the other five were just ahead"? However, deftly shifting the burden of proof or appealing to noble emotions does not constitute a justification for using proxy questions. Even if the quantifiable proxy question has been designed and evolved to catch as much as possible of the original question, as is often the case, there is still no guarantee that the proxy question is adequate, objective, or fair. Simply put, a complex system probably needs a complex appraisal.

To give an uncontroversial analogy, people use the volume of an object as a proxy for its mass. When asked to lift a box without knowing its contents, we make a mental estimate of how much effort it will take to do so; people often express surprise when the box is "lighter" or "heavier" than expected. This example illustrates three key observations: (1) using proxies is something we do all the time, without being instructed or trained, so it is likely to have some use; (2) you should not be surprised if the proxy is not adequate for the case on hand; but (3) regardless, despite many previous experiences that show the proxy is a vague indicator at best: you allow yourself to be surprised, time and again. To compound the problem in academia, the equivalent of lifting the box is missing: there is often no short-term verification of whether the proxy is adequate or not.

Of course, these proxies are rife and many have been there for a long time. We rank students by a score that is an aggregate of a multitude of assessments; yet I cannot think of a single ranking so obtained that matches anybody's assessment of all students in a class. We all know examples of students who "just" obtained a second class honours degree but went on to outshine their classmates in doing original postgraduate research, and first class honours students who turned out to be merely adequate followers of instructions during a disappointing Ph.D. project. Many academics have experienced this, and some prefer an unquantified, visceral impression of students' final year projects as better predictors for a successful career as a postgraduate researcher.

In the face of these examples, where proxy rankings appear to give a less-than-accurate reflection of what it is we want to know, another unquantifiable question poses itself: why do we seem to have only gone further down the path of quantification in the recent past?

Evaluating Academics

What makes for a good academic? The apparent need to rank people has made us familiar with quantifiable proxies such as the number of hours or modules taught, student feedback (preferably in the form of Likert-type questions, which are then treated as if they have interval scales), the number of postgraduate students supervised, the number of peer-reviewed publications and invited talks at conferences. All are indicators of some kind of academic activity, but few people would argue that these indicators capture all essentials.

For example, there are important aspects of the academic's job that are hard if not impossible to express numerically. Take the pastoral element to academic work. A few graduates from our programs credit me with having prevented them from dropping out; they claim that if they had not had some interaction that I provided, or had not some action been taken that I carried out, they would not have graduated. How this ranks with a good publication or graduating a Ph.D. student I do not know – not even in my own, very subjective view – as these are all achievements to be legitimately proud of. How to express this in a score that should convey objectively whether my colleague or I should get a promotion is even less clear to me.

However, it is not just that the ranking system fails to include important aspects of the job. The quantification of certain research-related aspects effectively biases the rankings. Some inputs now count as outputs. For example, quantities such as the number of grants and the amount of income obtained are part of the same magical formula that allows review committees to put a number on academic performance. When the number of grants and Euros are small, one may argue that, in practice this just weights certain outputs more heavily; for example, if each grant allows for the completion of one supervised Ph.D. and two publications, there is a one-to-one correspondence between grant money and these two categories. Hence taking income into account merely bestows more weight upon these two categories, without fundamentally changing the nature of the academic's work, and besides, it means that there is no three or four year delay between obtaining a grant and reaping the benefits in terms of output. Be that as it may, and leaving aside the question of how desirable this weighting is, a severe distortion takes place when the grants are much bigger and skewed towards certain areas of research, as is often the case in science-based disciplines.

Early 21st Century Science Funding In Ireland: Feast or Famine?

At first glance, it may seem that academic scientists in Ireland have never had it so good. Science projects have been very successful in the PRTLI programs, which have disbursed a total of 1.2 billion Euros to all areas of academic research in the period 1998–2011 (HEA 2011). In the first 8 years of its existence, Science Foundation Ireland (SFI) has disbursed more than one billion Euros in SET areas. The Irish Research Council for Science, Technology and Engineering (IRCSET) has added many more tens of millions into the mix, much of it targeted specifically at funding individual postgraduate and postdoctoral researchers. PRTLI money has been used to construct new buildings and put together international research teams; SFI alone has funded nearly 1000 postdoctoral researchers and more than 1000 postgraduate researchers, and has helped forge linkages with industry (SFI 2008).

It would be unfair to disparage the many improvements this funding has brought about, especially considering that even during the economic boom, per capita investment in Research & Development was still significantly below the OECD average

(OECD, 2006a; 77). However, I have to point out that these riches have come at a cost. In monetary terms, the core funding to universities, which is meant to underpin the general, broad, university functions, has been consistently cut in terms of per capita allocation by up to 2000 Euro in the period 1999-2006 (OECD 2006b; 175).

Moreover, funding levels have not increased to the same extent for all scientists. If you happen to carry out research in or related to the government-designated areas of ICT, BioSciences & BioEngineering, and Sustainable Energy, then Science Foundation Ireland has 160 million Euro per annum to disburse to you and your colleagues. All other researchers in SET can effectively apply for only a fraction of this money, about 10 million Euros, through the Research Frontiers Programme (RFP). As the name suggests, this fund is not there for you to obtain high quality data in an established field of research – words like "novel", "innovative", "new", and "progressive" often appear in the proposal so frequently as to make the epithet almost meaningless.

Putting that objection aside, if you want to spend that money on curiosity-driven research, that is fine, as long as you can do it by Gantt chart[2] of course. (At the time of writing, speculation is rife that this avenue may vanish, and that all of SFI's funding will go towards targeted research only.) The amount of RFP funding available to researchers in all areas of science, engineering, and technology, amounts to 50 projects per year to the tune of a maximum of 200,000 Euro for 4 years.

This inequity is somewhat mitigated by other funding mechanisms within Ireland and the EU that are not limited to the three areas supported by SFI. However, since these funding calls are open to all, researchers in other areas now find themselves competing with people who have been given a much greater opportunity to work in (large) teams, have more capital investment, more postdoctoral and postgraduate researchers... it is hard to argue that the playing ground is level, even concerning funding that is open to all. It is not easy to find exact numbers, but it is certain that research funding awarded to the three designated areas has significantly outgrown research in other areas. I am highlighting these inequities not to complain, but because I feel they have got lost somewhat in the public perception.

Curiosity-Driven Research, Targeted Research, and Socio-Economic Benefits

Research can be undertaken for many reasons. Research may be done out of sheer curiosity, to figure something out for the sake of figuring it out. Research may take place with an application in mind, to figure out if practical use can be made of an idea. Research may also aim to figure out how to go from prototype to mass-production. There is a place for all of these kinds of research – and I would even go so far as to contend that academic research has a role to play in all of them.

When it comes to research policy and research funding, however, things become a little murkier. There is a limited pot of money available, and how should one choose one project over another? Should decisions be based on an unquantifiable and highly subjective notion of beauty, as described by Poincaré, or on whether a pressing social or economic need is addressed? I pose the question deliberately as a dichotomy, since it is often presented as such by advocates on both sides. The dichotomy is false because, of course, it is perfectly possible to do both, or neither. Indeed, IRCSET's Embark Scholarship scheme, which coexists with SFI's programmes, is a personal award made to students to carry out research in any SET area.

The question of whether, and to what extent, academic funding should be curiosity-driven or oriented is not a simple one to answer. It must be said that when the government mentions "oriented research", they increasingly mean research with rather short-term socio-economic benefits in a limited area of research. Two extreme positions on this issue can be defined. On the one hand, it appears possible to espouse the demand for socio-economic benefit, seeing it as not only fair, but as a long overdue necessity: taxpayers' money must be accounted for, after all; academics are forced to peek out of their ivory towers and apply their brains to finding solutions to real-life problems; and industry is encouraged to make a financial contribution to a third level system that gets less funding per student. At the opposite end of the spectrum, some people insist that only curiosity-driven research should take place at universities, that the socio-economic impact of this research is both irrelevant and unquantifiable, and highlight the outrage of the government funding or co-funding research that is only going to make industry and venture capitalists richer. Most people find themselves somewhere in between these extremes.

It must be said that both sides make some rather exaggerated claims. For example, advocates of the Mode 2 (Gibbons 1994) or Triple Helix (Leydesdorff and Etzkowitz 1996) models of university-industry-government sponsored innovation claim that the taxpayer has a right to see that their hard-earned money is invested wisely. Opponents decry the falsity of claims of socio-economic benefits they feel forced to make in their proposals, and caution against the taxpayers' impending wrath when scientific research does not reap the rewards that were solemnly promised. In my experience, the taxpayer is rather lukewarm about, if not downright unaware of, the government-funded research we carry out – both before and after the recent economic downturn. (I admit that some do seem angry about the purportedly vast sums of money all academics get for what is perceived to be doing next to nothing all year. I fear that no amount of evidence to the contrary will change that perception.)

What about the pragmatic argument that in a time of shortage, the taxpayer has the right to prioritise even curiosity-driven research in areas of potentially viable short-term innovation, and if that stifles long-term benefits, then we will deal with that problem later? I think the situation here is akin to the age-old seed corn problem: if you have set aside a certain amount of corn for next year but your family are hungry now, what do you do? How much you need to eat now or invest in short-term projects is clearly a complex issue that cannot be solved by rhetoric.

Shaping Academic Recruitment

When big PRTLI and SFI grants (say of over 1 million Euro) started to come in, it became more common for academics to drastically reduce or even completely drop their teaching commitments. I am not implying that this was necessarily the academics' choice – there are many who sincerely miss teaching, but simply cannot find the time to combine teaching with a hugely increased research programme and concomitant administrative duties. However, the inevitable result was that those who were able to obtain big grants were less likely to teach than those who did not. The first changes to academia were upon us.

The advent of SFI Principal Investigator grants and Stokes lectureships and professorships brought about even greater changes. The impact of the latter came at a high enough price: these people were top researchers from abroad, hired as academics but explicitly recruited on their research track record, not on their qualities as teachers. The stated expectation was that they would, within five years, become sufficiently established to obtain their own grants and thus justify their salaries to their host universities, who were expected to keep them on. Thus, a subset of academics were now recruited solely based on their oriented research prowess, and teaching ability was de facto relegated to merely a pass/fail criterion. Lest I be misunderstood: it is the principle I have difficulty with, not the people thus recruited; and am I not implying that they are individually bad teachers or that they individually contribute less to schools or departments. The point I am making is that these considerations had less weight than they otherwise would have received. I admit that this change is not directly dictated by funding agencies, but argue that the climate change that has led to it has been caused by them.

Again the question poses itself: where does the balance lie? Should science schools be nothing but grateful to SFI, since:

> ...importantly, "The Stokes" should allow more flexible and proactive strategic recruiting by HEIs of key research personnel at junior and senior levels. It should allow Schools to strategically plan their staffing, to integrate quality research staff into the current base of permanent staff and to add to the School's net pool of expertise. (SFI 2008)

or should they be disgusted at the social engineering that takes place when they are offered to have high-quality research staff funded for five years, but only if they do the kind of research SFI want them to do? Emotions here run high, and the gamut of opinions is quickly covered.

Further changes to the balance were not long in coming. International Principal Investigators (PIs), up to 103 by 2008 (SFI 2008), were also brought in. These PIs are not obliged to do any teaching, but to carry out and obtain funding for oriented research, although they are expected to "contribute to the school". The upshot is that a not inconsiderable fraction of researchers currently working in SET areas in Irish universities have been appointed through various schemes that, in my view, implicitly undervalue undergraduate teaching.

In the interest of fairness, it must be said that funding agencies should not shoulder the blame alone. Quantification works at more levels than one. Rumour has it that some universities have on occasion based their shortlist for a lecturing position on the h-index of the candidates. (The h-index is a measure of the quality of one's publications: if the somebody's h-index has a certain value, say n, then this person has published n articles that have been quoted n or more times.) This is another example of shortlisting without any regard to teaching qualities whatsoever, determined by a single numerical proxy.

A point worth repeating is that, in pointing out what I see as debatable or deplorable in the current situation, I do not think that the fault lies with the people recruited in this way. Some even conform to my ideals of what an academic's job should be, but even those who do not can hardly be held responsible for promises being made to them. The people brought in tend to have good to excellent track records. My point is that the change in culture and the distribution of academic activities these developments have caused is often underestimated. And this is by no means the end of the changes in science in academia.

Research Centres and Faculties

Greater in impact still than the targeted appointments discussed above is the creation of research centres within universities. Mainly through the Program for Research in Third Level Institutions (PRTLI) and SFI Centres for Science, Engineering and Technology (CSET), every university now has a hybrid structure where research centres and schools coexist. (They go by a variety of monikers: for research centre you may have to read research institutions, and for schools you may wish to substitute departments.) Few, if any, written rules appear to exist; it is clear that one can be a member of one or more research centres and one school. (Lest I give the wrong impression, I am one of these people, albeit with a responsibility for a greater than average amount of teaching.)

Schools have indisputably been hit in every possible way by this development. Schools have been punished for their own success in attracting research funding, in that the people heading up the research often become unavailable for teaching. In an ironic twist, people with a strong teaching background can also get taken out of the pool of teaching academics – I admit that it hurts me that the expression is no longer a pleonasm – to head up what are essentially teaching indexation or quality assurance projects. There is perhaps nothing wrong with any of these roles per se, but the cumulative effect is inevitably that those who are still engaged in teaching tend to spend more time doing this, and can therefore only remain engaged in research either to a lesser extent or at the expense of personal time, while some of the people at the forefront of research spend less or no time teaching. If this redistribution of tasks were the result of people's individual choices, I would be only too happy; but it is caused, at least in part, by a policy of targeted research funding.

The advent of centres and, in science and engineering at least, a preponderance of well-funded postgraduate scholarships, has also affected postgraduate life in the schools. For example, where in 1998 postgraduate researchers would typically feel allied with a school; many now identify with the research centre they are working in. There probably is more friction now concerning postgraduate tutoring than ever before: if postgraduates do not need or get an income from it anymore, why would they engage in it? Of course, many still see the value of teaching and interacting with undergraduate students, but even they have to contend with competing pressures of meeting increasingly frequent and stringent research deadlines imposed by funding agencies.

Again, apart from the moral rights or wrongs, I would like to see evidence that putting together large research centres gives good value for money. I am not disputing that putting together small teams of researchers tends to increase their efficacy; but it does not follow that putting together large research teams is therefore better than, or even equally effective as, assembling small research teams. I will admit that I do not know what the answer is, or even whether there is a generally valid answer – but it seems fair to ask for evidence in favour of these investments. I am not alone in this – to quote Harnad, as recently as 2007, "nothing like standardized 'norms' or benchmarks has as yet emerged from scientometrics" (Harnad 2007).

A step too far?

In 2009, the UK government introduced the Research Excellence Framework (REF), which will be used by the Higher Education Funding Council for England (HEFCE) to provide accountability for public expenditure on research. Each university department was to submit evidence to be rated, with 60% of marks awarded for the quality of their research as judged by academic panels, 25% according to the socio-economic impact the research makes within a 15-year window, and 15% according to the quality of the department.

Many scientists railed against the timeframe, and quoted a plethora of examples where unpredicted and unpredictable socio-economic benefits emerged after much longer time spans: the laser, X-ray crystallography, carbon chains, etc. In my opinion, these scientists ceded too much ground by far, and they allowed the government to beg the question. It is not clear to me why or how academic research should be defined in terms of socio-economic benefit, on whatever timescale.

Others, supported by many academics from the humanities, wondered how one could hope to get funding for say a reinterpretation of Voltaire or a thorough investigation of a distant galaxy. They cried out for a critical evaluation of what academic research should entail. The net result of the storm of protest resulted in… a change of relative weightings to 65%, 20% and 15%. Once a proxy question is found, it is not easily discarded.

Conclusion

In summary, events over the last 10–15 years have significantly altered the scene in universities as a whole, and within the SET disciplines in particular. As detailed elsewhere in this book, on the teaching side, a loudly proclaimed but poorly evidenced need for quality assessment and quality control have led to the introduction of a vast number of measures that (i) are only quantifying what can be quantified and hence fail to capture some of the most essential aspects of university teaching and learning, and (ii) have led to hugely increased administrative loads. On the research side, vastly increased funds in some areas of SET have shifted the balance in academia, in that they have introduced a difficult coexistence between research centres and faculties, have hugely favoured three designated areas of research, and have *de facto* placed even more emphasis and value on the role of research and less on the role of undergraduate teaching.

In the present research climate, the potential for income or technology generation has been promoted to a level where it may determine whether a project gets funded or not. If there is funding for basic and applied research, then it seems wrong that one curiosity-driven piece of basic research in the sciences gets funded because luckily there happens to be potential for spin-off, where an otherwise equally interesting project in the humanities does not just because it lacks this potential. I am not making a sweeping generalisation here that no applied or commercially oriented research should be government-funded under any conditions. I contend that both types of research could and should coexist with education.

I may be accused of mostly sketching the situation or pointing out what I see wrong with the current academic climate, but offering little by way of an alternative. The reason for this absence is twofold. On the one hand, I have deliberately refrained from offering detailed alternatives for fear of offering a straw man. On the other hand, as I have been at pains to point out, the issues are complex and interrelated; a single change anywhere will have unforeseen and unintended consequences, and therefore changes must not be proposed lightly or without ample consultation with people from many backgrounds and diverse expertise. I am convinced that a combination of quantitative and qualitative data is the best default option. One quantitative indicator tells you next to nothing; several independent quantitative measurements indicating the same thing may tell you something; but these indicators must be complemented by a professional, if necessarily somewhat subjective, qualitative interpretation of these data and of non-quantifiable factors.

I strongly advocate an evidence-based reappraisal of the balance between teaching and research as a starting point for a discussion on the role of the university in the 21st century. This balance should not take place at individual level, but at school level. I promise to be open to proof of the necessity for the changes that have taken place in the last 13 years, especially in research funding, management structures and quality assessment, or even a compelling analysis after the fact that reveals that no matter what philosophical objections one might have, the benefits outweigh the costs.

A recent study carried out in the Netherlands found that, in the period between 1990 and 2008, when oriented research became the norm, even though the absolute number of publications per annum increased, the relative number of publications in these areas remained constant with respect to other areas of research (van de Besselaar and Horlings 2011). This finding may be interpreted for or against preferential funding, but I think it cannot be used against my argument that a high price was paid in terms of the fabric of academia.

I can only hope that the Forfás Research Prioritisation Exercise has taken notice, although its predefined aim was to identify up to 20 priority areas for the allocation of public funding of research and development over five years (Forfás 2010). Interestingly, the recent next EU Framework Programme for Research and Innovation, 'Horizon 2020', that will run from 2014 to 2020, has prioritized investigator-driven research that allows researchers to identify new opportunities in any field of research (EU 2011). I am personally happy with this development and its concomitant focus on non-oriented research in small groups, but I should also point out that this policy change seems to be as unsupported by evidence as earlier drives for oriented research were.

Until such proof emerges, I will continue to advocate the importance of universities in education, including postgraduate education. In doing so, I am not trying to bring universities back to where they were pre-PRTLI, nor am I disparaging the benefits of 13 years of relatively large investment into the SET area and the valuable work people have carried out as a result. However, I feel universities must find a new equilibrium where the roles of universities in education, curiosity-led research and targeted research are carefully evaluated, discussed and safeguarded, and long-term goals and ambitions regain priority over short-term benefits.[3]

Notes:

1. Includes "human capital".
2. A project schedule that lists milestones and start and finish dates of project components. Not ideally suited to open-ended research, but often required by proposal evaluators.
3. Two days after submitting the final draft of this chapter, I heard a recording of a 1975 interview with E.T.S. Walton (1903–1995), Ireland's only Nobel Prize winner in the sciences. His particular case for funding blue skies research – if people in the 1830s had oriented funding towards developing better street lighting, they would have invested in improving the technologies of the day, not in Faraday's pioneering experiments in electromagnetic induction that underpin today's street lights – is too nice not to be included. The interview may be retrieved at:
   http://www.rte.ie/radio/radioplayer/rteradiowebpage.html#!rii=9:3137904:67:11-12-2011:

References:

DeBoer, G. E. (1991). *A history of ideas in science education.* New York: Teachers College Press. EU. 2011.

http://erc.europa.eu/sites/.../erc_highlight_ec_proposal_Horizon2020_0.pdf. Accessed December 8, 2011.
Fermilab. 1969. http://history.fnal.gov/testimony.html. Accessed November 30, 2011.

Forfás. 2010. http://www.forfas.ie/newsevents/news/title,6828,en.php. Accessed December 2, 2011.

Gibbons, M., C. Limoges, H. Nowotny, S. Schwartzman, P. Scott, and M. Trow. 1994. *The new production of knowledge: the dynamics of science and research in contemporary societies*. London: Sage. ISBN 0803977948.

Harnad, S. 2007. Open access scientometrics and the UK Research Assessment Exercise Scientometrics 79: 147–156.

HEA. 2011. http://www.hea.ie/en/prtli. Accessed December 5, 2011.

Leydesdorff L., and H. Etzkowitz. 1996. Emergence of a triple helix of university–industry–government relations. Sci Public Policy 23: 279–286.

OECD. 2006a. OECD economic surveys: Ireland. ISBN: 9789264022195.

OECD. 2006b. Reviews of National Policies for Education: Higher Education in Ireland 2006. ISBN: 9789264014312.
Poincaré, H. 1908. Science and Method. Dover Publications; Dover Ed edition (2011).

SFI. 2008. Powering the Smart Economy: Science Foundation Ireland Strategy 2009-2013.

Solomon, J. 1994. The laboratory comes of age. In: Teaching Science. London: Routledge.

van den Besselaar, P., and E. Horlings. 2011. Focus en massa in het wetenschappelijk onderzoek. The Hague: Rathenau Instituut. ISBN: 978-90-77364-35-2.

CHAPTER 10
DEGREES OF NONSENSE

Dr. Brendan Walsh
School of Education Studies, Dublin City University

Yakademia
yak, verb (yaks, yakking, yakked) informal talk continuously about something unimportant. *Oxford Dictionary and Thesaurus*, OUP, Third Edition, 2009.

In March 2009 the Director of Commercialisation at NUI Maynooth wrote that the 'old model' of university education was 'no longer viable' as, traditionally, it was associated with a reluctance on the part of Irish universities to 'commercialise' their research (Scanlon, 2009). Henceforth, universities should, according to the writer, transform research into a thing of 'significant economic importance' thereby turning 'knowledge into money' (Ibid.). By leaving aside the problematic and contested nature of knowledge we must assume that the writer meant *specific* types of knowledge in other words knowledge that could be turned to profit. The 'commercialisation agenda' should henceforth 'shape the research agenda' and therefore NUIM would 'train' their postgraduates; 'upskill' their scientists, thereby 'feed(ing)' their 'pipeline', the purpose of which was 'to deliver' new 'spin-out opportunities' (Ibid.).

While it is tempting to present Scanlon's prose as parody, it in fact reflects European and Irish government policy regarding university and higher education. This is the new vernacular of Yakademia, a place where a type of Newspeak renders conversations about the nature and purpose of university education increasingly problematic. It is inhabited by middle-management former academics or "managers" and embraces "outcomes", "measurability", "quality assurance", "evaluation" and so forth, all of which have their origins in the world of corporate business, a place increasingly revealed as having a lose understanding of probity or effective management.

Making Knowledge into Money: The New Model University

Academics working within the Irish university community are familiar with the increasing influence of commercialisation in their work.[1] Informed by the neo-liberal notion of monitory productivity the commercialisation paradigm insists, just as the nineteenth century *laissez-fare* ideology did to the detriment of education and much else here and in England, that publically funded institutions must provide a quantifiable return on investment.[2] In Ireland this is because the state has become unwilling to continue subsidising universities at sustainable levels, hence it encourages the academy to seek funding outside of the public purse. Scanlon is joined by voices from outside the academy such as Craig Barrett, former CI of Intel and not, we gather, an authority on education, who suggested in March 2010 that teachers be paid on the basis of performance; a method first employed in Ireland in 1871 and later abandoned as the single most damaging element of the national and secondary education systems (Burns and Paul, *The Sunday Times*, 7.3.2010). Dermot O' Connell, general manager of Dell, has suggested modernising the Leaving Certificate as has John Herlihy of Google. By modernise they mean, of course, make more suited to the needs of corporate profit making; the notion that an education system might have inherent purposes belonging also, one assumes, to Scanlon's 'old model'. Competition is a central tenet of the corporate world and once corporate models were applied it followed that universities should be made to compete with one another. The community of scholarship, if such ever existed, had no place in the modern world and university managers became eager to see their institutions among the top 100 world universities, to be among the elite, such as Oxford perhaps? And yet, in 2009, when John Hood stood down as its Vice-Chancellor, having failed to persuade the Dons to implement a more business-like model, he noted that Oxford was a 'lively, argumentative place' (Griffiths, 2009). Are we to conclude, therefore, that a characteristic of an elite university is the rejection of business models and a tendency toward contrariness? Derek Bok, formerly President of Harvard University, is unconvinced about the benefits of commercialisation noting that 'universities have paid the price for industry support through excessive secrecy...and corporate efforts to manipulate and or suppress research results' (Bok, 77). Perhaps he was minded, for example, of the infamous study sponsored by Philip Morris in 2001 which reassured the Czech government that early mortality in smokers saves public money in medical care and pension costs? The much vaunted correlation between education and a buoyant economy is at best unproven and at worst troubling. Some of the wealthiest countries in the world deny education to all or part of their citizenry, indeed apartheid South Africa regularly sat atop development indices. Economic growth does not depend upon education, rather, as in China and parts of India for example, upon the use of particular interpretations of education - more specifically, training - to achieve the economic aims of the state (Nussbaum, 14-15). Indeed, a limited form of training is more useful as it tends to undervalue critical reflection, so characteristic of the Humanities; we can know that we cannot find work, but not *why* we cannot find work (Ibid, 125).[3] In this way universities become removed from culture in the liberal sense and become part of the political and economic norm (Evans, 19).[4] Historically, these influences have tended to instrumentalise university education 'at the expense of critical thinking and public engagement' (Burawoy, 3). In order to ensure that Irish universities, indeed universities world-wide, cease doing whatever it was they were previously doing that was evidently ineffective, they have been reconceptualised as a "sector" and part of the wider public service, of course there is no higher education sector, except as a government 'conceives it' (Maskell & Robinson, 65), the term is imported from the corporate lexicon and allows government to talk about investing in a "sector" rather than supporting it.[5]

That universities, like other publically funded institutions, are financially accountable is hardly contentious. However, to whom are they accountable and in what ways? Formerly, universities were understood as contributing to the public good through the disinterested pursuit of knowledge. In this, a degree of trust operated between society and universities, one that, given the development of Western Europe in particular since the late Middle Ages, was not misplaced. However, a number of factors served to make politicians re-evaluate the role of these institutions. The Cold War, the Space Race, the growth of Asian economic power, European integration, pressure from industry and, in Ireland, the growth of neo-liberal ideology as evidenced by government policy in the 1990s , are only some of the factors that have resulted in a new conceptualisation; one that seeks to turn 'knowledge into money.' In order that government secures a return on investment in universities, new mechanisms of accountability have been established through legislation (The Universities Act 1997) and a plethora of crude instruments designed to measure academic work or "output". The Act, described at bill stage by Garret Fitzgerald as 'an extraordinarily authoritarian, indeed Thatcherite Bill...profoundly contrary to, and openly dismissive of, our highly successful university system' finally secured the State's influence in the planning, evaluating and financing of the universities (White, 227-229). Irish universities are accountable under legislation, but that accountability exists within the paradigm of productivity that is monetarily identifiable, measurable and increasingly linked to public funding. While the Higher Education Authority spoke of the 'critical distance' (White, 227) between it and the universities in 1996, their *Strategic Plan 2008- 2010* demonstrated its position relative to government economic policy: 'Higher education' was concerned with the 'provision' of graduates equipped with the 'skills' needed to 'perform successfully' in a 'competitive environment' and 'contribute to fostering an enterprise culture' although this was prefixed with the usual empty reassurance that 'the student is the central focus of all higher education activities' (HEA, 2010. 12). Patently s/he is not, the economy is and the HEA has become its cheerleader.[6] In 2008 the government observed that a 'significant factor' behind Ireland's 'economic success' was 'the country's highly valuable human capital base...its young, well-educated and talented population' as the economy 'mature(d)' it would be 'necessary to emphasise the value added and the productivity per person' (Government of Ireland, 2008, 59).[7] The HEA repeated the mantra in its favoured corporate vernacular: 'Higher education...provides the economy with skilled human capital. The evidence is overwhelming of significant returns from investment in formal education and training for the individual, and OECD countries that have invested well in higher education have enjoyed positive growth rates' (HEA, 2010, 5); in short, those countries - now mostly suffering crippling national debt and/or social unrest and successive changes of government - that had turned knowledge into money. The economic growth vaunted by the HEA, *as late as 2010*, was not the product of education systems, but an illusion based upon indiscriminate lending by the global banking industry. This is the "new" model. Forms of knowledge which can be made to serve the global economy (graduates equipped with the 'skills' needed to 'perform successfully') are encouraged, as are those who are prepared to support that project. By implication, other forms of knowledge are not. Hence, the universities, funded by governments informed by the neo-liberal economic paradigm, are increasingly pressured to concentrate on those activities that either generate or promise the generation of income for (or from) their graduates. Not alone does this increasingly influence courses "offered" to undergraduates, but has the effect of equating research with income, either through funding or possible gain through student fees, patents or Scanlon's 'spin-out opportunities'.[8]

In order to establish which universities were best meeting the needs of the new model paradigm governments needed a means of identifying the best performers. One such formula, from which all books and publications in literature, the arts and humanities were excluded, was developed at the Shanghai Jiao Tong University (China) in 2004. Literature, always potentially dangerous, presumably belongs to the "old" model. Then again, while universities are eager to grasp massive post-graduate fees from Chinese students, there are those who consider China one of the most repressive regimes of the modern era (though not in the same league as its friend North Korea) and no lover of free-speech - hardly surprising Shanghai Jiao Tong University has little time for books. Five years after Shanghai University produced its criteria, the president of Harvard was lamenting the 'steep decline in the percentage of students majoring in the liberal arts and sciences' stressing that '(h)uman beings need meaning, understanding, and perspective as well as jobs' (see Nussbaum, 124). Shanghai Jiao Tong University had, as creators of league tables so often do, confused those actions which sustain life with those that make life worth sustaining (Graham, 22). As history has repeatedly and recently revealed, the neo-liberal economic paradigm is by no means reliable. Only five years ago it promised employment to, in particular, Engineering, Architecture and Construction Studies students, while failing to reveal that potential salary was based upon unsustainable credit, leaving them unemployed and now fodder for the new nonsense of re-credentialisation, whereby, upon paying fees, they can re-qualify as paid up members of the Lifelong Learning community; sold to them as the necessity to continue "up-skilling" due to, and informed by, the volatility of global labour , in turn, at the mercy of market uncertainty. In other words, whatever new skill they "up" to is just as likely to become superfluous tomorrow.

When universities limit their expertise to engaging with bodies of knowledge which are commercially attractive, either by fees income or otherwise, they exclude or limit education that has little or no evident market value. This is the new elitism, where those who wish to pursue blue sky (curiosity driven) research may be considered as non-contributory because they do not require or seek research funding or their work is not immediately recognisable as applicable, as Barrow has noted 'obviously...a person might conduct fruitful research for a lifetime without needing anything in the way of funding' (Burrow, 9). Either way they fail to contribute to the funding or profile of their School or university *within the new paradigm*. Fitzgerald's remark about Thatcherite policy was prescient because, by emphasising the commercial, government and university managers have persuaded academics to regard their colleagues as productive, not in terms of furthering knowledge *per se*, but in terms of specific types of knowledge i.e. those capable of being commercialised or attracting income.[9] This is a classic free-market ruse and will have devastating effects upon the discovery and dissemination of new knowledge by Irish universities (what 'spin out opportunities' Newton missed in failing to note the marketing potential for Flower of Kent apples!).[10] Ironically it is informed by a Soviet style predisposition toward tighter regulation of the university. Contradictions abound; tighter government control in the service of an ever more liberated market.[11] The neo-liberal paradigm cannot operate outside the limitations of utility, applicability and saleability and it is this paradigm the Irish university system is now being moulded to suit, one where industrialists, politicians, European policy-makers, aided and abetted by dazzled yakademics, are busily dismantling the institutions that have laid the foundations of the intellectual and social progress of Europe for 800 years.[12] Corporate branding, "outcomes" and "measurability" are the Tripos of the new yakademia.[13] Government no longer supports universities, it *invests* in them, therefore, like any other "provider" they must show a return, but one that is recognisable and measurable within the criteria set down by government, one that, if successful will help it be re-elected - hardly a very noble calling for institutions whose sole purpose was once the inculcation of critical thought, meaningful learning, disinterestedness, constructive scepticism and the public good.[14]

Selling Nonsense to Our Students

A more impressive ruse still is how this nonsense has been sold to university managers and staff and the indecent haste with which they have embraced it. Tony White notes that discussions about the Universities Act revealed, again, that 'there...existed a deep distrust of universities' in 'the upper reaches of public administration' (2001, 229). But rather than articulate this distrust, successive governments and civil servants have employed the catchphrases of the market and created a new lexicon that is seemingly reasonable and based upon notions of equity and openness. Public institutions must be accountable to the public, but who constitutes that public? Hardly the dispossessed, the indebted, the marginalised or the untalented, given the public pronouncements we noted at the beginning of this chapter. The "public" are those with a vested interest in the productivity of the universities: government – so that they are re-elected; business – so they can make profits, and industrialists – so their workers can be trained at the public expense. These groups are usually associated with the 'most pedestrian ideas about the function of universities' (Evans, 61). Their interests, while often couched in the vocabulary of "society" are, usually, specific and partial (Graham, 31). They are traditionally suspicious of discourses and forms of knowledge that exist outside the market paradigm, those that tend toward social justice and those that are not easily measurable, such as teaching (see Wrigley, in Hill, *passim.*). The trend in Ireland, as in the UK, is 'toward creating a uniform structure of expert knowledges ...based on the calculating sciences of actuarialism and accountancy' (Peters, 130) and of imposing measurability upon disciplines that sit stubbornly outside the paradigm such as Philosophy, History, Literature, Ethics, Theology, indeed the entire Humanities corpus and not a few of the sciences. Because scholars - traditionally clever people - can no longer be trusted to know what it is their students might be expected to master upon engaging for several years with their discipline, it has been deemed appropriate to force these, erstwhile unthinking clever people, to formulate specific learning outcomes for their students. This implies that all outcomes are the same for all students; another neat de-humanising echo of the Soviet system but ironically suited to the market paradigm as, presumably, it ensures parity of "quality" in the final product. The aim of all this is to homogenize learning throughout Europe so students can move with ease – the "transfer of knowledge" – at the service of the global economy (Burawoy, 3). Thus the lexicon of accountability, while sounding sensible, in fact disguises another agenda and subjects all discussion about the nature and purpose of learning to the imperative of economic efficiency. Having moved from under what, in retrospect, appears the benign shadow of Church authority, the universities, without a murmur, have embraced the new *credo* of the market and its attendant commandments: measurability; accountability; output, outcomes; applicability; relevance and competition. In this way, only that which can be measured within the criteria set by those outside the academy, may be deemed of value; if it cannot be calculated it must be spurious. Academics wanting to succeed (the career academic is a contradiction in terms) must publish in "high impact" journals (regardless of their relevance or readership; a type of battery farming where the chickens are forced to lay regardless);[15] secure research funding (increasingly confused with research) for any number of projects, and ensure that every article and utterance is posted on a Research Profile webpage, lest the opportunity of attracting post-graduate fees be missed; not for us the sanctuary of Descartes' maxim that 'to live well you must live unseen'.[16] The possibility that the inquisitive may discover what an academic has written within the covers of a book or journal seems not to have occurred to the purveyors of these Profile pages nor that, for many academics, the sole and cherished 'reward for teaching (is) the perpetuation of...taste' (Bloom, 65). Indeed we have even descended to the level where a member of staff, commenting on the recent inauguration of a renowned scholar as president of a Dublin university, remarked: '...he will not make the mark of his predecessor on the public mind unless he elects to fashion a more robust media persona' (*The Irish Times*, Education Today, 1.2.1011). Ultimately, the emphasis upon measurability replaces the notion of learning as a process of acquisition or engagement with that of a type of mechanical process whereby knowledge is "delivered" by "providers" and "outcomes" are achieved. This undermines and belittles the integrity of academic engagement and perpetrates a lie upon our students by encouraging them to believe that difficult, complex, incomplete and contested bodies of knowledge can be obtained through a process of teaching methodology combined with stated outcomes. It removes, as all neo-liberal theories seek to, the three-fold relationship between difficult ideas, their originators and those seeking mastery of their complexities.

One of the ways in which this falsity has been presented to students is in the guise of "service"; another reason why universities are now referred to as "providers" that "deliver" "programmes". One may deliver eggs; one cannot deliver knowledge, much less understanding. This is so because knowledge and therefore academic work is inherently endless; all knowledge is contested, especially so in the afterglow of post-modernism.[17] The notion of service sits well with market ideology; it means that students become customers. We have seen this happen in parts of the UK, where the Police Force has been re-designated as the Police Service, although we assume that that part of the public they expend most of their time, resources and expertise upon, i.e. criminals, are not primarily their customers. Hospitals too are now deemed to provide a service and have many "customers" although the service they "offer" must cause internal confusion as, ultimately, their objective must be to have no "customers", in other words, a healthy public. We must assume the Police Service and the

Courts are likewise confused about their mission being "services" dedicated to eliminating the need for "customers".[18] We may therefore assume that important institutions exist, which while dealing daily with the public, do not deal with "customers". A customer buys a product; we do not buy health or justice, regardless of the philosophical and ethical complexities of such an assertion. Hence, the term customer, although beloved of the neo-liberal paradigm because it reduces complex human interactions to provider/product/customer, is not always appropriate. Patients do not "access" health services and students do not access education, these are not products awaiting them; health and education are acquired through complex and often fraught interaction. One *becomes* educated, usually through the mastery of complex and challenging bodies of knowledge, we can have no idea how it will affect us or in what way it will shape our lives, it is not something we "get" or "do", it is a process and university is its beginning, a place where we are invited to rigorously test our suppositions, prejudices, certainties and discover the extent of our ignorance. Indeed I would submit that education should reinforce the realisation of how much we do not know and add to our unknowing; to paraphrase Mill, to be dissatisfied humans rather than satisfied pigs. At university we are invited to develop our capacity to critically engage with our world and to demonstrate this by the integrity and sustainability of our conclusions (Graham, 88-89) what Barnett calls 'creativity accompanied by critique' (Barnett, 2000, 69). This is not a service, it is an invitation and to pretend otherwise with nonsensical "outcomes" and Mission Statements concerning what students may 'expect' is a sham, one that is unworthy of a community of the intelligent.[19]

Relevant Nonsense

Because of the pressure being brought to bear upon universities to contribute to the project of reinvigorating the local and global economy, they have increasingly cloaked themselves in the vernacular of "relevance". Relevant and applicable modules are the offspring of the "new" model, heady with the aroma of opportunity and income; just as many technical studies did less than five years ago.[20] Relevance is informed by the notion of usefulness; if knowledge is useful then it is valuable, this is because the opposite of usefulness is uselessness. However, it is not that simple. The extent to which something is useful is defined by the use to which it is put and the context in which it is useful. The ability to speak German is of no use unless I find myself in conversation with another speaker, but in that context it is very useful. Hence what is useless in one context is useful in another. When universities are encouraged to offer relevant courses of study, relevance is defined by time and circumstance; what historians refer to as periodicity. Relevance is the new mania and O'Hear's observation that 'education is nothing'...unless it enables its initiates to 'distance themselves from their present concerns and perceptions and achieving the proper distances of the feeling intellect' allows us 'enter into those human achievements that have endured and which have...provided some distancing of the individual from his own greed and the greed of others' is replete with sense and relevance (O'Hear, 105). Because universities are no longer certain of their own purpose or the integrity of their traditional disciplines, they are susceptible to the imperative of perceived needs. Having jettisoned their critical, disinterested insistence on the search for truth, no longer viable after the assault of post-modernism, the Left's castigation of them as elite and the Right's continued parody of them as Leftist and unaccountable, they have, perhaps understandably, sought to present themselves as relevant. One outcome of this has been the rise in Peace Studies, Social Justice Studies, Development Studies and so forth although these are generally not accompanied, as far as we can tell, with studies founded in their opposite, hence, they become, not studies, but a type of propaganda that leave universities open to the accusation that they embrace selected forms of social engineering. If universities embrace one set of ideologies why not another? The decision is based, not upon the integrity of academic disciplines as traditionally understood, i.e. disinterestedness, but upon the ideology of the academic offering the particular course, a phenomenon that has allowed the Right, with justification, to accuse them of being ideologically compromised.[21] In fact, as O'Hear points out in his thought provoking "The Importance of Traditional Learning" both Left *and* Right 'are agreed in wanting to sweep traditional academic disciplines away in favour of instant 'studies' all of which are united 'in the fact that they do not involve any painstaking initiation into a traditional discipline and immersion in its achievements' (O'Hear, 104).

To return to "usefulness". As noted, "useful" is a relative term and rather a useless one at that. As Graham notes, '(c)ancer research...is often taken to be paradigmatic of 'useful' scientific investigation. However, the results of cancer research are no use whatsoever to those whose business is improving agriculture or reducing the number of traffic accidents...' (Graham, 25). Indeed, given that a small percentage of the public actually develop cancer, the vast amounts of funding allocated would surely be better spent elsewhere, however, as the son of cancer sufferers I am grateful it is not. Hopefully this illustrates the relevant/irrelevant thesis I am attempting to clarify. Again, 'mastery of ancient Greek is usually thought of as "useless" while it is in fact 'not merely useful, but essential, for those who want to study Plato in the original language' (ibid.). Hence, when governments or industrialists speak of "useful" or "relevant" they mean knowledge that is useful within their definition of "use". And if more people speak German than ancient Greek, it simply means that a knowledge of German is more useful to more people, not that one is more useful than the other. As Graham concludes; '...any subject may be useful to some people for certain purposes, and useless to others for others. What we can often say, for limited periods of time, is that certain subjects are more likely to be useful to a larger number of people than other subjects are' (Graham, 26). Lest the reader think this is merely semantic playfulness, consider the increasing cohort of unemployed graduates of erstwhile "useful" disciplines. One discipline is more "useful" than another only in terms of the use to which it is put; my Greek class may be imperative, because by it I gain access to an otherwise closed world (or indeed earn my living by it) but the motorway I use to get there, rather than a slower route, is merely convenient; for me, therefore, Greek trumps Engineering. Therefore, when a university promotes courses on the basis of "usefulness", potential employability, "relevance" and so on, what it is in fact doing is denying the *inherent* value of bodies of knowledge opting instead to tout those that appear useful to some people, for some of the time at a particular historic moment, a reflex of periodicity couched in the language of yakademia. A fulfilling life is replete with things that have no "use": Chopin's nocturnes; the Sistine Chapel ceiling; the plays of Shakespeare; the novels of Jane Austin; Ray Houghton's volley, the Parthenon....

Upskilling: It's Not So Simple

We mentioned above that the unpredictability of the global labour market has meant that governments tend to prefer the notion of skills or training to that of education. The latter is complex, contested and labour intensive while the former is, apparently, definable, measurable and immediately applicable. While there is a tendency to confuse the two, they are quite different. Training refers to the acquisition of a pre-specified skill set so that a particular task may be accomplished. This is not to say that elements of training may not be educational but the distinction was well captured by Pring: '(a) well trained teacher is useful, but an educated one is better...' (Pring, 72). For politicians and industrialists, training is "useful" because it provides people with skills, indeed, "transferable skills" as the new lexicon insists. A transferable skill, if we understand it correctly, is one which will be useful when applied in another field. This is convenient as, presumably, the same skills will work in future, different, settings. So, again, if we understand the idea, skills acquired while studying for an Engineering Degree, for example, might be transferable to, say, the teaching of History or Literature. This, of course, is nonsense. Skills, by definition are not transferable, they are specific combinations of expertise needed to complete specified tasks such as fix aircraft engines or build bridges. Some skills may be useful in more than one task but this is not because they are 'transferable' but because the tasks have inherent similarities. But because, culturally, vocational training has been deemed inferior to university education in Ireland and because policy makers do not know the difference, training has been undervalued and its integrities and purposes confused; one is not better than the other, one is different from the other. Universities will soon come under pressure to demonstrate the 'transferable skills' of "programmes" they "deliver". Hence we will have to watch the nonsense of scholars crowbar the idiocy of "skills" into their "programme descriptors" assuming 'the most servile of attitudes' as Virginia Woolf described it in a not dissimilar context, in order to 'submit' 'to the decrees' of the measurers' because policy makers and university managers are too obtuse or indifferent to protect their staff and students from having to engage with such humbug (Woolf, 105). A more poignant nonsense of course is the notion that a set of teachable skills will provide a student with fast-track entry into the labour market, as Brown and Scase pointed out 17 years ago 'in the context of rapid technological innovation and market uncertainty, the demonstration of high calibre is more important than the acquisition of applied skills, because much of what is learnt is soon out of date' (Brown & Scase, 44). Surely, this is more apparent now than ever. Educated sensibility, despite the lazy accusations of elitism aimed at the notion, not training, will prepare students to face the vagaries of contemporary life.

A Fine Outcome

A review of the anti-intellectualism inflicted upon contemporary universities would be incomplete without reference to learning outcomes. In short, these are the skills, content knowledge or competencies students should have mastered (acquired) at the end of a course (programme/module) of study (provision). We can say, I believe, with a fair degree of certainty, that over the centuries, scholars have identified those elements of knowledge they wished their students to master upon completing a course of studies. After all, there seems little point in teaching these bodies of knowledge unless students were committed to learning at least parts of them. Again, it seems that progress in scientific enquiry, medicine, law, education and so forth indicates that the academics involved in these disciplines had a more than vague notion of what it was they wished their students to be aware of, prioritise and learn. Yet, despite overwhelming evidence to the contrary as witnessed by the evolution of disciplines such as those just mentioned, academics were, apparently, fumbling about in the dark, with little notion of what they were doing or why they were doing it. Therefore in contemporary Irish universities a lecturer must, before teaching a course, detail its learning outcomes; in effect, the details of the transaction - those things the students will "get" by attending the module. The lecturer may not change the content of the course unless s/he updates the outcomes to include the new content. It is sold to the student body as evidence that the transaction is traceable, transparent and can be accounted for. The product "outcome" is described so that the student "customer" knows what s/he is going to get but the entire practice is based upon a fundamental misunderstanding of the academic endeavour. Academics habitually revisit, test, scrutinise and challenge their disciplines. Reading, thought, reflection and peer review goad them into intellectual uncertainty and hesitation. Bodies of knowledge appear incomplete, incompatible and unreliable. Academic life is, for many, a way of *being* in the world, a process of coming to terms with its complexities as manifest through intellectual disciplines or new modes of thought. Reflection, discovery, disproof and the advent of new knowledge lead to the modification if not absolute rejection of previously held convictions, sometimes within the course of days or hours. However, for now, this should not occur mid-module for if a mathematician, for example, were to find that a proposition that formed part of his or her module was fundamentally flawed, s/he would, if the flaw significantly altered the module, have to seek permission to alter the course content and learning outcomes and in at least one Irish institution would be asked to provide reasons for wishing to do so before being allowed to progress.[22] To add to the nonsense, it is possible that students could complain that they are now engaged in a module that differs from the one they registered for. This unlikely but not impossible scenario demonstrates the risk to true scholarship, perhaps more so in the Sciences were 'accidental discovery is, entirely typical.'[23] The process is authoritarian, stridently antithetical to serious critical enquiry and the norms of academic endeavour. It seeks to transform the relationship between lecturer and student into a parody of open, critical, mature two-way inquiry. It is characteristic of the increasing dominance of instrumentalism within academia which in 'attempting to specify in advance the knowledge and research necessary for...action...limits the action to known boundaries' thereby limiting research and enquiry but 'also the very action that it would promote' (Barnett, 2000, 90).This 'technologization of discourse' (see Evans, 83) is a means of altering and undermining long held understandings (long held because humanity has deemed them inherently valuable and therefore transmitted them) of the engagement with knowledge which it presents as fixed, unproblematic and somehow deliverable. This is a lie practised upon students who are shielded, therefore, from the reality of learning as complex, unpredictable and often anarchic; toward consumption rather than creation and toward conformity rather than dissent. It pretends that students attending the same module will achieve the same outcomes, this must be so, otherwise lecturers would be compelled to write outcomes for individual students. It is Soviet in conception and based on a wholly inappropriate cognitive-behaviourist understanding of human interaction – the same so beloved by companies engaged in marketing. It doesn't matter why a product is purchased or why something is learnt; only that it is. At a new level of nonsense it means that university Schools can be judged not on how well they facilitate the engagement with learning but on how well they meet their objectives and outcomes. It is hardly surprising then that an uncertain academic or School should simply create the narrowest, achievable outcomes possible – the very antithesis of what, traditionally, academics strove to do.[24]

Verbiage

European governments and their agencies have attempted to increasingly influence and adapt university education to their purposes, pointing, ironically, to their control of the ever reducing funding they grudgingly provide. In doing so they have imposed a 'quasi-democratic ethos of collusion with the values of a market economy' (Evans, 23). It is not our concern here to condone or condemn free-market ideology, rather to discuss its appropriateness as employed to regulate education. We are repeatedly told that the market dislikes uncertainty but that is precisely what lies at the heart of all meaningful education and one of the ways governments have attempted to overcome the troublesome intellectual nature of universities is to create and/or adopt a new language to describe them. Yakademics, equally troubled by the vagueness of intellectual enquiry, were smitten (not for them the Dons' strident vote of no confidence in the government educational policy that rang through the Sheldonian Theatre Oxford in June 2011). Naturally, aspects of the "old" model, such as university terms, were jettisoned in favour of semesterisation; university departments were re-named Schools, courses became modules and so on, none of which, of course, made a jot of difference to students' engagement with learning.[25] Modularization, in some universities, appears little more than an attempt to dupe students into believing that engaging with learning comes about through the amalgamation of disconnected parts of different disciplines and that, knowing almost nothing about them (hence, "student") they are in a position to make informed decisions about what to study - a type of unguided pick and mix. This represents another way in which universities have abdicated their responsibility to their students because it forces students to engage with "modules" in which they have no interest or inclination and/or presents serious knowledge as a type of popular download of seemingly interesting stuff.[26] Again, titles such as Doctor or Professor were dropped from common usage as they implied a hierarchy of knowledge. Presumably students would find it disconcerting that their lecturers knew more than them and offensive if touted in such an obvious manner.[27] But language is important; we need only look to Orwell's great *1984* to understand its potential to re-brand nonsense as sense or, in our time, for example, death as "collateral damage". Governments have altered the language; they don't support, they invest; learning is not the disinterested pursuit of worthwhile knowledge but the acquisition of useful skills. University education has become an almost magical proposition because it is simultaneously intellectually enriching and also economically useful; it can foster culture *and/or* equip people for work; it can encourage a love of knowledge *and/or* put that knowledge to economic use; it can, as Maskell and Robinson say of developments in the United Kingdom, 'both promote...the values which characterize itself *and also* turn them into programmes that can be marketed in the global marketplace. Good leads to goods' (Maskell and Robinson, 69, original emphasis throughout).

In Ireland, the universities, according to the HEA's succinct Soviet paradox, are 'autonomous' yet 'fully accountable to Government for...delivery of national objectives' and to do so the Higher Education institutions (a homogeneous mass) must 'enhance the quality of learning' not to mention 'deliver(ing) higher education using more innovative and flexible approaches' (HEA, 2010, 5 & 13). In this way the then government's aspiration to locate Ireland 'as a location of choice in the International Education market' might be achieved (Government of Ireland, 2008, 14). The meaning, so to speak, of this nonsense is simple. The Higher Education Authority and its political masters are either unfamiliar with the fundamental attributes of learning (engagement, uncertainty, difficulty...), or they have chosen to abandon them as informing the practices of institutions dedicated to learning, or they wish to conceal these attributes in an attempt to force a different agenda for learning upon those institutions. The government's 2008 *Building Ireland's Smart Economy* (i.e. wealthy economy) outlined the priorities for university and higher education using the Strategic Innovation Fund to 'instil a commercialisation culture in third-level institutions' prioritising 'entrepreneurship, mathematical, science and language skills...' (Government of Ireland, 2008, 15). The poverty of political understanding regarding the scientific and mathematical disciplines, their theoretical application and magnificently compelling research *cul-de-sacs* or 'accidental' discoveries cannot be dealt with in a chapter of this length.[28] Suffice to say that, after decades of underfunding for science and mathematics in schools, in initial teacher education and in Higher Education institutions, it must strike the scientific community as a tiresome irony to discover that, yet again, they are charged, with re-invigorating the economy.

The value of the "useless": recovering learning

Ever increasing control of universities is exercised through government funding. As Casey has pointed out elsewhere in this book, the reintroduction of some form of funding from student fees is unavoidable. It seems inequitable that those who do not directly benefit from university education should bear its cost while the present level of underfunding is not sustainable. Again, the notion that all should receive a university education is far from convincing. Traditionally graduates were guaranteed higher incomes and more fulfilling careers. The more common university education becomes, the more common graduates become and so, logically, a new hierarchy will appear in terms of remuneration and employment. Universities should not flatter themselves about the increasing demand for undergraduate places; that is simply government policy, long ago mocked by Sir Humphrey Appelby (Oxon) as a means of massaging the unemployment figures. Demand will increase in times of economic difficulty such as the present, not because school leavers hunger for education, but because politicians tell them that universities will provide training, increasingly those universities are promulgating the same fraud and by doing so undermining the worth of what they *can* do - facilitate the development of an educated, critical, reflective citizenry.

Universities should seek to recover their identity as part of the historic academy. Language is important in this process. Rather than adopt the verbiage of outside agencies, might we not return to using the lexicon traditionally associated with intelligent communities of critical minds. Might we not disinterestedly critique what it is that is being asked of us and respond in a vernacular appropriate to our purpose, even if that is, occasionally, cerebral. Might we not admit that learning is in fact a complex and uncertain human endeavour, one that necessitates caution and by definition is not "delivered"; might we not seek to constructively unsettle rather than infantilise our students in a manner that will allow them humbly approach life knowing theirs is not the only truth? Might we not rediscover the 'rewards of occupying a more collective public space...if (our) august institutions are not to become empty parodies of their former selves we might wish to recover some of the rich possibilities of academic disorder' (Evans, 151-52). Indeed, the 'lack of dissent' concerning the changes to higher education in Ireland, is, Lynch believes 'a reflection of the deadening consumerism that has beleaguered Irish education for decades' (in Lavin (ed.) 2006, 88). Might we not, as a community, scrutinise and keep in check the often inappropriate understandings of and intrusions into our work (Barnett, 1990, 90). Indeed, if we are to offer our students education in the true sense of the word then it must be 'subversive...in the sense of subverting (their) taken-for-granted world' (Ibid, 155). In this way we invite our students to engage in an unsettling experience, one where certainties are scrutinised, where our disposition is intelligent doubt. Only in this way can we help them not simply find employment but, the value of that employment and of its purpose within the wider human family, employment and ways of living which can be defended in the light of living within that family. Perhaps had this been our Mission Statement we might have been less hasty in consigning so many thousands of our recent graduates to the vagaries of a neo-liberal paradigm that had, ultimately, no use for them, while we left them seemingly incapable of articulating, re-imagining or re-creating a new social order. Rather we left them with "skills" to carry on-board the immigrant ship, again.

Universities must begin again to ask the hard questions, questions 'that society does not want to ask' and 'generate ideas that help invent the future' (Shapiro, 4). They need to free themselves from 'unexamined commitments' especially those emanating from authorities and recover the disinterested examination of what is valuable rather than "useful" (Ibid., 98). Above all, they must encourage their students to discern between 'logical and illogical arguments' (between sense and nonsense), to 'detect rot when they hear it' (Barrow, 9) regardless of its origin, including, of course, that originating in the university itself. Higher education is not at the service of anything other than itself, it is inherently valuable. Its interests are its own and its purpose emancipatory - to move from ignorance to knowledge, it is a process of liberation, a freeing from unknowing to knowing, it cannot be "delivered" and the extent of this freeing cannot be measured, it is a disposition, a capacity for intelligent discernment and it is this characteristic that makes it so loathed by fanatical regimes. It was once withheld from women, the poor, Irish Catholics, Dissenters and African Americans. Those who wish to position citizens in pre-ordained categories of production and consumption are contemptuous of its capacity for discernment. What, after all, if there was nothing we wanted from the market? The hope of the 'true educator' might rather be that his or her students might 'resist the lure of the current fashions and ephemera, both in politics and in the market place, and...see their lure for what it is' (O'Hear, 105).

Might not the university consider itself anew – being in the world but not of the world, offering 'what it has been doing for eight hundred years; perpetual critical scrutiny of what it encounters...' encouraging its students to distinguish enlightenment from ideology? (Barnett, 2000, 69 & 71). If Irish university managers persist in offering students merely a regurgitation of the narratives and descriptions of the world already found in any party broadcast or corporate recruiting brochure they trivialise their institutions and deny students the possibility of discovering alternatives that are contested, challenging, uncertain but *theirs.* Let them be responsible citizens of course but 'not uncritical' ones (Walford, 62).This surely is the function of liberal education, to help students to bridge the gap between that which is valuable for living and that which makes living valuable. When Faust noted that people needed 'meaning' as well as 'jobs' he continued: '(t)he question should not be whether we can afford to believe in such purposes in these times, but whether we can afford not to' (in Nussbaum, 124). Education based on a corporate, mercantile model runs the risk of, and, we contend has contributed to, the creation of 'a greedy obtuseness...a technically trained docility that threaten the very life of democracy itself and...impede the creation of a decent world culture' (Ibid.). This, it seems, is becoming the model for Irish universities and if income, regardless of origin, is the dominant imperative then we must prepare for "programmes" in Astrology, Wiccan Studies, Reality Television Studies and any other nonsense people may be willing to pay for. It will rid the yakademics of the messy burden of culture and herald the dawn of super-humbug. The tragedy is, to paraphrase Chesterton, not that the university will believe in and peddle nothing, but that it will believe in and peddle anything.

Conclusion: On Being Useless

While 'all attempts to conserve things come too late' even a short review, such as this, hopefully demonstrates that the common theme of the "new model" is the economically productive citizen (Scruton, 56). The obligation placed upon educators and students being to engage in a process, erroneously labelled education, whereby graduates will become human capital - a Soviet style product: a worker for the State but in the new dispensation; competitive, capitalist and entrepreneurial. Gradually, this is the role universities are assuming, that of political handmaiden and facilitator for corporate interest. Employing corporate models, European governments have brought pressure to bear upon its universities, many of them ancient and outstanding institutions, in an attempt to remould them to suit current economic imperative. In this they have donned the corporate American (formerly Soviet) pathology of work as meaning. This is not to say that work does not lend meaning to our life, in many cases wonderfully so, but there must remain places where to do is actually to think and thinking is not a passive activity. History demonstrates that the distrust of intellectualism finds rich soil: the Khmer Rouge, the Nazis, the Soviet Union, Al Qaeda... The Humanities, in particular, are increasingly presented as an indulgence, unconnected with productivity as if we should not allow people to study those things which humanity deems significant, thereby reinterpret, reinvigorate and internalise them, acting as messengers, as carriers, of cultural significance to the next generation. When Margaret Thatcher was informed by an undergraduate at Oxford that she was reading History, the future PM is reputed to have replied 'What a luxury'. While this seems a startling response from a young woman so anxious for the embrace of history, the implication that the Humanities are a luxury is profoundly dangerous. It forms the manifesto of every repressive regime; attempts to deny people serious access to their cultural heritage; stultifies the development of imaginative, artistic, linguistic and even political sensibility and returns the Arts to the preserve of a cultured elite. As Michael Wood has pointed out, those who believe that supposedly unpractical university courses are a luxury which the State should not support are 'right in a quite wretched way. They won't have to pay for them. But their children will…and not with money' (Wood, 2011).

The issue is not whether education is useful, rather, useful to what end? A high earning graduate spending his or her money on cocaine is hardly an ideal outcome. Earning power alone is not a key consideration in education, indeed as Cottom notes '(I)f education only serves the purpose of employability, it simply makes us into chumps...' and someone else's chump at that (Cotton, 203). Rather, what uselessness means, is that we accept the possibility of 'risk without reward' and that we resist the 'tyranny of stupidity in any form: the market, technocracy, the state...' (Ibid.). Utility, as presently understood, is not about the liberation *from*, rather, an induction *into* specific economic and political forms of thought and European and domestic educational policy is directed at their reproduction despite mounting evidence that the economic paradigm is seriously flawed. Let multi-nationals finance the training of their workers using their own profits rather than the public purse and let universities go about what it is they are best placed to do, that which was traditionally the purpose of academic freedom: objective, critical, sceptical, purposive inquiry, not at the expense of preparation for working life but neither at the expense of those things that make life worth working to preserve.[29] To paraphrase Cottom: if we are not doing our best to create dissatisfaction among our students, we may be serving our customers, but we are most certainly not doing our job (Ibid., 206).

Notes:

1. I have purposely employed the term community over 'sector'. Like all Newspeak, this designation encourages the notion of productivity, making unproblematic the notion that the purpose of a university is to generate money.
2. For a brief historic overview of the rise of Neoliberalism and the notion of intellectual capitalism see P. Roberts and M. A. Peters, *Neoliberalism, Higher Education and Research,* Chs. 1 & 2.

3. Nussbaum relates how Indian Institutes of Technology and Management reinstated liberal arts courses 'partly to counter the narrowness of their students...' p. 125.
4. Writing in the 1940s Robert Maynard Hutchins reflected 'I do not believe that industrialization and democracy are inherently opposed. But they are in actual practice unless the gap between them is bridged by liberal education for all.' Cited in Jaroslav Pelikan, *The Idea of the University: a re-examination*, p. 189.
5. On universities acquiescing with the designation "sector" see Padraig Hogan, "The Promise of Untimely Mediations: Reflections on University Education in the Early Twenty-First Century, in T. Kelly (ed.), *What Price the University?* , p. 140.
6. I recently attended a workshop where an academic working in the UK encouraged us to try to persuade potential post-graduate students to relinquish their areas of interest in favour of those our School was working on in order to help build 'research capacity'. This, he admitted, was the lamentable outcome of the Research Excellence Framework.
7. What role the talentless may have played is not considered but this sentence implies its marginal if not superfluous nature. In the world of competitive individualism there is, seemingly, no place for those born empty handed. We now know of course that the truth was rather different; economic success was founded upon our banks lending money they did not possess.
8. Derek Bok, former President of Harvard University, an institution with an impressive record of attracting funding notes 'Most universities have not earned much money from royalties; the odds of making anything substantial from patenting a new discovery are extremely small'. *Universities in the Marketplace*, p. 77.
9. On the potential for disharmony between those who resist change and management see K. Lynch, "International league tables and ranking in higher education: an appraisal", *Level* 3, Issue 6, May 2008.
10. The variety of apple reputed to have fallen on Newton.
11. This was the experience of academics in the UK, the 'paradox of Thatcherism' was greater government control in order to achieve greater deregulation, see Jonathan Bate, The Wrong Idea of a University, *Standpoint*, June 2008.
12. I am not ignorant of the role of amateurism in this development, particularly with regard the development of science, technology and medicine in the late eighteenth and early nineteenth century.

However, much that was discovered was later refined and broadcast by universities.

13. Alumni must have wept at witnessing the former crest of University College, Dublin being replaced with the ugly, corporate and institutionally meaningless "UCD Dublin" – an embarrassing tautology similar to that formerly employed by AIB Bank.
14. On the ideological nature of funding even within a well supported discipline such as Science, see van Kampen in this volume "Early 21st Century funding for Science in Ireland: feast or famine?"
15. I borrow this image from Keith Thomas who writes that the Research Excellence Framework (UK) has 'generated a vast amount of premature publication and an even larger amount of unnecessary publication by those who have nothing new to say at that particular moment, but are forced to lay eggs, however addled.'
16. In at least one Dublin university the requirement to populate and update this Profile page is, essentially, mandatory.
17. Before his death Newton famously wrote 'I do not know what I may appear to the world; but to myself I seem to have been only like a boy, playing on the seashore, and diverting myself, in now and then finding a smoother pebble or a prettier shell than ordinary, while the great ocean of truth lay all undiscovered before me.' A more eloquent summary of the nature of intellectual enquiry could hardly be imagined. Cited in Carl Sagan, *Cosmos*, p. 91.
18. On the notion of the student as customer see Graham, pp. 45-46.
19. Mission Statements are, in effect, admissions of failure in that we may suppose that an institution that is achieving these goals does not need to aspire to do so. They are, of course, more evidence of the nonsense permeating contemporary public life.
20. This is not in any way to undervalue the integrity of these disciplines, rather to highlight that that integrity is vulnerable to factors outside the academy. School leavers and their parents are easy prey to the mantras of industry and business regarding "safe" employment options but these should be understood within the context of radically uncertain socio-economic variables.
21. America has long suffered the rise of such courses. Writing in 2001 about of their colonisation of Departments of English Literature John Hollander reminded readers that 'there are still people who love and want to write about and teach literature, rather than some preprogrammed mode of social history or bracketed X Studies framed by a quasi-religious sectarianism, identity politics, *et cetera*.' Cited in Daniel Cottom, p. 50.

22. Permission is not, as one would expect, granted or withheld by a panel of expert peers but by a committee of academics from often unrelated disciplines.
23. Carl Sagan, *Cosmos*, 180.
24. In a similar way, in order to push a School collectively up the citations rankings all colleagues have to do to is cite one another; nonsense structurally embedded in nonsense.
25. It is remarkable that the elite universities, those Irish university managers crave parity with, such as Oxford and Cambridge, retain their three term academic year. One wonders if retaining ones institutional culture in the face of meaningless changes is a characteristic of institutional success.
26. Scruton is thought provoking on such matters commenting that Foucault's 'vision of European culture as the institutionalized form of oppressive power is taught everywhere as gospel, to students who have neither the culture nor the religion to resist it.' *Gentle Regrets*, p. 36.
27. Yakademics (and many others who consider their views deeply egalitarian) labour under the illusion that these titles refer to them, rather than to the intellectual heritage to which they belong, this is why it may have been useful for students to remain aware of them, but in a parody of equality, these rich reminders of the community into which they have entered have also now been denied them. Of course strident censoriousness is not an uncommon characteristic of the pseudo-liberal position.
28. The discovery of radio emissions from Jupiter by Burke and Franklin in the 1950s being one such "accident "and utterly unconnected with their work on cosmic radio background sound.
29. Academic freedom has, traditionally, had two aspects 'First, individual scholars and scientists should be free to pursue the truth...to teach and to publish...following rigorous intellectual criteria and subject to what is today called 'peer review' which would, secondly 'immunize universities from religious or political interference.' Robert Anderson, "The 'Idea of a University' today", http://www.historyandpolicy.org/papers/policy-paper-98.html. Accessed, 2.2.2011.

References:

Government of Ireland, *Building Ireland's Smart Economy: a framework for sustainable economic renewal*, 2008

Higher Education Authority, *HEA Strategic Plan 2008-2010*, Dublin, 2010
Ronald Barnett, *The Idea of Higher Education*, Open University Press, UK, 1990
..........................*Realizing the University in an age of supercomplexity*, Open University Press, UK, 2000
Robin Barrow, "The higher nonsense: some persistent errors in educational thinking", OpEd, Taylor & Francis, 1999. http://faculty.ed.uiuc.edu/westbury/JCS/Vol31/BARROW.html. Accessed 7.14.2006.
Phillip Brown & Richard Scase, *Higher Education & Corporate Realities: class, culture and the decline of graduate careers*, UCD Press, 1994
Derek Bok, *Universities in the Market Place: the commercialization of Higher Education*, Princeton University Press, 2003
Harold Bloom, *The Closing of the American Mind: How Education has failed Democracy and Impoverished the Souls of Today's Students*, Simon and Schuster, New York, 1987
Phillip Brown & Richard Scase, *Higher Education and Corporate Realities: class, culture and the decline of graduate careers*, UCL Press, UK, 1994
Michael Burawoy, "A New Vision for the Public University", Social Science Research Council, publicsphere.ssrc.org/burawoy, accessed 29.8.2011
John Burns and Mark Paul, "Everyone's a Winner", *The Sunday Times, Focus*, 7.3.2010
Daniel Cottom, *Why Education is Useless*, University of Pennsylvania Press, Philadelphia, 2003
Mary Evans, *Killing Thinking: the death of the universities*, Continuum 2005
Drew Faust, "The University's Crisis of Purpose", *New York Times Book Review*, 6.9.2009
Gordon Graham, *Universities: The Recovery of an Idea*, Imprint Academic, UK, 2002
Dave Hill (ed.), *Contesting Neoliberal Education: Public Resistance and Collective Action*, Routledge, UK, 2009
Sian Griffiths "This place needed a shake-up" *The Sunday Times, Education*, 12.7.2009
Thomas Kelly, *What Price the University?* NUI Maynooth, 2007
Luciana Lolich, "...and the market created the student in its image and likening: Neo-liberal governmentality and its effects on higher education in Ireland, *Irish Educational Studies*, Vol. 30, No. 2, June 2011
Kathleen Lynch, "International league tables and ranking in higher education: an appraisal", *Level 3*, Issue 6, May 2008

Duke Maskell & Ian Robinson, *The New Idea of a University*, Imprint Academic, 2002

Martha Nussbaum, *Not For Profit: Why democracy needs the Humanities*, Princeton University Press, 2010

Anthony O'Hear, "The Importance of Traditional Learning", *British Journal of Educational Studies*, Vol. XXV, No. 2, June 1987.

Jaroslav Pelikan, *The Idea of the University: a re-examination*, Yale University Press, 1992

Michael Peters, "The New Prudentialism in Education: Actuarial Rationality and the Entrepreneurial Self", *Educational Theory*, Vol. 55, No. 2, 2005

Richard Pring, "The Context of education: monastery or marketplace?' in *Philosophy of Education: Aims, Theory, Common Sense and Research*, Continuum, UK, 2004

P. Roberts and M. A. Peters, "Neoliberalism, Higher Education and Research", *Educational Futures: Rethinking Theory and Practice*, Volume 26, Sense Publications, Rotterdam, 2008

John Scanlon, "Commercialisation should not be regarded as a dirty word", *Irish Times*, 25.3.2009

Roger Scruton, *Gentle Regrets*, Continuum, 2005.

Harold Shapiro, *A Larger Sense of Purpose: Higher Education and Society*, Princeton University Press, 2005

Keith Thomas, "Universities Under Attack", *London Review of Books*, December, 2011

Tony White, *Investing in People: Higher Education in Ireland from 1960 to 2000*, Institute of Public Administration, Dublin, 2001

Michael Wood, "Must We Pay for Sandskirt?" *London Review of Books*, December, 2011

Virginia Woolf, *A Room of One's Own*, Penguin Classics, 1928 (this edition 2000)

CONTRIBUTOR BIOGRAPHIES

Ronald Barnett is Emeritus Professor of Higher Education at the Institute of Education, London. In his work, he has been trying to advance a social philosophy of the university and higher education. His books include *Realizing the University in an Age of Supercomplexity*, and *A Will to Learn: Being a Student in an Age of Uncertainty*. Recently published (2011) is *Being a University* (Routledge). Several of his books have been prize-winners and have been translated into other languages. He is the inaugural recipient of the EAIR Award for 'Outstanding Contribution to Higher Education Research, Policy and Practice' and has had both a higher doctorate of the University of London and a Fellowship of the Society for Research into Higher Education (SRHE) conferred upon him. In 2009, he was a Special Adviser to the UK's Select Committee Inquiry into Universities and Students; he is a visiting professor in China and Australia and has been an invited speaker in around 35 countries.

Dr. Gerard Casey is an Associate Professor in the School of Philosophy at University College Dublin, Adjunct Professor at the Maryvale Institute (Birmingham, UK) and an Adjunct Scholar at the Ludwig von Mises Institute (Auburn, AL, USA). He was Head of the Department/School of Philosophy in University College Dublin from 2000 to 2006. He previously taught at the University of Notre Dame, 1980-1981 and was a Professor at The School of Philosophy, The Catholic University of America in Washington. He is the NUI Consultor to the State Examination Commission in Religious Education. He received his B.A. from University College Cork, then went on to receive an MA and PhD from the University of Notre Dame, a Bachelor of Laws from the University of London and a Master of Laws from University College Dublin. His most recent book is *Murray Rothbard, Vol. 15 in the Major Conservative and Libertarian Thinkers Series* (Continuum, New York, 2010) and *Libertarian Anarchy:*

Against the State will be published (also by Continuum) in July 2012.

Tom Garvin is Professor Emeritus of Politics at University College, Dublin. He has taught Comparative Politics, Nationalism and American Politics. He is the author of many articles and books on Irish and American politics. His most recent books are: *Judging Lemass*, Dublin, Royal Irish Academy (2009) and *News from a New Republic*, Dublin: Gill & Macmillan (2010).

Professor John G. Hughes has been Vice-Chancellor of Bangor University in Wales since 2010. From 2004 to 2010 he was President of National University of Ireland, Maynooth. He was educated at Queens University Belfast where he obtained a BSc with First Class Honours in Mathematics and a PhD in Theoretical Physics. Following appointments at Queens and at the International Atomic Energy Agency, Vienna, he became Professor of Information Systems Engineering at University of Ulster in 1991. He held a range of senior academic positions at Ulster including Dean of Informatics and Pro-Vice-Chancellor (Research & Development). Professor Hughes is a Fellow of the British Computer Society and was elected by the Society as IT Professional of the Year in 1997. In 1999 his research team won the prestigious European Grand IST prize for software innovation. Professor Hughes has extensive international links in Europe, the US and Asia.

David Limond holds a professorship at Trinity College in the University of Dublin was previously Registrar for the School of Education there. He obtained his PhD at the University of Glasgow and has studied and taught in several universities and colleges in Scotland, England and Ireland. He has published work on a range of topics in six previous books and various journals.

Dennis O'Keeffe is Professor of Social Science at the University of Buckingham and Senior Research Fellow in Education at the Institute of Economic Affairs. He has published widely in the area of education and the Social Sciences and has made a particular study of truancy in English secondary schools. His books include *The Wayward Elite* (1990) and *Political Correctness and Public Finance* (1999) More recently he has been influential in bringing attention to French 19th century conservative and liberal thinkers, through his translations of *Principles of Politics Applicable to all Governments* by Benjamin Constant (2003) and of the Collected Works of Frederic Bastiat. The first volume of this six volume Bastiat translation (*The Man and The Statesman*) was published in 2011. His translation of *Evenings on the Rue Saint – Lazare* by Gustave de Molinari is forthcoming. His previous translations include Alain Finkelkraut's *The Undoing of Thought*. His book on Edmund Burke which is Volume 6 of the series Major Conservative and Libertarian Thinkers edited by John Meadowcroft was published in 2010. In the 1980s he was active in the Jagiellonian Trust which gave succour to the intellectual opposition in Eastern Europe especially in Poland. Two chapters of *Economy and Virtue* which he edited for the Institute of Economic Affairs in 2004 are shortly to be translated and published in China for a book entitled *The Morality of Capitalism.*

Dr. Aidan Seery is currently Director of Research and lectures in the philosophy of education, higher education and education research methods in the School of Education, Trinity College Dublin, He is a member of the Cultures, Academic Values and Education (CAVE) research grouping in the School and his research interests include: higher education and self-formation, narrative philosophy and biography, and the philosophical foundations of educational research.

Dr. Paul van Kampen completed an ir. (M.Sc. or M.Eng. equivalent) in Engineering Physics at Eindhoven University of Technology in 1994. He obtained his Ph.D. in Experimental Physics from University College Dublin in 1998. Since

November 1997, he has been working at Dublin City University, first as a postdoctoral research fellow, then as a lecturer and senior lecturer. His areas of research are atomic physics (now dormant), physics education, science education and science teacher education. He is a former chair of the B.Sc. in Science Education at DCU. Recently he has given several invited and contributed talks and workshops at international physics education conferences, and was awarded the DCU President's Award for Teaching and Learning in 2010. His current focus is on inquiry-based teaching at second and third level, which he sees not as a panacea but as one of several avenues to make teaching and learning an even more worthwhile enterprise.

Dr. Brendan Walsh lectures in the History of Education at the School of Education Studies, Dublin City University. His *Teaching in Ireland 1878-2010* will be published in 2015.

Also Available from Glasnevin Publishing

Reinventing the University

Edited by Prof. Ronaldo Munck & Prof. Kathryn Mohrman

2010

ISBN: 978-0-09555781-5-1

"Business as usual" is no longer a viable way of running a 21st Century university. The impact of globalization, the growing complexity of the university mission and the still uncertain impact of the 2008/09 global recession all point towards a future characterised by uncertainty. Against the pessimistic scenario, however, we can discern some good reasons for optimism in regards to the university re-inventing itself for the new millennium. This book demonstrates the need for the modern university to move beyond narrow disciplinary boundaries and to become more socially embedded in order to succeed in the current competitive climate. The universities are uniquely positioned to bridge the needs of the citizen and the emerging technologies in a democratic and participatory manner. Science and technology is leaping ahead at an unprecedented pace due to globalisation, but often social needs and human ethics are not to the fore. While universities cannot retreat to an 'ivory tower' which no longer exists, they can engage with technology and the market to help make science serve social need and advance democratic citizenship in a most turbulent global era.

Visit: www.glasnevinpublishing.com for more titles and information

Also Available from Glasnevin Publishing

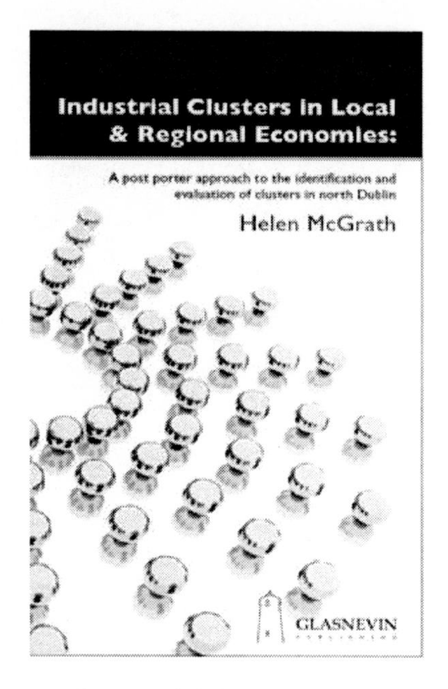

Industrial Clusters in Local & Regional Economies
By Dr. Helen McGrath
2008
ISBN: 978-0-9555781-1-3

In a departure from the predominantly Porter (1990; 1998) influenced cluster studies that were performed on Irish manufacturing throughout the 1990s i.e. studies which examined primarily market based relationships in the national context, this book focuses on local and regional industry concentrations and the nature of inter-firm relationships within those concentrations. Underpinning this approach is a broad theoretical framework that combines three streams of related literature: industrial districts, Porter's clusters and regional systems of innovation.

This book offers empirical insight into industrial clustering in the Irish context and in particular inter-firm dynamics in traditional, local industrial sectors: fish processing; printing; and bakery. By compiling and reviewing the relevant theoretical and empirical cluster literature and offering a step-by-step guide as to how to identify clusters at a local and regional level this book appeals to both academic researchers and policy makers who wish to undertake similar studies.

Visit: www.glasnevinpublishing.com for more titles and information

<this page is intentionally blank>

Lightning Source UK Ltd.
Milton Keynes UK
UKOW051321020412

190015UK00001B/26/P